Epistemic Paternalism

Collective Studies in Knowledge and Society

Series Editor:

James H. Collier is Associate Professor of Science and Technology in Society at Virginia Tech, USA.

This is an interdisciplinary series published in collaboration with the Social Epistemology Review and Reply Collective. It addresses questions arising from understanding knowledge as constituted by, and constitutive of, existing, dynamic, and governable social relations.

The Future of Social Epistemology: A Collective Vision
Edited by James H. Collier

Social Epistemology and Technology: Toward Public Self-Awareness Regarding Technological Mediation
Edited by Frank Scalambrino

Socrates Tenured: The Institutions of 21st Century Philosophy
Adam Briggle and Robert Frodeman

Social Epistemology and Epistemic Agency
Edited by Patrick J. Reider

Democratic Problem-Solving: Dialogues in Social Epistemology
Justin Cruickshank and Raphael Sassower

The Kuhnian Image of Science: Time for a Decisive Transformation?
Edited by Moti Mizrahi

Taking Conspiracy Theories Seriously
Edited by M. R. X. Dentith

Overcoming Epistemic Injustice: Social and Psychological Perspectives
Edited by Benjamin R. Sherman and Stacey Goguen

Heraclitus Redux: Technological Infrastructures and Scientific Change
Joseph C. Pitt

Epistemic Paternalism: Conceptions, Justifications and Implications
Edited by Amiel Bernal and Guy Axtell

Epistemic Paternalism

Conceptions, Justifications and Implications

Edited by Amiel Bernal and Guy Axtell

ROWMAN &
LITTLEFIELD
———— INTERNATIONAL
London • New York

Published by Rowman & Littlefield International Ltd.
6 Tinworth Street, London, SE11 5AL, UK
www.rowmaninternational.com

Rowman & Littlefield International Ltd. is an affiliate of Rowman & Littlefield
4501 Forbes Boulevard, Suite 200, Lanham, Maryland 20706, USA
With additional offices in Boulder, New York, Toronto (Canada), and Plymouth (UK)
www.rowman.com

Copyright © Amiel Bernal and Guy Axtell, 2020
Copyright in individual chapters is held by the respective chapter authors.

All rights reserved. No part of this book may be reproduced in any form or by any electronic or mechanical means, including information storage and retrieval systems, without written permission from the publisher, except by a reviewer who may quote passages in a review.

British Library Cataloguing in Publication Data
A catalogue record for this book is available from the British Library

ISBN: HB 978-1-78661-573-2

Library of Congress Cataloging-in-Publication
Library of Congress Control Number: 2020940182

ISBN: 978-1-78661-573-2 (cloth)
ISBN: 978-1-5381-7123-3 (pbk)
ISBN: 978-1-78661-574-9 (electronic)

Contents

Introduction   1
Amiel Bernal and Guy Axtell

PART I: DIGITAL PATERNALISM AND OPEN SOCIETIES   **15**

1   Artificial Ignorance, Epistemic Paternalism, and Epistemic Obligations   17
Stephen John

    Epistemic Obligations 18
    Epistemic Paternalism 20
    Epistemic Solidarity 22
    Conclusion 26

2   Epistemic Paternalism Online   29
Clinton Castro, Adam Pham, and Alan Rubel

    Architectures of Control 29
    Unilateral Change 31
    Demoting Fake News 34
    Conclusions and Caveats 39

3   Expert Advice for Decision-Making: The Subtle Boundary between Informing and Prescribing   45
Marion Vorms

    Epistemic Deference and Inductive Risk 46
    Inductive Risk as a Challenge to the Neutrality of Expert Advice 46

How to Escape Moral Paternalism? 47
The Credibility and Relevance of Expert Evidence in the Courtroom 48
Credibility and Relevance of Testimonial Evidence: Pragmatic Issues 51
Scientific Reports: Navigating between Credibility and Relevance 52
Insights from the "Case Assessment and Interpretation" Framework 54
Conclusion 56

4 Political Epistemic Paternalism, Democracy, and Rule by Crisis 61
Lee Basham

Epistemic Paternalism 62
Epistemic Paternalism, Pathologizing, and Democracy 63
Toxic Truths and Rule by Crisis: *Realpolitik* 66
Child Abuse? Epistemic Paternalism and the Pathologizing Project 69
Conclusion 71

PART II: SCIENTIFIC AND MEDICAL COMMUNICATION   77

5 Epistemic Paternalism, Science, and Communication 79
Fabien Medvecky

Hors d'œuvre: A Mixed Plate of Definitions 79
Entrée: EP in a Suspicion Broth 80
Main: A Deconstructed Dish of EP: Interference and Intention 82
Cheeses: Intentionality, Ethics, and Communication 84
Dessert: A Bitter Sweet Sample of Concerns and Objections 86
Digestif: To Conclude 88

6 Persuasion and Epistemic Paternalism 91
Robin McKenna

De-Idealized Social Epistemology 92
The Science of Science Communication 93
Epistemic Paternalism and Epistemic Autonomy 96
Justifying Epistemic Paternalism 98
Conclusion 102

7 Expert Care in Mental Health Paternalism 107
Shaun Respess

For Their Own Good 108
Changing Lives with Magic Bullets 110
Knowing Your Patient 111
Care to Intervene? 115
Caring Authorities 118

8 Epistemic Paternalism in Doctor–Patient Relationships   123
Aude Bandini

Defining Epistemic Paternalism (EP) 126
Medical Epistemic Paternalism (MEP) And Epistemic Injustices 128
Do Patients Know Best? 130
Conclusion: The Clash Of Expertises 134

PART III: EPISTEMIC NORMATIVITY   139

9 Epistemic Paternalism and Epistemic Normativity   141
Patrick Bondy

Paternalism, Epistemic, and Otherwise 142
Justifying Epistemic Paternalism Instrumentally 147

10 Epistemic Paternalism, Personal Sovereignty, and One's Own Good   155
Michel Croce

Epistemic Paternalism Defined and Bullock's Dilemma 156
Soft Epistemic Paternalism and the Case of Education 160
Epistemic Paternalism Justified: On Personal Autonomy as Sovereignty 163

11 Epistemic Care and Epistemic Paternalism   169
Fernando Broncano-Berrocal

Epistemic Care 170
Epistemic Paternalism 171
The Justification of Epistemic Paternalism 174
Morally Permissible Epistemic Paternalism as Proper Epistemic Care 174

12 Epistemic Autonomy, Epistemic Paternalism, and Blindspots of Reason   183
David Godden

On the Permissibility of Epistemic Paternalism 183
Preliminary Considerations 184

Epistemic Paternalism 186
Intellectual Autonomy 186
Intellectual Autonomy and the "Freedom" of Inquiry 188
Paternalistic Interferences and the Blindspots of Reason 190
From Epistemic Self-Censorship to Epistemic Paternalism 192
Consent after the Fact: *A Permissibility Condition for Paternalistic Epistemic Interferences* 194
Conclusion 195

PART IV: EPISTEMIC IN/JUSTICE, VICE, AND VIRTUE 201

13 Epistemic Paternalism, Epistemic Permissivism, and Standpoint Epistemology 203
Liz Jackson

Defining Epistemic Paternalism 204
Justifying Epistemic Paternalism 205
Epistemic Permissivism 206
Standpoint Epistemology 210
Conclusion 213

14 Silencing, Epistemic Injustice, and Epistemic Paternalism 219
Valerie Joly Chock and Jonathan Matheson

Epistemic Paternalism 219
Epistemic Injustice and Silencing 223
Silencing as Paternalism 226
Conclusion 228

15 Epistemic Paternalism as Epistemic Justice 233
Amiel Bernal

Epistemic Paternalism, Conditions, and Justifications 234
Epistemic Injustice: From Objectification to Disrespect and Unfairness 238
The Apparent Tension between Epistemic Justice and Epistemic Paternalism 241
Resolving the Tension: Ideal Theory and Non-Ideal Theory 242
A Final Analysis 246

16 Epistemic Vices and Epistemic Nudging: A Solution? 249
Daniella Meehan

Epistemic Nudging Introduced 250
Epistemic Vices Introduced 251
Epistemic Nudging as Successful Vice Combat 252

Epistemic Nudging as Insufficient for the Mitigation of
Vice 253
A "Deep" Understanding of Epistemic Vice 253
Epistemic Laziness 255
Concluding Remarks 259

17 Paternalism and Epistemic (Non-)Violence   263
    Adam Green

    The Route of Epistemic Injustice 264
    Kinds of Paternalism 266
    Non-Violent Paternalism? 271

18 Paternalistic Knowers and Erroneous Belief   279
    Shaun O'Dwyer

    Two Ideal Doxastic Domains 282
    An Ideal Schema for the Rebuttal of Erroneous Belief 284
    Epistemic and Ethical Injustice in Rebuttals of Erroneous
    Belief 288
    Conclusion 290

19 Paternalism and Intellectual Charity   293
    Charlie Crerar

    The Puzzle of Charity 293
    Charity as Paternalism 295
    The Paternalistic Account: Problems 297
    Charity as Corrective 299
    Charity and Paternalism: Final Thoughts 301

Notes on Contributors   307

About the Editors   311

Index   313

Introduction

Amiel Bernal and Guy Axtell

Epistemic practices which have a paternalistic profile affect our private and public lives, often in ways of which we are not aware. Quite often, due to our own inattention or unconcern, we just may *not know* how selectively information is being presented to us, and how much more is being left out. But in other cases, due to a designed interference of some kind, there is information we *may not* know.

The *may not* could still mean that people voluntarily adhere to norms of disciplinary objectivity, as when someone plays the social role of scientists adopting protocols for a *blinded* design for their scientific experiment, or the role of citizens assenting to be jurists in a court case presided over by a judge. Accepting such a social role, people willingly consent to having certain information withheld, information which they admit might bias either their judgment, of that of similarly-situated role players. What they accept is that these norms are in place for the epistemic aims of the practice, so that abiding by them is for their own epistemic good, individually or at least collectively.

But the *may not* could also mean that people's inquiry is interfered with not only by design, but also without their consent; indeed, part of what they remain ignorant of includes the interference itself, who designed it, and for what aims or purposes. This introduces a matter of much debate. In such cases what does it mean to say the design of the practice is for their own good, individually or collectively? Arguments for and against epistemic paternalism recur throughout the history of philosophy. Plato's *noble lie* justified by "need" and "good effect," and John Stuart Mill's insistence on maintaining a *market place of ideas* are just two of the most significant examples, insofar as their arguments highlight tension between deference to purported expertise and democratizing knowledge.

It is important first to distinguish description from advocacy. *Epistemic Paternalism* (hereafter EP) is in its primary sense a normative thesis, a thesis of advocacy for, or justifiable participation in, some range of specific epistemic practices which have a descriptively paternalistic profile. Alvin Goldman introduced and defended EP early in social epistemology's emergence (1991; 1999). Restricted access to information sometimes improves people's reasoning and supports veritistic outcomes, as for instance in "blinded" scientific experiments and in judicial rules prohibiting the disclosure of a defendant's past criminal profile to a jury. Goldman argued that while these norms produce a kind of ignorance, they arose in recognition that it is good for scientists and jurors and sometimes others to be protected from their own biases—"their own 'folly'" (126). On the issue of the legitimate extent to which others may interpose their own judgment upon us for our own epistemic good, Goldman placed himself in conversation with Thomas Scanlon (1972) who "expressed doubts about epistemic protectionism by appeal to the value of autonomy." While taking issue with Scanlon, Goldman acknowledges that legitimate instances of EP must be qualified by such serious concerns as the status and power of the controlling agent, the scope of control, and the rights of citizens.[1] Recent defenders (Kristoffer Ahlstrom-Vij 2013) as well as critics of EP (Emma Bullock 2016) define a paternalistic epistemic practice as any practice which (i) interferes with someone's inquiry, (ii) without their consent, (iii) for their own epistemic good.[2] While varied definitions might be possible, and some of our contributors consider alternatives, this shared manner of profiling paternalistic epistemic practices supplies substantial common-ground for debating the normative issues of advocacy and reproach.

Ahlstrom-Vij (2013) modifies Goldman's characterization of EP but carries its defense forward especially against Scanlon's reliance on notions of epistemic autonomy, and on acts of interference with others' expression or inquiry. These concepts he finds do not allow us to locate or analyze the genuinely problematic cases of EP. Epistemically paternalistic practices which deserve support or censure seem "relevantly and in some cases radically different from paradigmatic cases of unjustified or otherwise problematic suppressions of expression" (87). EP is often not just compatible with, but enabling of informed inquiry: "[I]t is exactly the purpose of epistemically paternalistic practices to provide an environment that makes it easier to form beliefs and desires in an informed manner" (86). Scanlon's answer to these normative questions may be incompatible with EP, but his approach seems limited to actions by the government which constrain the self-expression of citizens. Ahlstrom-Vij locates his defense of EP in *ameliorative* epistemology, and tries to show how effective amelioration "needs to be informed by the psychology of cognition" (7). Other extant accounts of autonomy, including those of Joel Feinberg and Joseph Raz, are not in conflict with the two normative conditions, the *Alignment Condition* and the *Burden-of-Proof Condition*, which Ahlstrom-Vij places on justified EP.

Interest in the concept of EP highlights how *caring for* and *controlling* others are descriptions of actions that are sometimes harmonizing and sometimes incongruent.[3] Aspirations for the intelligent design or modification of practices to improve voter competence must find its way through this debate. For while there is an apparent tension between epistemic paternalism and epistemic justice, EP's defenders think that the tension is only apparent, and that intelligent interventions can in fact be a form of epistemic justice insofar as applications of epistemic paternalism respect persons as actual knowers, facilitate their epistemic capacities, and ameliorate epistemic injustice. Traditionally, paternalistic actions are divided between positive interferences (laws or policies forcing/re-enforcing people to benefit themselves) and negative interferences (laws or policies forcing/re-enforcing people not to harm themselves). If we must use the language of interferences, EP conceivably has instances of both types. Controversial instances of EP are debated in law, medicine, education, news, journalism, social media, scientific method and science communication. Just with respect to news and social media, concerns about EP might include the aims and consequences of policies, whether governmental or corporate, for censoring or abstaining from censoring hate speech, real-time posting of acts of terror, jihadist recruitment videos, deep fakes, political propaganda, etc.

This list of examples shows why paternalistic policies are of immediate social and political concern in the present era. The promises/perils of Big Data allow unprecedented ways of predicting, monitoring, and manipulating behaviors. New technologies may aid or hinder open access to information and perspectives; they may assist or impede the mass manipulation of behavior and belief. If *ought implies can*, and the range of what we *can* do is expanded by new technologies, then concern with how we *ought* to design information technologies to respect democratic values while encouraging veritistic results from inquiry, is expanded also. So, this collection engages interest in emerging technologies and what they portend, interest shared by policy makers and gatekeepers of all kinds, philosophers, and STS researchers (science studies; science, technology and society).

Our project began with asking for contributions which highlight contemporary social epistemology and help clarify several shared questions. First, the collection asks whether and why it is a helpful to treat EP as a distinctive form of paternalistic practice, and if it is, then what new questions and concerns are identified in the small but growing literature on EP. Second, what entities are entitled to undertake a paternalistic practice, and in virtue of which features does such entitlement accrue to them? State neutrality to citizens' comprehensive conceptions of the good, and the "Who is watching the watchmen?" problem are far from trivial concerns. These are considered alongside arguments from justice, amelioration, and care in support of EP. Third, while acknowledging a large exiting literature and debate over paternalism among not just philosophers but also cognitive and social psychologists, behavioral economists, and legal theorists (see, for example, Grill and Hanna eds. 2018), the collection creates a forum which invites more social epistemologists to the discussion. Social epistemology brings unique resources for advancing both the liberal hope for an enlightened or de-biased democratic citizenry through the intelligent re-design of choice architectures, and critical concern for real and potential illiberal and unjust abuses of EP.

Questions of the content, scope, justification, and application of EP direct the organizing themes of this anthology. Rather than engaging just in conceptual analysis, the collection utilizes sometimes quite detailed case studies of epistemic justice or injustice through paternalistic practice; it contains discussions of information overload, the value or disvalue of ignorance, intellectual virtues and vices, civic rights, inductive risk, moral risk, human bias, collective interest, social modes of knowing, and power. Which EP practices are likely to increase democratic participation and representation, and which are likely to curtail it? Citizens may be error-prone and biased, as situationist psychologists and vice epistemology-centered proponents of EP often allege, such that we cannot rely upon ourselves for epistemic improvement. At the same time, liberal principles clearly cannot support any such prescription as that "France must be free of all vice" (Robespierre). If interpretation of bias studies is not to become a new "reign of error," the justification of paternalistic practices must remain a question beholden to democratic values and principles. Ambiguity in the defense of EP can relatedly arise from failing to acknowledge the distinction between "epistemic value" and "the value of the epistemic" (Pritchard 2013). Not all of the chapters take a definite stance on the normative question of permissible EP and its limits, but many of those which do take a stance draw upon not only the existing literature on "nudging" (associated with general paternalism), but also the expansive literature on epistemic justice and injustice (see Sherman and Goguen eds. 2019; Kidd, Medina, and Pohlhaus eds. 2017).

The collection consists in four Parts. Part I addresses fundamental questions of how to negotiate information conveyance in open societies, and especially in the context of an ever-changing digital landscape. Concerns include Big Data and how information is collected, stored and presented. Questions of how to appropriately modify search algorithms, are questions regarding the appropriate scope of digital epistemic paternalism. For example, does Google or Facebook have normative grounds for censoring false news outlets without their consultation, for perceived greater goods? Part II regards problems of scientific and medical paternalism. Reference to social roles and location play prominently in this section. Part III engages in conceptual and applied analyses of EP in relation to cognitive constraints of people, and normative concerns with autonomy and morality. Part IV connects epistemic paternalism to epistemic in/justice, as contributors consider charity, intellectual vice, and standpoint theory, among other topics.

In Part I's first chapter, Stephen John examines the emerging field of Personalized Medicine and the prospect that developments in Machine Learning technologies will allow better predictions about individuals' propensities to develop disease. But should patients always receive uncurated information and predictions? If not, how should we decide when such controls on the flow of information are permissible? John develops an answer to this question in terms of "epistemic obligations"; he contrasts this approach with one framed in terms of individuals' epistemic freedoms, which he finds implicit in current debates around EP. The chapter suggests quite a different way of looking at the issues since he argues that the received approach obscures the complex web of social-epistemic norms which bind and structure communicative practice. Good informing, he argues, "requires careful curation of a communicative encounter, tied to an understanding of a subject's epistemic and practical needs and limitations."

Clinton Castro, Adam Pham, and Alan Rubel are concerned with *new media* (highly interactive digital technology for creating, sharing, and consuming information). After providing multiple examples, they focus in on Facebook's efforts to counter "epistemic bubbles" and fake news. The chapter argues that while paternalistic, this effort is morally permissible, and indeed that "many epistemically paternalistic policies can (and should) be a perennial part of the internet information environment."

Marion Vorms examines what she sees as the moving boundary between informing and instructing, and how it affects the legitimacy of paternalistic epistemic practices. The cases she considers focus on the function and use of evidence in the criminal justice context. These uses are not all of one type, and the ensuing holistic appraisal of evidence in the courts draws attention to "the strikingly complex inference networks fact finders must construct so as to marshal a mass of evidence, which may or may not cohere." The distinction between credibility and relevance, Vorms argues, highlights "a difficulty of experts' task in advising decision-makers," namely "to provide the best and most relevant information, without encroaching upon their recipient's decisional autonomy." Imprinting their own values upon their audience is one way that experts are likely to exceed their duty. But other and more specifically epistemic threats of paternalism also abound, some related to "the very structure of inference networks in complex evidential reasoning."

Lee Basham's historical exposé and critique of what he terms *political epistemic paternalism* broadens the collection further. Epistemic paternalism is a political tool, but one which democracy does not effectively constrain. "In the context of real politics, on a global level, there is little political epistemic paternalism cannot justify in the constraining of public knowledge and the hierarchical decisions it enables. Outrages against domestic democracy must almost become the norm if we pursue the inexorable logic of political epistemic paternalism." Basham offers historical evidence for this thesis in repeated incidents of "rule by crisis." Especially when public trust lapses, governing by crisis rationalizes the censoring and manipulation of information, and is often sought by corrupt political authorities as the most effective way to achieve their desired projects.

Part II of the collection focuses on scientific and medical communication. Here again we find that those who take sides in the debate over epistemic paternalism are often concerned with the relationship between vertical and horizontal, or again, epistocratic and democratized modes of knowledge distribution.

In the first chapter of Part II, Fabien Medvecky points out how recognition of the ubiquity of peoples' cognitive biases motivates arguments for interfering in their inquiry for their own epistemic good, while the need for agents to develop skills and virtues of good inquiry on their own motivates criticism of EP as creating some of the same conditions of citizen incompetence which it ostensibly aims to correct. But while epistemic paternalism is often viewed with suspicion, and defenders have typically supported EP only "in certain circumstances," while agreeing that, all things being equal, EP is less than desirable, Medvecky argues for turning this received view on its head: "it is not EP that we ought to be suspicious about, but rather, we should be suspicious of testimonial practice that fails to give due consideration to EP." Medvecky develops this view by explaining how mundane, and how needful it is for us to interfere with one another's epistemic states, and by drawing attention to "the interplay between interference and intentionality in communicative practice." This leaves him substantially at odds with the language of interference which defenders of EP such as Goldman, Ahlstrom-Vij, and Croce employ, and which EP's critics are happy to share. For at the core of suspicion of EP lies an assumption Medvecky thinks we should challenge, the assumption of epistemic autonomy: that individuals can and want to know things independently, without interference from others.

"Many of us hold false beliefs about matters that are relevant to public policy such as climate change and the safety of vaccines.... What can be done to rectify this situation?" Robin McKenna's chapter focuses on two quite different readings of this question. The *descriptive* reading concerns which methods will be *effective* in persuading people that their beliefs are false, while the *normative* reading involves assessing methods we are *permitted* to use in the service of persuading people. After articulating the distinction and its relevance, McKenna's chapter focuses in on this second question. A "de-idealized" approach to normativity is required to appropriately assess this question. This approach recognizes that human beings are not ideal epistemic agents. De-idealized social epistemology enables more concrete suggestions for improving our epistemic situation, while insisting that reasonable proposals be *evidence-based* (that is, based on an answer to the first, descriptive, question). On the basis of both reason and evidence, McKenna argues that "marketing methods" are an acceptable response to the normative question. Marketing methods are both more effective and less ethically and politically problematic than are the "rational persuasion methods" of EP as approached through notions of agent irrationality flowing from assumptions of idealized epistemology.

Shaun Respess examines expert care in mental health paternalism. Medical professionals and practitioners acting as experts in the mental health field make many decisions regarding the epistemic needs of their clients/patients. Some of these decisions appropriately qualify as *epistemic paternalism,* including "concealing particularly unpleasant test results from patients, promoting certain studies and methods over others, and sanctioning official diagnoses over a client's experiential testimony." But what constitutes valid expertise, and how might expertise be leveraged paternalistically in better or worse ways? In a manner highly informed by feminist epistemology, the author argues that an ethics of care should supplant utilitarian, libertarian, and virtue-based accounts of paternalism. On this account, the ethics of care helps articulate "a more accurate representation of how one may or may not appropriately intervene." Care ethics, Respess finds, depreciates agential epistemology, which is argued to root in methodological individualism; it instead makes central a theoretical approach more attuned to inter-dependent agents and dominant *networks* or *ecosystems* of knowledge.

Aude Bandini's chapter focuses on doctor-patient relationships and the devaluation of the expertise of patients—especially "non-compliant" patients. Such patients are usually suspected of "not getting" how serious their disease is, or what treatment options should be foremost. Otherwise, the argument goes, they would whole heartedly collaborate and take better care of themselves (take their medication, exercise more, quit smoking, etc.). The non-compliant patient's refusal or inability to behave is then primarily explained as the outcome of various epistemic flaws: ignorance or some other sort of cognitive frailty (irrationality, short-sightedness, overwhelming emotions or stress due to the disease, etc.), worsened by some vicious character features (recklessness, laziness, weakness of the will, etc.). Bandini questions these assumptions, while defending patients' lay expertise and elaborating the relationship between standard paternalism and more recent arguments cast in terms of EP.

Pat Bondy defends the view that there is a justifiable form of epistemic paternalism (EP) that falls under general paternalism. These cases of EP are epistemic because they are directed at generating epistemic goods, but the reason for generating those epistemic goods is because they bring about other goods, either for the subject, or for people whom the subject will affect, or for society at large. After clarifying this conception of epistemic paternalism, Bondy develops an instrumental approach to epistemic normativity at the individual level. Epistemic reasons are evidential in character, and epistemically rational beliefs are those that are held on the basis of good evidence. Epistemic rationality is not instrumental in character; it's just determined by the quality of the evidence. But epistemic normativity is instrumental: it is a matter of taking the appropriate means to achieve a goal that one has a normative reason to try to achieve. Often, though not always, one has normative reason to try to get true beliefs and avoid false ones. Believing what the evidence supports is the appropriate means to take for achieving that goal. To illustrate how that approach applies in the interpersonal context of EP, consider this example. S1 might be a legislator sitting on an environmental sub-committee;

S2 might be another legislator who would prefer to remain uninformed on the issue; p might be the proposition that climate change poses a serious threat to our survival and way of life; the body of evidence might be that possessed by relevant scientists; and a paternalist action might be to corner S2 during a coffee break and present a bullet-point summary of the recent report issued by the Intergovernmental Panel on Climate Change, which S2 had been avoiding. Bondy takes this to be a justified case of epistemic paternalism insofar as S2 is better off epistemically, and their epistemic improvement improves policy making for the public. Of course, normative reasons can be defeated, yet this analysis shows that some forms of epistemic interference can be justified.

Michel Croce's (2018) article added significantly to attempts to offer an account of legitimate or justified epistemic paternalism (Ahlstrom-Vij 2013; Goldman 1991 and 1999; Pritchard 2013, and others). In his chapter in this collection Croce continues to develop his unique account of features in virtue of which this entitlement comes or goes. Croce addresses Emma Bullock's dilemma for EP, and in particular how she a) singles out cases to which the dilemma applies, and b) interprets the notion of "personal autonomy." He then presents a solution to the dilemma on behalf of those who find scope for justification of epistemic paternalism "in the distinctive value of some interferences." More specifically, he shows that there are cases of (hard) epistemic paternalism that do not fall prey to Bullock's dilemma if one is willing to go beyond the *personal sovereignty* model of autonomy. Articulating it, Croce responds to Bullock's challenge "in a way that safeguards the legitimacy of epistemic paternalism, albeit restricting its scope to a limited range of cognitive projects."

Fernando Broncano-Berrocal, like Robin McKenna and Charlie Crerar, approaches normative questions about EP through an ethics of care. Caring practices, as those involved in parenting, health care or teaching, have epistemic dimensions. But to what extent is epistemic care compatible with epistemic paternalism, and can some epistemically paternalistic acts be considered instances of epistemic care? The author discusses several different conditions on the justification of paternalistic practices, including an *Expert condition* (Goldman 1991), an *Alignment condition*, a *Burden-of-proof condition* (both Ahlstrom-Vij 2013), a *Balancing-goods condition* (Ahlstrom-Vij 2013; Bullock 2016), and a *Virtue condition* (Croce 2018). Ultimately, he develops and defends an *Epistemic care condition*, a condition roughly, on which A acts permissibly toward B if A's epistemically paternalistic act is an instance of proper epistemic care.

David Godden focuses debate over permissible EP on different conceptions of the epistemic autonomy of agents. Prevailing arguments about the permissibility of paternalistic epistemic interventions tend to adopt a conception of epistemic autonomy as epistemic self-reliance. For example, Ahlstrom-Vij explains epistemic autonomy as "the freedom of inquirers to conduct inquiry *in whatever way they see fit*" (2013: 61 emphasis added). Godden argues, however, that autonomy is better understood as epistemic self-governance, and that, so understood, certain kinds of paternalistic epistemic interventions are permissible. Each of us has epistemic blind spots—contingently true claims inaccessible to us because of our constitution or situation. Yet an awareness of our epistemic blind spots, such that they are "known unknowns" to us, can be part of self-governance and provide people with reason to consent to paternalistic epistemic interventions. Godden takes his analysis to suggest stricter standards than Ahlstrom-Vij for the permissibility of epistemic paternalism. Yet he argues that people's commitment to the norm of belief can still license even paternalistic epistemic interventions inquirers themselves would not consent to, "specifically, when their epistemic circumstance blinds them to the reasons licensing the intervention."

Liz Jackson explores the relationship between epistemic paternalism and two other epistemological theses—epistemic permissivism and standpoint epistemology. These two recent theses interact with normative questions about epistemic paternalism, and Jackson argues they provide a sufficient condition for *unjustified* epistemic paternalism. Epistemic permissivism is the view that there are evidential situations which rationally permit more than one attitude toward a proposition. Standpoint epistemology is the view that one's social situation gives one unique access to certain epistemic goods. Part of what interpersonal permissivism and standpoint epistemology have in common is their denial that there is one privileged way of interpreting a body of evidence. The burden of Jackson's argument is to show how permissivism and standpoint epistemology overlap, and how each "provides us with a class of cases of unjustified epistemic paternalism." Jackson's paper highlights the epistemic latitude or slack we owe one another with respect to many of our beliefs, and thus the need for caution and for considering "whether we might be in an epistemically permissive case before engaging in epistemic paternalism."

Valerie Joly Chock and Jonathan Matheson are also concerned with the epistemic justice or injustice of EP. They utilize Kristie Dotson's concept of "testimonial smothering," which obtains when a speaker feels obliged to limit her testimony due to the reasonable risk of it being misunderstood or misapplied by the audience. Testimonial smothering is seen by the authors as a form of epistemic paternalism since the speaker is interfering with the audience's inquiry for their benefit without first consulting them. Your silencing of your own testimony may well be the result of an epistemic injustice. For example, it is because their testimony is often unsafe and risky that pressure to remain silent about domestic violence exists for women of color. Yet cases of one's withholding testimony from an audience due to testimonial smothering fit the standard conditions for epistemic paternalism. Ironically perhaps, a kind of epistemic injustice, self-silencing due to testimonial smothering, offers a vivid case of permissible epistemic paternalism. For when someone is the victim of epistemic injustice, it clearly be permissible for them to withhold further testimony to those who have demonstrated pernicious ignorance and testimonial incompetence regarding the subject. "To think otherwise would be to think that individuals are required to provide testimony that will contribute to even more epistemic injustice."

Amiel Bernal's "Epistemic Paternalism as Epistemic Justice" first develops the case that epistemic paternalism is *in principle* an impermissible form of epistemic injustice, before arguing against this view. Appealing to the distinction between ideal and non-ideal theory, Bernal argues that the normative standards which generate this ostensive tension are inappropriate for social epistemology. Recognizing that social epistemology and epistemic injustice are only possible in non-ideal theory leads to the conclusion that, in some instances, epistemic paternalism can constitute restorative epistemic justice. This thesis is demonstrated by two cases of epistemic paternalism which promote epistemic justice, while respecting the parties involved.

Daniella Meehan's chapter begins with attitudes and thinking styles identified by vice epistemologists as epistemic or intellectual vices. 'Bad' epistemic behavior, is, unfortunately commonplace, and the 'predictably irrational' behavior of humans, is often the backdrop for calls for paternalistic interventions. Meehan examines whether "epistemic nudging" (EN) can be employed as a successful practice to combat our epistemic vices. Nudgers like Cass Sunstein argue that when well-designed nudges are in place, human agency is retained while freedom of choice is not compromised. But despite its *prima facie* appeal, Meehan argues that epistemic nudging "at the very best amounts to a superficial and short-lived way of addressing epistemic vices." Situation management masks vices without eliminating them. Worse, recurring nudges are likely to lead to the atrophy of desirable epistemic capacities of agents. Indeed, the practice of EN "can often lead to the creation of further vices, specifically the vice of epistemic laziness." If so, EN, rather than being a cure-all, actually contributes in no small way to what Meehan and other authors describe as *reflective incapacitational injustice*.

Adam Green's chapter is akin to Meehan's in that both articulate how paternalistic interventions into epistemic practices are often "at significant risk of committing wrongs of the sort they seek to redress." Incorporating the literature on epistemic violence, Green turns the discussion to a contrast of epistemically violent and non-violent interventions. We are tempted to meet epistemic violence with violent interventions or interferences. Yet, the cost of an epistemic intervention goes up the more violence the intervention involves. "Epistemic injustice is rooted in epistemic violence, but paternalism can take the form of violence." By contrast, non-violent action, which involves more deeply listening to the perspective of the other person, also resists epistemic injustice. Non-violent approaches hold great promise as a way of overcoming the "tension between ineffective and violent intervention" which Green finds so pervasive in the debate over EP.

Shaun O'Dwyer's chapter aims to provide an ideal schema for evaluating efforts proceeding from epistemically paternalist motivations: efforts at persuading members of disadvantaged groups to inquire into, modify or abandon demonstrably erroneous beliefs. Asking whether these efforts are themselves just or unjust, O'Dwyer makes an interesting distinction between epistemic and *thumetic* values (after the Greek *thumos*, "feeling," "spirit" or "passion"), a distinction (but not a dichotomy) that any ideal schema should make. The ideal schema provides for co-operative dialogue to rectify erroneous belief, but is also valuable for identifying where epistemic injustice is most likely to occur in interventions that fall short of that schema's standards. This approach aims to avoid the pitfalls of epistemic versions of what Jonathon Quong terms "judgmental paternalism." This is when some person or collective is motivated to take action to improve the "welfare, good, happiness, needs, interests or values" of another agent, but on the basis of a "negative judgement" about the latter's ability to decide competently. O'Dwyer concludes that paternalism is a philosophy which appears at loggerheads with itself: "The profound tension the epistemic variety of this paternalism gives rise to is that similarly motivated efforts to ameliorate the cognitive disadvantage that results in violation of an agent's right to know x can also impinge on her right to be taken seriously."

"Entrenched polarisation and partisanship, 'take-down culture' on social media, break-downs in inter-cultural dialogue: we are all familiar with the array of problems presently afflicting public discourse in societies across the world." But how best to assuage them? Charlie Crerar's chapter, which closes out the anthology, suggests that "A greater willingness to be charitable across viewpoints would not provide a panacea for these problems, but it would help." An intuitive understanding of intellectual charity is as a form of EP: a listener assigns excess credence as a way of encouraging epistemic improvements. This, though, generates a whiff of arrogance around charity, of assuming a position of intellectual superiority, along with the deeper worry that "unless the charitable agent does occupy some relevant position of superiority, the paternalistic defence of charity cannot perform the task for which it was called upon." Instead, Crerar proposes an account of intellectual charity as a *corrective virtue,* that helps compensate for shortcomings elsewhere in our intellectual character. Charitably allotting more credence to others than you think they deserve actually serves us all well. Amongst other things, Crerar's "corrective account" differentiates justified EP from EP motivated by uncharitable judgment about others.

To summarize, the points of view expressed in this collection are highly diverse. The collection includes scholars quite conversant with analytic epistemology, and who partly for reasons of clarity focus their chapters on examination of specific conditions for the justification of paternalistic practice, however rare or widespread they see this as being. The collection also includes scholars whose work largely eschews analytic methods in favor of broader historical or political critique of epistocratic manipulations as threats to individual liberty of conscience, and to democracy. Some of these differences may be ones of style, but a more interesting concern for readers could be the *different conceptions of social epistemology itself* found advocated or implicitly assumed by contributors to the collection. Thus, our contributors draw readily upon both virtue and vice epistemology, and together with this, research on epistemic injustice. We also suggest that the issues raised in debate over epistemic paternalism overlap with (and perhaps shed new light upon) what differentiates epistemic and deliberative accounts of democratic legitimacy.

Such divergence in approaches to social epistemology have been an ongoing concern in this book series (Sherman and Goguen eds. 2019; Reider ed. 2018).[4] With contributors from such different camps raising issues and concerns which should be of genuine concern to all readers, this collection hopes to reconcile these 'in house' divisions among self-described social epistemologists. At the least it may aid the articulation of these differences, through shared attention to a common set of issues, and through leading all readers to rethink some very basic disagreements about the value, or the tyranny, of ideal theory.[5]

NOTES

1. Goldman (1991, 127) writes, "Epistemic paternalism on the part of isolated individuals is quite a different matter from paternalism exercised by the state, or any other powerful organ of society. There are historical reasons for being very cautious about state control of information."

2. As Liz Jackson notes, this definition is found in Ahlstrom-Vij (2013, 51) and Bullock (2018, 434). Goldman's descriptive sense of EP is: "I shall think of communication controllers as exercising epistemic paternalism whenever they interpose their own judgment rather than allow the audience to exercise theirs (all with an eye to the audience's epistemic prospects)" (1991, 119). His advocacy is framed in terms of arguments for rejecting the thesis that communication controllers should never interpose but (assuming low personal cost of effort) should always disseminate to inquirers all the evidence relevant to their inquiries.

3. Competence theories often aim to justify strong paternalism, while consent-based theories may aim either to support or censure it. But the suggested mediation of these normative claims might be anticipated by John Dewey, for whom "freedom of mind is the fundamental and central freedom in the maintenance of a free society" (*LW* 15: 175). Tan Sor Hoon (1999) points out that for Dewey, it is not freedom from interference, but free and full participation, that is important: "No man and no mind was ever emancipated by merely being left alone" (*LW* 2: 340). Dewey held great

hope for experimentalism, and for extending a progressive and pro-social "method of operative intelligence" to the direction of life. But Dewey clearly held strong paternalists to err in assuming that the good for a person is achievable without their cooperation.

4. On vying conceptions of social epistemology, and prospects for their reconciliation, see also Susan Dieleman (2016) and David Coady (2010).

5. For some social epistemologists 'the tyranny of the ideal' is brought about by a Platonist rationalism that forgets Arendt and Foucault. Different conceptions of social epistemology as we find them among our contributors have also been variously exhibited in other volumes in this book series. We hope that this collection helps not just to articulate these differences, but also to commensurate them.

BIBLIOGRAPHY

Ahlstrom-Vij, Kristoffer. *Epistemic Paternalism: A Defence*. New York: Palgrave Macmillan, 2013.

Bullock, Emma. "Knowing and Not-Knowing for Your Own Good: The Limits of Epistemic Paternalism." *Journal of Applied Philosophy*, 35(2), 2018: 433–447.

Coady, David. "Two Conceptions of Epistemic Injustice," *Episteme* 7(2), 2010: 101–113.

Dewey, John. *The Later Works of John Dewey: 1925–1953* (*LW*). Edited by Jo Ann Boydston. Carbondale, IL: SUI Press, 2008.

Dieleman, Susan. "Responsibilism and the Analytic-Sociological Debate in Social Epistemology," *Feminist Philosophical Quarterly* 2(2 #6), 2016: 1–14.

Goldman, Alvin I. *Knowledge in a Social World*, Oxford: Oxford University Press, 1999.

———. "Epistemic Paternalism: Communication Control in Law and Society." *The Journal of Philosophy* 88(3), 1991: 113–131.

Grill, Kalle and Jason Hanna. *The Routledge Handbook of the Philosophy of Paternalism*. London: Routledge, 2018.

Kidd, Ian James, Jose Medina, and Gaile Pohlhaus, Jr. (eds.). *The Routledge Handbook of Epistemic Injustice*. London: Routledge, 2017.

Pritchard, Duncan. "Epistemic Paternalism and Epistemic Value," *Philosophical Inquiries* 1(2), 2013: https://doi.org/10.4454/philinq.v1i2.53

Reider, Patrick J. (ed.). *Social Epistemology and Epistemic Agency: Decentralizing Epistemic Agency*. Lanham, MD: Rowman & Littlefield, 2016.

Scanlon, Thomas. "A Theory of Freedom of Expression," *Philosophy and Public Affairs* 1(2), 1972: 204–26.

Sherman, Benjamin R. and Goguen, Stacey (eds.) *Overcoming Epistemic Injustice: Social and Psychological Perspectives*. Lanham, MD: Rowman & Littlefield, 2019.

Tan, Sor Hoon. "Paternalism: A Deweyan Perspective," *The Journal of Speculative Philosophy* 13(1), 1999: 56–70.

Part I

DIGITAL PATERNALISM AND OPEN SOCIETIES

Chapter 1

Artificial Ignorance, Epistemic Paternalism, and Epistemic Obligations

Stephen John

Proponents of personalized medicine (PM) claim that developments in machine learning technologies will allow us to make better predictions about individuals' propensities to develop disease, hence allowing for more effective prevention and treatment options (Frohlich et al. 2018; Mesko 2017). Consider two (of the very many) reasons to be sceptical of such claims. One is that patients will misunderstand personalized predictions, leading them to make worse medical decisions. Another is that increased knowledge of personalized risk scores will undermine citizens' willingness to contribute to socialized healthcare, as the "low risk," will realise that participation is not, in fact, in their best interests. Both concerns, if valid, imply reasons to control the flow of information from personalized medical tests: the first implies that results should be available *only* when they are interpreted and contextualized by intermediary experts, such as trained genetic counsellors; the second implies reasons against allowing test results to be available *at all*. How should we decide when such controls on the flow of information are permissible?

In this chapter, I propose an answer to this question in terms of "epistemic obligations" and contrast this approach with one framed in terms of individuals' epistemic freedoms. The latter perspective, is, I suggest, implicit in current debates around "epistemic paternalism," and is problematic because it obscures the complex web of social-epistemic norms, which bind and structure communicative practice. Section 1, "Epistemic Obligations," illustrates the obligation-first approach to the ethics of information control through a study of the "understanding" worry about PM, and section 2, "Epistemic Paternalism," explores its implications for work on epistemic paternalism more generally. Section 3, "Epistemic Solidarity," extends my approach through an analysis of the solidarity concern about PM in terms of duties of ignorance. The conclusion suggests that many worries about epistemic paternalism are, in fact, best understood as worries about the possibility of abuse of power. We do need to ask when risks of abuse are serious enough that we should reject controls on information; what we do not need to do is to justify the control of information per se.

EPISTEMIC OBLIGATIONS

One way of thinking about controls on the flow of information is as violations of free inquiry. A different starting point is as enabling fulfilment of our epistemic obligations. This section develops the second, less familiar approach. By "epistemic obligation," I refer to demands of ethical, rather than epistemic normativity: obligations to seek knowledge, understanding (or other epistemic states), which derive from our broader ethical obligations (rather than, say, obligations to believe only on the basis of the evidence). It seems clear that our ethical obligations can generate epistemic obligations; if my son makes a solemn promise to his teacher that he will learn the capital cities of Europe, then he has a prima facie obligation to do so. At a first pass, we can distinguish two major kinds of epistemic obligations.

First, *self-directed epistemic obligations*—that is, obligations to ensure we achieve certain epistemic states (knowledge, understanding, etc.), grounded on our more general ethical obligations: as a parent, I am obliged to find out which foods are suitable for young children; as a voter, I am obliged to be well informed about the policies of different parties; and so on. Second, *other-directed epistemic obligations*—that is, obligations to ensure that others are well informed about certain topics: as a parent, I am obliged to ensure that my children know how to cross roads safely; a physician is obliged to ensure that her patients are well informed about the risks of some procedure and so on. Note that we can have *other-directed* obligations, which do not match-up with any correlative *self-directed* obligations; for example, a physician might have an obligation to inform her patients, even if her patients have no obligation to ensure that they are well informed. However, some *other-directed epistemic obligations* are grounded in reciprocal *self-directed* epistemic obligations: for example, a climate scientist may have an obligation to inform voters about climate change, such that they meet their obligation to be well informed about political matters. I will use the term *epistemic enablement obligations* for this subset of *other-directed* obligations.

We can frame both self- and other-directed epistemic obligations in terms of *informing*: self-directed obligations are obligations to become *informed* about some subject matter; other-directed obligations are obligations to *inform* others. As Neil Manson and Onora O'Neill (2007) have explored in their discussion of informed consent procedures, informing is a complex activity, bound by both ethical and epistemic constraints. Their key insight for this chapter is that good informing should be distinguished from merely providing information; a physician who gives you 10 pages of small-font information about a drug, with the fact that it might cause a fatal heart attack hidden on page 7, has not discharged her obligation to inform you of the risks of taking the drug.

Why not? I suggest that good informing requires careful curation of a communicative encounter, tied to an understanding of a subject's epistemic and practical needs and limitations. To make this metaphor more vivid, imagine a museum worker charged with curating an exhibition. Simply stacking a pile of exhibits in a room may be an (apparently) neutral way of presenting the past, but doing so is likely to leave visitors, at best, bemused, rather than enlightened! Rather, a good curator will organize and contextualize exhibits in ways, which help visitors understand their significance and value. In turn, the ways in which she does this will be sensitive to her audience's epistemic background and practical needs: for example, information cards designed for children will differ from cards designed for connoisseurs. I suggest that similar considerations apply to communication more generally. For example, maybe a good physician would focus on telling the patient about the heart attack risk and making this salient, even if doing so involves leaving out other, epistemically well-established, claims about the drug. A one-page information sheet might leave out lots of information about the drug—say, that it was manufactured in Switzerland, or that it is precisely 1 cm long—but be far preferable as an aide to informing than the 10-page manual that includes this information.

Consider, then, the case of PM. There are long-standing worries that patients find it hard to interpret and understand predictions about their risk of disease (Edwards and Elwyn, 2001). These worries have only intensified as risk-scoring tools have become ever more "personalized"; for example, it seems that when patients are told that, in virtue of possessing certain genomic variants, they have a risk of disease, they tend to adopt a "genetic determinism"; that is, they interpret this information as implying that their risk is fixed (Kaphingst et al. 2012). Such an assumption is, however, false: for example, even if you have a genetic propensity to heart disease, you can still reduce one's overall heart disease risk through exercise and diet.

What are the implications of our knowledge of how patients (mis)understand personalized risk scores for the regulation of PM? The general framework sketched above suggests that there may be good reasons to require that test results are *only* available when they can be contextualized or explained by trained professionals. To see why, consider two ways in which personalized tests might relate to epistemic obligations. First, if we think that individuals have (broadly) ethical obligations to maintain their health, then they have derivative epistemic obligations to become informed about health risks, and PM tests are one way of discharging these obligations. Second, we might (in my mind, quite rightly) deny that anyone has an obligation to be healthy but think that there is a general obligation to ensure that everyone has the capability to be healthy, which, in turn, grounds an *other-directed epistemic obligation*—typically borne by medical professionals—to ensure that they are well informed about health risks; the provision of PM test results is one way of discharging this obligation. Either way, mere provision of uninterpreted results is unlikely to succeed in genuinely informing patients; rather, it is far more likely that uninterpreted results will merely confuse patients. We can, then, think of regulations demanding that test results are always contextualized and explained as ways of enabling individuals to meet their self-directed epistemic obligations or of ensuring that experts' other-directed duties to inform are properly discharged. Of course, this is a truncated version of a complex argument. I hope, though, that my main point is clear enough: thinking in terms of "epistemic obligations" provides a simple and powerful framework for thinking through how worries about patient understanding might justify controls on the flow of information.

EPISTEMIC PATERNALISM

Here is an alternative way of thinking about the policies outlined in the previous section: they place limits on freedom of inquiry—that is, they prevent patients from accessing raw test results—because such freedom will not be in patents' best epistemic interests. That is to say, they seem to be instances of "epistemic paternalism" (Goldman 1991; Ahlstrom-Vij 2013), structurally analogous to cases where, for example, we limit peoples' ability to access alcohol on the grounds that prohibition is in their prudential best interests. The second kind of paternalism is, however, highly controversial, because it seems to interfere with individuals' autonomy. We might think, by analogy, that something similar is true of the first kind of case: that the starting point for thinking about limits on freedom of inquiry is that they are prima facie wrongful, even when they promote epistemic well-being. This kind of set-up seems assumed in some recent work on the concept of "epistemic paternalism"; for example, consider Emma Bullock's claim that (in cases of epistemic paternalism) "there will always be a non-epistemic reason against interfering, namely, the harm it would cause to the individual's personal sovereignty" (Bullock 2018: 441). As Bullock notes, although discussions of epistemic paternalism often focus on the narrower concept of "epistemic autonomy," such practices may seem worrying because they interfere with our more general ability to inquire as we see fit. Although not how Bullock frames her claim, we can express this concern as that epistemic paternalism infringes our "right to free inquiry," grounded in our more general sovereignty. This approach has a prima facie appeal. However, I suggest that it distorts our understanding of socio-epistemic norms. (The end of the section suggests a possible explanation of its initial plausibility.)

Consider, again, the example of the physician who curates a consent form to ensure her patients are truly informed of the risks of taking the drug. In constructing this form, the physician might make various, ethically relevant mistakes: for example, she might underestimate her patients' ability to understand complex information, or she may try to influence her patients' decision through how she frames the information she provides. Good informing is, undoubtedly, an ethically and epistemologically complex activity. Still, once we think in terms of a physician's obligations to ensure that her patients are informed, it seems odd to think that the very practice of curation *at all* stands in need of some special justification, because it violates hearers' sovereignty. (Or, more precisely, thinking this way seems to render the concern ethically empty, because such "violations" are such a ubiquitous aspect of our socio-epistemic lives.) Starting from the alternative perspective of personal sovereignty seems to conceive of information as akin to something which is floating around "out there" in the world, which we then try to control. This is a mistake: rather, the creation and flow of information is always already embedded in social contexts and institutions, governed by complex ethical norms. To think that curating the flow of information is *always* problematic is to ignore that the flow of information is *always* already shaped by ethical norms.

Of course, matters become more complex once we move to cases such as the regulation of personalized medical test results, because it can be harder to identify who counts as a speaker, and, hence, who bears which epistemic obligations. Still, a similar lesson is true: while we can discuss the ethical issues involved in particular decisions about how information should be curated, the curation of information itself is simply a core function of a reasonable regulatory structure.

With these comments in place, we face two questions: Which ways of curating information are better or worse? How does this obligation-first approach to thinking about "epistemic paternalism" relate to everyday paternalism? These are complex questions, which I cannot answer fully here. However, both challenges point us to an important worry about curating the flow of information: that it *can* easily involve an (illegitimate) over-riding of personal sovereignty. To explain: for speakers to discharge their obligations to inform hearers, they will have to make certain sorts of assumptions about their audiences. Typically, these assumptions will include not only assumptions about their audience's epistemic capabilities ("Will they understand this?") but also their practical interests ("Is this something they want to know or should know?"). For example, a physician might assume that her patient wants to know about a heart disease risk but not that a drug was manufactured in Switzerland. However, there may be systematic differences between what a hearer really does or should want to know, and what a speaker thinks her hearer really does or should want to know. For example, in virtue of her religious convictions, a hearer may think that it is particularly important to know whether an operation carries a risk—however small—of requiring a blood transfusion, whereas a speaker might think that the hearer is irrational or misguided in wanting this information. Hence, we face a general problem: systems that allow speakers to discharge their epistemic obligations to inform must allow leeway—to include or exclude certain information—but this leeway can be abused by overruling the subject's personal value judgments; a system that allows the physician to make the ethically proper decision not to report the fact that the drug was manufactured in Switzerland may also allow the physician to make the ethically improper decision not to report the potential need for a blood transfusion. Such abuses constitute a clear example of the kind of substitution of judgment, which marks paternalistic interference (Begon 2016). An important desideratum on ethical information curation is that speakers avoid such abuses. It is, then, certainly true that practices of epistemic paternalism *can* instantiate the same wrongs, which make standard paternalism wrong; however, to think that *all* instances of epistemic paternalism are problematic in the same way as standard paternalism is to flatten the complex ethical landscape that structures information flow.

EPISTEMIC SOLIDARITY

We can distinguish between a descriptive sense of "epistemic paternalism"—to describe a set of practices, which structure the flow of information with the aim of improving subjects' epistemic state—and an evaluative sense—as a set of practices, which prima facie stand in need of justification. I have suggested that we should structure our thinking about informational control policies around the concept of epistemic obligations, rather than restrictions on epistemic subjects' free inquiry. If so, the descriptive concept is useful—because it describes a set of strategies for meeting our obligations, hence reminding us of the complexities of good informing (John 2018)—but the evaluative concept is not—curating the flow of information is not always prima facie wrongful. Still, one might wonder whether we really should adopt an obligation-first approach; one application is, after all, not an argument. In this section, I suggest a further advantage of starting from epistemic obligations rather than epistemic rights: that doing so provides a more elegant way of thinking about a core topic in debates over information control, the creation and maintenance of ignorance.

Consider, again, the case of PM. One worry is that personalized predictions are easily misunderstood or misinterpreted by audiences, such that untrammelled access to raw test results might worsen individual and population health. A second worry about improved prediction techniques in general (and, hence, relevant to PM specifically) is that patients might understand PM all too well; through gaining personalized medical information, they may lose solidaristic motivation (Kavka 1990; Launis 2003; Nuffield Council on Bioethics 2010, Chap. 3). This is a complex concern, but the core thought is simple. Two claims seem prima facie plausible: first, that justice demands a form of socialized healthcare, where healthcare provision is, at least partially, funded through general taxation. Second, most of those who contribute to actual socialized healthcare systems do so, at least partly, on the assumption that such contribution is in their own expected interest, because there is a good chance that they will need to access such a system in the future. In turn, the second thought seems to rely on citizens being behind a "natural veil of ignorance," where they lack detailed knowledge of their own future health. Behind this "natural veil," it is both rational and natural to make an "equal risk assumption": that we are each at roughly equal risk of needing healthcare in the future. PM may undermine this "equal risk" assumption; at least some will realize that, given their unique risk pattern, they are likely to be "net losers" from contributing to shared systems, and, as such, what seems like a prudent investment will come to seem more like a burdensome subsidy to others. Allowing access to personalized medical results will undermine the solidaristic attitudes necessary for sustaining institutions that are demanded by justice.

Leading writers in the field are sceptical that PM *must* undermine solidarity (Praisanck and Buyx 2017). Furthermore, even if these concerns are valid, they could, in principle, be responded to in many ways. For the sake of argument, however, I will assume that these concerns are valid, and that the only way in which they could be resolved would be through banning access to PM results. How should we assess such an information-control policy?

Clearly, it would not count as an instance of epistemic paternalism, because it would not promote subjects' epistemic interests. Still, the general evaluative framework associated with the concept of epistemic paternalism provides one way into thinking about this policy. Just as there are non-paternalist reasons why we might limit personal sovereignty—for example, we might ban alcohol sales because of the harms caused to others—so, too, we might think of this policy as imposing a limit on individuals' epistemic sovereignty as a way of preventing "harms" (or, strictly, undermining social justice). In turn, just as we might debate whether restrictions on alcohol sales are a proportionate response to the harms caused by consumption, so, too, we might try to assess whether limits on access to personalized predictions is a proportionate response to the dangers to socialized healthcare.

Note that this framing seems to imply that there is nothing interesting or distinctive about the fact that the second policy involves restrictions on *epistemic* autonomy and affects our *epistemic* well-being. Rather, our problem becomes a familiar problem—perhaps the most familiar problem—within moral and political theory: how to balance concerns about individual freedom against concerns about maximizing the good. Bullock (2018) has argued convincingly that discussions around epistemic paternalism face a problem: either they assume a *eudaimonistic* view of the value of epistemic wellbeing or they collapse into familiar ethical debates. She argues—convincingly to my mind—that the *eudaimonic* option is problematic. My example seems to add more grist to her mill: it does not seem that debates over information control are fundamentally different from more familiar debates around paternalism merely because they involve "epistemic" states.

However, Bullock herself seems to think that, in framing these problems, we should start from thinking in terms of agents' sovereignty and, hence, free inquiry. In this regard, she shares the same underlying starting-point for thinking about "epistemic paternalism," which I challenged in section 2. From this starting point, debates over information control are framed as problems of how to commensurate between (broadly) deontic and (broadly) consequentialist concerns; between the "right" to access personalized data and the "harms" to the community of such access. Such commensuration is notoriously difficult. Interestingly, this problem is even worse if you think that the *eudaimonic* option is plausible: debates over information control involve balancing not only concerns about consequences and sovereignty but also the quasi-deontic good of epistemic autonomy and a quasi-consequentialist good of knowledge. Regardless of whether they view knowledge as intrinsically valuable, in framing information control policies *as if* they involve constraints on inquiry, standard debates over epistemic paternalism lead us to problems about how to commensurate freedom and the good. I will now suggest that an advantage of the alternative, "obligation-first" approach is that it avoids this problem.

In the first section, I introduced the concept of a self-directed epistemic obligation: that is, an obligation to acquire or maintain some epistemic state, derived from a more fundamental ethical obligation. Typically, when we think about our epistemic obligations, we think about obligations to *improve* our epistemic situation: for example, obligations to become more informed about certain topics. However, we can also have obligations to *fail to improve* our epistemic situation. For example, in virtue of my more general obligations to respect my friend's privacy, I have an obligation not to read his secret diary, which he has left open on the table. I can have obligations to remain ignorant (Manson 2012). (Note a complexity here: we might think of some of the empirical data that underlie work in epistemic paternalism as also suggesting certain sorts of obligations of ignorance: obligations not to acquire information that we know will mislead us. Knowing that, in virtue of her own epistemic frailties, she is likely to be misled by reading observational studies, a physician might have an obligation not to read such reports. This is a different kind of obligation of ignorance, however: in the diary case, reading the diary really *will* improve my epistemic situation—in a way in which reading the observational reports would not—but the point is that I *still* should not do so.)

In the first section, I suggested that we can also have "epistemic enablement obligations," that is, obligations to enable others to meet their epistemic obligations. Just as we can have obligations of ignorance, I suggest that others can have obligations to enable us to maintain our ignorance. For example, a third party, who knows that I am insatiably (but improperly) curious about my friend's private life, finds my friend's diary open on the table. She has, I suggest, an obligation to hide away the diary as a way of enabling me to ensure that I meet my obligation of ignorance. (Of course, she may also have an obligation to hide the diary as a way of protecting my friend's right to privacy, but the two motivations are reinforcing, not exclusive.)

With this backdrop in place, we have a framework for thinking about the "solidarity" concern about PM, centered around two questions: first, do citizens have obligations—grounded in their broader duties to support just institutions—not to gain more personalized information? Second, if they do have such duties, does the state have correlative duties to enable them in the fulfillment of these obligations? My tentative answer to both of these questions is "yes": I suggest that we have the first obligation because it is typically recognized that our obligation to support just institutions can place limits on our pursuit of our prudential interests (in this case, acquiring potentially useful health information). I suggest that the second obligation follows as a result of states' duties to cultivate citizens' dispositions to advance justice (Macedo 1992). Of course, both of these claims could be contested, and there may be other, competing concerns which overrule these obligations. I will not discuss these substantive issues here. What I want to suggest, rather, is that reframing the solidarity concern in terms of our epistemic obligations allows us to avoid the tension we identified in the "epistemic paternalism" framework. On my proposed approach, by contrast, rather than conceptualize information control policies in terms of a clash between rights and consequences, we can, instead, think about them as embedded in wider patterns of socio-epistemic obligation. Of course, weighing and assessing different obligations is not an easy task, but it is easier than balancing freedom against the good.

CONCLUSION

In this chapter, I have done two things. First, I have made a preliminary exploration of two topics concerning the regulation of PM, arguing that a proper response to new forms of artificial intelligence may be to maintain states of artificial ignorance. Second, I have suggested that, despite its use as an analytical tool, the concept of "epistemic paternalism" is not a useful guide to the evaluative and normative issues concerning information control policies. We should, instead, think in terms of interlocking sets of epistemic obligations. To stress: this is not to say that all processes of information control are ethically fine, with nothing to worry about. Rather, it is to point to a genuine, unresolved tension: there are excellent reasons why various agents should have the power to control the flow of information, but such powers can easily be abused. For example, there may be ethical reasons why the state should control the flow of personalized information, maintaining a just healthcare system, but, also, good ethical reasons to worry that these powers might be abused to maintain unjustifiable forms of ignorance. As such, there may well be pressing ethical, political, and practical reasons to resist controls on the flow of information. We shouldn't, however, confuse those powerful reasons with reasons to think that controlling the flow of information is itself something that requires justification.

BIBLIOGRAPHY

Ahlstrom-Vij, Kristoffer. *Epistemic Paternalism: A Defence*. Basingstoke: Palgrave Macmillan, 2013.

Begon, Jessica. "Paternalism," *Analysis* 76(3), 2016: 355–373.

Bullock, Emma. "Knowing and Not-Knowing for Your Own Good: The Limits of Epistemic Paternalism," *Journal of Applied Ethics* 35(2), 2018: 433–447.

Edwards, Adrian and Glyn Elwyn. "Understanding Risk and Lessons for Clinical Risk Communication about Treatment Preferences," *BMJ Quality & Safety* 10(1), 2001: 19–113.

Fröhlich, Holger, Rudi Balling, Niko Beerenwinkel, Oliver Kohlbacher, Santosh Kumar, Thomas Lengauer, Marloes H. Maathuis et al. "From Hype to Reality: Data Science Enabling Personalized Medicine," *BMC Medicine* 16(1), 2018: 150.

Goldman, Alvin. "Epistemic Paternalism: Communication Control in Law and Society," *The Journal of Philosophy* 88(3), 1991: 113–131.

John, Stephen. "Epistemic Trust and the Ethics of Science Communication: Against Transparency, Openness, Sincerity and Honesty," *Social Epistemology*, 32(2), 2018: 75–87.

Kaphingst, Kimberly A., Colleen M. McBride, Christopher Wade, Sharon Hensley Alford, Robert Reid, Eric Larson, Andreas D. Baxevanis, and Lawrence C. Brody. "Patients' Understanding of and Responses to Multiplex Genetic Susceptibility Test Results," *Genetics in Medicine* 14(7), 2012: 681.

Kavka, Gregory S. "Some Social Benefits of Uncertainty," *Midwest Studies in Philosophy* 15, 1990: 311–326.

Launis, Veikko. "Solidarity, Genetic Discrimination, and Insurance: A Defense of Weak Genetic Exceptionalism," *Social theory and practice* 29(1), 2003: 87–111.

Macedo, Stephen. "Charting Liberal Virtues," *Nomos*, 34, 1992: 204–232.

Manson, Neil. "Epistemic Restraint and the Vice of Curiosity," *Philosophy*, 87(2), 2012: 239–259.

Manson, Neil, & Onora O'Neill. *Rethinking Informed Consent in Bioethics*. Cambridge: Cambridge University Press, 2007.

Mesko, Bertalan. "The Role of Artificial Intelligence in Precision Medicine," *Expert Review of Precision Medicine and Drug Development* 5(2), 2017: 239–241.

Nuffield Council on Bioethics. *Medical Profiling and Online Medicine*. London: Nuffield Council on Bioethics, 2010.

Prainsack, Barbara, & Alena Buyx. *Solidarity in Biomedicine and Beyond*. Cambridge: Cambridge University Press, 2017.

Chapter 2

Epistemic Paternalism Online

Clinton Castro, Adam Pham, and Alan Rubel

ARCHITECTURES OF CONTROL

In 1995, Nicholas Negroponte introduced the idea of *The Daily Me*, a virtual newspaper custom-fitted to each reader's particular taste. As Cass Sunstein elaborates:

> If your taste runs to William Shakespeare, your Daily Me could be all Shakespeare, all the time. . . . Maybe your views are left of center, and you want to read stories fitting with what you think about climate change, equality, immigration, and the rights of labor unions. . . . With the Daily Me everyone could enjoy an *architecture of control*. Each of us would be in fully charge of what we see and hear. (Sunstein 2017: 1)

At the time, *The Daily Me* may have sounded like an improvement on traditional news. But we now know it has substantial drawbacks. Consider the Michigan resident who received media attention for being "surprised to hear there was anything negative in the Mueller Report at all about President Trump" (Golshan 2019). The resident made her statement over a month after the report, which contained many negative revelations about the president and received much media attention for this, was made available to the public (USDOJ 2019). When the resident made her statement, it was hard to imagine that any American could think that the report was anything but negative for the president. Yet, she thought it exonerated him.

When the resident did learn that the report was negative, it was through serendipity. At the time, the only Republican representative calling for impeachment on the basis of the report happened to be hers. He held a town hall to share his thoughts about the report. Were it not for this, the resident would have gone on believing that there was no evidence that the president had obstructed justice.

The Michigan resident is not unique. Many of us have been made epistemically worse off through our exercise of the powers granted to us by *new media*, highly interactive digital technology for creating, sharing, and consuming information. Among its affordances, new media fosters *epistemic bubbles*, social epistemic structures that leave out relevant sources of information (Nguyen *forthcoming*).[1] It does this by ferreting out our preferences and adapting to them automatically. As Eli Pariser explains,

> The new generation of Internet filters look at the things you seem to like . . . and tries to extrapolate. They are prediction engines, constantly creating and refining a theory of who you are and what you'll do and want next. Together, these engines create a unique universe of information for each of us and . . . alters the way we encounter ideas and information. (Pariser 2012: 9)

It's worse than this, though. New media feeds us information designed to influence us based on those preferences and proclivities. It doesn't merely reinforce our beliefs, it seeds and nurtures new ones (cf. Alfano et al. 2018).

YouTube, for example, will recommend videos to you based on what you have watched. This is done using a machine learning algorithm that is responsible for more than 70% of the time people spend on the site (Roose 2019). The YouTube algorithm is good at showing users what they are inclined to keep watching. For instance, watching videos from the liberal, progressive Young Turks is likely to lead to recommendations from CNN, and the channels of Barack Obama, Elizabeth Warren, and Bernie Sanders (Kaiser and Rauchfleish 2018). Viewing videos from the Fox News channel is likely to lead to recommendations from alt-right, men's rights, and conspiracy theory channels (Kaiser and Rauchfleish 2018). Given that two-thirds of Americans get news through social media (with one in five getting news from YouTube) (Pew Research Center 2018b), it is no wonder we can consume a lot of news but be misinformed or underinformed about current affairs of monumental importance.

Combine this with new media's immense popularity, and there is cause for concern.[2] Consider "vaccine hesitancy." The reluctance or refusal to vaccinate has surged in recent years and made its way to the World Health Organization's list, "Ten threats to global health in 2019" (World Health Organization 2019). Much of the popularity of "anti-vaxxing," a movement that aims to spread vaccine hesitancy, is owed to new media (specifically, sites such as Facebook, Twitter, and YouTube) (Hussain et al. 2018). And now, two decades after the federal government declared it "eliminated," measles has returned to the United States (Joy 2019). Epistemic bubbles can have dangerous material consequences.

This raises questions about the responsibility new media developers have to alter the architecture of control that its users enjoy. This, in turn, raises questions about the latitude that social media developers have here. On the one hand, we might think developers should lead their users to consider a more diverse array of content than they currently do, even if that is not in line with users' wishes. On the other, there might be something objectionably paternalistic about this: users should decide their information diets for themselves.

We will argue that because so much of the Internet information environment is epistemically noxious, there is lots of room and opportunity for epistemic paternalism (acting to improve the epistemic lot of another, regardless of the others' wishes). In fact, we argue, epistemically paternalistic policies should be a perennial part of the Internet information environment. We proceed as follows. First, we motivate a framework for guiding developers' changes to their technologies. We then use the framework to show that an epistemically paternalistic policy Facebook enacted to combat fake news on its site is permissible. We close with reasons for thinking that epistemically paternalistic policies like the one we discuss should be a common feature of Internet information environments.

UNILATERAL CHANGE

Developers make unilateral changes to their technologies all of the time. They must in order for their products to function in the dynamic social, economic, and technological environments in which they operate. But which unilateral changes are developers permitted to make? Begin by considering two cases.

Mundane Update

In April of 2018, Facebook updated their plan to restrict data access on Facebook. This involved eliminating the Events API, which enabled users to grant apps access to events they attended or hosted (which made it easy to add these events to one's calendar).[3] The update phased out this functionality because the Events API allowed applications to access private information about users without their consent. The functionality will be accessible again, to applications that meet stricter requirements than the site previously had (Schroepfer 2018).

Emotional Contagion

For a week in 2012, Facebook ran a psychological experiment on 689,003 unwitting users. Some of these users had content with "positive" emotional content filtered from their experience of the site. Others had content with "negative" emotional content filtered out. The study showed "that emotional states can be transferred to others via emotional contagion, leading people to experience the same emotions without their awareness" (Kramer et al. 2014: 8788).

In thinking about the limits of unilateral decision-making, it is helpful to keep both of these cases in view. We take it that Emotional Contagion was morally wrong and that Mundane Update was not. We'll explain our judgments of these cases to shed some light on the ethics of making unilateral changes to large social media platforms.

Why, exactly, was Mundane Update not morally wrong? We think that a good explanation is that it exposes no one to treatment they can reasonably reject.[4] The only parties that might have a claim to rejecting the treatment they receive are the users of apps that depend on the Events API and the developers of those apps. Both parties are inconvenienced and have options taken away from them (the users cannot add events to calendars automatically; the developers will eventually have to accommodate Facebook's stricter requirements or cease to use the API). But these inconveniences are minor. No one seems to be harmed (the inconvenience does not rise to this level in either case), nor is anyone's freedom or autonomy threatened (they are still able to do the underlying thing that matters, that is, put important events in calendars and interface with Facebook). Further, the reasons that favor the update—that is, protecting third parties from having their private information exposed—are weighty. Given that the imposition is minor and the claims in favor substantial, the update exposes no one to a treatment they can reasonably reject. So, it is permissible.

Using the same framework, we can explain why Emotional Contagion was morally wrong. Begin by asking what reasons the experimental subjects have for rejecting the treatment. Much of the criticism of the experiment focused on the idea that users may have been harmed by the experiment. One critic conjectured that Facebook could very well have killed users with their experiments, stating, "At their scale and with depressed people out there, it's possible" (Goel 2014). While these considerations weigh against Emotional Contagion, there is a stronger objection.

A weightier reason experimental subjects have to reject the treatment is that it used them without their permission. Facebook's experiment is in tension with what we'll call *Consent*, the idea that there is a strong prima facie reason to avoid using people in ways that precludes them from consenting to that usage (cf. Kant 1998; Korsgaard 1996; O'Neill 1989). The experiment precluded users' consent by exploiting their assumption that they would be interacting with a normal version of the site and surreptitiously exposing them to a faux version of the site in order to run the experiment. It did this without asking them whether they wanted to be part of an experiment and without letting them know about it, thus using them while precluding them from consenting to that usage.

A possible objection to our assessment of Emotional Contagion is that *A/B testing*, the process of experimenting with different options in order to measure the relative success of each one (Deswal 2012), is known to be a common method for developing web-based products. Thus, the experimental subjects were not used without their consent: they were being used in exactly the way they tacitly consented to being used when they signed up for the site. According to this objection, Facebook didn't exploit users' assumption that they would be interacting with a normal version of the site. Rather, it did something they consented to by using the site, that is, being exposed to different versions of the site in order to gain information about how it affects them and improve the site's functionality.

We find this response uncompelling. In ordinary A/B testing, users are exposed to slightly different versions of a site, *each version of which is a candidate version of the site*. In Emotional Contagion, users were not exposed to candidate versions of the site. Instead, they were exposed to defective versions of the site. That is, they were exposed to versions of the site that were systematically stripped of the content that they logged on to see (i.e., news about their friends). So, even savvy users who interacted with Facebook in full awareness that the site might be in A/B testing would have had their expectations upset in Emotional Contagion. Whatever tacit consent to testing users gave when using the site, it did not extend to this treatment.

Now, the experimentees' claims against experimentation could be outweighed if the reasons for the experiment were weighty enough. But the reasons in favor of Emotional Contagion do not seem to be weighty at all. Facebook did not run the experiment because its users were at any substantial risk of harm (e.g., contrast this with Mundane Update). Rather, the company was simply curious about how much positive and negative posts influenced their users.[5] Further, Facebook had options available to them that did not involve surreptitious testing. As Facebook chief technology officer (CTO) Mike Schroepfer would later announce, "We should have considered other non-experimental ways to do this research" (Schroepfer 2014). Facebook also could have simply asked users if they wanted to volunteer for experimentation.

Now that we have explained our judgments of Mundane Update and Emotional Contagion, we are in a position to step back and highlight a few features of the framework we have used. In thinking about whether some intervention is permissible, it is helpful to think about whether anyone who will be affected by it will be exposed to treatment they can reasonably reject. When thinking about reasons for rejecting some treatment, it is helpful to think of whether the treatment will harm them, whether it respects their personhood, and what the reasons for the intervention are.[6] These factors can push and pull against each other to make a treatment permissible or impermissible.

DEMOTING FAKE NEWS

Let us now consider a unilateral decision Facebook has made in their fight against fake news. In April of 2019, Facebook announced that it would use a new metric, Click-Gap, to determine where to rank posts in one's News Feed.[7] Click-Gap measures the gap between a website's traffic from Facebook, compared to its traffic from the Internet at large. The idea here, as explained by Facebook, is that "a disproportionate number of outbound Facebook clicks . . . can be a sign that the domain is succeeding on News Feed in a way that doesn't reflect the authority they've built outside it" (Rosen 2019). Click-Gap is part of a measure to demote low-quality content, such as fake news, in the News Feed and prevent it from going viral on the website (Rosen 2019).

We'll argue that this measure, call it Demoting Fake News, is an instance of permissible epistemic paternalism. We'll begin by explaining why it is an instance of epistemic paternalism. We'll then argue that it is permissible, despite being paternalistic. We'll close with reasons for thinking that epistemically paternalistic policies like this one should be common.

A prima facie intuitive, standard definition of paternalism, owed to Gerald Dworkin (2017), is as follows:

Paternalism. S acts paternalistically toward R by doing (omitting) Z *iff*:

(C1) Z (or its omission) interferes with the liberty or autonomy of R.
(C2) S does so without the consent of R.
(C3) S does so just because Z will improve the welfare of R (where this includes preventing his welfare from diminishing), or in some way promote the interests, values, or good of R.

Were we to accept this definition, Demoting Fake News would not be an instance of paternalism because (C1) is not met.

It's worth pausing to explain why. We follow John Christman (2018) in understanding an individual as *autonomous* when she is not directed by doxastic or conative attitudes that are not simply imposed externally on her, but are hers, authentically (i.e., she can reflectively endorse them), and *free* when she can act without external or internal constraints and has the resources to effectuate her desires. So, to determine whether Demoting Fake

News is paternalistic, we must ask whether they undermine users' autonomy or freedom.

Begin with autonomy. If the policy works, it will play a role in shaping users' doxastic attitudes (e.g., their beliefs about whether vaccines are safe). The crucial question, then, is whether the resulting attitudes will be authentic. It seems that they will be. Whatever effect the interventions will have on users' attitudes, it will be by way of shielding users from misinformation masquerading as information. Users affected by the policy will then be *prevented* from forming inauthentic attitudes. This is because people (typically) will that their doxastic attitudes are justified and accurate. Now, there might be users who want to be anti-vaxxers, come what may. Perhaps they value being a member of the conspiracy-theorist community more than good epistemic hygiene. However, such users are not going to have their considerations changed by an intervention like Demoting Fake News.[8] The touch of this intervention is far too light for that.

We take it that a similar conclusion holds with respect to freedom. Demoting Fake News does not constrain what users can do. The policy may bring about a state of affairs that some might not like, namely one where an unvarnished experience of Facebook is not possible. But bringing about a state of affairs that is not desired hardly consists in constraining what one can do, and under this policy, users can still post what they were able to post before, follow whomever they were able to follow before, and so on. The claim that Demoting Fake News limits users' freedom strains credulity.

Despite failing to meet (C1), we think that Demoting Fake News is an instance of paternalism. This is because we reject the common definition of paternalism. To see why, consider the following case from Shane Ryan (2016).

The Smoke Alarm Case

Suppose that a mother is worried about the safety of her son in his new apartment. It's his first time living away from home and his mother knows that there is no smoke alarm in his apartment. She thinks that if she were to suggest that he get one, then he would agree, but knowing him as she does, she doesn't believe that he would actually get one. She knows that he is very proud of his new-found independence, and she thinks that if she were to ask him whether he would like her to buy him one, he would say no. She decides to buy him one anyway and, by offering it to him already bought, tries to make his acceptance of it a fait accompli (Ryan 2016: 126).

In this case, (C1) does not obtain. Yet, the mother acts paternalistically toward the son.

That Paternalism is susceptible to counterexamples like the Smoke Alarm Case is the primary reason that we are motivated to accept a less standard account of paternalism, owed to Ryan (2016):

Paternalism*. S acts paternalistically toward R by doing (omitting) Z *iff*:

(C1) S does so irrespective of what S believes the wishes of R may be.
(C2) S does so just because S judges that Z may or will advance R's ends (her welfare, interests, values or good).

By the lights of this definition, Demoting Fake News could qualify as a paternalistic intervention, so long as it is motivated by Facebook's judgment that improving people's epistemic lot improves their welfare.

Now, the relationship between having true (or accurate, etc.) or justified (or rational, etc.) doxastic attitudes and one's welfare is complicated (e.g., see Hazlett 2013). Knowing a fact can be irrelevant to our ends (e.g., knowing how far two randomly selected grains in the Sahara are from one another, Sosa 2000). It can even be detrimental (e.g., knowing how a movie ends before you've seen it, Kelly 2003). So, we find it helpful to couch the remaining discussion in terms of epistemic paternalism.

Epistemic Paternalism. S acts epistemically paternalistically toward R by doing (omitting) Z *iff*:

(C1) S does so irrespective of what S believes the wishes of R may be.
(C2) S does so just because S judges that Z may or will make R epistemically better off.

We will follow Kristoffer Ahlstrom-Vij (2013: 50–61) in understanding someone as *epistemically better off* when she undergoes an epistemic Pareto improvement with respect to a question that is of interest to her, where an *epistemic Pareto improvement* is an improvement along at least one epistemic dimension of evaluation without deterioration with respect to any other epistemic dimension of evaluation.

By the lights of Epistemic Paternalism, Demoting Fake News is epistemically paternalistic. As Adam Mosseri, vice president of News Feed explains, Demoting Fake News aims to fight fake news's effect of making the world less informed (Mosseri 2017). That is, the policy has been enacted because Facebook believes that they will make users epistemically better off (i.e., (C2**) is met). In explaining the responsibility Facebook has for doing its share in the fight, Mosseri likens Facebook's responsibility to the responsibility teachers have to fight misinformation. This is apt. Teachers are often epistemically paternalistic toward their students. And, like teachers, Facebook would not change course were it to learn that Demoting Fake News was unwelcomed (i.e., (C1**) is satisfied). This is because of the kind of pressure Facebook is reacting to when it demotes fake news, that is, pressure from the public and, increasingly, governments[9] to fight fake news. Having articulated the ways in which Demoting Fake News is paternalistic, let us now turn to the moral question: Is it permissible?

To answer, consider the two constituencies that might have a claim against the policy: users of Facebook and purveyors of fake news.

Begin with the users. What claim might they have against the policy? Well, it's not plausible that they are harmed, so they can't appeal to that. Nor is the policy in tension with Consent. Facebook has been open about its campaign to fight fake news, and in any event, it is reasonable to expect curators of news feeds to exercise discretion, especially against misleading content.

Disgruntled users might retort that the opportunity to see more fake news than they would under this policy has been taken away without their consent. But, importantly, Consent does not speak against *affecting* people without their consent. Rather, it speaks against *using* them in ways they are not able to consent to. And using someone—as opposed to merely affecting them—involves intending their presence or participation to contribute to achieving the end (Guerrero 2016; Kerstein 2013, 2019; Scanlon 2008). Removing the option to see more fake news does not violate this standard, because eliminating it does not intend the presence or participation of users who would like to have the option.

As a last recourse, users might appeal to autonomy or liberty. But as we argued earlier, the policies do not undermine users' autonomy or liberty. They do not instill in users inauthentic attitudes, nor do they limit users' abilities to effectuate their desires. So, it does not seem that there are users who could reasonably object to Demoting Fake News.

Let's, then, turn to the purveyors of fake news. They might claim that this policy harms them, and that this is morally relevant. It is hard to know how much weight, if any, this appeal should have. This is for several reasons. One is that fake news is an affront to users' autonomy: it is misinformation masquerading as information, and thus doxastic attitudes based on it are inauthentic. Another reason is that the purveyors are left with alternatives under this policy. It leaves them free to promote vaccine hesitancy (or whatever cause they seek to advance), so long as their methods do not subvert user autonomy in the way just described. So, they are left with the options that allow them to minimize (or eliminate) any harm done to them. They just have to do it in ways that is more respectful to users.

Purveyors may try to appeal to Consent. We do not think they will get any traction here either. Consent, recall, stated that there a strong prima facie reason to avoid *using* people in ways they cannot consent to. Demoting Fake

News does not use purveyors. It does not require their presence or participation. To better demonstrate this, it might be helpful to consider a policy that would use purveyors of fake news. Facebook could institute a policy where any person or organization caught promoting fake news was digitally strung up and shamed for reasons of deterrence. The deterrence policy in that case requires using the purveyors of fake news.

Finally, purveyors might appeal to considerations of autonomy or liberty. It is difficult to see how purveyors' autonomy might be compromised, as Demoting Fake News does not involve anything that might affect purveyors' attitudes. The liberty of purveyors is not compromised either. We have already seen why: under Demoting Fake News, purveyors are free to advance the ideas they support (they just might not be able to pursue these aims quite as effectively, if they do not change their current approaches).

Let us now turn to the reasons that speak in favor of Demoting Fake News. It is reasonable to think that it will prevent significant harms to individuals. Policies like Demoting Fake News have proved to be quite effective. For instance, in November 2016 Facebook, updated its Facebook Audience Network policy, which banned ads that contain or promote fake news (Wingfield at al. 2016). As a result, the sharing of fake news among users on the site fell by roughly 75% (Chiou and Tucker 2018). Given that fake news is a driver of harmful movements, such as vaccine hesitancy, there is a strong consideration in favor of the policy. After all, those who wind up sick because of vaccine hesitancy are significantly harmed.

Harm reduction is not the only effect Demoting Fake News has. It also supports user autonomy. Consider:

> A growing body of evidence demonstrates that consumers struggle to evaluate the credibility and accuracy of online content. Experimental studies find that exposure to online information that is critical of vaccination leads to stronger anti-vaccine beliefs, since individuals do not take into account the credibility of the content (Nan and Madden, 2012; Betsch et al., 2010, 2013; Allam et al., 2014). Survey evidence . . . shows that only half of low-income parents of children with special healthcare needs felt "comfortable determining the quality of health websites" (Knapp et al., 2011). Since only 12% of US adults are proficient in health literacy with 36% at basic or below basic levels (Kutner et al., 2006), Fu et al. (2016) state that . . . "low-quality antivaccine web pages . . . promote compelling but unsubstantiated messages [opposing vaccination]." (Chiou and Tucker 2018)

Far from being disrespectful to agents' autonomy (something paternalistic policies are often accused of), epistemically paternalistic policies like Demoting Fake News are an important element of respecting it. The policy, if successful, will protect users from internalizing attitudes that would be inauthentically held.

Demoting Fake News is a policy no one could reasonably reject; further, there are compelling reasons to enact it. So, it is justified. In fact, it is for these reasons that Facebook *must* engage policies like Demoting Fake News: users who adopt unwarranted beliefs because of fake news and individuals who contract illnesses because of vaccine hesitancy have a very strong claim against Facebook's taking a laissez-faire approach to combating fake news on its site.

Since much of the Internet information environment is epistemically noxious, there is lots of room and opportunity for interventions, such as Demoting Fake News, that are epistemically paternalistic. Hence, many epistemically paternalistic policies can (and should) be a perennial part of the Internet information environment. What should we conclude from that? One thing is that we should recognize that developers should engage in epistemic paternalism as a matter of course. Another is that our focus in evaluating epistemically relevant interventions should not be on whether such actions are epistemically paternalistic. Rather, it should be on how they relate to other values (e.g., well-being, autonomy, and freedom).

CONCLUSIONS AND CAVEATS

What we have offered here are really only the opening moves of a longer discussion about how, exactly, to manage new media in ways that appropriately balance the interests of everyone involved. The policy we have discussed governs with a fairly light touch. But initiatives like Demoting Fake News may be limited by the same fact that makes them justifiable, that is, that they govern with a light touch. These policies may be able to pop epistemic bubbles, but they may not be able to dismantle sturdier structures, such as *echo chambers* (epistemic structures that, like epistemic bubbles, leave relevant sources of information out; but, unlike epistemic bubbles, actively discredit those sources (Nguyen *forthcoming*)). There is good reason to look into what we may do to chip away at these structures. Social media sites foster echo chambers that light-touch policies will likely be ineffective against. This raises questions about which interventions can dismantle echo chambers and which (if any) of them may be enacted.

NOTES

1. The term "epistemic bubble" bears some semblance to a more popular term, "filter bubble" (which was coined by Pariser). A *filter bubble* is a kind of epistemic bubble that is created by internet filters that attempt to show you what you want

to see, by extrapolating from your past behavior and the behavior people like you (Pariser 2012).

2. To give a sense of this: In the United States, 69% of adults are on Facebook, 73% use YouTube, and 45% are on Twitter, and the median American uses three social media sites (Pew Research Center 2018a; 2019). Usage is even higher among teens. As of 2015, 97% of 12th graders used social media sites (Twenge 2017).

3. An application programming interface (API) is a program that allows different applications to communicate to each other.

4. This approach is inspired by Scanlon (1998).

5. In a vague apology for the experiment, Facebook's chief operating officer (COO) said, "This was part of ongoing research companies do to test different products, and that was what it was" (Gibbs 2014). In a blogpost promising more transparency and greater care in research, Facebook's CTO said that the emotional contagion hypothesis was "important to look into" (Schroepfer 2014).

6. There, of course, can be other factors and we cannot mention them all here (e.g., we have made no mention of considerations of justice or special relationships).

7. "News Feed is a personalized, ever-changing collection of photos, videos, links, and updates from the friends, family, businesses, and news sources you've connected to on Facebook" (Facebook 2019).

8. This isn't to say that the architecture of social media sites can't influence users in important ways. We take it that the "technological seduction" that sites like YouTube exhibit (cf. Alfano et al. 2019) *can* encroach on autonomy by, for example, seeding and nurturing convictions that either can't be endorsed upon reflection *or* have been seeded and nurtured through methods that agents are alienated from.

9. Germany is proposing a law to fine Facebook for advertisements containing fake news (Olsen 2016).

BIBLIOGRAPHY

Ahlstrom-Vij, Kristoffer. *Epistemic Paternalism: A Defense*. Basingstoke: Palgrave Macmillan, 2013.

Alfano, Mark, Joseph Adam Carter, and Marc Cheong. "Technological Seduction and Self-Radicalization." *Journal of the American Philosophical Association* 4, no. 3 (2018): 298–322. doi:10.1017/apa.2018.27

Chiou, Lesley and Catherine Tucker. "Fake News and Advertising on Social Media: A Study of the Anti-Vaccination Movement," 2018. https://ssrn.com/abstract=3209929 or http://dx.doi.org/10.2139/ssrn.3209929

Christman, John. "Autonomy in Moral and Political Philosophy." *The Stanford Encyclopedia of Philosophy*, Spring 2018 Edition. https://plato.stanford.edu/archives/spr2018/entries/autonomy-moral/

Deswal, Siddharth. "A Web Designer's Introduction to A/B Testing," 2012. https://webdesign.tutsplus.com/articles/a-web-designers-introduction-to-ab-testing-web design-9056 Facebook. "News Feed." Accessed August 1, 2019. https://www.facebook.com/facebookmedia/solutions/news-feed

Gerald Dworkin. "Paternalism." *The Stanford Encyclopedia of Philosophy* Fall 2019. https://plato.stanford.edu/entries/paternalism/

Gibbs, Samuel. "Facebook Apologizes for Psychological Experiments on Users." *The Guardian*, March 2, 2018. https://www.theguardian.com/technology/2014/jul/02/facebook-apologises-psychological-experiments-on-users

Guerrero, Alexander A. "Appropriately Using People Merely as a Means." *Criminal Law and Philosophy* 10, no. 4 (2014): 777–94. https://doi.org/10.1007/s11572-014-9346-x

Hazlett, Allan. *A Luxury of the Understanding*. New York: Oxford University Press, 2013.

Hussain, Azhar, Madiha Ahmed Syed Ali, and Sheharyar Hussain. "The Anti-Vaccination Movement: A Regression in Modern Medicine." *Cureus*, March 2018. https://doi.org/10.7759/cureus.2919

Goel, Vindu. "Facebook Tinkers with Users' Emotions in News Feed Experiment, Stirring Outcry." *The New York Times*, June 29, 2014. https://www.nytimes.com/2014/06/30/technology/facebook-tinkers-with-users-emotions-in-news-feed-experiment-stirring-outcry.html

Golshan, Tara. "Republicans' Successful Campaign to Protect Trump from Mueller's Report, in One Quote." *Vox*, May 30, 2019. https://www.vox.com/2019/5/30/18646048/republican-protect-trump-mueller-report-amash

Joy, Kevin. "What's Causing the Latest Measles Outbreak?" *Michigan Health Blog*, January 31, 2019. https://healthblog.uofmhealth.org/whats-causing-2019-measles-outbreak-symptoms-perfcon

Kaiser, Jonas and Adrian Rauchfleish. "Unite the Right? How YouTube's Recommendation Algorithm Connects the U.S. Far-Right," 2018. https://medium.com/@MediaManipulation/unite-the-right-how-youtubes-recommendation-algorithm-connects-the-u-s-far-right-9f1387ccfabd

Kant, Immanuel. *Groundwork of the metaphysics of morals*. Cambridge: Cambridge University Press, 1998.

Kelly, Thomas. "Epistemic Rationality as Instrumental Rationality: A Critique." *Philosophy and Phenomenological Research* 66, no. 3 (2003): 612–40. https://doi.org/10.1111/j.1933-1592.2003.tb00281.x

Kerstein, Samuel. *How to Treat Persons*. Oxford: Oxford University Press, 2013.

Kerstein, Samuel. "Treating Persons as Means." *The Stanford Encyclopedia of Philosophy* Summer 2019. https://plato.stanford.edu/archives/sum2019/entries/persons-means/

Korsgaard, Christine M. *Creating the Kingdom of Ends*. Cambridge: Cambridge Univ. Press, 2004.

Kramer, Adam D.I., Jamie E. Guillory, and Jeffrey T. Hancock. "Emotional Contagion through Social Networks." *Proceedings of the National Academy of Sciences* 111, no. 24 (2014): 8788–90. doi:10.1073/pnas.1320040111.

Mosseri, Adam. "Working to Stop Fake News." *Facebook Newsroom*, 2017. https://newsroom.fb.com/news/2017/04/working-to-stop-misinformation-and-false-news/

Negroponte, Nicholas. *Being Digital*. New York: Vintage, 1995.

Nguyen, C. Thi. "Echo Chambers and Epistemic Bubbles." *Episteme* forthcoming: 1–21. https://doi.org/10.1017/epi.2018.32

Obar, Jonathan A. and Anne Oeldorf-Hirsch. "The Biggest Lie on the Internet: Ignoring the Privacy Policies and Terms of Service Policies of Social Networking Services." *SSRN Electronic Journal*, 2016. https://doi.org/10.2139/ssrn.2757465

Olson, Parmy. "Germany Wants Facebook to Pay for Fake News." *Forbes*, December 19, 2016. https://www.forbes.com/sites/parmyolson/2016/12/19/germany-wants-facebook-to-pay-for-fake-news/

O'Neill, Onora. *Constructions of Reason: Explorations of Kant's Practical Philosophy*, Cambridge: Cambridge University Press, 1989. doi:10.1017/CBO9781139173773.

Pariser, Eli. *The Filter Bubble: How the New Personalized Web Is Changing What We Read and How We Think*. New York: Penguin Books, 2012.

Pew Research Center. "Social Media Use in 2018." 2018a. https://www.pewinternet.org/2018/03/01/social-media-use-in-2018/

Pew Research Center. "News Use across Social Media Platforms 2018." 2018b. https://www.journalism.org/2018/09/10/news-use-across-social-media-platforms-2018/

Pew Research Center. "Share of U.S. Adults Using Social Media, Including Facebook, Is Mostly Unchanged Since 2018." 2019. https://www.pewresearch.org/fact-tank/2019/04/10/share-of-u-s-adults-using-social-media-including-facebook-is-mostly-unchanged-since-2018/

Roose, Kevin. "The Making of a YouTube Radical." *New York Times*, June 8 2019. https://www.nytimes.com/interactive/2019/06/08/technology/youtube-radical.html

Rosen, Guy. "Remove, Reduce, Inform: New Steps to Manage Problematic Content." *Facebook Newsroom*, 2019. https://newsroom.fb.com/news/2019/04/remove-reduce-inform-new-steps/#reduce

Ryan, Shane. "Paternalism: An Analysis." *Utilitas* 28, no. 2 (2016): 123–35. https://doi.org/10.1017/s0953820815000254

Scanlon, Thomas M. *What We Owe to Each Other*. Cambridge, MA: Harvard University Press, 1998.

Scanlon, Thomas M. *Moral Dimensions: Permissibility, Meaning, Blame*. Cambridge, MA: Harvard University Press, 2008.

Schroepfer, Mike. "Research at Facebook." *Facebook Newsroom*, 2014. https://newsroom.fb.com/news/2014/10/research-at-facebook/

Schroepfer, Mike. "An Update on Our Plans to Restrict Data Access on Facebook." *Facebook Newsroom*, 2018. https://newsroom.fb.com/news/2018/04/restricting-data-access/

Sosa, Ernest. "For the Love of Truth?" in Linda Zagzebski and Abrol Fairweather (eds.). *Virtue Epistemology: Essays on Epistemic Virtue and Responsibility*, 49–62. Oxford: Oxford University Press, 2000.

Stewart, Emily. "8chan, a Nexus of Radicalization, Explained." *Vox*, May 3, 2019. https://www.vox.com/recode/2019/5/3/18527214/8chan-walmart-el-paso-shooting-cloudflare-white-nationalism

Sunstein, Cass R. *#republic: Divided Democracy in the Age of Social Media*. Princeton, NJ: Princeton University Press, 2017.

Twenge, Jean M. *iGen: Why Today's Super-Connected Kids Are Growing Up Less Rebellious, More Tolerant, Less Happy—and Completely Unprepared for Adulthood (and What This Means for the Rest of Us)*. New York: Atria Paperback, 2017.

United States Department of Justice. Special Counsel Report on the Investigation into Russian Interference in the 2016 Presidential Election. Washington, DC. March 2019. https://www.justice.gov/storage/report.pdf

Verma, Inder M. "Editorial Expression of Concern: Experimental Evidence of Massive Scale Emotional Contagion through Social Networks." *Proceedings of the National Academy of Sciences*. July 2014, 111 (29) 10779; DOI:10.1073/pnas.1412469111

Wingfield, Nick, Mike Isaac, and Katie Benner. "Google and Facebook Take Aim at Fake News Sites." *The New York Times*, November 15, 2016. https://www.nytimes.com/2016/11/15/technology/google-will-ban-websites-that-host-fake-news-from-using-its-ad-service.html

World Health Organization. "Ten Threats to Global Health," 2019. https://www.who.int/emergencies/ten-threats-to-global-health-in-2019

Chapter 3

Expert Advice for Decision-Making: The Subtle Boundary between Informing and Prescribing

Marion Vorms

A difficulty of experts' task in advising decision-makers is to provide the best and most relevant information, without encroaching upon their recipients' decisional automony. The boundary between informing and prescribing is a subtle one, especially when the science at stake is complex and pervaded with uncertainty. As studied by the philosophical literature on "inductive risk" and the role of values in science, what may appear as purely informative is often imprinted with value judgments. I will however show that there is another way experts are likely to exceed their duty, which is not reducible to imprinting their own values upon their audience. This other threat of undue paternalism lurking on experts' function is more specifically epistemic, and potentially harder to deal with, as it is more surreptitious and likely to go unnoticed, including to the experts themselves. It is related to the very structure of inference networks in complex evidential reasoning, which is often overlooked in the literature on scientific confirmation.

After highlighting some central issues arising from consideration of the requirement for experts reports to be "value-free," I will draw from analyses of evidential reasoning in criminal inquiry and the courtroom, as well as from instructions given to forensic experts in England and Wales, so as to shed light on that other, subtler difficulty experts must overcome in reporting their results. This consists in finding the right balance between actually drawing inferences that are within the scope of their competences, and which they can therefore legitimately endorse, and refraining to draw further inferences that would exceed the scope of such competences. As we will see, such fine-tuning is made particularly tricky by the fact that, in complex decisional tasks, expert and common knowledge are often intertwined in their contribution to evaluating the inferential bearing of the available evidence for a given issue.

EPISTEMIC DEFERENCE AND INDUCTIVE RISK

The Role of Expert Advice in Decision-Making: Informing without Prescribing

Many of our decisions, at either the individual or group level, have to be grounded on scientific knowledge that is beyond our reach. Even though one may feel reluctant to consider beliefs acquired through the words of others as fully justified—hence to count them as genuine knowledge—when it comes to making practical decisions, especially those that are highly consequential, we have no choice but to defer to experts' advice. Patients having to decide whether or not to undergo a surgery, jurors in criminal trials in charge of deciding whether to convict or not, as well as policy-makers having to take action regarding greenhouse gases emission regulations, need to rely on (medical, forensic, climate) experts to make the best-informed decisions.

Decision, however, is supposed to be the subject's own. A commonly shared ideal of individual freedom relies on a prima facie clear-cut distinction between informing and prescribing: experts must guide the subjects' decision by providing them with the best available knowledge regarding their case, but the resulting decision should depend on the subjects' own preferences. At the societal level, the democratic ideal dictates that the values guiding policies should be the people's own, rather than the experts'. We expect experts to neutrally tell us what it is rational to believe, not to prescribe our actions.[1]

INDUCTIVE RISK AS A CHALLENGE TO THE NEUTRALITY OF EXPERT ADVICE

As clear-cut as it may seem, such boundary between informing and prescribing is blurred by what Hempel (1965) first coined "inductive risk": since empirical confirmation of any claim is doomed to be relative, accepting, as well as rejecting such claim, involves a risk of error. Which risk is worth taking cannot be objectively determined on empirical grounds. Some decision has to be made, based on an appraisal of the relative costs of accepting the claim if it is wrong (false positive), and of rejecting it if it is right (false negative). In other words, some consequence-dependent confirmation threshold has to be set, beyond which a claim is considered warranted enough to be accepted, and publicized.[2] But, as Rudner (1953) had already argued, appraisal of the relative costs and benefits of the various outcomes (accepting the claim if it is true / false / rejecting it if it is false / true) depends on values.

One could argue that, in scientific research, such values are shared by the whole community, and result in very high, and subject-independent, standards of proof (think of the *p*-value, as well as all institutional practices governing scientific publication). Those warrant that no claim can be scientifically published unless maximally confirmed, thus somehow saving the "value-free ideal of science," according to which scientific claims should be justified on the basis of epistemic criteria only (Betz 2013; John 2015b; Kitcher 2011).[3] But, as soon as we are dealing with practically consequential claims, and even more so with policy-advising and decision-informing contexts, the question arises as to whether such an ideal can, and should, be saved.[4] Indeed, in such cases, scientists' decision to assert something will ground their recipient's decision to take such or such consequential action. Douglas (2000, 2009) argues that scientists are morally obliged to take into account the practical consequences of their claims—hence, for issues of public interest (e.g., the toxicity of a given substance), they should factor in the expected costs and benefits of a policy based on each type of possible error (false positive and false negative) in setting their own standards of assertion. Those would therefore be "floating standards" rather than fixed ones (John 2015a). Moreover, as Douglas has argued, such risk assessment does not only impact scientists' final decision whether to publicize a claim, but their whole methodology: according to her, it is both ethically desirable, and practically unavoidable for scientists to make value judgments throughout the process of hypothesis testing (e.g., through test sensitivity setting, see Douglas 2000). From such a perspective, the distinction between informing and prescribing is far from clear: as scientific conclusions are already shaped by the ensuing decisions, they must (both normatively and descriptively) contain prescriptions.

HOW TO ESCAPE MORAL PATERNALISM?

The "floating standards" conception, as coined by John (2015a), raises several problems. As I endorse most of John's criticisms, I will not recast them here, and will rather highlight a few further points, which are relevant for the rest of this chapter.

First, unless assuming that she shares the same values as her intended audience, the scientist's setting of her standard of assertion according to her own appraisal of the relative costs of false positives and false negatives would just be a way to impose her own values onto the decision-maker. This would be, so to speak, disguised moral paternalism under the pretense of legitimate epistemic authority.

One could therefore be tempted to prescribe that experts should take their audience's values into account when setting their own standards of assertion.[5] This, however, seems hardly workable. Even if we assume that experts have some secure access to such values (which is a strong, and doubtful assumption), it is by no means clear what they should do. Should they adopt the standards they assume their recipients would have adopted in their place? Consider a case for which the recipient's values imply that false negatives would be much worse than false positives: scientists should adopt a low standard, and assert the corresponding hypothesis as soon as there is some tiny evidence in its favor. But what would the recipient's own understanding of the scientist's report consist in? If she is not aware that the scientist herself has already applied a low standard, she might understand her claim as outright ascertaining something, which in fact is of very low probability. Hence, there might be some kind of "double counting" of her own values, lowering even more her (actual) standard of acceptance. This is only one example of the pragmatic puzzles lurking in such situations. There is no room in this chapter to explore the endless difficulties contained here, but this should be sufficient to claiming that the idea of a standard tuned to the intended audience's expected interpretation is by no means trivial, to say the least.

What then should experts do in order to report their results so as to help the recipient's making the decision that corresponds best to her values, without presuming anything about those values? The most tempting answer may seem to lie in an attempt to state the results as precisely as possible, hence to report degrees of evidential support, and, where applicable, to be explicit about probabilities.[6] This again raises several problems, one of which being that, even to reach a probabilistic conclusion, one has to make outright decisions in the course of the inquiry.[7] Moreover, such a strategy is more akin to a way of protecting oneself by not committing too far, than to an attempt at offering full understanding and information to the recipient.[8] It might be the least bad solution in many situations, but it is far from being the panacea.

Even setting aside the question of values, and hence of the threshold that has to be reached to consider a claim acceptable, how a given claim (be it outright or probabilistic) grounds our decisions is far from trivial, and is not reducible to a cost-benefit calculus. As will appear in the following, the relevant distinction to understand the boundary within which scientists should remain might not be best thought in terms of value judgements only. There are indeed other ways for experts to encroach upon their audience's decisional autonomy, which are more specifically epistemic in kind. In order to highlight them, I will now concentrate on the duty of expert witnesses in criminal trials.

THE CREDIBILITY AND RELEVANCE OF EXPERT EVIDENCE IN THE COURTROOM

Judges and jurors in criminal trials are expected to make highly consequential decisions based on the evidence presented to them in court. But the evidential basis, of which they must appraise the probative force so as to decide whether or not the suspect is guilty of the alleged crime, is far from being a single piece of evidence. It is rather a complex, incomplete, and partially contradictory set of evidence of heterogeneous types. Among those, forensic expert reports may be a key component, but they cannot be conclusive: experts are asked to report on specific issues, but they should not give their opinion on the final one, namely whether the suspect has indeed committed the facts alleged (not to speak about their legal qualification).

To be sure, there is a role for values as described in the inductive risk discussions here. At each step, whether a claim is considered to be enough proven, so as to be accepted, surely depends on what is at stake.[9] But here, I will highlight other aspects of the difficulty of setting the boundary within which expert reports should stay, which are not reducible to values issues, as I will argue.

In order to do so, I will first introduce some tools of analysis from the so-called New Evidence Scholarship (see Twining and Stein 1992), and more precisely from David Schum's (1994) study of the properties and uses of evidence in probabilistic reasoning—which is aimed at applying to any domain and discipline, but whose core object is criminal inquiry and judicial reasoning.

Complex Evidential Reasoning: Inference Networks and "Cascaded" Inference

Confirmation theories in the philosophy of science (Crupi 2020; Hajek and Joyce 2008; Hartmann and Sprenger 2010) study the relation between a given piece of evidence E, and the hypothesis H on which E may or may not have confirmatory bearing. In particular, Bayesian theories usually take E as unproblematically given, and attempt at formalizing the quantitative relationships between E and H—the crucial quantity for assessing the probative value of E for H being the likelihood ratio $p(E|H) / p(E|-H)$.

However, considering the function and uses of evidence in the criminal context draws attention to the strikingly complex inference networks fact finders must construct so as to marshal a mass of evidence, which may or may not cohere. As Schum (1994) has shown, the study of the probative value of a given piece of evidence for a hypothesis cannot be exhausted by a quantitative analysis. In addition, and as a preliminary to such analysis, the *structural* relationships among evidence items, and the subtleties of the inferential routes that fact finders may take, are worth studying in detail.

One major point is that the probative value of any evidential item is highly dependent on the rest of the available evidence. There are many different ways a piece of evidence may have inferential bearing on a given hypothesis, either directly (e.g., a threatening letter addressed by the suspect to the victim is directly relevant—though not conclusive—on whether she killed him) or indirectly (e.g., a report questioning the authenticity of such letter). In some cases, one single, prima facie neutral piece of information may turn some non-significant information into key evidence, or dramatically change the meaning of another piece of evidence, turning some exonerating evidence into incriminating one, or the other way around (see Schum 1994, Chap. 3, for a detailed analysis, and examples).

Another important point is that the inferential path that may lead from a given E to a given H is potentially infinitely decomposable. Even the most "direct" piece of evidence does not automatically and unquestionably lead to the final conclusion; any (inductive) inferential step is in principle defeasible, as resting on some implicit assumption or generalization that can be put in question. Consider a mobile phone geolocation report. In most cases, it seems reasonable to somehow automatically infer that the mobile's owner was herself geolocated. However, where the stakes are high, and if other pieces of evidence suggest that the suspect might have been in the area where the crime took place at the alleged time of the crime, while his mobile was located somewhere else, it sounds highly reasonable to put into question the implicit generalization that mobile phones are where their owners are.[10] Depending on what level of granularity one chooses—which clearly has to depend on the stakes—one can put in doubt every little step, which may appear as obvious and secure in most contexts.

It is worth noting that the generalizations warranting inferences may themselves be of different kinds, from common knowledge (which assumedly is shared among people of the same community) to personal-life experience (less likely to be widely shared) and expert knowledge. As forcefully highlighted by Schum, each agent constructs her own inference network from her very standpoint. To be sure, some generalizations may appear well warranted, while others are clearly prejudicial, and, of course, there are wrong reasoning paths (whose graphic representation, as proposed by Schum in the line of Wigmore [1913], helps figure out). But even though there might be better routes than others, there is not *the* "good" route; probabilistic, evidential reasoning is doomed to being uncertain.[11]

To summarize, another way to cast the idea of inductive risk is to say that each inferential step is grounded on a defeasible generalization, which different agents may be more or less willing to accept. Whether one takes it or not has to depend on the stakes of the inferential process, but also on how much the underlying generalization seems grounded. To grasp the subtleties of the complex inferential relations between different nodes of a network, and how those may shed some light on the role of experts, let me now turn to the distinction, proposed by Schum, between the credibility and the relevance of evidence.

The Credibility and Relevance of Evidence

In order to be of any probative value for a given conclusion (e.g., the hypothesis that the suspect is guilty of the alleged crime), a piece of evidence (e.g., the victim's neighbor's report that she saw the suspect in the staircase one hour before the alleged crime) has to be both *credible* and *relevant*.

Credibility

In order to clarify the notion of credibility, it is useful to follow Schum in noting E^* the evidence item itself, as it is received by the subject (the neighbor's oral or written report; a threatening letter; a CCTV recording; an expert report on fingerprints, etc.), and E the fact that this item attests to (the presence of the suspect in the staircase one hour before the alleged crime, the suspect's writing of the letter, the happening of the recorded scene, the match between fingerprints collected on the crime scene and the suspect's fingerprints, etc.). The credibility of E^* warrants inference from E^* to E. Credibility of a given piece of evidence is composed of several elements, depending on the type of evidence at stake. The credibility of an eyewitness report, for instance, can be decomposed at least into the witness's truthfulness (willingness to report what she actually believes she saw), objectivity (ability to correctly interpret what she perceived) and observational accuracy (see Schum 1994).

Clearly, credibility is a matter of degree. A maximally credible E^* would make it certain that E is the case (if E^* is maximally credible, then it is conclusive with regard to E). But, unless E is the final issue, one must also assess its relevance for this issue (or any intermediary hypothesis that might be of some relevance for it).

Relevance

E is relevant for H when it matters in some way for evaluating H; it is also a matter of degree. A piece of evidence can be highly relevant for a given hypothesis while being minimally credible; on the other hand, one can have a highly credible report on a matter that is of very little relevance for the question at stake. Relevance itself can be assessed along many different lines and, as already emphasized, it is strongly dependent on the rest of the available evidence. Moreover, it can and is often diversely evaluated by different people with different background knowledge and life experience, without necessarily one of them being "right" and others being "wrong."

CREDIBILITY AND RELEVANCE OF TESTIMONIAL EVIDENCE: PRAGMATIC ISSUES

Although the distinction may seem clear-cut with regard to (lay) testimonial reports, it soon blurs when one considers some pragmatic subtleties of linguistic communication. Even if we assume that a witness's report is perfectly accurate—hence maximally credible—it is worth acknowledging that a human witness is not a mere tape recorder, and that she chooses to report some details, and ignores others. Even if we assume that she is entirely willing to be cooperative, such choice depends on her own appraisal of the relevance of those items. Hence, she may keep silent on some aspects of what she saw that she finds insignificant, but which might have turned out to be highly relevant from another standpoint. Not telling them might thus be misleading. And this is just one example of how the subtleties of human communication may turn a perfectly accurate report into a misleading inferential basis for its recipient. Should one say that such a report is not credible after all? Or is it up to the recipient's to correctly interpret it and evaluate its relevance?[12] It would be beyond the scope of this chapter to further explore those pragmatic issues. Suffice it to say that even what could prima facie be considered as a maximally credible report may be misleading in some cases (for reasons independent to confirmation threshold and values).[13] This has to do with the very *relevance* of the content conveyed—or not conveyed, and with the inferences the recipient will feel entitled to draw on this basis. Let us now consider the specific case of expert testimony.

SCIENTIFIC REPORTS: NAVIGATING BETWEEN CREDIBILITY AND RELEVANCE

The pragmatic issues highlighted above may seem less likely to arise in the case of expert reports, at least in the court context: expert witnesses are expected to provide their conclusion on a given issue—they are, so to speak, more constrained in choosing the information they deliver. Hence, there seems to be less room for a diverging interpretation of the implicatures of what she says, or does not say. As soon as the issue on which she is expected to report—call it E—is clearly defined, an expert's task can be described as follows: she should give a maximally credible report on E, without infringing on her audience's appraisal of the relevance of E to H (the final issue on which decision has to be made). If a judge asks a forensic expert to tell whether or not the fingerprints found on the crime scene match the suspect's own, her expertise does not go until assessing whether and how much this speaks in favor of guilt. Let me now quickly articulate such a view and highlight its limits.

What does a maximally credible report on E consist in? Consider fingerprints analyses. First of all, the expert engages her responsibility with regard to the whole chain of events, processes, and analyses, which led from the collection of the samples from the crime scene and the suspect, to the conclusion about a match between them. Given inductive risk, such conclusion is doomed to be uncertain: there is a risk of error at each step of the process. But it seems to belong to the expert's duty to take responsibility on all the decisions that lead to a conclusion on E. Up to E, she chooses the relevant standard of proof at each step, independent from considerations of her audience's values. Here, the standards that apply seem to be defined by the relevant scientific discipline, and to be independent from what is at stake in this particular context. This certainly does not solve the problems arising from the fact that most issues experts are asked to report on are not an all or nothing matter, and are probabilistic in character (this is obviously the case for fingerprints and DNA match, but could be generalized to most cases). As highlighted earlier, the most precise scientific report might not be the most intelligible and usable one, and may even be misleading in some cases (see endnote 8). But providing an outright conclusion might override the expert's remit, by taking one more step toward the final conclusion. This problem however can be reduced to a value question, as studied in the first part of the chapter. Another kind of problem arises when one considers the question of the relevance of the expert's (supposedly maximally credible) conclusion to the final issue at stake.

Following the image proposed earlier, the expert should not go beyond expressing her conclusions on E—she should not commit on the *relevance* of E for H. The reason for that is not specifically related to an attempt at preventing her own values from impacting her inferential process. Rather, being an expert in, let's say, fingerprints analysis, there is no reason to assume that she is better placed than the judge or jurors to assess the relevance of a match to the final issue at stake in the trial. Or is she?

It is worth noting that finding a match does not exclude the possibility that the fingerprints come from someone else with similar fingerprints (this again is generalizable to any kind of "trace" found on a crime scene). This is a separate issue from the appreciation of the quality of the match itself; this rather seems to concern the relevance of a match for the final issue of finding the defendant guilty or innocent. However, this is clearly a point the expert has something to tell about. She is definitely better placed than non-experts to formulate both the probability of finding such traces if the suspect was on the crime scene, and the probability of finding them if they came from someone else. In other terms, her expertise encompasses both the analysis of the trace, and more general knowledge about fingerprints in the general population. One apparently straightforward solution is to actually define E (the issue on which the expert has to bring a conclusion) as a likelihood ratio encapsulating all relevant information, rather than some conclusion on the quality and precision of a match. After all, the expert should give a maximally credible report on what is on her remit. As we will see in the last part of the chapter, this solution, though sensible, does not entirely solve the crucial and tricky problem of defining the exact level at which experts should give their report, which, I will finally argue, should ideally be done through concertation between experts and judges.

INSIGHTS FROM THE "CASE ASSESSMENT AND INTERPRETATION" FRAMEWORK

"Case Assessment and Interpretation" (CAI) is a model originally developed in 1998 by an interdisciplinary team of forensic practitioners and statisticians employed by the Forensic Science Service in England and Wales (Cook et al. 1998a, 1998b), which has been continuously developed since, and is at the core of forensic scientists' training. It is aimed at providing them with a conceptual framework and practical protocols for structuring the investigation process, and most importantly for us, for producing reliable and useful expert reports of their results, which are most often pervaded with probabilistic reasoning and statistics.

The first and fundamental prescription of the model, which is based on the principles of Bayesian inference, is that scientists should never concentrate on a particular proposition, without considering at least one alternative. Hence, one crucial task is to precisely frame a pair of propositions to be addressed. In the forensic sphere, those correspond to a prosecution proposition and a defense proposition. At the end of the process, the interpretation of the evidence—the assessment of its probative value—should take the form of the likelihood ratio $p(E|Hp) / p(E|Hd)$, where Hp and Hd are the prosecution and defense hypotheses, respectively.

However, as Cook et al. (1998a) highlight, the specification of the (pair of) propositions to be addressed "is rarely a trivial matter" (153). Following Cook et al. (1998b), one can distinguish between three levels of propositions, called *Source*, *Activity*, and *Offence*. An example of an Offence level pair of propositions would be, "Mr A committed the burglary / Another person committed the burglary"; corresponding Activity level propositions could be, "Mr A is the man who smashed window X / Mr A was not present when window X was smashed"; and Source-level propositions would be, "The glass fragment came from window X / They came from some other broken glass object." As appears here, the propositions of a given pair must be exclusive; they must also be exhaustive "within the framework of circumstances as they are perceived by the scientist at the time of examination" (1998b, 234). This means that they need not exhaust all conceivable scenarios, but only those that are possible, given other hypotheses one takes for granted (e.g., here, the facts that there exist actually someone who committed the burglary, and that he was acting alone, with no one else around—which could be established by a CCTV footage).[14]

At which level should experts be asked to bring their conclusions? As Cook et al. (1998b, 231) note, "The higher the level of the propositions, the greater the assistance that will be given to the court but, of course, the scientist may not stray outside the bounds of his/her expertise nor, indeed, into the realms of advocacy." So, where exactly do those bounds lie?

It is clear that offence-level propositions are "completely outside the domain of the scientist" (ibid., 233), not only because they imply specifically legal notions in order to (legally) qualify the found facts, but also because legal fact finding seldom relies on one and only piece of evidence. Even when one expert report is key to the case, other pieces of evidence must be relevant, which impact the expert's report relevance—for reasons that may rely on common, or any specific knowledge that is not within the expert's competences. It is also clear that, at the lowest end of the spectrum, source-level propositions should be addressed by the scientist, whose expertise provides her with all legitimacy to draw conclusions on them. Hence, the problem of adjusting the exact level of propositions, which the scientist can, and should address, rather arises when one considers activity level propositions.

> Level I [source] propositions generally require little in the way of circumstantial information, but level II [activity] propositions cannot be addressed without a framework of circumstances. For example, the transfer/persistence issues relevant to the question "what is the probability of finding this quantity of matching glass if Mr A is truly the man who smashed the window X?" require information about how the window was smashed and the time interval between the incident and the taking of the clothing. Likewise, to address the question "what is the probability of finding this quantity of matching glass if Mr A were unconnected with the smashing of the window?" then it is necessary to know if there is something about Mr A which would predispose him to have glass on his clothing. In the absence of such information, assumptions will need to be made about the relevance of [background surveys about glass transfer and persistence]. The more information that is available to the scientist, then the more effective he/she can be in exercising judgement in relation to level II propositions. In this regard there needs to be a degree of interaction between scientist, investigator and/or advocate which is probably not required for level I propositions. (Cook et al. 1998b, 233)

Moreover, because more circumstantial information is required for higher-level propositions, "The interpretation is more vulnerable to change if, later, that information fails to become evidence" (ibid., 234). More generally, the higher the proposition, the riskier it becomes to draw conclusions, and the more "mixed" (i.e., expert and common) is the background knowledge needed to draw inferences. In the absence of enough information for a scientist to conclude on a higher-level proposition, prosecutors and advocates may ask him to "contribute to the argument by answering questions about hypothetical situations such as, for example, 'is this the quantity of glass you would have expected if Mr X had smashed the window ten minutes before he was picked up?' . . . There is a blurring of the roles of scientist and advocate here" (ibid., 236). As a consequence, the expert herself might be the "victim" of the questions asked.

Hence, expert and common knowledge are often intertwined in their contribution to evidential reasoning. Ideally, defining the exact level at which she can actually commit—which, as we have seen, is highly case-dependent, should be interactive. One could consider that it is the judge's job to find the right question on which she expects the expert to answer; but experts themselves should know until where they can go, which might actually be part of their credibility as experts. It is their duty to fine-tune between giving the best warranted information, while guiding agents in their evaluation of the relevance of such information to the issue at stake.

CONCLUSION

Experts are expected to deliver reports that are intelligible and usable, without going beyond evidential support. One main obstacle to meeting this requirement can be formulated in terms of "inductive risk": at each and every step of their inquiry, scientists have to make choices. Discussions about inductive risk, and how this impacts experts' task in advising decision-makers, usually focus on the problem of value judgments: whether or not one advocates the desirability and feasibility of value-free scientific expertise, one acknowledges that, if scientific conclusions are already shaped by the expected costs and benefits of the ensuing decisions, they already contain prescriptions.

I hope to have shown that the question of value-judgments, and the associated decision-theoretic image of a cost-benefit-dependent confirmation threshold, might not be the best—and definitely not the only—way to think of the difficult boundary for experts not to infringe. As soon as one takes seriously the extreme subtleness of inference networks in complex evidential reasoning, as the example of criminal inquiry and trials shows, one realizes that there is another way expert advice runs the risk of becoming (unduly) paternalistic, and one which is at least partially independent from any value judgment. Whereas they are definitely expected to commit on all the aspects of their conclusions within their domain of expertise—the "credibility" side—their tasks complexifies when it comes to finding the right level at which their expertise allows them to express their conclusions—how far they can and must commit on "relevance." As we have seen, whether, and how some scientific conclusion allows for one more inferential step may depend on both expert, and common knowledge.

NOTES

1. Of course, there are cases where the expert is expected to prescribe us some particular course of action, as a way of achieving some goal—which we have explicitly or implicitly acknowledged as desirable. But by no means are they expected to tell us what our ultimate goals should be.

2. In the context of an analysis of the norms of scientific experts' communication, John (2015b) insists that one should distinguish between standards of acceptance (which might be immune to inductive risk) and standards of assertion. However, whether there is something like "acceptance" or "outright belief," independent from any particular action to be taken (assertion in a given context being one of them), is a difficult issue, which is discussed in Vorms and Hahn (2019).

3. One could indeed consider that the value according to which admitting a false hypothesis within collective scientific knowledge is far worse than not accepting one which in fact is true, and wait until it is better confirmed, is just a warrant of the good functioning of the epistemic values that govern scientific inquiry (see John 2015a; Levi 1960). Moreover, this can be described as a way to regulating scientists' epistemic paternalism: a scientist's making a claim (within her field of expertise) imposes to any rational being the epistemic duty to accept it (in the absence of specific reasons not to), but such duty is itself grounded in the existence of epistemic warrants intrinsic to scientific practice and institutions. To designate such a maximal confirmation, many authors borrow the phrase "beyond a reasonable doubt" (see Betz 2013; Hempel 1965; John 2015a) from the judicial domain. However, whether this legal standard of proof should be considered fixed or moving is itself a discussable issue (see Picinali 2013; Vorms & Hahn 2019).

4. It is not even clear that such a distinction between "pure," and practically orientated science, exists. Any scientific claim, even the most remote from any practical considerations, is likely to have some practical consequences at some point. However, one can follow John (2015a) in distinguishing between different contexts of communications: scientific publications are in principle not directed to a specific audience, but rather to the "world at large," whereas reports made in private contexts (including public bodies policy-advising), are addressed to a specific audience, in a specific decisional context. See John (2015a) for a criticism of the idea that standards should be different in those two contexts.

5. John (2015a) temporarily considers, before rejecting it, such a reformulation of Douglas's proposal: "Scientists should consider their audience's proper epistemic standards for acceptance when setting their own epistemic standards for assertion."

6. This is Betz's (2013) suggestion to save the "value-free ideal," in the line of Jeffrey's (1956) point that scientists do not have to accept outright hypotheses.

7. Even if scientific acceptance is graded rather than outright, one has to accept a series of intermediary hypotheses at each and every step (e.g., about the good

functioning of instruments, or about the reliability of other scientists' results). Moreover, the very structure of intellectual inquiry relies on decisions to be made as to what hypotheses are still worth investigating, what hypotheses can be relied on for the rest of the inquiry, and what hypotheses can be safely rejected. To this regard, even the most theoretical inquiry does not mark off so clearly from a consequential-goal orientated one such as criminal inquiry (see Vorms & Hahn 2019).

8. As John (2015a) notes, "Claims like 'given the evidence, it is extremely likely that neonicitinoids deplete bee populations' or 'given the evidence, it is unclear that neonicitinoids deplete bee populations' do not go beyond the available evidence. However, we know that the former is likely to be heard as 'neonicitinoids deplete bee populations' and the latter as 'neonicitinoids do not deplete bee populations.' The moral status of making a claim turns not only on what we say, but on how others (foreseeably) interpret what we say" (Saul, 2013). See McCready (2015) about the pragmatic role of evidential language as being primarily plausible deniability.

9. In fact, the very standard of proof in common law criminal trials, according to which guilt must be proved *beyond a reasonable doubt* for the suspect to be actually convicted, can be interpreted as embodying the very ratio between the relative costs of sending an innocent man to jail and letting a guilty man free.

10. Here is where values get into the picture again: if the stakes are high, you may scrutinize each and every step. But my point here is that the resulting acceptation or rejection of the inference is not entirely accountable in terms of confirmation thresholds.

11. More recently, Bayes nets have been proposed and developed as a reasoning aid for criminal inquiry, forensic and judicial reasoning (see Lagnado et al. 2012).

12. In a work in progress with Anouk Barberousse, we discuss the consequences of such a blurring between credibility and relevance of testimony for the reductionism/anti-reductionism debate in the epistemology of testimony.

13. Stephen John's (2018) criticism of "honesty" as a virtue in scientists' communication may shed a new light on such analysis of credibility—understood as the property of yielding the right epistemic states in the recipient (and, assumedly prompting her to make the right decision).

14. See Fenton et al. (2013) for a criticism of the common uses of likelihood ratios in forensic inquiries and reports. Quite notably, a piece of evidence may be neutral at one level, and become diagnostic at another one, which requires to manipulate resulting likelihood ratios with great care.

BIBLIOGRAPHY

Betz, Gregor. 2013. "In defence of the value free ideal." *European Journal for Philosophy of Science* 3: 207–220.

Cook, Robert, Ian W. Evett, Graham Jackson, Peter J. H. Jones, and Jim A. Lambert. 1998a. "A model for case assessment and interpretation." *Science and Justice* 38 (3): 151–156.

Cook, Robert, Ian W. Evett, Graham Jackson, Peter J. H. Jones, and Jim A. Lambert. 1998b. "A hierarchy of propositions: Deciding which level to address in casework." *Science and Justice* 8 (4): 231–239.

Crupi, Vincenzo. 2020. "Confirmation." In Edward N. Zalta, ed., *The Stanford Encyclopedia of Philosophy.* https://plato.stanford.edu/entries/confirmation/

Douglas, Heather E. 2000. "Inductive risk and values in science." *Philosophy of Science* 67 (4): 559–579.

Douglas, Heather E. 2009. *Science, policy, and the value-free ideal*. Pittsburgh, PA: University of Pittsburgh Press.

Fenton, Norman E., Daniel Berger, David Lagnado, Martin Neil, and Anne Hsu. 2014. "When 'neutral' evidence still has probative value (with implications from the Barry George Case)." *Science and Justice* 54 (4): 274–287.

Hajek, Alan and James Joyce. 2008. "Confirmation." In Stathis Psillos and Martin Curd, eds., *Routledge Companion to the Philosophy of Science*. London: Routledge, 115–129.

Hartmann, Stephan and Jan Sprenger. 2010. "Bayesian Epistemology." In Sven Bernecker and Duncan Pritchard, eds., *Routledge Companion to Epistemology*. London: Routledge, 609–620.

Hempel, Carl G. 1965. "Science and human values." *Aspects of Scientific Explanation*. New York: Free Press, 81–96.

Jeffrey, Richard. 1956. "Valuation and acceptance of scientific hypotheses." *Philosophy of Science* 23, no. 3: 237–246.

John, Stephen, 2015a. "Inductive risk and the contexts of communication." *Synthese* 192, no. 1: 79–96.

John, Stephen. 2015b. "The example of the IPCC does not vindicate the Value Free Ideal: A reply to Gregor Betz." *European Journal for Philosophy of Science* 5, no. 1:1–13.

John, Stephen. 2018. "Epistemic trust and the ethics of science communication: Against transparency, openness, sincerity and honesty." *Social Epistemology* 32, no. 2: 72–87.

Kitcher, Philip. 2011. *Science in a Democratic Society*, New York: Prometheus Books.

Lagnado, David, Norman Fenton, and Martin Neil. 2012. "Legal idioms: A framework for evidential reasoning." *Argument & Computation*, doi:10.1080/19462166.2012.682656

Levi, Isaac. 1960. "Must the scientist make value judgments?" *The Journal of Philosophy* 57 (11): 345–357.

McCready, Eric. 2015. *Reliability in Pragmatics*. Oxford: Oxford University Press.

Picinali, Federico. 2013. "Two meanings of 'reasonableness': Dispelling the 'floating' reasonable doubt." *The Modern Law Review* 76, no. 5: 845–875.

Saul, Jennifer. 2013. *Lying, Misleading, and the Role of What Is Said*. Oxford: Oxford University Press.

Rudner, Richard. 1953. "The scientist qua scientist makes value judgments." *Philosophy of Science* 20, no. 1: 1–6.

Schum, David. 1994. *The Evidential Foundations of Probabilistic Reasoning*, Evanston, IL: Schum.

Twining, William, and Alex Stein, eds. 1992. *Evidence and Proof*, New York: Twining.

Vorms, Marion, and Ulriek Hahn. 2019. "In the space of reasonable doubt." *Synthese*, forthcoming.

Wigmore, John H. 1913. "The problem of proof." *Illinois Law Review* 8, no. 2: 77–103.

Chapter 4

Political Epistemic Paternalism, Democracy, and Rule by Crisis

Lee Basham

The day I found out that three physicians wanted me dead was heart wrenching. I sobbed.[1]

—Rachel Mary

Our focus should be practical when we advocate a moral practice, and not merely a theoretical ideal. I wish to argue that we should embrace the opportunities of a historically informed, horizontal structuring of public, political epistemology. Not the hierarchical one we live under, with, and through today. Here our concern is *political* epistemic paternalism. By political epistemic paternalism I mean decision-making by elements of our political hierarchies that have powerful influence over both information disseminated, or not, to the public and therefore the resultant popular response and the political projects that result.

Consider epistemic divine providence; we know exactly what we ought— an epistemic ideal. A construct of endless theological interest for its own sake, but useless in our world and lives, except, perhaps, as an expedient of solace. Much of the literature surrounding the issue of epistemic paternalism might strike us as quite similar. Its attempts at empiricism are incomplete when we review recent civilizational history, especially the twentieth and twenty-first centuries. Our interest is not epistemic paternalism "as such." We live on a dangerous planet of many uncertainties. Instead our interest is in how epistemic paternalism undermines functioning democracies to the point of frequent, repetitive episodes of dysfunction. Political epistemic paternalism collapses into *realpolitik*, by its own internal logic. We are not talking about raising children but the course of state. The fundamental *realpolitik* problem with the political application of political epistemic paternalism is found in some of the many violent conflicts in which we have engaged.[2]

Our thesis is simple and if correct, of interest. Epistemic paternalism is an ethical and political tool; in the politically real, the context of current representational democracies it can be of great moment. Democracy cannot and does not effectively constrain it. Instead, epistemic paternalism constrains and controls democracies. The twentieth century has unfolded by punctuated, catastrophic events. Much of this is arguably produced by paternalistic considerations that stand apart from democratic oversight. We will review examples of this pattern in what follows. The *realpolitik* of political epistemic paternalism, by definition as a practice of withholding information, cannot be constrained democratically. Particularly at our most momentous points of decision.

EPISTEMIC PATERNALISM

Political epistemic paternalism has been defended, in an attenuated way, by authors like Kristoffer Ahlstrom-Vij. In Ahlstrom-Vij's concise, readable and controversial book, *Epistemic Paternalism, a Defence* (hereafter, *Defence*) we find both clarity and avoidance about the political momentousness of the issues he approaches.[3] It is, in this, illuminating. There are a number of thoughtful, complex conditions placed by Ahlstrom-Vij and others on the proper deployment of epistemic paternalism. These are desirable in many contexts. For the purposes of our discussion, consider these familiar five:

1. The interference condition: This practice actively or passively interferes with a reasoner's ability to conduct inquiry in whatever way the reasoner desires for the benefit of making more likely an accurate or fair decision.[4]
2. Absence of consultation: The reasoner is not consulted on whether she ought to be interfered with in particular cases, or even generally.[5]
3. An improvement goal: A motivation for paternalizing the reasoning of the subject is that this renders the reasoner epistemically better off.[6]
4. The alignment of the moral and epistemic: Both the epistemic and non-epistemic reasons we have for applying the paternalistic practice are not at odds with each other.[7]
5. A "burden-of-proof" requirement: The evidence indicates that it is highly likely that *everyone* impacted by the paternalistic practice(s) will benefit epistemically from it.[8]

It is not so much that we tell people what to think, as we tell them how to and when not to. Naturally, one concern might be that the conclusion is foregone: They will, if rationally informed by our lights, conclude and believe what we wish them to, and do what we wish them to, accordingly.

When certain truths undermine the stability of a particular epistemic paternalist nation-state or civilization, economically, morally, socially and politically, they are, both in revelation and in investigation, dis-incentivized. This is the problem of *toxic truths*. Some truths are too toxic in their potential to generate destabilization. We will not hear of them, except in outlining media and by our own devices. This point has been discussed at length in the epistemic literature and seems secure.[9] The suppression of toxic truths is, equally, fundamental to political epistemic paternalism. The historical examples we will review below illustrate this.

Democracy's fundamental feature and motive is epistemic. Popular knowledge and concerns shape policies the polis both enjoy and are willing, after reflection on the relevant facts, that suffer for. Part of this process is public vigilance. Skeptical public communities of inquiry monitor official claims and submit official pronouncements to rational scrutiny. This suggests an alternative to epistemic paternalism in many cases: horizontal systems of discussion and epistemic evaluation that avoid the need and even advantages of employment of epistemic paternalism.

If democracy's fundamental feature and motive is epistemic, then whatever subverts this, for instance, epistemic paternalism, It may easily, and ought to put into motion processes that lead to wide-scale and permanent erosion and trivialization of democratic practice. A rigorous system of information "curating" and exclusion from the public is now, as always, being advocated by powerful forces. One ubiquitous in civilizational history, both in theory, as we see in Plato and Machiavelli, and in our daily lives; an ordinary fact.[10]

EPISTEMIC PATERNALISM, PATHOLOGIZING, AND DEMOCRACY

An important distinction, one we should track carefully, is between deception by commission—lying and other misleading information (recall Kant's famous example of putting luggage outside the front door to fool a neighbor into thinking Kant was taking a trip) and deception by omission (simply not revealing information critical to the judgments of others if they are to be accurate).

Political epistemic paternalism must, to succeed, resort to both in our more critical, momentous contexts. First, omission in the initiation of the deceit (conditions 1 and 2), second, commission in the denial the deceit ever occurred (condition 2). If the latter is admitted, the former is revealed, undermined, and even obliterated. Such omissions of fact are to be kept, at least until they appear to be antiquities. This tandem constitutes some of the most powerful tools of control over humans ever devised, whether for benevolent or malevolent purposes, or the vast space of what we find hard to distinguish, even as we resort to it.

Is such an epistemic, paternalistic pathologizing project consistent with a functional, representational democracy? An argument to the contrary:

(P1) In the political realm, functional representative democracy requires democratic oversight concerning the standards and actual applications of epistemic paternalism.
(P2) Epistemic paternalism in the political realm functions by suppressing information to the polis, both about what the polis is being prevented from knowing in general and in particular instances, and the motives for this suppression.
(P3) When information about what a polis is being prevented from knowing and the motives for suppression is withheld, the polis cannot contest or modify this withholding.
(P4) By its very nature the political epistemic paternalism project cannot proceed if what it is preventing knowledge of is revealed to the polis; this is intrinsic to the political epistemic paternalism project.
(C) Political epistemic paternalism is intrinsically contrary to democratic oversight.
(P5) What is contrary to democratic oversight is contrary to functional representative democracy.
(C2) Political epistemic paternalism is contrary to functional representative democracy.

Apply this to the perspective of our epistemic betters, our historically and politically situated epistemic elites. In order to maintain their credibility and effective paternalistic control, they must obscure their methods, purposes, and failings.

Epistemic paternalism of necessity requires epistemic elites to exercise control, and with political power impose it. So if its being deployed at any time entails the existence of these epistemic elites, they must be must be able to lead us and to produce a willingness to be led by them. One might, in her political piety, believe our political institutions have epistemic experts inclined to function in this way. Or one might decidedly not, upon historical reflection.

Epistemologists like David Estlund have strongly questioned the larger impact of epistemic paternalism on democracy, arguing that it leads to the erosion of democracy into a Plato-style *Epistemocracy*.[11] While I do not share the Rawlsian orientation we might think Estlund does, his concerns about the political implications of epistemic paternalism appear generally sound. I largely concur with Estlund and in what follows will attempt to explain why.

Estlund argues, in short, that political epistemic paternalism is an all-consuming doctrine.

(P1) For any polis, it is true that there is a small group of people—the epistocrats—who know those normative standards better than others and, thus, know better what the decisions that conform to those standards are.

(P2) For any polis, if it is true that the epistocrats know those standards better than others and so forth, then these people should have political authority over others.

(C) Thus, for any given polis, epistocrats should have political authority over others.

I owe this admirable concision to Kasper Lippert-Rasmussen (2012). Lippert-Rasmussen goes on to critique the argument by imagining middle grounds where the conclusion is "softened." Indeed, these may exist, but given the premises, *only in virtue* of maintaining an effective epistemic ruling elite. This would be an elite that requires, for its success, that it promote the illusion of democracy and obscure the reality of epistomocracy.[12] Again, the parallel to Plato is striking. Also, as we will see, it can be deadly. Conditions (3) and (5) trade in largely non-contextual probabilities for epistemic, and given alignment, moral improvement. But life is highly contextual and fluid in its diverse situations and the people within these so situated. Condition (5) becomes at times rudderless, especially in times of change that affects different persons and groups differently. Imagine you are a soldier, voluntary or conscript. Perhaps in the requisite contexts, knowingly sacrificing your life for your country improves, in the final analysis your situation. Many believe so, and not without noble reasons. Die well. But this sentiment is also easily abused. Epistemic paternalism's reliance on after-action reports deems it deeply suspect in the diverse contexts of real life.

Epistemic elitism is powerfully challenged by the all too often and all too true Voltairean remark concerning power.[13] The position is untenable with humans in the political realm, and probably with any imaginable being, biological, technological or perhaps, even divine. Only a few individual exceptions, unforced confessions by those in epistemic power, appear in history. But they are frequent enough in our cautionary lore. We might imagine even Stalin, with his conspiratorial show trials upon his brow, went to his own death with a smirk.

This undermines the usual integrity defense—a form of political piety—that epistemic elites will not, on general principle, harmfully manipulate the facts they deliver, or fail to, to the public. This is naïve in a political context, and it is the topic of political epistemic paternalism. The paradox is that when we combine epistemic experts' potential political power with real-world politics, as we might wish to, both politics and its uncertainties corrupts the epistemic status of elites. Perhaps on first contact. There are many cases of this in contemporary history. Below we will review two of these. The doctrine of epistemic elitism required by its paternalism not only lends itself to hubris, but to conspiracy against those they claim to benefit.

These arguments against political epistemic paternalism and politically empowered epistemic elites are just formulations of common sense. They gain credibility in that, and in the long history that illustrates their soundness. There are two aspects here: deceit by hierarchy and receptivity by those subject to it.

TOXIC TRUTHS AND RULE BY CRISIS: *REALPOLITIK*

We will use two dire, actual examples to signal and demonstrate the untenability of any significant political epistemic paternalism. These are not exhaustive of the history here by any means. This is not to say political epistemic paternalism interferes at every level of government, no matter how trivial, but more egregious examples establish the urgency of the problem.

The *public trust approach* is the view that government abuses will, in proportion to the severity of the abuse, be revealed by mainstream media and national law enforcement. It is provably false, both analytically and historically, and as this has been done elsewhere, we will move on without a lengthy examination.[14] It is easy to show a small group can wield vast resources, particularly "informational" because almost all of the persons involved do not understand the real goal and nature of what they are doing. Stunning resources can be brought to bear when the real reasons for the orders and policies are disguised by a small number, if well placed, from those they control.

The inscrutableness of condition (4) is unmistakable. Gulf of Tonkin is a now established, tragic example, as is, arguably, the apparent US allowance of the Japanese attack on Pearl Harbor on December 7, 1941, as a pretext for entering World War II. Today, this is a valid and often well-received position among academic historians.[15] Here the main concern, as documents now show, was not the Japanese, but by leveraging the Axis treaty of mutual support, to enter into the war in Europe against Nazi Germany. If the British fall so goes all—including the United States. In a memorandum of 1940 to President Roosevelt, Lieutenant Commander Arthur McCollum explains,

> In the Pacific Japan by virtue of her allegiance with Germany and Italy is a definite threat to the security of the British Empire and once the British Empire is gone [by Nazi conquest of the British Isles] the powers of Germany-Japan and Italy will be directed against the United States. . . . If by these means Japan could

be provoked to commit an overt act of war, so much the better. In all events, we must be fully prepared to accept the threat of war.[16]

McCollum outlines many ways for the United States to provoke an attack by Japan. Most of these ways were implemented; the essential thrust was resource denial, particularly of iron and oil.[17] And Japan was, accordingly, provoked in the manners outlined. McCollum concludes that we must provoke this war for Europe's sake. Captain Joseph Rochefort styled it a "pretty cheap price to pay for unifying the country."[18] The truth was toxic, the pay-off, immense. Only now can we reflect on this with relative dispassion.[19]

Rochefort appears to be right, if a gamble on consequences is our leading light. Added to information we now have on the details of US knowledge of the exact movements of the main task force of the Japanese navy carriers toward Hawaii and Pearl Harbor (we now know they did break radio silence and monitored accordingly), the sudden withdrawal of US carriers from Pearl Harbor, the careful omission of intelligence information to the main naval commander at Pearl Harbor, Admiral Husband E. Kimmel of the US Pacific fleet, and additional evidence, the case that the United States wisely provoked and then intentionally allowed the Japanese attack, by design, is well on its way to success.[20] It is, in fact, by far the simplest explanation of the evidence before us today. As it was also, then, had that evidence been made public. But of course, it was not, for a multitude of reasons, even if known, as it was, by scores of military officers and intelligence analysts.[21]

The consensus was that US intervention in the war in Europe was absolutely necessary, and Japan should be used to ignite massive popular support. The plan succeeded brilliantly, even if the task was far more perilous than imagined in 1940. This is a classic case of well-contrived, but profoundly anti-democratic, epistemic paternalism. Arguably mass-murderous, it achieved important results, and if we follow both the officers mentioned earlier, did so "cheap." Ahlstrom-Vij and similar thinkers argue that we do not enjoy a right to epistemic autonomy.[22] But clearly, like most all rights, what is at issue is a general right and is conditioned by context. Consider the closely related right to self-defense. What the epistemic paternalist misses is how urgent this can be in certain contexts.

Are we prepared to argue that the 2,300 young men and women killed that day, both military and civilian, had no right to epistemic autonomy and as a consequence, to know how they were going to be used?[23] We well might, if we are political epistemic paternalists, as the entrance into World War II by the United States against Germany was critical at that moment, yet unpopular. But it is unclear that the populace could not be swayed, or Japan triggered at least by the far more limited provocation approach; not the intentioned mass killing of US Navy personal and civilians that is now seriously contemplated to have occurred by the circles of academic historiography.

When we turn to the US war in Vietnam and the fraud of Gulf of Tonkin, Guenter Lewy uses conservative official reports to document approximately 1,353,000 killed, including more than 50,000 US citizens.[24] This is consistent with political epistemic paternalism, and is a consequent of it. Are we similarly prepared to invoke epistemic paternalism? And argue the US citizens had no right to epistemic autonomy and as a consequence, to know why they would be expended?

Here champions of epistemic paternalism might be more hesitant, as Vietnam was a catastrophe both political and moral. But infallibility is not a necessary condition of non-divine epistemic paternalism. The epistemic paternalism exercised by the political hierarchy in this case radically backfired, but what is that to the general position of political epistemic paternalism as *generally applied*? And if we construe political epistemic paternalism as nation-centric (as it largely is today), the cost was still fairly insignificant to the United States in "body-count" and the counts to come. If this strikes you as a reduction to absurdity of the moral claim to superiority ("better") epistemic paternalism makes in the *political* realm, I find myself in good company. Suppression of evidence in jury trials are one thing, the course of state rather another. But let us return to the broader pattern: Rule by crisis appears a predictable practice on the basis of epistemic paternalism. The argument for recourse is straight forward:

(P1) Leadership in Western-style democracies, if it is to pursue certain rationally and evidentially desirable projects within what it views as a timely manner, must on occasion consider the option governance by crisis.
(P2) The opportunities for governing by crisis are constant and numerous within Western-style democracies, and frequently governing by crisis is the most timely and effective way to achieve the desired project.
(P3) The *public trust approach* fails to undermine such governing by crisis projects because the *public trust* approach fails for a number of reasons, including its question-begging nature, its extreme exaggeration of the number of people that might need to be intentionally involved and the problem of toxic truths.[25]

Leadership in Western-style democracies is aware that *public trust* fails and so is often neither constrained nor constrainable by popular accountability *via* mainstream media and national law enforcement.

(P4) Leadership in Western-style democracies is often instrumentally rational.

At least we should hope,

(C) Leadership in Western-style democracies will routinely govern by crisis when it believes this is a superior, secure, and sustainable method of achieving aims it views as very desirable, aims that cannot be nearly as easily (if ever) obtained *via* lengthy democratic processes like public debate and legislation.

Governing by crisis has a very seductive feature for leadership: That of *dispatch*. And as noted earlier, it can even seem to have a dimension of moral obligation. The benefits of *unaccountability* in effective leadership cannot be dismissed.

The general pattern of concerns applies to 9/11 alternative conspiracy theory. It is difficult to overstate how epistemic paternalism generates suspicion, and does so rationally, in a population who knows they are subject to epistemic paternalism at the most fundamental level; for instance, the engineering of wars.

CHILD ABUSE? EPISTEMIC PATERNALISM AND THE PATHOLOGIZING PROJECT

Under a consistent regime of political epistemic paternalism, public activities contrary to information elimination, manipulation, and cognitive ability reduction are enemies of the political epistemic paternalism program. These contrary activities are classified, and publicly portrayed, as personal and social *pathologies*. That is, medicalized then socially marginalized.[26] They reflect socially dangerous activities and the people who are apt to practice them are to be portrayed as subject to various irrational and emotional disorders; dehumanized, if rationality is definitive of human. Taken all together, and in light of its institutional support, political epistemic paternalism is the foundation of what is known, in recent literature, as the *pathologizing project*. Resistance to the project is medicalized; conceived as a medical disorder. It is one to cure when possible, or socially isolated and managed, rather like a spreading virus, when not curable.

Here, information is withheld and manipulated, and abilities undermined, to produce a more desirable social outcome. But for whom? Influential elements within academia, particularly a faction of social scientists, as well as national governments and corporate media, of recent endorse developing this aggressive stance. They support a large-scale project of information denial to the public, access-exclusion of content creators to the public sphere, and cognitive disabling ("immunization") of children to disrupt receptivity of alternative, non-official narratives. In sum, they support social isolation of citizen researchers, elimination of sources of dissent, and strict regulation of emerging, organized public discussion *via* the Internet and other media.[27]

Most ominously, they endorse the development and application of sophisticated psychological techniques to undermine the public's ability to entertain significant doubts about corporate media and government pronouncements and actions, "targeting children."[28] This is, presumably, motivated by epistemic paternalism on the political level. The recent anthology *Taking Conspiracy Theories Seriously* revolves around the controversy concerning this proposed social engineering project.[29]

Political epistemic paternalism, active but confronted by resistance in public, and by nature unable to reveal its specific knowledge, reasoning and rationales, must resort to emotional abuse. It proceeds like child abuse. The main and overall goal of the pathologizing project is to curtail popular doubt about the reliability of our information hierarchy by, ironically, curtailing information and communication about its suspect methods and its flaws. The semblance of respectable, orderly, and honest government and corporate adventure is desirable, when the reality is at critical moments none of this. We will be drawn to constructs and clumsy, illusion-confirming construal of the facts with a growing intensity and authoritarian imposition to create this semblance. The emotional aspects of epistemic paternalism are powerfully cognitively distorting. The emotional component cannot be ignored. We cannot dismiss the emotional mechanisms of political epistemic "paternalism," the abuses it and requires and resorts to for success within the public. Ginna Husting explains,

> Especially in popular and political culture, contempt is a performative emotion—the expressing of it in public effects the movement of another to a status that is both beneath the contemnor's [person targeting others with contempt] and unworthy of attention or recognition as fully human. . . . When we perform contempt in public, we *emotionally* push people from the realm of belonging, toleration, and worthiness of interaction.[30]

That is, political epistemic paternalism must socially vanish them. Husting concludes,

> They fall from the state of being recognized by us—of being worthy even of attention or consideration. To earn contempt is to be marked as un-reasonable, as unworthy of rational interaction. In that way to hold another in contempt is to hold his/her humanness in abeyance, to radically decouple him-her from what Hannah Arendt would call our "life in common."[31]

Such are the wages of political epistemic paternalism.

We also cannot ignore terror management as a feature of epistemic paternalism.[32] Terror management is an explanatory theory that posits much human behavior is a response to extreme, usually unmentionable, fears. For instance, fear of our death. Calming an immature person, or an entire polis, is a fundamental feature of parenting, of paternalism. Terror management theory is not merely an existential issue, as in our avoidance of thoughts of death, and our contrivances when they arise—"meant to be" statements and resort to the divine and other constructs—but a deeply political one. Terror management is as pressing for, and between, we the living. Rational fear is experienced when confronting the reality of our political and military system, now possessed with world-killing devices. And deploying increasingly complete networks of automated AI surveillance over most all methods of communication, especially the Internet. This situation is properly terrifying. Especially if we see epistemic paternalism lurking behind the entire enterprise. Political epistemic paternalism is terrifying. And this is a severe moral objection. Terror management deals with it through epistemic and metaphysical imponderables, the sum of which is our public trust in epistemic elites, our "political piety." This looks rather like a religion, and like religion, tempts enforcement.

The increasingly strident retreat to political piety we now witness in mainstream media, academia and Internet exchanges concerning popular growing doubts about our information hierarchy and government actions is a wholly unsurprising response to the terror of living under what is, at best, political epistemic paternalism. At base, this response seems a faith declaration. A new *Catholic Index* style of epistemology. Almost a cry for mercy; epistemic elites will do what they have to, in order to protect us.

Husting's forthright observations are recognizable to most of us. In the real world, the adage, "No plan survives first contact" comes to mind.[33] Political epistemic paternalists may mean well. But their overarching strategy is, in both practice and when challenged, of necessity cruel.

CONCLUSION

Political epistemic paternalism undermines, at several levels, the exercise of representational democracy. Our prior examples are extreme only to alert us. The real misfortune is constant, chronic and ubiquitous, even if not momentous in the instant, but in its entirety. The awesome and ominous power of omission/commission deception is demonstrated by the phenomenon of *rule by crisis*. It has arguably led to more millions of human deaths than any other anthropogenic force in history.

The objection to, and proper target of, epistemic paternalism is democracy itself. Plato knew this and so should we. Tempting, continuing, and perilous, we must choose, as we always have needed to: Either democracy or an intrinsically unaccountable political epistemic paternalism. As in the Gulf of Tonkin. Can careful contrivances be introduced to stabilize this hybrid of epistemology and consequentialist action at the highest levels of state, and throughout it? We might be doubtful. There seems no useful compromise that does not commit illogical violence to both. Democracies are the realms of collective, not contrived, uncertainties. They are not ruled from the pinnacle cool-air heights of paternalistic manipulation and deception—both by omission and commission—but by shared reasoning and accurate information. These vast, horizontal regions are the waters we travel as members of a real and functional democracy.

The answer may be found in the insight that originates representational, legally constrained, democracies. Here *horizontal* mechanisms of information distribution, not vertical conversation eliminators, guide and control the course of societies. These mechanisms operate by largely unregulated and uncensored discussion, response, and counter-discussion across billions of human beings. When unencumbered, horizontal systems operate by the statistical mechanism of trillions of decisions and responses, based upon full access to information, speculation, and interpretive viewpoint. They do not operate by the carefully curated and hierarchical contrivances of our past and present. While epistemic paternalism may be appropriate in limited venues, such as jury trials, on the global political stage, its benefits become more and more questionable. It no longer appears to be a useful tool. When a society is open, it opens by the mutuality of reason and evidence operating within in this statistically powerful horizontal system; not the epistemic manipulations that provide the regrets we inherit from our twentieth century. Rules of behavior are in order, but they are inferential, not informational. We should embrace the opportunities of a historically informed, horizontal structuring of public, political epistemology. Without this, in the rush of contemporary civilization, memories remain short, attention fractured, and concentration quickly perishes. With our open horizontal system, we can prevent new, profound tragedies and accomplish great things.[34]

NOTES

1. This both fortunate and unfortunate story can be found in the video https://www.youtube.com/watch?v=rqJfQg-E8Tg (retrieved June 7, 2019). While I neither endorse nor reject the intent of this display, it is an example germane to a discussion of epistemic paternalism and its potential failings.

2. I define "realpolitik" as political actions motivated by practical and material factors, perhaps morally justifiable, perhaps not.

3. Ahlstrom-Vij, *Epistemic Paternalism, a Defence* (2013). See also the recent collection of papers *Epistemic Consequentialism*, Kristoffer Ahlstrom-Vij and Jeffrey Dunn (eds.), 2018, for a wide-ranging set of positions, including a large discussion of ethical consequentialism in the context of epistemic paternalism.

4. *Defence*, pp. 40–41.

5. Ibid., pp. 50–53.

6. Ibid., p. 114.

7. Ibid., p. 117.

8. Ibid., p. 122.

9. See Basham, Lee, "Joining the Conspiracy" (hereafter "Joining"), *Argumenta* 3, 2 (2018): 271–290. The view that the public can trust the media in critical events is often questionable. One of many examples, "If you approached American conspiracy theorists of the 1950s who claim mass media and law enforcement are purposely ignoring the real dangers of radioactive fall-out to the down-wind public caused by the Atomic Energy Commission's nuclear bomb testing—including a mass die-off of live-stock—with the reply that all can rest assured, the Department of Agriculture will no doubt hold a press conference to correct the deception, they would not be impressed. Nor should they be. It never happened" (p. 280). Any indulgence in "that was then, this is now" (what I term the "United States of Amnesia" syndrome), is insufficient in light of recent events.

10. *Republic*, Books 3, 8.

11. Estlund, David, *Democratic Authority: A Philosophical Framework*, Princeton University Press (2008). Also see his interesting reply to critics, "Replies to Saunders, Lister and Quong." *Representation* 46: pp. 53–67.

12. *Res Publica*, 2012, Volume 18, Issue 3, pp. 241–258. Almost a perfect pun, if we focus on "mocracy."

13. As we all recall, "Power corrupts, and absolute power corrupts absolutely."

14. This failure has been much discussed in the literature, beginning with Keeley, Brian, "Of Conspiracy Theories," *Journal of Philosophy* 96 (3), pp. 109–126 (1999) and Basham, Lee, "Malevolent Global Conspiracy, *Journal of Social Philosophy*, volume 34, pp. 91–103. For a detailed summary of these and the subsequent critiques of the public trust approach, see M. R. X. Dentith's *The Philosophy of Conspiracy Theory*, Palgrave Macmillan, 2014, and "Joining."

15. Hanyok, R, "Skunks, Bogies, Silent Hounds, and the Flying Fish: The Gulf of Tonkin Mystery, 2–4 August 1964," *Cryptologic Quarterly*, 19, 4, 20.1, pp. 1–50, 1998 (derived from NSA/CSSM 123-2, redacted, approved for release by NSA, 11-03-2005).

16. Stinnett, Robert, *Day of Deceit* (hereafter *"Deceit"*), Simon and Schuster, 2000, McCollum's Action Proposal," Appendix A, pp. 271–277.

17. Note that a number of *realpolitik* arguments for the invasion of Iraq at that time also invoked resource denial, targeting, among others, Iran and China.

18. See Rochefort's *Reminiscences of Capetian Joseph J. Rochefort* (US Naval Institute Oral History Division, 1970), p 163.

19. Again, the "United States of Amnesia" syndrome.

20. Admiral Kimmel's family applied to the US Navy to posthumously reinstate his rank, decades after he was court-martialed for "gross incompetence" concerning the attack on Pearl. They argued this alleged incompetence was intentionally manufactured by Washington. Predictably, the US Navy dismissed their well-evidenced appeal with a terse rebuke of the very idea.

21. See *"Deceit"* appendixes B through E, pp. 278–318.

22. *"Defence,"* Chapter 4.

23. https://visitpearlharbor.org/pearl-harbor-visitors-bureau-review-submission/ retrieved August 7, 2019.

24. Guenter, Lewy, *America in Vietnam*, Oxford University Press, 1980 (see statistical appendix).

25. Again, this has been argued for in several epistemic quarters. See "Joining" for a summary.

26. Again, see *Taking Conspiracy Theories Seriously*. Much of this anthology, and other recent work in epistemology, richly illustrate the manipulative pathologizing project emerging in Social Science and particularly Social Psychology. Also see Basham, Lee. 2019, "'They' Are Back (and Still Want to Cure Everyone): Psychologists' Latest Bid to Curtail Public Epistemology." *Social Epistemology Review and Reply Collective* 8 (7): 23–33, Wagner-Egger, Pascal; Gérald Bronner, Sylvain Delouvée, Sebastian Dieguez, Nicolas Gauvrit. "Why 'Healthy Conspiracy Theories' Are (Oxy)morons: Statistical, Epistemological, and Psychological Reasons in Favor of the (Ir)Rational View." *Social Epistemology Review and Reply Collective* 8, no. 3 (2019), pp. 50–67 and Dentith, M. R. X., "The Iniquity of the Conspiracy Inquirers." *Social Epistemology Review and Reply Collective* 8, no. 8 (2019), pp. 1–11. See Martin, Brian, *Suppression Stories*, Fund for Intellectual Dissent, 1997. Martin, a physicist, authors an "on the ground" classic in the social epistemic literature. His work continues in advocating citizen research and researchers, most recently concerning vaccination debates, for instance, *Australia's Vaccination Panic*, https://www.bmartin.cc/pubs/18vpa/18vpa.pdf.

27. Notoriously, Cass Sunstein endorses this tactic, where governments routinely conspire against citizens who accuse the government of conspiring against them; he terms this "cognitive infiltration." See *Journal of Political Philosophy*, Volume 17, Issue 2, 2009, pp. 202–227. The watch word of the Sunstein piece is "crippled" epistemologies, and the cure was to immunize, confuse, or socially isolate those so crippled. His advocacy of "cognitive infiltration" was widely criticized in philosophical circles. In his subsequent book, *Conspiracy Theories and Other Dangerous Ideas* (Simon and Schuster 2014), he vanishes the project of government "cognitive infiltration" from mention, while maintaining, almost verbatim, his other dubious recommendations.

28. This is the special, and especially disturbing, contribution by the *Le Monde* group of Social Scientists. See Basham, Lee and M. R. X. Dentith, "Social Science's Conspiracy-Theory Panic: Now They Want to Cure Everyone." *Social Epistemology Review and Reply Collective* 5, no. 10 (2016), pp. 12–19; and Basham, Lee, "Pathologizing Open Societies: A Reply to the *Le Monde* Social Scientists." *Social Epistemology Review and Reply Collective* 6, no. 2 (2017), pp. 59–68.

29. *Taking Conspiracy Theories Seriously*, M. R. X. Dentith, ed., Rowman & Littlefield, 2018. Expanded versions of the above mentioned (see endnote 27) are found within.

30. Husting, Ginna, "Governing with Feeling: Conspiracy Theories, Contempt, and Affective Governmentality" in *Taking Conspiracy Theories Seriously*, M. R. X. Dentith, ed., Rowman & Littlefield, pp. 118–119.

31. Ibid.

32. For a simple introduction to terror management theory as applied to physical death, see Solomon, Greenberg and Pyszczynski, *The Worm at the Core*, Random House, 2015, and https://ernestbecker.org/resources/terror-management-theory/, retrieved July 4, 2019. The application to political terrors is easy to extend. Terror management theory in its inception is "research that investigate the role of terror management processes in physical and mental health. Specifically . . . research that elucidates the role of death concerns in (1) conscious threat-focused defenses, (2) self-esteem striving, (3) depression, (4) anxiety disorders, (5) discomfort with the physicality of the body and (6) neuroticism." All of this also characterizes political debate and I would suggest, at a new level of intensity.

33. Originally, to my knowledge, a claim about combat.

34. *Acknowledgments.* I would like to thank Amiel Bernal and Guy Axtell for their helpful and attentive comments, Terry Laborde and Nydia Guzman Ramirez-Basham for additional ideas, and, of course, Otto Blaast for his sustaining insights.

BIBLIOGRAPHY

Ahlstrom-Vij, Kristoffer. *Epistemic Paternalism, a Defence*. Palgrave-Macmillan, 2013.
Ahlstrom-Vij, Kristoffer and Jeffrey Dunn (eds.). *Epistemic Consequentialism*. Oxford: Oxford University Press, 2018.
Basham, Lee. "Malevolent Global Conspiracy." *Journal of Social Philosophy* 34 (2003): 91–103.
———. "Social Science's Conspiracy-Theory Panic: Now They Want to Cure Everyone." *Social Epistemology Review and Reply Collective* 5, no. 10 (2016): 12–19.
———. "Pathologizing Open Societies: A Reply to the *Le Monde* Social Scientists." *Social Epistemology Review and Reply Collective* 6, no. 2 (2018a): 59–68.
———. "Joining the Conspiracy." *Argumenta* 3, no. 2 (2018b): 271–290.
———. "'They' Are Back (and Still Want to Cure Everyone): Psychologists' Latest Bid to Curtail Public Epistemology." *Social Epistemology Review and Reply Collective* 8, no. 7 (2019): 23–33.
Dentith, Matthew R. X. *The Philosophy of Conspiracy Theory*. London: Palgrave Macmillan, 2014.
———. "The Iniquity of the Conspiracy Inquirers." *Social Epistemology Review and Reply Collective* 8, no. 8 (2019): 1–11.
Estlund, David. *Democratic Authority: A Philosophical Framework*. Princeton, NJ: Princeton University Press 2008.
———. "Replies to Saunders, Lister and Quong." *Representation* 46 (2010): 53–67.

Guenter, Lewy. *America in Vietnam*. Oxford: Oxford University Press, 1980.
Hanyok, Robert J. "Skunks, Bogies, Silent Hounds, and the Flying Fish: The Gulf of Tonkin Mystery, 2–4 August 1964," *Cryptologic Quarterly* 19, no. 4, 20.1 (1998/2005): 1–50. (Derived from NSA/CSSM 123-2, redacted, approved for release by NSA, 11-03-2005.)
Husting, Ginna. "Governing with Feeling: Conspiracy Theories, Contempt, and Affective Governmentality," in Matthew R. X. Dentith (ed.), *Taking Conspiracy Theories Seriously*, 118–119. Lanham, MD: Rowman & Littlefield, 2018.
Lippert-Rasmussen, Kasper. "Estlund on Epistocracy: A Critique." *Res Publica* 18, no. 3 (2012): 241–258.
Keeley, Brian. "Of Conspiracy Theories," *Journal of Philosophy* 96, no. 3 (1999): 109–126.
Martin, Brian. *Suppression Stories*. Wollongong, Australia: Fund for Intellectual Dissent, 1997. Australia: Wollongong, https://www.bmartin.cc/dissent/documents/ss/ssall.html
———. *Australia's Vaccination Panic*. Sparsnäs, Sweden: Irene Publishing, 2018. https://www.bmartin.cc/pubs/18vpa/18vpa.pdf.
Plato. *Republic*. Cambridge Texts in the History of Political Thought by Plato. Cambridge: Cambridge University Press, 2000.
Rochefort, Joseph. *Reminiscences of Captain Joseph J. Rochefort* (US Naval Institute Oral History Division, 1970.
Solomon, Sheldon and Jeff Greenberg and Tom Pyszczynski. *The Worm at the Core*. New York: Random House, 2015.
Stinnett, Robert. *Day of Deceit* (with Appendix A, 271–277). New York: Simon & Schuster, 2000.
Sunstein, Cass. *Conspiracy Theories and Other Dangerous Ideas*. New York: Simon & Schuster, 2014.
Sunstein, Cass and Adrian Vermeule. "Conspiracy Theories: Causes and Cures." *Journal of Political Philosophy* 17, no. 2 (2009): 202–227.
Wagner-Egger, Pascal, Gérald Bronner, Sylvain Delouvée, Sebastian Dieguez, and Nicolas Gauvrit. "Why 'Healthy Conspiracy Theories' Are (Oxy)morons: Statistical, Epistemological, and Psychological Reasons in Favor of the (Ir)Rational View." *Social Epistemology Review and Reply Collective* 8, no. 3, 50–67 (2019).

Part II

SCIENTIFIC AND MEDICAL COMMUNICATION

Chapter 5

Epistemic Paternalism, Science, and Communication

Fabien Medvecky

Epistemic paternalism (EP) is generally viewed with suspicion, and when it is defended, the focus turns to defending EP "in certain circumstances," while still holding the view that, all things being equal, EP is less than desirable. But such suspicion fails to take into the mundaneness of epistemic interference, whether paternalistic or not. EP can be viewed as a two-step dance; one step is a "(non-consultative) interference" move, and the other an "intentionality (of epistemic improvement)" move. And the interference condition is much more pervasive than we might like to admit; it is inescapable, and, I will argue, often desirable. But epistemic interference on its own is not EP. It's the intentionality move that distinguishes EP from other forms of epistemic interference. Looking more closely at the interference–intentionality dance leads me to turn the whole business of being suspicious about EP on its head and conclude that it is not EP that we ought to be suspicious about, but rather, we should be suspicious of testimonial practice that fails to give due consideration to EP. I pepper the chapter with cases and examples from the scholarship and practice of science communication as a way of grounding this debate in real world practice as I make the argument over a six-course meal.

HORS D'ŒUVRE: A MIXED PLATE OF DEFINITIONS

While Goldman first opened the black box of EP, describing it as "communication controllers as exercising epistemic paternalism whenever they interpose their own judgment rather than allow the audience to exercise theirs (all with an eye to the audience's epistemic prospects)" (Goldman

1991), Ahlstrom-Vij's more precise 2013 definition has become the go-to. Ahlstrom-Vij (2013) presents EP as having three conditions:

1. A does X, which interferes with the epistemic autonomy or freedom of B to conduct inquiry in whatever way she sees fit (interference condition);
2. A does so without consulting B on whether B should be interfered with in the relevant manner (non-consultation condition); and
3. A does so for the purpose of making B epistemically better off (improvement condition).

He also expands Goldman's veritistic (truth-seeking) aspirations by taking the term "epistemically better off" to also include to improve (or avoid worsening) understanding, and to acquire intellectual virtues (or avoid forming epistemic vices) (Ahlstrom-Vij 2013).

Importantly, this definition of EP locates the practice very clearly in the space of social practice; an agent can't be epistemically paternalistic toward themselves due to the second (non-consultation) condition. EP as it is defined, then, is a social practice, and most often, part of testimonial practice. Following from Lackey (2008), we can define testimony as:

> S testifies that p by making an act of communication a if and only if (in part) in virtue of a's communicable content, (1) S reasonably intends to convey the information that p, or (2) a is reasonably taken as conveying the information that p.

From Goldman's "communication controllers" through to Lackey's "act of communication," we get that EP is inherently linked to communicative acts, and being about epistemology, it is also about knowledge. This makes science communication a good field to draw upon for examples. Science communication is closely linked to knowledge from its relationship to science (which, at the very least, is space involved in knowledge creation), and it is also deeply engaged in testimonial practice, given it is a communication field. Indeed, science communication has proved a fruitful space to think concretely through some related topics in social epistemology from epistemic justice (Medvecky 2018) to epistemic trespassing (Ballantyne 2018).

ENTRÉE: EP IN A SUSPICION BROTH

Testimonial practice is not controversial, it is not especially praised or blamed, it just is something that happens. EP, however, is generally viewed with suspicion (Grill and Hansson 2005) and "is commonly regarded as a harmful practice that could undermine our freedom, epistemic autonomy, or both" (Croce 2018: 305). At the core of this suspicion lies an assumption of epistemic autonomy: that individuals can and want to know things independently, without undue interference from others; that as epistemic agents, the ideal is akin to being fully informed (or as fully as possible) and rational—something close to ideal rational agents. Goldman terms this the *Requirement of Total Evidence* (RTE), which he gives as, at a minimum, "A cognitive agent X should always fix his beliefs or subjective probabilities in accordance with the total evidence in his possession at the time" (Goldman 1991: 113).[1] Of course, as Goldman, Ahlstrom-Vij, and others have noted, this principle can't always be adhered to, nor would we want to always adhere to it.

There are some instances where this ideal of epistemic autonomy is viewed as problematic, and more relevantly for us, there are spaces where EP has been strongly defended, most notably in health and legal settings. Goldman (1991) makes a case for why EP is defensible in some legal cases, most notably restricting evidence when the latter might mislead the jury. This is a view shared by Ahlstrom-Vij, who also makes a claim for EP in health settings, from randomization to prediction models. In the health setting, EP has been positioned as (potentially) defensible for genetic testing (Bullock 2018; Medvecky and Leach 2019). Other examples include curriculum selection in teaching, blinding processes in job applications (and peer review?), and the news (Croce 2018; Goldman 1991).

Indeed, EP can be, and has been, defended in such contexts, but the fact that defending EP takes so much work (tellingly, Ahlstrom-Vij's 2013 book is titled *Epistemic Paternalism: A Defence*), makes it explicit that the starting position is to view EP suspiciously. Yes, it is acknowledged that epistemic autonomy is may not be as blanketly desirable, nor indeed as broadly viable as might be thought, so some degree of interference is tolerable. And in some context, this interference should extend to EP. As Goldman states, "Even if we concede a measure of (intrinsic) epistemic value to autonomy, a value compromised in epistemic paternalism, it is questionable whether the loss always outweighs the gains" (Goldman 1991: 126). But still, while EP can be defended (in some instances, under certain conditions), all things being equal, it's best to not think about engaging in EP except in these excused cases. I think this is misguided and I want to make the claim that epistemic interference is in fact so normal and every day that the starting position should be flipped around. I will make the case that while we should sometimes be suspicious of engaging in EP (in some instances, under certain conditions), *thinking about engaging in EP* and normalizing EP as one of many tools in testimonial practice, should be praised as ethical communicative practice.

MAIN: A DECONSTRUCTED DISH OF EP: INTERFERENCE AND INTENTION

If we are to be suspicious of EP, what, exactly, should we be suspicious of? More precisely, which of the condition(s) should we be suspicious of? *Interference, non-consultation,* or *improvement*? We might sometimes be suspicious of the first condition, *Interference*, but if this was truly the source of the concerns, communication and testimony would be not only incredibly limited, it would be nigh impossible. Firstly, epistemic interference is utterly trivial and common, from incomplete claims to shortcuts to rounding off. Take the mundane task of answering the question "What time is it?" We usually respond to such a question somewhat inaccurately by rounding off the answer to the nearest quarter hour or to the nearest five minutes (if asked the time at 10:53 and 28 seconds, we'll respond either "11 o'clock" or "5 to 11," but almost never the exact time). And every day, we carry out such interference constantly. But interference is not only trivial; it is also essential and necessary for meaningful testimonial practice.

Epistemic interference is necessary for testimony because of epistemic scarcity (we have a greater demand for knowledge than we can satisfy), a paucity stemming from both material and epistemic costs. There are material costs to knowing, from the time it takes to gain and access knowledge to the resources needed to gain knowledge such as books, computers, and so forth (Medvecky 2016). Then there are epistemic costs to knowing, which Radnitzky and Bernholz (1987), quoted in Yalcintas (2013: 1134) as "epistemic resources forgone, resources which would have been available if one had opted for the competitor of the theory." Put simply, we can't know everything because we have neither the material nor the epistemic capacity to do so; therefore something, some epistemic content, some potential knowledge must *not be gained* for some other knowledge to be gained. Note this goes both ways: we can't communicate every piece of knowledge because we have neither the material nor the epistemic capacity to do so; therefore something, some epistemic content, some potential knowledge must *not be communicated* for some other knowledge to be communicated.

Take the recent reporting of the first black hole image, which received significant press coverage. A black hole is one of science's most fascinating and complex phenomena, but when reporting it, no press outlet could provide the full information. There is simply too much there to be said, much of which would be technically beyond the majority of readers. When explaining what a black hole is, each journalist had to choose what to include and what *not to include*, such as the BBC's description (Ghosh 2019) provided here:

What is a black hole?

- A black hole is a region of space from which nothing, not even light, can escape;
- Despite the name, they are not empty but instead consist of a huge amount of matter packed densely into a small area, giving it an immense gravitational pull;
- There is a region of space beyond the black hole called the event horizon. This is a "point of no return," beyond which it is impossible to escape the gravitational effects of the black hole.

The BBC and other media outlets' descriptions are not inaccurate per se, but they are incomplete. In leaving information out, science journalists interfere (albeit in a mundane way) with their reader's epistemic autonomy. When communicating technically complex information, from earthquake risks to an individual's genetic make-up, assessing which information is relevant, which is meaningful, and which would simply be unhelpfully confusing is part of parcel of the testimony. Given that not all the details can be given (since there is always more depth that can be provided), and not every detail understood (since some information requires time, prior technical knowledge, etc.), testimony almost always includes some element of interference.

In a world of epistemic scarcity, where our demand for knowledge is greater than what can be satisfy given both material and epistemic limitation, testimony that simplifies, rounds off, and so on allows us to gain more helpful, relevant, interesting knowledge and to communicate more helpful, relevant, and interesting knowledge. Such practices do interfere with one's epistemic autonomy and, importantly, these interference are also rarely consultative (I doubt the BBC ran a poll with readers to see which version of a description of black holes they felt would be most epistemically beneficial). Fundamentally, this points to one thing: that (non-consultative) interference in an agent's epistemic autonomy is part and parcel of testimony. So either we reject testimony (which would be tragic epistemically given how much we rely on it) or we accept that we aren't ever really epistemically autonomous. We are, as Gelfert (2014) puts it, "epistemically dependent." And epistemic dependence means there will necessarily be epistemic interference. Epistemic autonomy, and the idea that we can be free from (non-consultative) interference, is a myth. This should not lead us to conclude that interference is therefore always permissible. But rather, that given non-interference is a myth, the debate about interference ought to turn on the circumstances in which such interference is problematic (perhaps when the interference is be severe, pervasive, and harmful) and when it is irrelevant (most mundane cases).

With non-consultative interference ruled out as a meaningful source of generalized suspicion about EP given its triviality and epistemic necessity, this leaves the improvement condition as the likely culprit. It may seem strange (and I believe misguided) to think that aspiring to make another agent epistemically better off might be viewed suspiciously. Certainly, the intention is good. But in fact, this is exactly what separates the third condition (improvement) from the first two (interference and non-consultation): intention. Whereas (non-consultative) interference can and does often occur without much thought or reflection, purposefully making another epistemically better off obviously requires purpose, it requires intention. The improvement condition, may not, in fact, be the real culprit, but I believe it highlights where the suspicion stems from: intentionality (the garden variety of intentionality, meaning the fact of being deliberate or done on purpose, not the philosophical variety). So we can separate two moves that flow through the conditions: an (non-consultative) *interference* move, and an *intentionality* move.

CHEESES: INTENTIONALITY, ETHICS, AND COMMUNICATION

We seem to be largely unconcerned by everyday, trivial forms of non-consultative interference (this should not be read as a justification of the latter), and one important factor that separates such interference from EP is the intentionality demanded by the third condition. Because the third (improvement) condition requires intentionality, it also invites an intentional scrutinizing of the other two conditions. EP, then, requires the interfering agent to intentionally interfere, to intentionally not consult, and to intentionally aspire to make the interfered-with agent epistemically better off. But while intentionality is necessary for EP, it is not sufficient. We can intentionally interfere (non-consultatively) without aiming to make the interfered with party epistemically better off. For example, restricting access to information about how to make chemical weapons is a form of intentional, non-consultative interference that isn't aspiring to make anyone epistemically better off.

Armed with this tripartite distinction between unintentional interference, non-altruistic intentional interference, and EP, we can reconsider the question of where our suspicions might lie and parse our candidates for suspicion more clearly. Are we suspicious of any interference? Suspicious of any sort of intentional interference (whether paternalistic or not)? Or is it really EP specifically what we find so problematic? Given epistemic autonomy is a myth, interference is going to happen whether we like it or not. Indeed, we can't not interfere, so it seems incoherent to suggest we should (by "ought implies can"). The only way to not interfere is to avoid testimony, which is neither possible nor desirable, so we can rule out the first option. Accepting that it makes no sense to be suspicious of epistemic interference per se, this leaves two options on the table: (1) Suspicion of intentionality in interference simpliciter (irrespective of whether it is in the form of non-altruistic intentional interference or EP), or (2) Suspicion of EP specifically (intentionality is fine; it's the paternalistic move where the moral issue really lies). I'll consider these in turn.

The first suggestion is that what we might be suspicious of is intentionality. Put another way, this equates preferring unintentional interference over II. Not only does this seem deeply counter-intuitive—all things being equal, it seems it's better to be thoughtful and considered about what we do; it also runs against the rationale for why we are concerned with epistemic interference in the first place. Recall, at the core, the suspicion over EP stems from an assumption of the inherent value of epistemic autonomy, not just with regard to interference, but with regard to testimony more broadly. This was Goldman's Requirement of Total Evidence (RTE): that "A cognitive agent X should always fix his beliefs or subjective probabilities in accordance with the total evidence in his possession at the time" (Goldman 1991: 113). But RTE isn't just about epistemic autonomy in terms of content. It's also about reasoning. While interference might run contrary to the autonomy of content gathering (but, as has been established, interference is inescapable), intentionality is part and parcel of reasoning. It takes intentional, considered, purposeful judgment to "fix [our] beliefs or subjective probabilities in accordance with the total evidence." It seems, then, that we better embrace intentionality, we better prefer intentional interference (whether or not it's done for the epistemic betterment of the other or not) to unintentional interference.

Given interference on its own can't be the source of our suspicion (because of its inevitability), and since intentional interference is preferable to unintentional interference, this leaves one option as to where the suspicion over EP should lay (if we are to be suspicious at all): with the paternalistic move. This view of the suspicion entails preferring non-altruistic intentional interference to EP. I think this view is misguided and makes explicit why suspicions over EP more broadly are equally misguided. It seems there are many cases where non-altruistic intentional interference is absolutely reasonable. The above example of restricting access to information about how to make chemical weapons seems perfectly well justified; so does the blinding of authors in academic peer-reviews, and so do many others, and the use of simplifications in science journalism, museums and so on down, due to space limits (non-epistemic reasons). These are fine, and given the discussion earlier, it is better if these, or any instances of interfering, are done intentionally. In order to, for us, be intentional, we should, when we engage in testimony, think about many things, from who our audience is, to how are testimony is going to be received and interpreted. We ought to think about the implications of our testimony; think about the capacity of our interlocutors to interact with our testimony; think about what we include and what we leave it out (our inevitable interference); and think about how our testimony will affect the epistemic state of our audience.

As part of this last point—thinking about how our testimony will affect the epistemic state of our audience—it seems unquestioningly good to consider the possibility of testifying so as to make our audience epistemically better off. Indeed, it would be a moral travesty to *not* consider the epistemic impact of our testimonies or the capacity for these to make "epistemically better off" those we interact with. This is not to say we need to engage in EP; it is to say that EP ought to be viewed as one of many paths we have available to us when testifying, and one that we ought to think about seriously. Indeed, anyone who has ever taught a class, given a presentation, written a paper, or such like would have had to, at some stage, make a decision over what to include and what to leave out, with a thought to explanatory clarity. Not everything can be said—not every version, not every detail—and some versions, some details lead to less clarity, to possible confusion in the intended audience. Choosing what to state and what to leave out in order to maximize comprehension and clarity (e.g., as opposed to maximizing argumentative force) is unquestioningly EP, and this chapter is full of it, as are most other academic papers. Put simply, suspicions over EP *because it is paternalistic* are misplaced. We ought to accept EP as one of the avenues open to us when we testify. Given we are going to interfere, interfering with open eyes and intentionally seems better than interfering blindly or out of habit. And if interference is better carried out with open eyes, then better still doing so with an eye to the potential for epistemic betterment in our audience.

DESSERT: A BITTER SWEET SAMPLE OF CONCERNS AND OBJECTIONS

The argument I've put forward is that (non-consultative) epistemic interference is not only trivial, it's also necessary in an epistemic landscape where testimony looms large. Given we're going to have interference, we should prefer intentional, considered interference to unintentional, accidental interference in our testimonial practice. If we are to prefer intentional, considered interference, then part of such consideration ought to be to consider the possible impact of our testimony on the epistemic state of our audience. Doing so requires we, at the very least, consider EP as part and parcel of good testimonial practice. Contrary to the common stance taken on EP, from defenders like Ahlstrom-Vij and Goldman to critics like Grill and Hansson

(Ahlstrom-Vij 2013; Goldman 1991; Grill and Hansson 2005), we therefore shouldn't start from a position of suspicion toward EP; our starting position should be that EP is just one of the options we have, one that is neither more nor less inherently problematic than any other. There are three challenges to this view I want to briefly flag.

The first concern is that the focus on intentionality is as misguided as the concerns about interference, and for largely the same reason: unintentionality is as trivial as interference. We have attention scarcity as much as we have epistemic scarcity; it's unrealistic (and implausible) to demand we act with considered intention about every aspect of every act we perform. As much as we can't help but interfere, we can't help but act on heuristic, habit, etc. The unavoidability of unintentionality (like that of interference) might be correct. There is a difference, though, in that interference is also a necessary and desirable part of testimony, and testimony is epistemically enriching. Unintentionality doesn't seem likely to lead to any epistemic improvement.

The second concern is that the view I take is so broad it becomes banal. Given I include things like rounding off the time to the nearest five minutes as a form of interference, it's no wonder I find the latter to be trivial; I've been too generous with my reading of the term *interference*. However, the reverse argument can be made that if interference is only used to mean non-trivial cases (cases that have significant impact or insert your favorite restricting qualifier here), then it's no wonder there's concern about it. But why should interference only apply to such cases and not also to trivial cases? Without a good reason to restrict the scope of interference, trivial cases also ought to be included.

Lastly, perhaps much of what seems like EP is not actually non-consultative. Granted, there isn't an explicit consultation going on, but there might be something like implicit agreement to the interference. When students enter a classroom, part of the deal of being taught is that the teacher does have a say in what is and isn't presented. Likewise when watching a nature documentary, part of the deal is that the filmmaker decides what is and isn't shown. And the same is true when I ask you for the time, the same is true of jurors and judge, the same is true of entering a museum, and so on. If there is such implicit agreement, then are these really cases of EP? Maybe, then EP should be restricted to cases where there is no implicit agreement, however such cases are likely to be much harder to find. Indeed, most of the cases rehearsed in the literature on EP (jury, medical, teaching, all have some level of implicit agreement). This "contractual" objection isn't particularly an objection to my argument, but rather an objection to much of the debate over EP in the first place. Perhaps this should invite a reimagining of EP either as something more trivial (by accepting "contractual" interference) which, in many ways, is also what I hope to suggest, or as something much more restricted (by excluding contractual interference), though this would require a complete revisiting of the existing literature and debate on EP.

DIGESTIF: TO CONCLUDE

Why are we suspicious of EP? While there has been some defense of EP, there is no doubt it is generally viewed with suspicion. Indeed, why bother provide a defense for it (see Ahlstrom-Vij's book's title) if it weren't viewed as problematic to begin with. The starting position with EP, then is that, all things being equal, it's best to not think about engaging in EP except in the excused/defended cases. I've argued this is misguided and that instead of being suspicious of EP and viewing it with inherent concern, EP should be viewed as a normalized part of testimonial practice, and (positively) considering engaging in EP should be praised as good communicative practice.

Why normalize EP? Because the basis for being suspicious of EP is flawed. The source of the suspicion is the view that non-consultative epistemic interference is wrong; it's an affront to RTE and epistemic autonomy. But such interference is both unavoidable and desirable in a social world where testimony forms a large part of our epistemic landscape. Such interference can be wrong only in a fictional world, a world imagined as populated by informed rational agents with unlimited epistemic and material resources. It is wrong in a world that's not quite ours, populated with people who aren't quite us. In *this* socially imbedded world—the world we actually inhabit—we are and want to be epistemically dependent (lest we be tragically epistemically impoverished), and we will engage in non-consultative epistemic interference.

Why praise thinking about engaging in EP as ethical communicative practice? Because thinking about engaging in EP shows that we are being thoughtful and considered about how we communicate and testify. All things being equal, when we interfere, given we will interfere, we ought, at the very least, to consider the implications of our interferences, including the epistemic implications. This implies considering EP as an option. If we ought to consider EP as part of our testimonial practice, then EP ought not to be viewed as inherently wrong or problematic. In fact, considering the epistemic implications of our interferences—considering EP as one of our options in our testimonial practice—should be praise; it shows that we are being thoughtful and considered about how we communicate and testify and about the epistemic state of our audience. EP should be more than just food for thought; it ought to be taken seriously as an integral part of our testimonial diet.

NOTE

1. Goldman also offers a stronger version of RTE: "A cognitive agent X should collect and use all available evidence that can be collected and used (at negligible cost)."

BIBLIOGRAPHY

Ahlstrom-Vij, Kristoffer. *Epistemic Paternalism: A Defence*. New York: Palgrave Macmillan, 2013.

Ballantyne, Nathan. "Epistemic Trespassing." Mind 128, no. 510 (2018): 367–395. doi: 10.1093/mind/fzx042

Bullock, Emma C. "Knowing and Not-Knowing for Your Own Good: The Limits of Epistemic Paternalism." *Journal of Applied Philosophy* 35, no. 2 (2018): 433–447. doi: 10.1111/japp.12220

Croce, Michael. "Epistemic Paternalism and the Service Conception of Epistemic Authority." *Metaphilosophy* 49, no. 3 (2018): 305–327.

Gelfert, Axel. *A Critical Introduction to Testimony*. London: Bloomsbury Academic, 2014.

Ghosh, Pallab. "First Ever Black Hole Image Released." BBC (2019). Retrieved from https://http://www.bbc.com/news/science-environment-47873592

Goldman, Alvin. I. "Epistemic Paternalism: Communication Control in Law and Society." *The Journal of Philosophy* 88, no. 3 (1991): 113–131.

Grill, Kalle and Sven Ove Hansson. "Epistemic Paternalism in Public Health." *Journal of Medical Ethics* 31, no. 11 (2005): 648–653. doi: 10.1136/jme.2004.010850

Lackey, Jennifer. "Learning from Words: Testimony as a Source of Knowledge." Oxford: Oxford University Press on Demand, 2008.

Medvecky, Fabien. "The Cost of Being Known: Economics, Science Communication and Epistemic Justice," in James Collier (ed.), *The Future of Social Epistemology: A Collective Vision*. Lanham, MD: Rowman & Littlefield, 2016.

Medvecky, Fabien. "Fairness in Knowing: Science Communication and Epistemic Justice." *Science and Engineering Ethics*, 24, no. 5 (2018): 1393–1408. doi: 10.1007/s11948-017-9977-0

Medvecky, Fabien and Joan Leach. "An Ethics of Science Communication." London: Palgrave Pivot. https://doi.org/10.1007/978-3-030-32116-1_11

Radnitzky, Gerard and Peter Bernholz. 1987 "Cost-Benefit Thinking in the Methodology of Research: The 'Economic Approach' Applied to Key Problems of the Philosophy of Science." In Gerard Radnitzky and Peter Bernholz (eds.), *Economic Imperialism*. New York: Paragon House, pp. 283–334.

Yalcintas, Altug. "The Problem of Epistemic Cost: Why Do Economists Not Change Their Minds (about the 'Coase Theorem')?" *American Journal of Economics and Sociology* 72, no. 5 (2013): 1131–1157. doi: 10.1111/ajes.12037.

Chapter 6

Persuasion and Epistemic Paternalism

Robin McKenna

We all hold some false beliefs. Many of these false beliefs are inconsequential. Sadly, others are rather more consequential. According to a recent report, 18% of Americans think either that the Earth's climate is not changing, or that human activity is not responsible for any change that is taking place.[1] While this is hardly the only obstacle to the implementation of policies to reduce greenhouse gas emissions and mitigate climate change impacts, it is one reason why politicians and other policy makers have been reluctant to act. Similar remarks could be made about the consequences of public misperceptions about the safety of nuclear power or GMOs, or the efficacy of vaccines. This prompts a question: What (if anything) can we do about the problem of consequential false beliefs?

It is important to distinguish two issues. The first, which is empirical, concerns which methods are *effective* in persuading people that they hold false views about issues like global warming. The second, which is normative, concerns which methods we are *permitted* to use in the service of persuading people to change their minds. (Brainwashing the public to accept the science on global warming might be effective, but it wouldn't be ethical.)

In answering the first question, we can draw on multiple empirical literatures, including work on (the science of) science communication, the psychology of persuasion and motivated reasoning.[2] In answering the second, I advocate adopting the perspective of a de-idealized social epistemology. A de-idealized social epistemology makes concrete suggestions for improving our epistemic situation that are *evidence-based* (i.e., based on an answer to the first, descriptive, question). The de-idealized social epistemologist recognizes that human beings are not ideal epistemic agents, and this has consequences for the normative prescriptions we should make.

Here is the plan for the chapter. I start by saying a little more about the methodology of de-idealized social epistemology. I then canvass the empirical literature to draw up a list of suggestions for how to improve public understanding and acceptance of scientific issues like global warming. Many of these suggestions depart from the familiar view that the main task for science communicators (and science educators) is to improve the public's scientific literacy and general critical thinking skills.[3] They involve attempts to structure the "epistemic environment"[4] in such a way that epistemic agents are more likely to form true beliefs about the relevant scientific issues than they would otherwise be. As such, they involve various forms of interference with inquirers' cognitive endeavours, and this, in turn, raises the question whether these forms of interference are problematic for the reasons that paternalistic interference is regarded by many as problematic. After sharpening this worry, I attempt to address it.

DE-IDEALIZED SOCIAL EPISTEMOLOGY

What does epistemology have to contribute to the problem of consequential false belief? One strand in contemporary epistemology—a strand initiated by W. V. O. Quine's "Epistemology Naturalized" (Quine 1969)—views epistemology as *ameliorative*. The task for the epistemologist is to, first, draw on the empirical sciences to form an understanding of how we go about forming beliefs (and, more generally, conducting our inquiries) and then, second, to identify ways in which we could do a better job of forming beliefs (and inquiring in general). What counts as "better" depends on one's epistemological views: some hold that what matters is holding more true beliefs (Goldman 1999), some that what matters is gaining more knowledge (Williamson 2000), and still others that what matters is improving understanding (Kvanvig 2003). For my purposes, we can set this debate aside, though for simplicity I'll talk as if the first, "veritistic," view is right.

Viewed from this perspective, the task for the epistemologist is to, first, gain an understanding of how people go about forming beliefs about issues like global warming and then, second, to identify how we can make it more likely that they form true beliefs about these issues. An epistemology that is adequate to this task needs to do certain things. First, it needs to pay attention to the multifarious ways in which we rely on others in our inquiries. We don't figure out what to think about global warming by conducting our own research (and even if we did, we would also need to rely on research conducted by others). We draw on what others (climate scientists, the media, friends and acquaintances) tell us about the issue. Thus, it needs to be a *social* epistemology (Goldman and Blanchard 2018).

Second, it needs to be *evidence-based*. There is a (large) empirical literature on what sorts of interventions are likely to correct public misperceptions about issues like global warming (and what sorts aren't). This has consequences for the sorts of suggestions for ameliorating our epistemic situation that the social epistemologist should make. Suggestions that might seem plausible in the abstract may not prove so effective in the "real world" (see further for examples). If our aims are genuinely ameliorative, it is no good coming up with a list of prescriptions that work in the abstract but not in practice. Thus, we need a *de-idealized* social epistemology: an epistemology that issues prescriptions that take our cognitive limitations and the environments we inhabit into account.

But what would a de-idealized social epistemological approach to the problem of consequential false belief look like? The rest of this chapter illustrates it.[5]

THE SCIENCE OF SCIENCE COMMUNICATION

So how do people form views about issues like climate change, and how can we go about correcting any misperceptions they may have? In this section, I give an overview of some empirical research on this question.

According to Cook et al. (2016), 97% of climate scientists agree that human activity is a major cause of global warming. But most people think that the level of consensus is in fact far lower. The numbers vary from country to country, but in the United States, only 13% think the level is higher than 90% (Ballew et al. 2019).[6] There are, of course, many ways in which one might try to narrow this gap. Which strategies one recommends will depend on what one takes the explanation for this "consensus gap" to be. One explanation cites the public's lack of scientific understanding and literacy (Bak 2001; Sturgis and Allum 2004). If this is right, then narrowing the consensus gap requires providing the public with the relevant facts—by telling them that global warming is happening, and explaining some of the mechanisms involved.

There is ample evidence that some ways of providing the public with relevant facts are effective (see further). But there is also ample evidence that it does not suffice to correct these misperceptions (Downing and Ballantyne 2007; Gardner and Stern 1996). As Moser and Dilling (2011) put it:

> Clearly, much can be said for broad public education in the principles and methods of science in general and in climate science specifically. A sturdier stand in science education may leave lay individuals less susceptible to misleading, factually untrue argumentation. But ignorance about the details of climate change is NOT what prevents greater concern and action. (163)

This is for two, importantly different, reasons. The first is the influence of political ideology on information processing. The evidence suggests that the strongest influence on estimates of the level of consensus on global warming is political ideology, not level of scientific literacy (Hamilton 2011; Hamilton et al. 2015; Hardisty, Johnson and Weber 2010; Hornsey et al. 2016; Kahan, Jenkins-Smith and Braman 2011; Lewandowsky and Oberauer 2016; Tranter and Booth 2015). We don't generally process and evaluate the information we receive in a neutral or unbiased way. Rather, our background beliefs, views, and values—including our political beliefs, views, and values—influence our information processing. Thus, liberals (in the US sense) generally tend to form a more favorable view of the scientific evidence on global warming than conservatives (again, in the US sense), no matter how much conservatives know about the underlying science (Kahan, Jenkins-Smith and Braman 2011).

The second is the prevalence of misinformation on global warming in the public sphere (Cook 2016, 2017; Cook et al. 2018). While liberals tend to think the level of scientific consensus on global warming is higher than conservatives, they still underestimate the true level (Ballew et al. 2019). This illustrates that the influence of political ideology on information processing is only part of the story. Even those not driven to deny that there is scientific consensus on global warming for ideological reasons are affected by the misinformation spread by global warming deniers. This is because (put roughly) misinformation tends to "drown out" information. There is good evidence that informing the public that scientists agree on certain issues (e.g., global warming) can be very effective in increasing public acceptance, even among those who, for ideological reasons, are disposed to deny the existence of consensus on global warming (Cook and Lewandowsky 2011; Lewandowsky, Gignac and Vaughan 2013; Toby Bolsen, Leeper and Shapiro 2014; van der Linden et al. 2014). But there is also evidence that this effect is drastically reduced when there is also widespread misinformation about the level of scientific consensus (and the integrity of climate scientists) (Cook 2016, 2017; van der Linden et al. 2017). As van der Linden et al. (2017) put it:

> Results indicate that the positive influence of the 'consensus message' is largely negated when presented alongside [misinformation]. Thus, in evaluating the efficacy of consensus messaging, scholars should recognize the potent role of misinformation in undermining real-world attempts to convey the scientific consensus. (5)

This suggests that the problem is not just that the public lack understanding of climate science, or are scientifically illiterate (and, insofar as the public do lack understanding, this is not because of lack of education). Public lack of understanding and scientific illiteracy is exacerbated by, first, the ubiquity of ideologically driven cognition and, second, the prevalence of misinformation. If this is right, then strategies for dealing with public misperceptions that assume the task is to correct misunderstandings by providing relevant facts are not going to solve the problem.

What can we do? I will canvass three sets of strategies from the literature. First, a common strategy with global warming misinformation is to *debunk* it. While debunking consequential false beliefs *can* work, it needs to be done carefully because misperceptions can be difficult to dislodge once they take hold (Lewandowsky et al. 2012; Seifert 2002). A different strategy is what you might call *prebunking*. Where debunking involves refuting misinformation once it has been taken on board, prebunking involves pre-emptively refuting it before it can be taken on board. The prebunking strategy is based on a key idea in inoculation theory, which is that exposing someone to refuted misinformation conveys resistance to it, in much the same way that exposing someone to a virus in a weakened form conveys resistance (Compton 2013). There is growing evidence of the effectiveness of prebunking, both in the specific case of misperceptions about global warming, and in general (Cook, Lewandowsky and Ecker 2017; Ivanov et al. 2015; Pfau 1995; Pfau and Burgoon 1988; Tony Bolsen and Druckman 2015; van der Linden et al. 2017). So, for instance, you might present someone with a common climate sceptic argument along with a refutation of it. Take the claim that human CO_2 emissions are tiny in magnitude compared to natural emissions. You would accompany a presentation of this argument with the refutation: human CO_2 emissions interfere with the natural carbon cycle, putting it out of balance.

Second, we can consider how issues like global warming are *framed*. There is a large body of evidence suggesting that whether individuals are willing to accept specific global warming mitigation policies—and even the underlying science—depends on how those policies are described (Campbell and Kay 2014; Corner et al. 2015; Dahlstrom 2014; Dryzek and Lo 2015; Hardisty, Johnson and Weber 2010; Kahan 2014; MacInnis et al. 2015). For instance, discussions of what to do about climate change are often framed in terms of what we can do to reduce carbon emissions. This leads to a situation where (put crudely) conservatives need to choose between the science and their conviction that business should be free from government interference. There is evidence that framing the problem as amenable to technological solutions (e.g., geoengineering) can make those who are ideologically opposed to regulating carbon emissions more willing to accept that action is needed to combat global warming (Kahan et al. 2015). Or, to take another example, there is evidence that framing charges for environmental costs as "carbon offsetting" rather than as a "carbon tax" increases public acceptance of the necessity of the charges (Hardisty, Johnson and Weber 2010).

Third, as well as considering the content of the message, we can look at who delivers it. Climate scientists have generally been the messengers of choice. This makes sense, given that public trust in scientists is quite high (American Academy of Arts & Sciences 2018; Ipsos MORI 2014). But scientists are not the most trusted source on every issue, or the best people to communicate key messages on a politically contentious issue such as global warming (Cvetkovich and Earle 1995; Cvetkovich and Löfstedt 1999; Kahan et al. 2010; Moser and Dilling 2011). This is in part because of a fact noted earlier: our background ideological beliefs influence how we process information. This extends to our assessments of expertise. Put crudely, we would often rather rely on someone we perceive to share our ideological beliefs and values than an "expert" with different values from our own (Kahan, Jenkins-Smith and Braman 2011). While this has its downsides—we would rather listen to someone who is like us than someone who isn't, even if we have reason to think they are less likely to be right—it has potential upsides in the present context. If we take steps to ensure that a politically diverse group make the case for action on climate change, we have reason to think that this would be more effective.

This completes my survey of possible strategies for combatting the problem of consequential false beliefs. Put broadly, these strategies involve attempting to construct a better epistemic environment—an environment in which it is more likely that individuals form true beliefs about climate science than it would be otherwise. We have reason to think that each strategy will be successful, both in general and in the particular case of misperceptions about climate science.

EPISTEMIC PATERNALISM AND EPISTEMIC AUTONOMY

In the previous section, I canvassed three strategies for correcting public misperceptions about climate science. The general message was that solving the problem of consequential false beliefs is going to require conscious efforts to construct an epistemic environment in which it is more likely that people will form accurate beliefs about climate science. But the fact that a strategy is likely to be effective is not conclusive reason for deploying it. Maybe there is something ethically problematic about some (or all) of the strategies I discussed. In this section, I try to make this worry more precise, before addressing it in the final section.

We can frame the worry here in terms of *paternalism*. Specifically, we can frame it in terms of *epistemic* paternalism. Put roughly, a practice is paternalistic if it involves interfering with someone's choices or actions for their own good, but without their consent. If I hide your cigarettes because I know you'll smoke the whole packet, which will be bad for your health, then I act paternalistically toward you. Equally roughly, we can call a practice epistemically paternalistic when it involves interfering with someone's cognitive activities—primarily, with the conduct of their inquiries—with the aim of improving their epistemic position, but without their consent.[7] For example, if a judge withholds information about the defendant's criminal record from the jury because they think knowing this would bias their deliberations and so make them less likely to arrive at the right verdict, then the judge engages in epistemic paternalism because she interferes with their cognitive activities (by withholding information) with the aim of making it more likely that they arrive at the right verdict.

Many think that paternalistic interference is always prima facie objectionable.[8] This is because any form of paternalistic interference infringes on our right as autonomous individuals to make our own choices and our own decisions about how to act. The point is not that *any* sort of infringement on our autonomy is prima facie objectionable. If I have autonomously decided to murder my neighbour, then there seems nothing prima facie objectionable about your calling the police to stop me because you are concerned for my neighbour's safety. The point is rather that it is always prima facie objectionable to infringe on someone's autonomy *for their own good*. If I hide your cigarettes, then I infringe on your right to decide for yourself if you want to smoke them.

One might think that many (if not all) of the strategies for improving the epistemic environment canvassed in the previous section are objectionable in much the same way that paternalistic interventions are objectionable. This is because they involve interfering with individuals' right to conduct their inquiries in the way that they see fit, with the aim of making them epistemically better off.[9] This is most obvious with inoculation theory. The analogy with vaccination suggests that inoculating someone against global warming misinformation without their consent would be like inoculating them against a disease without their consent.

But what about framing and the considerations about spokespersons? While neither of these strategies involve outright deception or the straightforward withholding of information (as when a judge withholds information about a defendant's criminal record from the jury), they all involve presenting information in ways that are designed to make it more likely that the audience will react in a desired way (here, form accurate views about climate science). As such, they are similar to the sort of interference proposed by adherents of "nudging" (Thaler and Sunstein 2008). A "nudge" is (according to Thaler and Sunstein) "any aspect of the choice architecture that alters behavior in a predictable way without forbidding any options" (6). An example of a "nudge" would be telling patients who are deciding whether to have an operation that 90% of those who have it are alive after five years, rather than that 10% of those who have it are dead after five years. These are two ways of presenting the same statistical information, but the former framing has been shown to make it more likely that patients will opt to have the operation than the latter (McNeil et al. 1982). Similarly, framing the issue of global warming in a certain way, or choosing a particular spokesperson to give a message, involves presenting information in ways that make it more likely that the audience will form accurate beliefs about climate science than they would otherwise.

To summarize: While there are several strategies for combatting the problem of consequential false beliefs that may be effective, some (or all) of them involve a sort of interference in the cognitive activities of individuals that one might think is prima facie problematic in the way that paternalistic interference is problematic. Indeed, one might think that they involve a form of (epistemic) paternalism. I finish by arguing that these forms of interference aren't prima facie problematic.

JUSTIFYING EPISTEMIC PATERNALISM

One way of arguing that the strategies canvassed earlier aren't prima facie problematic would be to argue that they aren't really paternalistic. I won't pursue this route, because I am inclined to think that they are. Another way would be to argue that they are both paternalistic *and* justified. Thus, there are justified instances of epistemic paternalism. Ahlstrom-Vij (2013) argues that there are justified instances of epistemic paternalistic interference. Rather than re-iterate this argument, I will construct my own. But let me emphasize that it complements rather than supplants Ahlstrom-Vij's work.

It is commonly assumed that there is a crucial difference between paternalism and *rational persuasion*. Rationally persuading someone to do (or think) something involves offering reasons, evidence and arguments; paternalistic interference with what they do (or think) involves manipulation of some form. In the present content, many would assume that there is a crucial difference between persuading someone to accept that human activity is the major cause of global warming through the provision of reasons, evidence and arguments, and persuading them to accept this through the sorts of strategies canvassed earlier.

In a recent paper, George Tsai (2014) has argued that this common assumption (that there is a crucial difference between rational persuasion and paternalistic forms of persuasion) is false:

> It is possible to rationally persuade someone to do something, yet treat her paternalistically. . . . Rational persuasion may express, and be guided by, the

motive of distrust in the other's capacity to gather or weigh evidence, and may intrude on the other's deliberative activities in ways that conflict with respecting her agency. (79)

Thus, for Tsai, rationally persuading someone to do something (e.g., stop smoking) can be problematic for reasons that paternalistically interfering with them to get them to stop (e.g., hiding their cigarettes) is problematic.

While I agree with Tsai that rational persuasion and paternalistic interference are far more similar than many suppose, I want to urge that we draw almost the opposite conclusion: paternalistic interference is often justifiable for precisely the reasons that rational persuasion is often justifiable. Thus, where Tsai sees the similarities between rational persuasion and paternalistic interference as casting doubt on the legitimacy of rational persuasion, I see these similarities as justifying many instances of paternalistic interference.

Tsai holds that there are two aspects of paternalistic interference that are problematic. The first is that it is guided by what Tsai calls a *motive of distrust* in the rational capacities of another person. The second is that it involves interfering with the deliberations and decisions of another person in ways that disrespect their agency. Tsai's claim is then that some (if not many) cases of rational persuasion also have these two aspects, and so are problematic for the same reasons that paternalistic interference is.

To illustrate this, he gives an example. Claire is trying to decide whether to go to graduate school in philosophy or to law school. Her father, Peter, is trying to persuade her to go to law school. To this end, he bombards Claire with information about the multiple ways in which law school is the better option. Peter is trying to persuade Claire to decide to go to law school through rational means; he isn't blackmailing her, tricking her into going, or anything of the sort. But Tsai thinks his actions are morally problematic because they interfere with Claire's ability to make the decision for herself:

> when others offer us reasons to persuade us at the wrong time or in the wrong way, they make it harder for us to be able to engage more purely and directly with the reasons most centrally tied to the choice-worthiness of our options. When our deliberations are *distorted* in this way, this potentially alters the self-determining and self-expressive aspects of our decision ... the point is that even the rational pressure of Peter's *reason-giving* (as distinguished from the rational pressure of the *reasons* themselves) might potentially alter the nature of Claire's deliberations in a way that results in a sense of loss for Claire. . . . Insofar as the timing of Peter's attempt at rational persuasion precludes Claire from having the purer, more direct engagement with the reasons most centrally relevant to her deliberative situation, this limits her exercise of epistemic agency. (95–96)

I think Tsai is right that Peter's behavior in Tsai's example is problematic. Peter is interfering with Claire's ability to deliberate and decide for herself because he has no trust in her ability to make this decision in a competent manner. That his interference takes the form of rational persuasion makes no difference. But I don't think this example shows what Tsai thinks it does. Tsai presumably thinks that this example generalizes: paternalistic interference (perhaps invariably) and rational persuasion (perhaps only very often) involve a lack of trust in the capacity of another person to deliberate and make decisions in a competent manner, which leads to interference in their deliberations and decisions. But I think this is wrong: neither paternalistic interference nor rational persuasion need be problematic in these ways.

First, part of the reason why Peter's distrust in Claire's capacity to make this decision is so problematic is that the decision in question (whether to go to law school or graduate school in philosophy) concerns Claire's life, and in particular, what she wants to do with it. Peter's distrust in her ability to make this decision for herself reflects not just a lack of respect for Claire's deliberative capacities but also for her ability to make life-choices, and his distrust is disrespectful in part for this reason. It is therefore unclear whether Tsai's point will generalize to cases where the decision has nothing to do with the life choices of the deliberator, whether these cases involve rational persuasion or paternalistic interference. (Thus, it is no surprise that hiding someone's cigarette packet strikes us as problematic: this involves the same sort of interference with their life choices that is so problematic in Tsai's example.)

Second, there are different *ways* of interfering with the deliberations and decisions of another person. The quoted passage given earlier suggests that Tsai's fundamental objection to Peter's behavior is that he has made it harder for Claire to engage with the reasons for and against her two choices. But this is a consequence of the way in which Peter has chosen to interfere with Claire's deliberations, not of him interfering at all. Peter could have "stated his case" in a way that didn't interfere with Claire's ability to engage with the reasons. He could have sat her down and told her why he thought law school was the right option, but made it clear that it was her decision to make, and he was just there to provide her with information, not to make the decision for her.

Third, while it is hard to see why you would interfere with the deliberations of someone you were confident didn't need your help, this doesn't mean that interference must always be guided by the sort of distrust that drives Peter to interfere with Claire's deliberations. In another version of the case, Peter might have simply been worried that Claire didn't have all the information she needed to make an informed choice, and have taken it upon himself to find some information about the benefits of going to law school.

You might object: this is all very well, but doesn't it just show that Tsai is wrong in thinking that rational persuasion is often problematic in the same way that paternalistic interference is? I have given us reasons to think that rational persuasion need not involve the sort of interference with the deliberations and decisions of another that is so problematic in Claire's case. What about paternalistic interference?

Consider the strategies for combatting the problem of consequential false beliefs canvassed earlier: inoculating people against climate misinformation, framing the issue in such a way as to make it more likely that they accept the scientific consensus, and choosing spokespeople so as to neuter ideological biases and blindspots. It can be argued that all of these strategies can avoid the problems Tsai identifies in his example.

First, our deliberations about what to believe when it comes to climate change don't directly concern our life-choices (though they do so indirectly, in that what we believe about climate change may inform our life-choices). Thus, interfering with people's decisions about what to think about climate change need not reflect any disrespect for their ability to make life-choices.

Second, someone utilizing these strategies is not aiming to interfere with people's abilities to engage with the scientific evidence pertaining to climate change. On the contrary: their aim is to facilitate engagement with this evidence, by drawing attention to what the evidence actually is and neutering ideological biases and blindspots that get in the way of engaging with it. As Dan Kahan (2010) puts it:

> It would not be a gross simplification to say that science needs better marketing. Unlike commercial advertising, however, the goal of these techniques is not to induce public acceptance of any particular conclusion, but rather to create an environment for the public's open-minded, unbiased consideration of the best available scientific information. (3)

The strategies identified earlier need not detract from our rationality. In fact, they may enhance it. The key message here is that, sometimes, we need a little help to think rationally in the first place.

Third, and finally, while the empirical literature I have canvassed in this chapter does engender a sort of distrust in the capacity of laypersons to form views about complex issues like climate change, it is important to note that this distrust is based on the evidence provided by the empirical literature. Moreover, the distrust is in our capacity to form views about these issues *in the complicated socio-epistemic environment in which we find ourselves*. This need not involve any sort of lack of respect for laypersons' epistemic agency. It is simply the consequence of the realisation that we are epistemic agents in an imperfect world.

I conclude that, while Tsai is right in arguing that rational persuasion isn't that different from paternalistic interference, he draws the wrong moral. Tsai argues that rational persuasion is often as problematic as paternalistic interference. I have argued that, on the contrary, in many cases, neither rational persuasion nor paternalistic interference is problematic.

CONCLUSION

The problem of consequential false beliefs is a problem for everyone. In this paper I have addressed it from the perspective of a de-idealized social epistemology. The task for a de-idealized social epistemology is to identify evidence-based strategies for improving the public's epistemic health. I have identified three strategies for improving the public's epistemic health with regard to scientific issues like global warming that have become politically contentious: prebunking, framing, and judicious choice of messenger. These strategies prompted an ethical concern: Do they constitute a problematic form of paternalism that infringes on epistemic autonomy? I argued that, while they are plausibly epistemically paternalistic, they are not ethically problematic.[10]

NOTES

1. See https://www.theguardian.com/environment/2019/may/07/us-hotbed-climate-change-denial-international-poll.

2. For references, see further.

3. One can find this view in both the philosophical literature (e.g., Kitcher 2011) and the non-philosophical literature (e.g., Ungar 2000).

4. I take this term from Ryan (2018).

5. I should emphasize that this approach is not new. It informs much of Elizabeth Anderson's work in social epistemology (e.g., Anderson 2011), and one can find manifestations of it in a large body of social epistemological work.

6. For some cross-national data, see Tranter and Booth (2015). The general message is that, while some countries do better than others, there is no country where most people have an accurate belief about the level of scientific consensus.

7. See Ahlstrom-Vij (2013). While Ahlstrom-Vij requires that epistemic paternalistic interference be with the aim of making the person interfered with epistemically better off, I myself would be inclined toward the view that an epistemic paternalistic practice merely involves interfering with someone's cognitive activities, whether it has the aim of improving or worsening their epistemic position. One might wonder why this qualifies as a form of epistemic paternalism (Bullock 2016). But perhaps epistemic paternalism is "epistemic" in roughly the same sense in which Fricker (2007) thinks epistemic injustice is "epistemic." Just as an individual experiences epistemic justice when they are harmed in their capacity as an epistemic agent, an individual is interfered with in an epistemic paternalistic way when they are interfered with in their capacity as an epistemic agent.

8. For discussion, see many of the essays in Grill and Hanna (2018). For a discussion of the legal case in particular, see Laudan (2006).

9. One might object that science communicators may not be interested in the epistemic health of the populace for its own sake, but merely as a means to the end of securing wider public support for policies to reduce greenhouse gas emissions and mitigate the impacts of global warming. I lack the space to discuss this objection here, but I refer the reader to Ahlstrom-Vij's discussion of this objection (Ahlstrom-Vij 2013, Chapter 2).

10. I would like to thank Amiel Bernal and Guy Axtell for very helpful comments on an earlier version of this chapter.

BIBLIOGRAPHY

Ahlstrom-Vij, Kristoffer. *Epistemic Paternalism: A Defence*. London: Palgrave Macmillan, 2013.

American Academy of Arts & Sciences. *Perceptions of Science in America*, 2018. Accessed http://www.publicfaceofscience.org/.

Anderson, Elizabeth. "Democracy, Public Policy, and Lay Assessments of Scientific Testimony." *Episteme* 8, no. 2 (2011): 144–164.

Bak, Hee-Je. "Education and Public Attitudes toward Science: Implications for the 'Deficit Model' of Education and Support for Science and Technology." *Social Science Quarterly* 82, no. 4 (2001): 779–795.

Ballew, Matthew T., Anthony Leiserowitz, Connie Roser-Renouf, Seth A. Rosenthal, John E. Kotcher, Jennifer R. Marlon, Erik Lyon, Matthew H. Goldberg, and Edward H. Maibach. "Climate Change in the American Mind: Data, Tools, and Trends." *Environment: Science and Policy for Sustainable Development* 61, no. 3 (2019): 4–18.

Bolsen, Toby, Thomas J. Leeper and Matthew A. Shapiro. "Doing What Others Do: Norms, Science, and Collective Action on Global Warming." *American Politics Research* 42, no. 1 (2014): 65–89.

Bolsen, Tony and James N. Druckman. "Counteracting the Politicization of Science." *Journal of Communication* 65, no. 5 (2015): 745–769.

Bullock, Emma C. "Knowing and Not-Knowing for Your Own Good: The Limits of Epistemic Paternalism." *Journal of Applied Philosophy* 35, no. 2 (2016): 433–447.

Campbell, Troy H. and Aaron C. Kay. "Solution Aversion: On the Relation between Ideology and Motivated Disbelief." *Journal of Personality and Social Psychology* 107, no. 5 (2014): 809–824.

Compton, Josh. "Inoculation Theory," in James P. Dillard and Lijiang Shen (eds.), *The SAGE Handbook of Persuasion: Developments in Theory and Practice*, 220–236. Thousand Oaks, CA: Sage Publications, 2013.

Cook, John. "Countering Climate Science Denial and Communicating Scientific Consensus." *Oxford Encyclopedia of Climate Change Communication*, 2016. Accessed doi:10.1093/acrefore/9780190228620.013.314

———. "Understanding and Countering Climate Science Denial." *Journal and Proceedings of the Royal Society of New South Wales* 150, no. 465/466 (2017): 207–219.

Cook, John and Stephan Lewandowsky. *The Debunking Handbook*. St. Lucia, Australia: University of Queensland, 2011. Accessed http://sks.to/debunk

Cook, John, Stephan Lewandowsky and Ullrich K. H. Ecker. "Neutralizing Misinformation through Inoculation: Exposing Misleading Argumentation Techniques Reduces Their Influence." *PLoS One* 12, no. 5 (2017): e0175799.

Cook, John, Sander van der Linden, Edward H. Maibach and Stephan Lewandowsky. *The Consensus Handbook*, 2018. Accessed http://www.climatechangecommunication.org/all/consensus-handbook/.

Cook, John, Naomi Oreskes, Peter T. Doran, William R. L. Anderegg, Bart Verheggen, Edward H. Maibach, J. Stuart Carlton, Stephan Lewandowsky, Andrew G. Skuce and Sarah A. Green. "Consensus on Consensus: A Synthesis of Consensus Estimates on Human-Caused Global Warming." *Environmental Research Letters* 11, no. 4 (2016): 048002.

Corner, Adam, Stephan Lewandowsky, Mary Phillips and Olga Roberts. *The Uncertainty Handbook*. Bristol: University of Bristol, 2015.

Cvetkovich, George and Timothy Earle. *Social Trust: Toward a Cosmopolitan Society*. Westport, CT: Praeger, 1995.

Cvetkovich, George and Ragnar Löfstedt, eds. *Social Trust and the Management of Risk*. Abingdon: Earthscan, 1999.

Dahlstrom, Michael F. "Using Narratives and Storytelling to Communicate Science with Nonexpert Audiences." *Proceedings of the National Academy of Sciences* 111, no. Supplement 4 (2014): 13614–13620.

Downing, Phil and Joe Ballantyne. *Tipping Point or Turning Point? Social Marketing and Climate Change*. London: Ipsos MORI Social Research Institute, 2007.

Dryzek, John S. and Alex Y. Lo. "Reason and Rhetoric in Climate Communication." *Environmental Politics* 24, no. 1 (2015): 1–16.

Fricker, Miranda. *Epistemic Injustice: Power and the Ethics of Knowing*. Vol. 69. Oxford: Oxford University Press, 2007.

Gardner, Gerald T. and Paul C. Stern. *Environmental Problems and Human Behavior*. Boston, MA: Allyn & Bacon, 1996.

Goldman, Alvin. *Knowledge in a Social World*. Oxford: Oxford University Press, 1999.

Goldman, Alvin and Thomas Blanchard. "Social Epistemology," in Edward N. Zalta (ed.). *The Stanford Encyclopedia of Philosophy (Summer 2018 Edition)*, 2018. Accessed https://plato.stanford.edu/archives/sum2018/entries/epistemology-social/.

Grill, Kalle and Jason Hanna, eds. *The Routledge Handbook of the Philosophy of Paternalism*. Abingdon: Routledge, 2018.

Hamilton, Lawrence C. "Education, Politics and Opinions about Climate Change Evidence for Interaction Effects." *Climatic Change* 104, no. 2 (2011): 231–242.

Hamilton, Lawrence C., Joel Hartter, Mary Lemcke-Stampone, David W. Moore and Thomas G. Safford. "Tracking Public Beliefs about Anthropogenic Climate Change." *PLoS One* 10, no. 9 (2015): e0138208.

Hardisty, David J., Eric J. Johnson and Elke U. Weber. "A Dirty Word or a Dirty World? Attribute Framing, Political Affiliation, and Query Theory." *Psychological Science* 21, no. 1 (2010): 86–92.

Hornsey, Matthew J., Emily A. Harris, Paul G. Bain and Kelly S. Fielding. "Meta-Analyses of the Determinants and Outcomes of Belief in Climate Change." *Nature Climate Change* 6, no. 6 (2016): 622–626.
Ipsos MORI. *Public Attitudes to Science 2014*, 2014. Accessed https://www.british scienceassociation.org/public-attitudes-to-science-survey.
Ivanov, Bobi, Jeanetta D Sims, Josh Compton, Claude H. Miller, Kimberly A. Parker, James L. Parker, Kylie J. Harrison and Joshua M. Averbeck. "The General Content of Postinoculation Talk: Recalled Issue-Specific Conversations Following Inoculation Treatments." *Western Journal of Communication* 79, no. 2 (2015): 218–238.
Kahan, Dan. "Making Climate-Science Communication Evidence-Based-All the Way Down," in M. Boykoff and D. Crow (eds.), *Culture, Politics and Climate Change*, 203–220. New York: Routledge, 2014.
Kahan, Dan, Donald Braman, Geoffrey L. Cohen, John Gastil and Paul Slovic. "Who Fears the HPV Vaccine, Who Doesn't, and Why? An Experimental Study of the Mechanisms of Cultural Cognition." *Law and Human Behavior* 34, no. 6 (2010): 501–516.
Kahan, Dan, Hank Jenkins-Smith and Donald Braman. "Cultural Cognition of Scientific Consensus." *Journal of Risk Research* 14, no. 2 (2011): 147–174.
Kahan, Dan, Hank C. Jenkins-Smith, Tor Tarantola, Carol L. Silva and Donald Braman. "Geoengineering and Climate Change Polarization: Testing a Two-Channel Model of Science Communication." *Annals of American Academy of Political and Social Science* 658 (2015): 193–222.
Kitcher, Philip. *Science in a Democratic Society*. Location: Buffalo, NY: Prometheus Books, 2011.
Kvanvig, Jonathan. *The Value of Knowledge and the Pursuit of Understanding*. Cambridge: Cambridge University Press, 2003.
Laudan, Larry. *Truth, Error, and Criminal Law*. Cambridge: Cambridge University Press, 2006.
Lewandowsky, Stephan, Ullrich K. H. Ecker, Colleen M. Seifert, Norbert Schwarz and John Cook. "Misinformation and Its Correction: Continued Influence and Successful Debiasing." *Psychological Science in the Public Interest* 13, no. 3 (2012): 106–131.
Lewandowsky, Stephan, Gilles E. Gignac and Samuel Vaughan. "The Pivotal Role of Perceived Scientific Consensus in Acceptance of Science." *Nature Climate Change* 3, no. 4 (2013): 399–404.
Lewandowsky, Stephan and Klaus Oberauer. "Motivated Rejection of Science." *Current Directions in Psychological Science* 25, no. 4 (2016): 217–222.
Linden, Sander van der, Anthony Leiserowitz, Geoffrey D. Feinberg and Edward Maibach. "How to Communicate the Scientific Consensus on Climate Change: Plain Facts, Pie Charts or Metaphors?" *Climatic Change* 126, no. 1–2 (2014): 255–262.
Linden, Sander van der, Anthony Leiserowitz, Seth Rosenthal and Edward Maibach. http://dx.doi.org/10.1002/gch2.201600008 "Inoculating the Public against Misinformation about Climate Change." *Global Challenges* 1, no. 2 (2017): 1600008.

MacInnis, Bo, John A. Krosnick, Adina Abeles, Margaret R. Caldwell, Erin Prahler and Debbie Drake Dunne. "The American Public's Preference for Preparation for the Possible Effects of Global Warming: Impact of Communication Strategies." *Climatic Change* 128, no. 1–2 (2015): 17–33.

McNeil, Barbara J., Stephen G. Pauker, Harold C. Sox Jr. and Amos Tversky. "On the Elicitation of Preferences for Alternative Therapies." *The New England Journal of Medicine* 306, no. 21 (1982): 1259–1262.

Moser, Susanne C. and Lisa Dilling. "Communicating Climate Change: Closing the Science-Action Gap," in John S. Dryzek, Richard B. Norgaard, and David Schlosberg (eds.), *The Oxford Handbook of Climate Change and Society*, 161–174. Oxford: Oxford University Press, 2011.

Pfau, Michael. "Designing Messages for Behavioral Inoculation," in Edward H. Maibach and Roxanne L. Parrott (eds.), *Designing Health Messages: Approaches from Communication Theory and Public Health Practice*, 99–113. Thousand Oaks, CA: Sage Publications, 1995.

Pfau, Michael and Michael Burgoon. "Inoculation in Political Campaign Communication." *Human Communication Research* 15, no. 1 (1988): 91–111.

Quine, W. V. O. "Epistemology Naturalized." In *Ontological Relativity and Other Essays*, 69–90. New York: Columbia University Press, 1969.

Ryan, Shane. "Epistemic Environmentalism." *Journal of Philosophical Research* 43 (2018): 97–112.

Seifert, Colleen M. "The Continued Influence of Misinformation in Memory: What Makes a Correction Effective?" In *Psychology of Learning and Motivation*, 41: 265–292. 2002.

Sturgis, Patrick and Nick Allum. "Science in Society: Re-Evaluating the Deficit Model of Public Attitudes." *Public Understanding of Science* 13, no. 1 (2004): 55–74.

Thaler, Richard H. and Cass R. Sunstein. *Nudge: Improving Decisions about Health, Wealth, and Happiness*. New Haven, CT: Yale University Press, 2008.

Tranter, Bruce and Kate Booth. "Scepticism in a Changing Climate: A Cross-National Study." *Global Environmental Change* 33 (2015): 154–164.

Tsai, George. "Rational Persuasion as Paternalism." *Philosophy and Public Affairs* 42, no. 1 (2014): 78–112.

Ungar, Sheldon. "Knowledge, Ignorance and the Popular Culture: Climate Change versus the Ozone Hole." *Public Understanding of Science* 9, no. 3 (2000): 297–312.

Williamson, Timothy. *Knowledge and Its Limits*. Oxford: Oxford University Press, 2000.

Chapter 7

Expert Care in Mental Health Paternalism

Shaun Respess

Operating as "experts," medical professionals and practitioners in the mental health field routinely make decisions regarding the epistemic needs of their clients/patients. These choices include concealing particularly unpleasant test results from patients, promoting certain studies and methods over others, and sanctioning official diagnoses over a client's experiential testimony. Many of these decisions appropriately qualify as *epistemic paternalism* (EP), which refers to the interference with a person's inquiry without consultation for the sake of that person's and others' epistemic good (Ahlstrom-Vij 2013: 4). Proponents and critics of EP debate the range of actions that may sufficiently meet its conditions and the moral permissibility of its regular practice. Among these questions are concerns of what may constitute valid expertise and how it may be leveraged paternalistically. Some have theorized possible epistemic and ethical conditions for experts who make interventions of this kind (Croce 2018; Goldman 1991). This chapter further engages these concerns by examining the peculiar form of paternalism present in American mental health care.

 I complicate the permissible parameters of EP by critiquing the ethical dimensions of "care" in paternalistic psychiatric treatment, and reimagine the concept of expertise by appealing to feminist epistemologies. I argue that care ethics should supplant utilitarian, libertarian, and virtue-based accounts of paternalism in articulating a more accurate representation of how one should or should not appropriately intervene. In my view, prior ethical evaluations of EP fail to appropriately situate "expertise" within the complex systems and relationships of knowing to which the status is dependent. In response, this analysis introduces care ethics into the EP literature and defends its distinct contributions. Within this inquiry, I depreciate the appeal of agential epistemology in favor of identifying dominant *ecosystems* and *relations* of knowledge. Experts will be portrayed as authoritative interferers within epistemic networks and will be examined according to their capacity to meet caring needs and to promote the epistemic and non-epistemic well-being of those in their care. The use of psychiatric interventions serves several purposes: (1) the focused subset diversifies examples of EP and demonstrates a unique form of interference that is both social and physiological; (2) it draws attention to unreliable norms within American medical practice; and (3) expertise in these scenarios is customarily accepted yet presents evident problems for analysis.

I first feature the conditions for EP as well as provide some initial explanations for sufficient epistemic authority. I then describe the paradigm of pharmacotherapy for illustration and context, afterward exposing some limitations and concerns with the representation of expertise in medical interventions. Ensuing critiques of expertise primarily originate from feminist epistemologies. The final substantive section proposes normative analyses of care in order to foster *caring commitments* for justifying expert paternalism. I conclude by stressing the implications of an expanded account of expertise for discussions of EP. A defense of care ethics is accentuated.

FOR THEIR OWN GOOD

Epistemic paternalism (EP), originally developed by Goldman (1991), involves one person (A) intervening on another's (B) decision-making or learning faculties in order to improve those capabilities or to shield B from troubling or unreliable beliefs. Most scholars insist that *both* B's epistemic and non-epistemic well-being should improve from the interference. Ahlstrom-Vij (2013) formally develops EP by detailing a set of necessary and jointly sufficient conditions for the concept; these conditions are as follows:

(1) *The Interference Condition*: A interferes with B's freedom to conduct inquiry; however, B desires or sees fit (40).
(2) *The Non-Consultation Condition*: A does not consult B when/before A interferes in B's inquiry, thus leaving them unaware of the interference (43).
(3) *The Improvement Condition*: The interference is done for the purpose of improving B's judgment or general epistemic abilities, or for improving those whom B influences (48).

Among those covering the topic, these three conditions are rather uncontroversial as standards, though there are discrepancies concerning what actions fit these requirements.[1] Typical examples of this kind include when an instructor hides a correct answer to a problem from a student so that the learner may benefit from discovering the answer on their own, or when a guardian protects their ward from bigoted language for fear that the dependent will be influenced negatively by baseless or hostile opinions.[2]

In health care, such decisions are considered justified if they protect a patient from harming themselves, panicking, or negatively affecting those around them. *Experts*, or people in privileged epistemic positions relative to us concerning some subject/topic D, possess the opportunity and capacity to make decisions in our and others' best interests by deciding which information is and is not valuable for us to know at particular moments. With respect to D, we value and rarely contest the epistemic positions of our experts. However, what is at stake in EP is whether such experts are justified in using their position to make decisions on our behalf. In order for an instance of EP to be justified, Ahlstrom-Vij proposes a *burden-of-proof condition*: where evidence indicates a high probability of everyone being epistemically better off by the interference as opposed to alternatives (122). Still, there is some dispute regarding how best to preserve one's well-being. Ahlstrom-Vij proposes the *alignment condition*, which requires that A's epistemic reasons be aligned with their non-epistemic reasons for interfering. As argued by Bullock (2018) and Croce (2018), this may not serve as a stable condition and is potentially overly restrictive.[3] Bullock thus replaces the alignment condition with the *balancing goods condition*, in which there are simply no strong reasons suggesting that B will be made worse off from the interference (440).

My critique not only considers how these conditions may reasonably be met but also examines who/what might meet these conditions. Observing the analysis provided by Croce (2018), one can accept that all conditions are met while still questioning A's authority to be paternalistic. Croce responds to Goldman's assertions that expertise is a necessary condition for one to conduct EP and that the expert's capacity to more effectively weigh circumstances and options sufficiently justifies their position.[4] In contrast, Croce argues that one is a *virtuous interferer* in their capacity for developing novice-oriented abilities: intellectual virtues that are sensitive to B's needs and epistemic dependency as well as are oriented toward what is ethically best for B (314–317). I generally agree with this amendment and endorse several of the values proposed (e.g., trust, sensitivity, or empathy). However, I diverge from Croce's ethical premise by suggesting that virtue theory is inadequate for grounding these values. I propose instead that we look toward the ethics of care as a more sufficient base. Thorough evaluations of EP must preserve the relational and interdependent foundations of social epistemology, which is somewhat deflated in virtue-based accounts that overemphasize the cultivation of individual excellence. The social uncertainties of EP practices demonstrated in the following sections support this assertion.

CHANGING LIVES WITH MAGIC BULLETS

Expertise is certainly not lacking in American mental health care: highly trained psychiatrists, psychologists, counselors, nurse practitioners, clinicians, therapists, and physicians are abundant. Yet the surplus of knowledge does not seem to produce better treatment outcomes: past studies conducted by the World Health Organization (WHO) regularly confirmed that those suffering from a psychotic disorder in a developed country like the United States faired significantly worse than those in underdeveloped or developing countries (Jablensky et. al 1992; Leff et. al 1992). Stated another way, psychiatrist Robert Post contends, "In the United States, people with depression, bipolar, and schizophrenia are losing twelve to twenty years in life expectancy compared to people not in the mental health system" (Whitaker 2010: 175–176). The primary suspect, empirically supported by several scholars, appears to be the excessive and misinformed endorsement of anti-psychotic medications in resolving the "broken" minds of incoming patients.[5] An approach now known as *pharmacotherapy*, this paradigm has also been labeled by Whitaker as "magic bullet psychiatry."

The following case offers some descriptive texture for this problem: in an interview with *Mad in America*, Jenna Fogle details her journey through the American mental health system. Experiencing moderate depression when she was a teenager, she was sent to a psychiatric clinic by her parents and then swiftly given a series of medications to balance her condition. Fogle was not consulted prior to receiving care, and neither her nor her parents were informed of any potential fallout from using these drugs long-term.[6] The drugs, thought to improve her epistemic capacities and regulate intense emotions, ultimately put her in a state of sedation that irreparably damaged motor functioning and altered her cognitive abilities. A condition labeled *tardive dyskinesia*, the effects include poor memory, slurred speech, muscle failure, uncontrollable tics, and diminished coordination; without early intervention, the condition is essentially permanent (Breggin 2008: 214–215). Other effects can include inner agitations associated with increased violence and suicide known as *akathisia* (Whitaker 2010: 232). Fogle's experience is typical of many psychiatric patients. Those who are depressive, bipolar, schizophrenic, or mentally abnormal are routinely hospitalized or prescribed medications for their epistemic and physical well-being, through evidence suggest that these interventions are detrimental and unreliable.

Pharmacotherapeutic interventions that withhold harmful information or disregard consent appear to rightfully qualify as EP, albeit an unjustified form. It is, however, worth noting that many counselors and therapists abstain from or limit these methods in favor of empathetic conversations. Many nurse practitioners and those in similar roles may also provide care but are not responsible for the paternalistic decision. While not all methods/persons may sufficiently qualify, interventions such as the anecdotal case meet the conditions: (1) expert A interferes with B's capability to fully inquire about her condition and appropriate treatment by limiting or removing alternative options or by forcefully "nudging" her in a desired direction;[7](2) though A might initiate a consultation, B is not always consulted regarding the efficacy or desirability of available options; and (3) A's choices are intended to benefit B epistemically, helping B "see clearly" or balance her emotions.

We trust in the decision-making capacities of A because of her relative expertise, even when broader evidence suggests that it might not be reliable. This form of paternalism would thus fail the burden-of-proof condition, even though the professional may not be aware of the evidence because of institutional or disciplinary constraints.[8] This may be viewed as an extended form of EP conducted by more powerful epistemic authorities. Whether omitted from public record or misconstrued in professional materials, the diminishment or absence of source material for experts may violate the alignment condition as well. If defensible scientific evidence of harm is withheld for the purpose of economic gain or academic hubris, then the case for justified paternalism would fail to produce sufficient non-epistemic motivations. An argument can be made for concealing public health information that may have drastic social consequences (Grill and Hansson 2005). This appears weak. Given the success of countries with less prescriptions and more transparency, no such harm to public welfare appears likely though the market for medications could suffer unfortunate fiscal losses. The misuse of pharmacotherapy exposes problems with the reliability of expert knowledge. Epistemic authorities in these instances can be both party to and victims of misleading information that ultimately causes harm despite an authority's best intentions. In this respect, the legitimacy of expertise is compromised.

KNOWING YOUR PATIENT

The paternalistic authority of experts is discursively justified by their credibility as knowers; their proficiency in some D subject matter is often the result of intense study and practice. Generally speaking, this is a safe assumption to promote. However, uncritically worshipping expertise can reinforce several social concerns such as falsely promoting epistemological individualism, credibility injustices, and patient objectification. In this section, I do not directly presume whether experts satisfy the third condition of desiring epistemic and non-epistemic improvement. Rather, I examine whether their procured position and methodological resources are sufficient enough to warrant their status as trustworthy authorities.

By preserving paradigms that identify *agents* as fundamental knowers, the wider ecosystem of knowledge becomes more obscure. As Nelson (1993) remarks, the theory that a knower can be epistemically independent and grasp objective truths in isolation is simply "implausible" (122). *Epistemological individualism* undermines or ignores our interdependency while suggesting that epistemic activity is simply a one-to-one interaction between knower and the abstract thing-to-be-known.[9] Nelson argues that *communities*, not solipsistic individuals, are the producers, proprietors, and appropriators of knowledge. She additionally refutes that these communities can be effectively broken down into assemblages of knowing individuals (150). Respectable theories, standards of evidence, and methodologies are dynamic and socially situated. Furthermore, they determine who is and is not an authorized knower within a given epistemic network (138–145). Communities also influence decision-making and intervention by implementing procedural guidelines that may absolve the expert of critical reflection. Using Goldman's (1991) example of EP in a court proceeding, I contend that judges conventionally do not actively reflect on epistemic reasons to intervene so much as they appeal to legal precedents and standards mandating that they do so in instances of unreliable facts or testimonies. Similarly, licensed psychiatrists are expected to know and abide by the definitions and classifications of mental disorders presented in the *Diagnostic and Statistical Manual of Mental Disorders: DSM-5* (2013). These norms create epistemological distance between interferers and the justifications for paternalistic actions.

While it is true that epistemic credibility (normally) needs to be earned and substantiated by the interferer in some manner, credibility and authority are not simply *taken* by an expert but are rather *conferred* onto them by an established community of knowers. Psychiatric experts, like most in health care professions, must meet the approval of their peers, be certified, and demonstrate an active participation in contributing to or upholding the reputation of the discipline. Experts are thus authorities in so far as their epistemic network holds some degree of respect and so long as those experts remain in good standing with that community. The credibility of psychiatrists is necessarily linked to the credibility of *psychiatry* as an established ecosystem of knowledge.

Psychiatric patients are not awarded the same degree of credibility, and regularly suffer from epistemic injustices when explaining their experiences. Fricker (2007) clarifies these harms: "testimonial injustice, in which someone is wronged in their capacity as a giver of knowledge; and hermeneutical injustice, in which someone is wronged in their capacity as a subject of social understanding" (7). Within medical relationships, credibility differences are quite transparent: A is given an excess of credibility based on her title and position within a credible community. We expect our medical professionals to have proficient answers even on subjects outside of their specialty (18). In contrast, B suffers from a credibility deficit: she is considered ignorant to the source and contingencies of her condition. Experts are indeed more credible on some matters. Years of formal education and applied practice are not futile. For Fricker, however, what is more concerning is the allocation of respect regarding these two persons: by discounting the testimonies of those whom we deem less credible, we disregard them as knowers.

In a recent publication, Gosselin (2019) critiques the medicalization of mental disorders in the United States and proposes principles of justice for diagnosis, treatment, and recovery. As she argues, the "medical model" of psychiatry perpetuates biases of patients as either dangerous and violent, incompetent, or weak-willed, thus making them less credible as persons (9). While I agree with her characterization of these perceptions, I do not believe that she carries this criticism far enough. The medical model, in my view, presents psychiatric patients as passive objects to be studied and treated rather than as speakers who disseminate knowledge. This is a type of injustice that Fricker (2007) calls *epistemic objectification* (133). Medicalization explicitly dehumanizes a person by diagnosing them as a collection of symptoms detached from their uniquely situated experiences and environments. Patients are not treated as *less credible*, but as *not worthy of demonstrating credibility*.[10]

As Code (1993) argues, isolating propositional knowledge (S knows P) as the paradigm for epistemology endorses the reduction of all-that-is-knowable into objects. Knowing others is distinct from knowing objects in that knowing others lacks the categorical simplicity and rigidity that many of us desire. In other words, observing and knowing unique persons is more complicated than studying "humans," "bodies," or any other formal grouping. Knowing-that similarly doesn't translate to *knowing-how*: engaging with complex bodies requires different skills than those needed for identifying symptoms (Dalmiya and Alcoff 1993). Despite these limitations, experts continue to study patients as objects rather than invite them in as credible informers. This is problematic: patients are knowers themselves, not just things to be known. Yet they rarely participate in the epistemic ecosystem.

This is, in part, why Croce's (2018) novice-oriented abilities are appealing, though I do not see them at complete odds with Goldman's (1991) account of expertise for EP. To incorporate these abilities is to redirect attention toward B. Within Goldman's account, the expert is simply a conduit concerning some D subject matter. Patients ("novices") are certainly well suited to provide testimony about their own health because health is partially about B and their experiences, not just about formal groupings established by health institutions. Psychiatrists often struggle in this regard under medicalization, viewing patients as a bipolar, schizophrenic, or depressive body rather than as a unique person with whom they are consulting. Epistemic interference on B's behalf is more scientifically predictable when B is an object who responds to certain stimuli. The problem is that subjects are not as predictable as objects.

Discriminatory norms like patient objectification negatively influence the epistemic and non-epistemic well-being of interferees while leaving interferers relatively immune. While experts may fail to communicate a desired belief to their subject or to satisfy internal or external pressures to provide quality care, the patient suffers considerably more.[11] Concealing or improperly framing information for a patient may result in much more dismal consequences than an instructor forcing a student to learn on their own. Gosselin (2019) clearly seeks to accommodate these risks: "People who have mental illness are vulnerable to coercion, exploitation, epistemic injustice, and other forms of oppression by agents that exercise power over them" (13). She rightfully notes a tension between patient autonomy and coercion that is prevalent in mental health: in order to do what is "best" for B, B is often compelled to begin and maintain treatment despite reservations or outright objections. The stigmatizing force of being "non-compliant" further aggravates the pressure to conform to an expert's directions. Framing care in terms of compliance maintains the institutional credibility of psychiatry by enforcing professional conventions irrespective of a patient's distinct needs or desires (16–17).

Patients may even oppress themselves through self-disciplining that reinforces false or harmful beliefs. Theoretically known as *biosociality* (Rabinow 2008), individuals will form a prominent identity around their diagnosis or condition; they come to believe that who they are is always inescapably determined by how they are afflicted. As patients *become* the object that psychiatry addresses them as their ability to form more accurate beliefs about their experiences or conditions remains subdued. Compliance is not always freely chosen either: normalization is most commonly a *survival strategy*. In Gupta's (2019) words, "Because of systemic inequality, many, if not all, mainstream medical interventions will simultaneously reinforce social inequality and alleviate some individual suffering" (3). Much like the long-term use of anti-psychotic medications, patients may opt for immediate relief while compromising their overall well-being. Regardless, we cannot condemn those suffering for seeking reprieve, or fault experts for providing it. Given the amplified effects on a patient's beliefs and physical well-being, justifications for expertise must be ethically situated better than previous accounts of EP have provided. Qualifying A as a knower of what is best for B requires a focused moral commitment that some scholars have pursued.

I propose that an ethics of care approach best orients and guides resolutions for unjustified paternalism.

CARE TO INTERVENE?

An expert interfering with someone for her own epistemic benefit is a form of care: the expert tends to the needs or desires of a (inter)dependent person for the sake of improving their judgment and well-being. Potentially framed as *epistemic care*, the complex process of helping others form desirable beliefs and judgments by manipulating information should be assessed according to an ethos revealed in practices of interference. Intervention is foremost a moral concern, though EP has significant epistemic ramifications as well. I contend that an ethics of care is best suited to address this concern, with an observable fit to the examples and complications highlighted in this chapter. The addition of care to discussions of EP validates *relations* of knowledge and provides guidance regarding epistemic obligations without being overly prescriptive.

Theories of care cultivate harmonious relations between interdependent persons and promote the well-being of those in caring relationships by sustainably fulfilling diverse needs. Ethics of care are not necessarily prescriptive, but more so evaluative. To use Puig de la Bellacasa's (2017) words, obligations of care are "constraints that get to endure across more or less changing relational fields. They transcend specific instances of production of care ethos but not necessarily to become moral norms, or even positions, but because they require engagement with an ongoing doing. These ethical obligations are commitments that stabilize as necessary to maintain or intervene in a particular ethos" (154). In ongoing practices, care ethicists assess *relationships* as the focus of moral inquiry and defend the premise of inevitable (inter)dependencies. As Kittay (1999, 2011) explains, there are moments in our lives (such as infancy, old age, and impairment) where we are significantly dependent/vulnerable. This should not overshadow the fact that we are generally always dependent to some degree. Expertise may not always be required to meet our needs, but in most cases, we rely on the strenuous and informed labor of others. Ethics of care situate our intricate connections to one another in order to foster values and demands for more flourishing lives.

Care ethics avoids the burden of relativism by asserting the universality of care as a necessary *doing*: providing and receiving care are naturally indispensable. Still, providing care to another with benevolent intention does not imply that it will be *quality care* or that it will be sufficiently justified, as I have previously demonstrated.[12] Care should not, however, be misconstrued as simply another virtue to be cultivated by the interferer. While virtue-based accounts like Croce's do share some similar motivations with care ethics, they lack the underlying relational premise. As Tronto (2013) illustrates, "They do not begin from the premise that the important ethical issues concern relationships and meeting needs, not the perfection of the virtuous individual" (36). The intellectual virtue of sensitivity suggested by Croce (2018: 317) appropriately draws attention to the unique needs of B but does so by accentuating an interferer's merit as an epistemic authority. Instead, the emphasis should be on the demands that A and B have within the contexts of the relationship.

Demands are unique to the fiduciary relationship that A and B have, thus producing distinct obligations and concerns. Experts and novices alike may choose to accept certain duties to one another but must also be cognizant of obscure demands that are not initially anticipated.[13] For instance, psychiatrists must be sensitive to the needs of a patient's families and close affiliates when intervening, along with treating the ailments suggested by the diagnosis. Trust must also be nurtured by both parties, both in the ethical sense of being sincere and in the epistemic sense of finding the other to be competent and informed (Fricker 2007: 76). To these ends, quality care requires an extended commitment to the construction of flourishing spaces that allow one's needs and desires to emerge safely.[14] In other words, we care for and in environments that facilitate essential resources and produce boundaries for mutual understanding and engagement.

The framework that I propose for EP and other forms of paternalism reconsiders epistemic responsibility and justification within a relational epistemology. Specifically, I explore the *process* of care as a model for positioning accountability and paternalistic authority. Tronto (2013) offers a general schema of the caring process:

1. *Caring about.* Someone or some group notices unmet caring needs.
2. *Caring for.* Once needs are identified, someone or some group has to take responsibility to make certain that these needs are met.
3. *Care-giving.* The third phase of caring requires that the actual caregiving work be done.
4. *Care-receiving.* Once care work is done, there will be a response from the person, thing, group, animal, plant, or environment that has been cared for. Observing that response and making judgments about it (for example, was the care given sufficient? successful? complete?) is the fourth phase of care. Note that while the care receiver may be the one who responds, it need not be so. Sometimes the care receiver cannot respond. Others in any particular care setting will also be in a position, potentially, to assess the effectiveness of the caring act(s). And, in having met previous caring needs, new needs will undoubtedly arise.

5. *Caring with.* This final phase of care requires that caring needs and the ways in which they are met need to be consistent with democratic commitments to justice, equality, and freedom for all. (2013: 22–23)

Those formally recognized as "experts" may or may not fulfill each part of the process. In fact, the responsibilities of step 3 are usually assumed by other caregivers. In accordance with steps 1 and 2, experts must recognize patients *as knowers* in order to identify their unique needs. Assuming responsibility also means determining whether such needs are within A's capacities and desires to provide care. Step 4 of the schema is somewhat vague, though it implies that the response by the receiver should be *positive* if caring is to be done well. Interference must sensibly solicit a response from B or others in a given setting that suggests that the intervention was appropriate and positive. I argue that the response should be predetermined by the goals of the unique relation in which A and B are engaged. For instance, the goal of psychiatric care is arguably not sedation, but rather the relief of mental suffering while maintaining B's autonomy and distinctiveness as a person.

The final step accommodates issues of testimonial and hermeneutical injustice, though much more effort is required to challenge systemic biases than the modification of individual relations can sufficiently achieve. This step also shares overlapping ambitions with Gosselin's approach to mental health. Gosselin (2019) promotes a model of justice that is more inclusive of those with mental disorders and seeks to bolster their social capital (25). Her self-assessment of the psychiatric process does not call for an eradication of medications or invasive treatment so much as it correctly clarifies the necessity to see patients as just knowers in the treatment process: "By inviting me into conversation my psychiatrist creates epistemic space for us to develop hermeneutical resources for understanding the situation together. Antipsychotics are essential for alleviating symptoms of psychosis; whether the marketing and prescribing of them is just to the people who take them depends on how these practices are done" (18). A relation in which EP may be justified requires sufficient discursive space for both the interferer and interferee to participate as knowers.

Psychiatrists have a duty to meet the needs of their clients but must know how to effectively carry out care. Advocating for a care-based epistemology, Dalmiya (2016) defines the firm relation between caring and knowing: "Whether knowers always need to care or not, *carers* always need to know. We cannot attend to a person's needs in caring for her without grasping what they are" (7). The right way to know (forming reliable beliefs) does not necessarily require good care, but if one expects to provide good care, then one will have to be good knower. In this respect, expertise is necessary but not sufficient for quality epistemic care. Caring encounters are themselves spaces of knowledge production (8–9), in which experts must be inclined to learn, modify, and reflect on their values and presumptions through relational activity. I have provided room in this analysis for expertise to exist outside of socially authorized domains, where one's situated knowledge is not completely defined by processes of legitimation.[15] I contend that expertise is ultimately realized and refined in bilateral or multilateral relations of knowledge where the conditions of dependable beliefs are shaped by the fluid commitments of those engaged. Therefore, an ethic to be developed and promoted by experts in paternalistic entanglements requires: (1) obligations to locate decisions and responsibilities in intricate caring arrangements and (2) normative commitments to foster the epistemic/non-epistemic well-being and respect of those in our care.

CARING AUTHORITIES

The use of epistemic paternalism by experts may be valuable for improving the epistemic and non-epistemic well-being of those in their care. However, this chapter challenges discussions of EP to refocus evidential conditions in relations rather than in individuals, and proposes commitments of care as ethical guidelines for assessing justified interventions. I examine psychiatric interventions in order to reveal complications with normative practices and to cast doubt on the reliable certainty of expert recommendations. I argue that epistemic authorities inevitably acquire their expertise from complex relations and ecosystems of knowledge production. Thus, approaches in social epistemology must continue to account for the circulation of epistemic capital when assessing the credibility of an interferer. The significance of care ethics in this regard should not be understated, as they provide a necessary orientation for navigating these endeavors while further supplying desirable values that our interventions should accommodate. Justifiably intervening in the inquiry of another for their own prosperity should require trust, respect, and safe/flourishing environments for epistemic care to occur. If we fail to meet these conditions, injustices and misunderstandings negatively affecting the interferee become more evident. Therefore, epistemic care will be an ongoing negotiation with unsettled exchanges and conventions where conditions of expertise, authority, and benefit will have to be regularly critiqued.

NOTES

1. Bullock (2018) notes a disagreement between scholars on what qualifies as "epistemically better off" in the third condition (435). The dispute is whether

adopting true beliefs is sufficient or if it's a manner of improving one's overall understanding. My argument does not rest on this distinction, though I favor the latter over the former. For more on this debate, see Goldman (1991), Ahlstrom-Vij (2013), and Pritchard (2013).

2. The first example is examined extensively by Croce 2018, 312–318.

3. See Bullock 2018, 441; Croce 2018, 310.

4. See Goldman 1991, 128–131. He addresses the problem of identifying experts by way of their knowledge in domains of prediction, facts, repair, and design. Croce (2018) positions these as *research-oriented* functions that he believes are commonly overstated (312).

5. I provide a sample of these scholars here; this is in no way exhaustive: Hengartner et Al. (2019); Kramer (1993); Whitaker (2010); Breggin (2008); Shorter (2009); Kirsch (2010); Lewis (2006); Herzberg (2010).

6. For the full interview, see Fogle 2013.

7. For more on nudging practices and their relevance to paternalistic interference, see Thaler and Sunstein (2008). They detail what is coined as "libertarian paternalism": manipulating choice architecture "alters people's behavior in a predictable way without forbidding any options or significantly changing their economic incentives" (6). This approach has been further examined and modified by Barton and Grüne-Yanoff (2015), as well as critiqued by Conly (2013) who is in favor of a more coercive form of paternalism.

8. Whitaker (2010) critiques the worship of psychiatric drugs and the concentrated political efforts used by institutions such as the *American Psychiatric Association* (APA) and *National Institute of Mental Health* (NIMH) to dismiss alternative programs or non-flattering research (283–312).

9. Broncano-Berrocal (2017) discusses our epistemic dependence on cognitive resources beyond our belief forming abilities. I would push this inquiry to engage even further with the persons, spaces, and mechanisms that we must account for when forming beliefs.

10. Beeby (2018) has also characterized this as *hermeneutical marginalization*: "when powerless knowers are excluded from full and equal participation in the practices through which shared meanings are generated; it happens when some knowers are not given equal opportunity to contribute to the shared epistemic resource" (236).

11. Within the EP literature, the first failure is commonly referred to as *doxastic disconnection*: though one is interfered with, the interferee fails to form the belief recommended by the practice and thus is not epistemically better off (Ahlstrom-Vij 2013, 125).

12. Caring is intrinsically both a *value* within our moral consciousness and a *practice* that is carried out on particular bodies. These are inherently mutual: for if one fails to act then they are not actually fulfilling care, and if one provides care without the attitude of care, then it will be poorly done (Kittay 2011, 52).

13. Goodin (1985) notes that though we may freely accept special obligations to those close to us who are vulnerable, we also recognize that there are those who are particularly vulnerable to our actions and decisions that we have not made commitments to.

14. Mol (2008) demonstrates that high-quality medical facilities not only promote good communication with patients but also construct an environment in which desirable embodied interactions (e.g., handshakes, eye contact, pleasant facial expressions, and consensual physical contact) are normative (76).

15. In the contexts of mental health care, Jordan (2010) argues that therapeutic practices should affirm *fluid expertise*: "that both people in the therapy relationship have expertise they use to move the treatment forward" (53).

BIBLIOGRAPHY

Ahlstrom-Vij, Kristoffer. *Epistemic Paternalism: A Defence*. New York: Palgrave Macmillan, 2013.

Barton, Adrien and Till Grüne-Yanoff. "From Libertarian Paternalism to Nudging—and Beyond." *Review of Philosophy and Psychology* 6, no. 3 (2015): 341–359.

Beeby, Laura. "Epistemic Justice: Three Modes of Virtue," in Heather Battaly (ed.). *The Routledge Handbook of Virtue Epistemology*, 232–243. New York: Routledge, 2018.

Breggin, Peter Roger. *Medication Madness: The Role of Psychiatric Drugs in Cases of Violence, Suicide, and Crime*. New York: Macmillan, 2008.

Broncano-Berrocal, Fernando. "Epistemic Dependence and Cognitive Ability." *Synthese* 194 (2017): 1–18.

Bullock, Emma C. "Knowing and Not-Knowing for Your Own Good: The Limits of Epistemic Paternalism." *Journal of Applied Philosophy* 35, no. 2 (2018): 433–447.

Code, Lorraine. "Taking Subjectivity into Account," in Linda Alcoff and Elizabeth Potter (eds.). *Feminist Epistemologies*, 15–43. New York: Routledge, 1993.

Conly, Sarah. *Against Autonomy: Justifying Coercive Paternalism*. Cambridge: Cambridge University Press, 2013.

Croce, Michel. "Epistemic Paternalism and the Service Conception of Epistemic Authority." *Metaphilosophy* 49, no. 3 (2018): 305–327.

Dalmiya, Vrinda and Linda Alcoff. "Are 'Old Wives' Tales' Justified?" in Linda Alcoff and Elizabeth Potter (eds.). *Feminist Epistemologies*, 217–244. New York: Routledge, 1993.

Dalmiya, Vrinda. *Caring to Know: Comparative Care Ethics, Feminist Epistemology, and the Mahabharata*. Oxford: Oxford University Press, 2016.

Diagnostic and Statistical Manual of Mental Disorders: DSM-5. Arlington, VA: American Psychiatric Association, 2013.

Fogle, Jenna. "Open Paradigm Project—Jenna Fogle." *YouTube Video*, 7:20, "Mad in America," September 4, 2013. https://www.youtube.com/watch?v=6Zys52mFfBE.

Fricker, Miranda. *Epistemic Injustice: Power and the Ethics of Knowing*. Oxford: Oxford University Press, 2007.

Goldman, Alvin I. "Epistemic Paternalism: Communication Control in Law and Society." *The Journal of Philosophy* 88, no. 3 (1991): 113–131.

Goodin, Robert E. *Protecting the Vulnerable: A Re-Analysis of Our Social Responsibilities*. Chicago and London: University of Chicago Press, 1985.

Gosselin, Abigail. "'Clinician Knows Best'? Injustices in the Medicalization of Mental Illness." *Feminist Philosophy Quarterly* 5, no. 2 (July 25, 2019). 1–39.

Grill, Kalle and Sven Ove Hansson. "Epistemic Paternalism in Public Health." *Journal of Medical Ethics* 31, no. 11 (2005): 648–653.

Gupta, Kristina. *Medical Entanglements: Rethinking Feminist Debates about Healthcare.* New Brunswick, NJ: Rutgers University Press, 2019.

Hengartner, Michael P., Silvia Passalacqua, Andreas Andreae, Thomas Heinsius, Urs Hepp, Wulf Rössler, and Agnes von Wyl. "Antidepressant Use During Acute Inpatient Care Is Associated with an Increased Risk of Psychiatric Rehospitalisation Over a 12-Month Follow-Up after Discharge." *Frontiers in Psychiatry* 10 (2019): 1–9.

Herzberg, David. *Happy Pills in America: From Miltown to Prozac.* Baltimore: John Hopkins University Press, 2010.

Jablensky, Assen, Norman Sartorius, G. Ernberg, M. Anker, A. Korten, J. E. Cooper, R. Day, and A. Bertelsen. "Schizophrenia: Manifestations, Incidence and Course in Different Cultures. A World Health Organization Ten-Country Study." *Psychological Medicine. Monograph Supplement* 20 (1992): 1–97.

Jordan, Judith V. *Relational-Cultural Therapy.* Washington, D.C.: American Psychological Association, 2010.

Kirsch, Irving. *The Emperor's New Drugs: Exploding the Antidepressant Myth.* New York: Basic Books, 2010.

Kittay, Eva Feder. "The Ethics of Care, Dependence, and Disability." *Ratio Juris* 24, no. 1 (March 1, 2011): 49–58.

Kittay, Eva Feder. *Love's Labor: Essays on Women, Equality, and Dependency.* New York: Routledge, 1999.

Kramer, Peter D. *Listening to Prozac.* London: Fourth Estate, 1993.

Leff, Julian, Norman Sartorius, Assen Jablensky, A. Korten, and G. Ernberg. "The International Pilot Study of Schizophrenia: Five-Year Follow-up Findings." *Psychological Medicine* 22, no. 1 (February 1992): 131–145.

Lewis, Bradley. *Moving beyond Prozac, DSM, and the New Psychiatry: The Birth of Postpsychiatry.* Ann Arbor: University of Michigan Press, 2006.

Mol, Annemarie. *The Logic of Care: Health and the Problem of Patient Choice.* New York: Routledge, 2008.

Nelson, Lynn Hankinson. "Epistemological Communities," in Linda Alcoff and Elizabeth Potter (eds.). *Feminist Epistemologies,* 121–159. New York: Routledge, 1993.

Puig de la Bellacasa, María. 2017. *Matters of Care: Speculative Ethics in More than Human orlds.* Minneapolis: University of Minnesota Press.

Pritchard, Duncan. "Epistemic Paternalism and Epistemic Value." *Philosophical Inquiries* 1, no. 2 (July 31, 2013): 9–37.

Rabinow, Paul. "Artificiality and Enlightenment: From Sociobiology to Biosociality," in Jonathan Xavier Inda (ed.). *Anthropologies of Modernity: Foucault, Governmentality, and Life Politics,* 179–193. Malden, MA: Blackwell Publishing, 2008.

Shorter, Edward. *Before Prozac: The Troubled History of Mood Disorders in Psychiatry.* Oxford: Oxford University Press, 2009.

Thaler, Richard H. and Cass R. Sunstein. *Nudge: Improving Decisions about Health, Wealth, and Happiness*. New Haven, CT: Yale University Press, 2008.

Tronto, Joan C. *Caring Democracy: Markets, Equality, and Justice*. New York: NYU Press, 2013.

Whitaker, Robert. *Anatomy of an Epidemic: Magic Bullets, Psychiatric Drugs, and the Astonishing Rise of Mental Illness in America*. New York: Broadway Books, 2010.

Chapter 8

Epistemic Paternalism in Doctor–Patient Relationships

Aude Bandini

If there are situations in which paternalistic attitudes might seem to be justified, doctor-patient relationships surely are to be included amongst them. Imagine an endocrinologist trying to persuade a type 2 diabetes patient to shift from her anti-diabetic pills to a much more intensive treatment involving multiple daily injections of insulin. For various reasons, the patient may be reluctant, or even refuse, to comply. From the physician's perspective, she is clearly making the wrong choice in terms of foreseeable health outcomes. Yet, she is an adult and there is nothing to suggest that she is mentally impaired or unable to make her own decisions. End of story? Probably not. For whereas the respect of the patient's autonomy is a gold standard in contemporary clinical practices, physicians are also expected to act benevolently and be personally committed to restore or maintain their patient's state of health: this commitment is historically and socially constitutive of medicine as a profession.[1]

The issue of epistemic paternalism is of special interest in the context of healthcare. Indeed, in order to elucidate cases such as the one offered above, it is necessary to articulate an assumption common among healthcare professionals according to which patients' disagreement with the latter's recommendations are just the negative outcome of a variety of epistemological shortcomings: perhaps the patient does not really know or understand the nature of her disease and its devastating consequences; or maybe she somehow refuses to know because she is anxious and annoyed.

In each of these cases and others, the patient's autonomy is questioned on epistemological grounds: since her conclusion comes out wrong, there must be something either in her premises or in her way of reasoning itself that is amiss. The physician may therefore feel justified in not taking her decision at face value, and in resorting to whatever means she thinks appropriate to bring her to her senses. For instance, the endocrinologist may set another appointment a couple of weeks later, so as to give her patient some time to think things through. The objective is to resume the discussion once the patient has processed the information, discussed it with her relatives, and eventually arrived at a decision all things duly considered.

However, in the physician's perspective, informing and giving time to the patient is but an instrumental means to eventually obtain her consent and compliance. This means that, as autonomous as she can be, the patient has virtually no real possibility to disagree with her doctor's already formed conclusions, for the latter are in principle epistemically sound, relying on evidence-based data and supported by clinical experience. Any rational and sufficiently informed agent should acknowledge that as far as health and disease are concerned, doctors know best. Of course, they also happen to be wrong. However, the length and quality of their training warrant their institutional status as experts or specialists. In other words, they are socially endowed with the highest degree of epistemic authority on the matters pertaining to their field, and this sets at least partially the stage for the kind of relationships they have with their patients. For instance, in their recent book on "Physicianship," Boudreau *et al.* claim: "At the most basic level, every clinical encounter involves the coming together of someone who is vulnerable and has particular needs with someone who is an expert and has access to special resources."[2]

Epistemically speaking, doctor-patient relationships are by definition uneven: they involve an encounter between an expert in medicine, and a lay sick person seeking help, explanations, and care. Her ignorance and distress may make her epistemically vulnerable to lies, manipulation, or abuse. But in most cases, she has hardly another choice than that of trusting her healthcare professionals on their words. And trust is indeed a perfectly fine epistemic attitude when legitimately earned and appropriately granted. In principle, both conditions are satisfied in any relationship whose distinctive feature is that it involves a person caring, helping out, in other words doing some good, to someone else – as in doctor-patient relationships, where medical resources and expertise primarily aim at eliciting, maintaining or improving patients' health and well-being. Especially when enforced by the institutional surroundings of clinical and research settings, physicians' epistemic authority is deemed legitimate and intrinsically valuable by the general population, as empirical surveys suggest.[3]

On the other hand, the patient has the possibility to withdraw her confidence at all time. The respect of her moral and intellectual autonomy is supposed to warrant her right to think, trust or doubt, and to make her own final decision as she pleases, so to speak. The requirement of a free and informed consent before any medical procedure is performed on her is a necessary counterbalancing principle with regard to medical authority, both epistemic and practical. The point of contention here is that this autonomy principle also authorizes the patient to make what, from the medical perspective, are clearly wrong decisions: vaccine or transfusion refusals, use of alternative therapies whose safety and efficiency remain unproved, choice of the most hazardous treatment amongst the alternatives offered, *etc*. In such cases, one may wonder how good a doctor can still be: her commitment to promote the patient's health and wellbeing is obviously incompatible with her obligation to not interfere, even though the patient is apparently putting her health in jeopardy. Understandingly, physicians may be puzzled and challenged, if not offended, by some of their patients' decisions and behaviors, and feel professionally compelled to intervene. It is within such a delicate context of conflicting demands that the issue of medical epistemic paternalism emerges.

Imagine a patient suffering from an aggressive breast cancer. The best therapeutic option may involve a mutilating surgery (*e.g.* a mastectomy), which the patient claims she wants to avoid at all costs. Healthcare professionals may have perfectly fulfilled their epistemic task towards her: explaining what was "wrong," informing her about the nature of the tumor and its probable development over time, and eventually telling her what, from their point of view and to the best of their knowledge, would be the best course of treatment, namely a mastectomy, *etc*. However, she refuses, and as a result significantly increases the risk of cancer proliferation and mortality. If giving her more time, explanations, clarifications, or guidance does not bring her to change her mind, healthcare providers might feel justified to resort to some more constraining – that is, covertly manipulative – strategies of persuasion (playing on the patient's fears about the future, or on her sense of responsibility towards her loved ones; engaging in some emotional bargaining involving either promises or threats, *etc.*), for the patient's own good.

The core issue here is the definition of the patient's best interests, and more precisely who is in the best epistemic position to determine them. Arguably, a person's health and sense of well-being relates to a vast array of subjectively experienced states that cannot be grasped from an external, disembodied, and third-person perspective. However, it is also hardly disputable that healthcare professionals rely on a genuine knowledge concerning health, the means to promote and preserve it, and also to prevent, control, and in some cases overthrow various illnesses. Modern medicine succeeded in eradicating smallpox or bubonic plague, saving thousands of lives. Then, who knows best, between the patient actually living and experiencing the disease, and the physician well-trained in biomedical sciences as well as in clinical practice?

DEFINING EPISTEMIC PATERNALISM (EP)

In the next sections, I will claim that *medical* epistemic paternalism (hereafter MEP) derives from the dubious assumption that a patient, because of her illness, is not cognitively up to the task of determining what her best medical interest is, and therefore cannot be considered an autonomous, virtuous epistemic agent whose decisions reflect a valid view of one's wellness. But before I can defend this claim, I need to clarify what epistemic paternalism (hereafter EP) in general amounts to.

Granted that paternalism broadly construed refers to any intervention an agent A imposes on another agent B without B's consent but for the sake of B's best interest (usually unbeknownst to her), EP would occur when:

i. An epistemic agent A considers she has sufficient evidence that another epistemic agent B's best cognitive state all things considered would be to believe that p;
ii. Epistemic agent B does not believe that p;
iii. A makes it so that B believes that p.

Now this definition is way too comprehensive, since it would encompass any teaching or training activity. For it to count as paternalistic, the epistemic autonomy of agent B should be somehow impinged upon or subverted, whether or not B is aware of it. An intervention qualifies as epistemically paternalistic if it involves shaping or altering an agent's beliefs (what she, otherwise, would subjectively hold true and/or justified) but without giving her the actual reasons, for otherwise the strategy would be blatantly self-defeating. Thus, the agent's B epistemic good does not necessarily coincide with the maximization of her true justified beliefs as she would see it. It rather amounts to the maximization of the beliefs B would be, all in all, better to hold true and justified according to A, who, allegedly, knows better.

Crucial to EP is that whereas it is *prima facie* epistemically benevolent and altruistic, the means employed are clearly questionable, both morally and epistemically: even if the belief eventually acquired by agent B turns out to be true, it is the outcome of an act of cognitive deception performed upon her. If this is correct, we should then add a fourth clause to our earlier previous definition of EP.

EP occurs when:

i. An epistemic agent A considers she has sufficient evidence that another epistemic agent B's best cognitive state all things considered would be to believe that p;

ii. Epistemic agent B does not believe that *p*;
iii. A makes it so that B believes that *p*;
iv. A willfully resorts to deceptive or manipulative means to make it so that B believes that *p*.

Clause iv. aims at capturing the fact that B's epistemic autonomy is impinged upon to the extent that she is brought to acquire, endorse and hold a belief *p* (be it true or not) about what A knows to be actually wrong or insufficient reasons. The deception, and the epistemic wrongness, may consist in an outright lie, but also in the disclosure of only some selected parts of the truth. This would be acceptable though, the argument goes, since had B been fully rational, unbiased, and able to take all relevant factors into account appropriately, she would have acquired exactly the same conclusion *p*. For the sake of time and energy, resorting to roundabout means (like oversimplified explanations, or selected omissions) in order to obtain the occurrence of the targeted belief is therefore permissible.

Of course, this course of reasoning may strike us as epistemically wrong. Just like in Gettier's famous cases, epistemic agent B ends up with beliefs that are perhaps actually true and justified, but not for the reasons she subjectively thinks make them so. She has been fooled twice: first, subjectively her belief turns out to be true and justified by mere epistemic luck; second, and in third person perspective, she has been willfully deceived by the epistemic authority, that is agent A, whom she trusted and thought reliable. In both cases, her resulting belief seems something far from what we would intuitively count as an optimal epistemic state.

If this is correct, EP is intrinsically an epistemic wrong done by an agent to another, as are lies and deceptions. However, one might immediately draw a parallel with the field of ethics, and object that whereas practices like lies and deceptions are intrinsically wrong from a deontological, Kantian, perspective, they can appear morally justified under certain circumstances, on a consequentialist interpretation. Along the same line, it could be argued that EP may be epistemologically justified, and even turn out to be the right thing to do, depending on the circumstances and considering the beneficiary's greater epistemic good. This claim probably captures the rationale of EP and its *prima facie* appealing force.

But even if we embrace a consequentialist approach concerning what one ought to do as an epistemic agent (what and how one ought to believe, but also how one ought to relate to other epistemic agents), EP's defense still hinges upon two strong and ill-grounded assumptions concerning the benefiting agent B's epistemic states and agency: first, it is taken for granted that epistemic agent B cannot achieve the right cognitive state – namely believing *p* – either by her own means or even if she was provided with all the relevant evidence. Accordingly, EP is not only motivated by a will to compensate for her ignorance or to correct her false beliefs, but also justified as a necessary intervention aiming at counterbalancing B's shortcomings in terms of epistemic agency. This leads us to the second assumption, articulated counterfactually, according to which in a possible world where B would be a better epistemic agent, she would rationally believe that p (and then possibly stop believing not-p) anyway. As a consequence, B would eventually agree with A that believing p was indeed the best epistemic state for her.[4] Both assumptions are of course two sides of the same coin and exemplify, or so I will argue, a clear-cut kind of epistemic injustice.[5] In the context of doctor-patient relationship however, the wrongs caused by epistemic paternalism are characterized by specific features we need to clarify.

MEDICAL EPISTEMIC PATERNALISM (MEP) AND EPISTEMIC INJUSTICES

The idea that patients, *qua* patients, are regularly victims of epistemic injustices has been recently championed by Havi Carel and Ian James Kidd.[6] They suggest that

> an ill person may be regarded as cognitively unreliable, emotionally compromised, existentially unstable, or otherwise epistemically unreliable in a way that renders their testimonies and interpretations suspect simply by virtue of their status as an ill person with little sensitivity to their actual condition and state of mind.[7]

Although Carel and Kidd do not address the issue of MEP as such, it certainly makes sense to follow their lead in our attempt to understand what is amiss with it. In order to capture that element, it will be helpful to rely on the following excerpt from a famous French obstetrician of the mid-twentieth century, Louis Portes:

> As the patient can never truly grasp, in the strictest sense of the term, the actual extent of his own misfortune, neither can he consent to what is being told or offered to him. [. . .] In front of the patient, inert and passive, the physician can by no means feel like he is interacting with a being endowed with free will, an equal or a peer he could properly educate. In his view, any patient is and ought to be like a child he ought not to deceive, but befriend – a child to soothe, not to take advantage of – a child he ought to save.[8]

Although this excerpt defends an extreme form of paternalism that virtually all health professionals would now condemn, it highlights an important assumption about the patient's epistemic position that remains widely endorsed, especially amongst physicians.⁹ In a nutshell, they argue that the patient *qua* sick is, to varied degrees, in a physical and emotional state – of say, pain, fear, distress, denial, or on the opposite, disproportionate confidence or hope to heal – that necessarily alters her intellectual faculties and hinders rational thinking. For instance, Boudreau *et al.* reject recent patient-centered, "contractualist" models in which the clinical encounter is construed as a "peer-to-near-peer" kind of relationships as a means to protect patient's autonomy. This is simply wrong, according to them, for it stems from the dubious idea that sick people are

> similar to the healthy in most respects, including the ability to make decisions unfettered by the impact of (say) severe illness, emotional turmoil, or existential concerns or the clouding of cognitive functions. Metaphorically, it is as if patients carried sickness on their backs – like a knapsack that is external and that does not affect the person.¹⁰

Such views, they insist, actually lead to an inacceptable transfer of responsibility from healthcare professionals to the patient, whereas this responsibility is not hers to bear, not to mention that her condition would make it impossible or detrimental for her to do so anyway. Theoretical claims aiming at balancing the authority relationships in clinical encounter are mistaken because "they erode the agency (intellectual and moral) of the physician and ignore the vulnerability and the impairments of function that are always present in the sick patient."¹¹

Epistemologically speaking, this entails that patients are likewise cognitively impaired, hence the reason why "fully functional" doctors ought to quit the posture of benevolent neutrality, step in, and make decisions on the behalf of their patient, including regarding what it is better or worse for her to believe. In other words, Boudreau et *al.* epitomize a clear endorsement of medical epistemic paternalism (MEP). Given the characterization of EP sketched in the previous section, MEP would be a special case of fully justified EP, because of the distinctive epistemic features of the agents involved.

According to this line of thought, doctors are in a legitimate epistemic privileged position, not only regarding health, disease, treatments and corresponding technical skills broadly speaking, but also as knowledge gatekeepers and information providers for their patients. In the clinical encounter, the decision whether a patient is apt to understand, process information, and think rationally, is theirs. More precisely, they are entitled (and as a matter of fact professionally expected) to educate their patients. In other words, they are granted the epistemic privilege of assessing what a patient knows, ignores or is wrong about; of determining what she should rather believe and how much she needs to know; and finally of making sure that her beliefs are adequately corrected, that some knowledge and understanding are gained, and how much of the latter is appropriate. Thus, as Boudreau *et al*. also emphasize, doctors may sometimes be entitled to be "authoritative and prescriptive, even quasi-dictatorial" depending on what they identify as "the patient's specific needs at a given moment in time and in a particular circumstance."

Again, the epistemic relation is here constitutively asymmetric: first, one (the expert, the doctor) is detaining truth and knowledge, whereas the other (the lay person, the patient) is presumed ignorant, uneducated or wrong; second, the former is conferred the "meta-epistemic" power and authority to evaluate and sanction the cognitive states and epistemological aptitudes of the latter. This is where MEP is the most likely to occur, especially if a disagreement emerges between them. The alleged intrinsic epistemic vulnerability of the patient, often worsened by other social factors and prejudices (related to race, age, income, education, language, social background, and so forth), is dangerously likely to result in testimonial and hermeneutical injustices against patients, as Carel and Kidd suggest. The deleterious influence of illness-related emotions may be overestimated and refered to in order to undermine patients' credibility, whilst their abilities to understand, discuss, form and maintain reliable beliefs are objects of suspicion.[12]

Of course, this does not amount to saying that no patients are ever never emotional, ignorant, cognitively vulnerable to all sorts of biases and misunderstandings. Neither is this a way of bringing all healthcare professionals into disrepute. Our goal here is rather to track epistemic paternalism in the context of doctor-patient relationships, in order to shed light on its main features, and explain its occurrence and persistence.

DO PATIENTS KNOW BEST?

Medical epistemic paternalism has certainly existed for a very long time. However, it has progressively emerged in plain sight under the influence of some quite recent and contingent historical factors. The most decisive of those is probably the so-called "epidemiologic transition," that is, roughly, the fact that as the health and life expectancy of populations improved in Western countries, chronic diseases, like type 2 diabetes, cancers, cardio-respiratory conditions, *etc.*, have now by far replaced acute – especially infectious – diseases as the typical kind of illnesses general practitioners and specialists face on a daily basis.[13] This shift has involved dramatic changes in the modalities of care deliverance, since outpatients are now the largest population compared to inpatients in clinical settings. It has also affected the kind of relationships doctors have to initiate and maintain with their patients in order to achieve therapeutic goals. In particular, the relevance of MEP can be seriously challenged, for when it comes to the treatment of chronic conditions, its grounding assumption about patients' epistemic dependence and vulnerability turns out to be inadequate.

Of course, there are still conditions under which patients' epistemic capacities are clearly impaired: a patient admitted to the ER or ICU because of a heart attack, or suffering from multiple injuries after a car accident, can certainly not act as an epistemically autonomous agent. She may just be simply unconscious. Arguably, there are also certain categories of patients whose cognitive abilities can be questioned, like babies and young children; elderly persons with advanced senility or Alzheimer; patients with severe mental health issues, and so forth.[14] But such situations of critical epistemic dependence are far less frequent amongst patients with chronic illnesses. While living with long standing and often incurable conditions, many of them manage to go to school, work, vote, or have children. Some of them are even physicians. In many respects, they appear to be as rational and epistemically autonomous as healthy people. Yet they are unquestionably ill, and it would certainly be a mistake for clinicians to treat them as if, to use Boudreau's words, they were carrying their illness (cancer, cystic fibrosis or diabetes) on their backs. But to what extent is MEP still appropriate then?

The clinical encounter, when the management of a chronic disease is at stake, exhibits some specific and common features: time constraints are usually less demanding, and the patient, though perhaps in pain or impaired to a certain extent, is there and well awake. Moreover, though most of frequent chronic diseases can fortunately be controlled, the majority of them still cannot be cured; chronic patients therefore usually engage in life-long term relationships with their healthcare providers. This means more opportunities for them to question, conduct their own inquiry, disagree, seek for a second advice, and so forth. Trust in the healthcare system can still be taken for granted at first, but then it has to be maintained over time, for it can be lost and sometimes needs to be restored. The balance of knowledge and epistemic authority in doctor-patient relationships is hence put in jeopardy.

Another specificity of chronic diseases that makes an important difference epistemologically speaking, is that they force patients to develop an intimate and extensive knowledge of *their* specific, individual, condition: not only *how it feels*, as the phenomenological tradition has emphasized, but also how to care for themselves and cope with the disease day after day, out of the clinical environment.[15] Most chronic patients play a crucially active and cognitively demanding role in the management of their illness: from taking pills, measuring blood glucose, to performing home blood transfusions or hemodialysis, cautiously adjusting treatment depending on symptoms and circumstances, *etc.*[16] Those are all medical, and sometimes quite complex and technical interventions that patients have nearly no choice but to perform by and on themselves without medical supervision. Either at home, at work, or on vacation, they have to make important therapeutic decisions that may put their life or others at risk, for instance in case of an accidental drug overdose. The outpatient becomes her own first and main healthcare provider, gaining experience and useful skills regarding how to recognize symptoms and act upon them, anticipate or manage acute episodes, finding a way to integrate their condition within their professional, social and family life. Accordingly, they have access to an important range of experiences and realities that neither textbook descriptions nor clinical trials (even when led in so-called "real life conditions") can properly capture. Of course, patients also happen to fail, sometimes dramatically. But in any case, they manage to foster a form of hybrid and unique understanding of their disease that is, in principle, inaccessible to non-sick people, including healthcare professionals, that stems from both the formal "one size fits all" therapeutic education delivered in healthcare institutions, and their ongoing experience of living with the disease.

An optimistic view is that both doctors and patients' knowledge could successfully complement each other. But so far, experience suggests otherwise: especially when patients fail at reaching the impersonal therapeutic goals, usually set by national or international health agencies, based on large-scale epidemiological studies, they often end up in the dock. Their self-management skills, health-related beliefs, understanding or overall rationality, are considered doubtful *a priori*.[17] The mere idea that patients could bring something epistemically valuable to the medical discussion, and to be to a certain extent entitled to disagree with healthcare providers and make their point, just as scientists and experts happen to do when they meet, has raised tremendous resistance within healthcare communities.[18] Presumably, MEP, as a mechanism of systematic exclusion and refusal of other forms of alleged medical knowledge and healing (e.g. so-called "alternative" medicines, traditional practices, home remedy, *etc.*), is the outcome of social and structural reasons that exceed by far individual considerations. What is at stake here are the types of knowledge production and knowledge keepers that are, historically, considered as legitimate and accountable in a given society. In Western countries, where the paradigm of biomedicine and evidence-based medicine prevails, chronic patients, as lay people who are additionally sick and crucially dependent on healthcare services, do not seem to fit the bill.

In the 1980s, however, an important public health crisis has brought the limits of biomedical authority in plain day light and played a key role in the rise of what has been eventually called "the patients' revolution."[19] Hereby, I of course refer to the infamous AIDS epidemic. This historical period is certainly unique in many respects, but at least two of its features prove particularly relevant for our reflection. On the one hand, the traditional hierarchy of knowledge between experts and lay people was suddenly suspended, for at least in the beginning health professionals turned out to be almost as clueless and as confused as their patients about the nature of the evil they were dealing with. On the other hand, a significant part of the patients were young adults, many of them belonging to marginalized and oppressed groups (gay, colored, sex-workers, drugs users, *etc.*), and for that reason already familiar with political activism. In the absence of treatment, facing the silence of public authorities and victims of severe social stigmatization, they felt the urge to take up the reins and joined in associations, like ACT UP (for AIDS Coalition to Unleash Power) in the United States. Numerous disruptive actions were carried out and unprecedented pressure was put on political and healthcare authorities.[20] ACT UP famous slogan, "Knowledge is Power," epitomized patients' firm determination to overthrow a long-standing top-down model of medical knowledge gathering and diffusion, where physicians and researchers exclusively (mostly males, whites, Christians, and wealthy compared to the general population, not to mention HIV victims) enjoyed the privilege of disclosing truth at their will, depending on what they thought patients needed or could handle, as MEP has it. However, irrespective of the socially established structure of authority however, activist patients were eager to get first-hand access to up-to-date knowledge, and to share and spread it out of the narrow and confidential settings of clinical research laboratories, science journals, and medical and pharmaceutical meetings. Their aim was to reach as many other patients and people at risk as possible, in order to stop, or at least slow down the disease's catastrophic spread.[21] Under such exceptional circumstances, as people were dying by the thousands and bio-medical sciences were caught short, MEP was simply not an option. This episode gave a striking illustration of the patients' underestimated capacities to take action, and epistemically, to investigate, gather, process, share, and make use of complex medical knowledge. Associations of HIV and AIDS victims have been playing a role model for most chronic patients' advocacy groups ever since. They cleared a path for the vindication of patients' rights, especially the right to know (or no to know), to play a crucial role in the process of therapeutic decision, and more broadly to participate in the determination of the goals of public medical research.

Finally, since the early 2000s, new information technologies have tremendously helped patients to reach one another, even remotely, and to engage in extended unformal discussions, involving testimonies and shared experiences. This common space, like others (peer support groups like AA), intends to provide patients with a secure place, where speech and opinions are free, or at least regulated by no one but themselves. Thus, they succeed in to eluding the medical gaze, often experienced as judgmental, authoritative and illegitimate. A point particularly worth noting here is that whilst doctor-patient relationship has only very recently been the subject of extensive scientific scrutiny (especially in the human and social sciences), it has been addressed, questioned and challenged for a long time by patients themselves, although via non-academic and unformal channels (novels, essays, and, nowadays, on online blogs, virtual group discussions, *etc.*) channels which, for that matter, hardly draw the attention nor the interest of professionals.[22] Even though the reliability of the pieces of information shared there may always be questioned, these actual or virtual communities of patients fulfill an important social role as they ensure peer support and mentorship to their members, helping them to cope with their conditions, and to navigate through healthcare and social services. By doing so, they have been generating a specific form of collective knowledge that social scientists now label "experiential knowledge."[23] Unsurprisingly, patients' claim to dispose of a "knowledge of their own," so to speak, sounds like a rejection of, or at least as a challenge to, the social and epistemic dominant paradigm of biomedicine, with its associated institutional rigid hierarchy between experts, professionals on the one hand, and lay and sick people, seen as mere knowledge users or consumers, on the other hand.

CONCLUSION: THE CLASH OF EXPERTISES

Despite all of the above, the genuine epistemic authority of patients' "experiential" knowledge still remains difficult to establish on solid grounds: within contemporary mainstream epistemology, which has inherited about 2,500 years of discussions about the contribution of empirical experience to knowledge, especially scientific knowledge, the blunt affirmation that the mere fact of having a first-person experience of something could be sufficient to foster some genuine knowledge about it, sounds at best very dubious. So, if patients *qua* patients actually know something about illness, treatment or recovery, it seems but only fair to ask them to justify their claims on shareable, rational and intelligible grounds.

This being said, pressing patients to provide their reasons and justify what they claim to know, if based on the mere *a priori* assumption that they are likely to be wrong or mistaken since they are neither medical experts nor healthy people, is strikingly unfair. For it amounts to endorsing an epistemic version of the presumption of guilt, rather than that of innocence. To the extent that healthcare aims at improving patients' condition and wellness, whilst taking their complex status of autonomous-yet-vulnerable individuals into account, it would seem misplaced to ask for their credentials, as it were, before the discussion even starts. Otherwise, an additional and unfair cognitive burden is put on the patients' shoulders. Accordingly, the physician's privileged position, both socially and epistemologically, commits her not only to listening to the patient first, but also to making an extra effort to give credit, by default, to what she is being told, if only provisionally. *Contra* medical epistemic paternalism, epistemic justice in patient-doctor relationships would ideally require that patients are believed as they should, neither more, nor less. The presumption of epistemic innocence should prevail, which entails in particular that being ill should never count as an *a priori* feature negatively affecting one's credibility or abilities as an epistemic agent. The burden of epistemic proof lies with the physician, although once again, this does not mean that it can never be successfully borne. Patients are not infallible. But as direct witnesses of what it actually is to be sick, sometimes for years, they might also, by default, be credited with significant epistemic resources that would be inaccessible otherwise.

NOTES

1. Edgar, "Professionalism in Health Care," 677–97.
2. Boudreau, Donald J. *et al. Physicianship*, 65.
3. Saunders, "Trust and Mistrust," 487–502.
4. Being a good or better epistemic agent is to be understood in the terms of virtue epistemology: it refers to the agent's dispositions to acquire, maintain and act upon the relevant belief, given the available evidence. This involves both a capacity to search for, spot and collect information and then to form her belief accordingly; and also an ability to grasp a certain mental content (say, the fact that p), and to exemplify the right cognitive attitude towards it: believing more or less strongly, doubting, assuming, giving more or less credit to, *etc.*
5. Fricker, *Epistemic Injustice.*
6. Carel and Kidd, *Phenomenology of Illness*. 180–203.
7. Carel and Kidd, *Phenomenology of Illness*. 184.
8. Portes. *À la Recherche d'une éthique médicale.* 163. Translation is mine.
9. See Hanna, "Hard and Soft Paternalism," 24–34; Bullock, "Paternalism and the Practitioner/Patient Relationship," 311–22.
10. Boudreau *et al.*, *Physicianship*, 2018. 70.
11. *Ibid.*
12. See for instance McMillan Cottom, *Thick.*
13. Omran, "The Epidemiologic Transition," 737–57.
14. Note however that a strong case could certainly be made against any MEP exerted over these patients too.
15. See in particular S. Kay Toombs, *The Meaning of Illness*. 1992.
16. In their meta-analysis, Jowsey *et al.* suggest that "Patients with chronic illness and informal carers may be spending 2 hours a day or more on HRA [Health Related Activities]." See Jowsey *et al.*, "Time Spent on Health Related Activities," 9.
17. For an example of patients living with diabetes being deemed short-sighted, self-deceived or irrational, see Reach, *The Mental Mechanisms of Patients'*

Long-Term Adherence, 2015. For an opposite view, see Jenny Ellison, "Weighing in," 55–75.

18. In their editorial for the *British Medical Journal*, Shaw and Baker report that for a quite large proportion of "anxious and overworked medics, the expert patient is the demanding patient, the unreasonable patient, the time-consuming patient, or the patient who knows it all." Shaw and Baker, "Expert Patient – Dream or Nightmare?," 724.

19. Richards *et al.*, "Let the patient revolution begin."

20. In France, the group AIDES was founded by Michel Foucault's partner, Daniel Defert, right after the philosopher's death. Defert discovered physicians had been deliberately lying to both Foucault and him about the latter's disease until the day he passed. See Defert, "Foucault. Les derniers jours."

21. See for instance David France, *How to Survive a Plague*.

22. To name but a few: Ivan Illich's *Medical Nemesis* or Susan Sontag's *Illness as Metaphor*.

23. Thomasina Borkman, "Experiential Knowledge," 446.

BIBLIOGRAPHY

Borkman, Thomasina. "Experiential Knowledge: A New Concept for the Analysis of Self-Help Groups," *Social Service Review*, vol. 50, no 3 (1976): 445–56.

Boudreau, Donald J., Cassell Eric, and Fucks Abraham. *Physicianship and the Rebirth of Medical Education*. New York: Oxford University Press. 2018.

Bullock, Emma. "Paternalism and the Practitioner/Patient Relationship." In *The Routledge Handbook of the Philosophy of Paternalism*, edited by Kalle Grill and Jason Hanna, 311–22. New York: Routledge. 2018.

Carel, Havi. *Phenomenology of Illness*. New York: Oxford University Press. 2016. Chapter VIII, "Epistemic Injustice in Healthcare," is a reproduction of Carel, Havi and Kidd, Ian James. "Epistemic injustice in healthcare: a philosophical analysis," *Medicine, Healthcare and Philosophy*, 17(4), 2014: 529–40.

Defert, Daniel. "Foucault. Les deniers jours." Interviewed by Éric Favereau. *Libération*, June 19th 2003.

Edgar, Andrew. "Professionalism in Health Care." In *Handbook in the Philosophy of Medicine*, edited by Thomas Schramme and Steven Edwards. Dordrecht: Springer. 677–97. 2017.

Ellison, Jenny. "Weighing In: The 'Evidence of Experience' and Canadian Fat Women's Activism," *Canadian Bulletin of Medical History*, vol. 31:1 (2013): 55–75.

France, David. *How to Survive a Plague – The Inside Story of How Citizens and Science Tamed AIDS*, New York: Alfred A. Knopf. 2016.

Fricker, Miranda. *Epistemic Injustice: Power and the Ethics of Knowing*. New York: Oxford University Press, 2007.

Hanna Jason. "Hard and Soft Paternalism." In *The Routledge Handbook of the Philosophy of Paternalism*, edited by Kalle Grill and Jason Hanna, 24–34. New York: Routledge. 2018.

Jowsey Tanisha, Yen Laurann and Mathews Paul. "Time Spent on Health Related Activities Associated with Chronic Illness: A Scoping Literature Review." *BMC Public Health*, 12 (2018): 1044–6.

McMillan Cottom, Tressie. *Thick and Other Essays*. New York: The New Press. 2019.

Omran, Abdel. "The Epidemiologic Transition: A Theory of the Epidemiology of Population Change." *The Milbank Quarterly*, Vol. 83, No. 4 (2005): 737–57.

Portes, Louis. *À la recherche d'une éthique médicale*. Paris: Presses Universitaires de France. 1954.

Reach, Gérard. *The Mental Mechanisms of Patients Adherence to Long-Term Therapies: Mind and Care*. Translated by Nastya Solovieva. New York: Springer International Publishing. 2015.

Richards Tessa, Montori Victor, Godlee Fiona, Lapsley Peter and Paul David. "Let the Patient Revolution Begin: Patients Can Improve Healthcare – It's Time to Take Partnership Seriously," *British Medical Journal*, (May 2013), vol. 346. https: doi: 10.1136/bmj.f2614.

Saunders, John. "Trust and Mistrust Between Patients and Doctors," In *Handbook in the Philosophy of Medicine*, edited by Thomas Schramme and Steven Edwards, 487–502. Dordrecht: Springer. 2017.

Shaw, Joanne and Baker, Mary. "Expert Patient – Dream or Nightmare?," *British Medical Journal*, vol. 328 (March 2007): 724–725.

Toombs, S. Kay. *The Meaning of Illness*. Boston: Kluwer Academic Publishers. 1992.

Part III

EPISTEMIC NORMATIVITY

Chapter 9

Epistemic Paternalism and Epistemic Normativity

Patrick Bondy

Paternalistic interferences in people's behavior occupy something of an unstable place in the way we think about our obligations to each other.[1] For example, when we suspect that a friend is possibly suicidal, we might quietly remove dangerous objects or substances from the vicinity, in order to protect our friend from himself. On the other hand, when a person is doing nothing that harms anyone else, who are we to interfere with the way she lives her life? It seems like an impermissible violation of people's autonomy to interfere with their actions and decision-making processes without their consent.

So it is understandable that the ethical status of paternalistic interventions is controversial. Frustratingly, however, what constitutes paternalistic behavior is itself not settled in the literature. Without a clear agreed-upon definition of the kind of behavior we're talking about, arguments about epistemic and non-epistemic paternalism run the risk of simply talking past each other.

There isn't space in this chapter to fully address the definition of paternalism in general, but I will offer what I take to be an interesting set of sufficient conditions for some behavior to count as paternalistic, largely following Bullock (2015). Interesting sufficient conditions are more important to have in hand than necessary conditions for the purpose of this chapter, because my goal here is to show that we can sometimes have normative reasons—good reasons, reasons of the kind which really justify actions—to engage in epistemic paternalistic behavior. To make the case for that claim, first we'll need to have in hand a set of conditions that are sufficient for behavior to count as paternalistic, and an understanding of the kinds of epistemic goods in light of which paternalistic interventions might be made. In the first section, I turn to those two tasks. The second section then articulates plausible principles regarding the normativity of our epistemic reasons at the intrapersonal level, and regarding the normative reasons we might have for promoting epistemic

PATERNALISM, EPISTEMIC, AND OTHERWISE

Paternalism in General

Paternalism can be characterized, roughly, as "the interference of a state or an individual with another person, against their will, and defended or motivated by a claim that the person interfered with will be better off or protected from harm" (Dworkin 2017). Paternalism is *epistemic* when the sense in which the other person will be better off is an epistemic sense.

Giving a rough characterization of paternalism in general, and epistemic paternalism in particular, is easy. More precise definitions are not so easy to settle on. Dworkin (2017, section 2) suggests the following analysis of "*X acts paternalistically toward Y by doing (omitting) Z*":[2]

(D1) Z (or its omission) interferes with the liberty or autonomy of Y.
(D2) X does so without the consent of Y.
(D3) X does so only because X believes Z will improve the welfare of Y (where this includes preventing his welfare from diminishing), or in some way promote the interests, values, or good of Y.

This definition is clearly on the right track but needs to be revised in at least two ways. An important revision for the purpose of this chapter is that, as Bullock (2015) argues, interventions that aim to promote *both* an individual's own good *and* some other important goal can still be paternalistic. These are cases of *mixed*, rather than *pure*, paternalism. So condition (D3) should be broadened to encompass cases where promoting an individual's own good is but one among several reasons for making an intervention. This revision is important in the context of epistemic paternalism, because promoting the subject's own epistemic good will typically not be the *only* reason for which one performs the intervention.

Another important revision is to condition (D2). It is not clear that lacking consent is enough to make an action paternalistic. Problems arise when a subject A performs an action that interferes with another subject B's choices or decisions, and B is not aware of the interference. In such cases, A *might* have implicit or standing consent from B to perform actions of this kind, in which case A's action is not paternalistic. But even if A does *not* have such standing consent, A's action is still not guaranteed to be paternalistic; it will depend on whether A believes that B *would* authorize A's action, *if* B were relevantly informed of A's action and the reason for it. If (i) B is unaware of A's action, (ii) B has not provided standing consent or a standing prohibition on interferences of this kind, and (iii) A believes that B, when relevantly informed, *would* authorize the interference, then A's action is not paternalistic—for in this case, A still aims to do only what B would authorize if B were relevantly informed. On the other hand, if A believes that B, when relevantly informed, would *not* authorize A's interference, then A's action *is* paternalistic. The analysis of paternalism offered by Bullock (2015) incorporates those revisions. On her analysis, A behaves paternalistically toward B iff:

(B1) A aims to bring it about that with respect to some state(s) of affairs which concerns B's good, B's choice or opportunity to choose is denied, diminished or discouraged. (7)
(B2) A's belief that this behavior promotes B's good is a reason for A's behavior. (10)
(B3) A discounts the fact that B would not authorize the interference if B were to be relevantly informed of A's interference with her choices. (17)

This analysis is intended to be "normatively neutral," which is to say that it aims to characterize paternalist behavior in such a way that the definition by itself does not settle the further question of whether such behavior is ever justified.

Let me just make three clarificatory remarks about these conditions, and one suggestion for a minor revision.

(i) In condition (B2), "a reason for A's behavior" should be read in a purely *motivating* sense of "reason." That is, A's belief (that the behavior promotes B's good) is at least part of what *motivates* or *prompts* A's behavior. (B2) does not involve the claim that this motivating reason is a *good* or *normative* reason for A's behavior.
(ii) Condition (B1) is also only a claim about A's motivations, and it allows that there can be failed attempts at paternalistic interventions. Even if one fails to promote another's good, the failed attempt can still count as paternalistic behavior.
(iii) Condition (B3) captures the sense in which A's action interferes with B's autonomy. It is formulated in this way because B might not even know that the intervention is taking place, and so B might not be in position to withhold her consent. What matters in such cases is whether a person would give her consent if she were relevantly informed.

The small revision I suggest is to condition (B3). The trouble is that (B3) leaves out any mention of B's actual attitudes toward A's intervention. And it could easily happen that B *would* authorize A's action if B were informed about the interference and the reason for it, but in B's imperfectly informed condition, she explicitly withholds her consent regarding A's intervention. Perhaps B does not know about A's intervention, but B explicitly wants no one to interfere. Or perhaps B knows that A is making the intervention, but B does not know why. In these sorts of cases, if B is such that she would consent to the intervention if informed of the interference and the reason for it, then A's action would not satisfy condition (B3), but, I suggest, it should still count as paternalistic. A is still ignoring B's explicit wishes, after all. So the following is a suitable replacement for (B3):

(B3*) A discounts either (i) B's actual refusal to authorize A's interference, or (ii) the fact[3] that B would not authorize the interference if B were to be relevantly informed of A's interference with her choices.

Of course, the conditions in Bullock's analysis are sufficient as they stand for behavior to count as paternalistic, and I am really only interested in articulating a set of conditions that are sufficient to explain a range of important cases of paternalistic behavior here. Still, I propose (B3*) instead of (B3) because there is an important class of cases of paternalistic behavior that (B1)–(B3) do not capture. These are cases where the subject actually withholds consent, but would give consent if informed of the reason for the interference. I think it is important that our analyses of general paternalism and epistemic paternalism account for such cases.

Epistemic Paternalism

What makes A's intervention *epistemically* paternalist is that it is an instance of paternalism, and that it aims to promote an epistemic good. For example, a judge (A) might block a jury (B) from acquiring evidence about a defendant's criminal history, in order to prevent the jury members from forming a biased opinion about the defendant and about the likelihood that he is guilty of the crime at hand. The point of withholding such evidence from jurors is to make it more likely that they will form *true beliefs* about the defendant's guilt or innocence.[4] And this is done, not only for the sake of the jurors' epistemic well-being, but also for the sake of arriving at a *just* verdict about the defendant's guilt or innocence. So, this is a case of *mixed* paternalism: it aims to promote the subject's own welfare, as well as to promote some further good as a result thereof.

Note that in that example, the judge does not proceed by first forming an opinion about the truth of the defendant's guilt, and then trying to bring the jury to accept that opinion. The judge paternalistically intervenes in order to put the jury in a good position to make the judgment for themselves. But epistemic paternalism can also take place when A thinks that there is very good evidence for the truth of a proposition, *p*, and A directly tries to get B to believe *p*. That can happen when we are selecting what to teach children, and how to teach them. It can also happen when the parties involved are all competent adults. For example, A might be a legislator sitting on an environmental sub-committee; *p* might be the proposition that climate change poses a serious threat to our survival and way of life; B might be another legislator who would prefer to remain uninformed on the issue; the relevant body of evidence might be that possessed by scientists who put together the recent report from the Intergovernmental Panel on Climate Change (IPCC); and A's paternalist action might be to corner B during a coffee break and present a bullet-point summary of the IPCC's report, which B had been avoiding. Here, A aims to force B to acknowledge evidence, which B would rather ignore, and to form a belief, which B would rather not form, for B's own epistemic good. (Perhaps A doesn't care about B's epistemic welfare just *for its own sake*, but A cares about the life and health of everyone else, which depends on the epistemic well-being of people just like B.) I take it that cornering and confronting B with a summary of the relevant evidence is a way of interfering with B's autonomy over her own inquiry and belief-formation, for B desired not to form the belief supported by that evidence, and she consequently desired to avoid looking at the evidence itself.

In the above examples, A undertakes an intervention in order to produce or promote the epistemic good of having true beliefs and avoiding false beliefs in B. In their influential discussions of epistemic paternalism, Goldman (1991) and Ahlstrom-Vij (2013a) characterize the epistemic good just in this way, that is, in purely veritistic (truth-directed) terms: epistemic paternalism involves paternalist control or intervention aimed at promoting the formation of true beliefs, or the avoidance of false beliefs, in the subject being interfered with. That's because Goldman and Ahlstrom-Vij are *epistemic value monists*: they think that there is only one kind of thing that is epistemically valuable, and that is true belief.[5] To the extent that other mental states or abilities are epistemically valuable, according to truth-monists about epistemic value, their value derives from the value of the true beliefs that those states involve. For example, *understanding* is an epistemically valuable state, and it is not identical with mere true belief, but for epistemic value monists, the epistemic value of understanding derives from the fact that understanding involves having many interesting true beliefs. (The true beliefs must fit together in the right kinds of ways in order for them to constitute understanding, but it is the many true beliefs, and not their fit, which a monist finds epistemically valuable in understanding.)

Some recent writers on epistemic paternalism have proposed broadening the set of epistemic goods in the service of which epistemic paternalist interventions might be made.[6] For example, perhaps understanding is epistemically valuable, in a way that does not derive entirely from the epistemic value of true belief. To illustrate: take two bodies of beliefs, *B1* and *B2*. Suppose they both contain the same number of true beliefs, but some of the beliefs in *B1* explain why others are true, while the beliefs in *B2* are unconnected. A monist about epistemic value might say that these bodies of beliefs are equally epistemically valuable,[7] while a pluralist might say that *B1* is more epistemically valuable; the value of the explanatory connections between those beliefs is over and above the value of the true beliefs themselves.

Of course, if there are epistemically valuable states or abilities the epistemic value of which does not entirely derive from the value of true beliefs, then we should expect that such epistemic goods can be the targets of epistemic paternalist interventions. But for our purpose here, it's not necessary to take a stand on the kinds of things that are epistemically valuable. The important points for us are that (1) whatever we want to count as epistemically valuable, we can build into the account of epistemic paternalism; (2) epistemic value pluralism subsumes epistemic value monism (pluralists think that true beliefs, and other things as well, are epistemically valuable); and (3) epistemic value monists can also say that many things aside from true beliefs are epistemically valuable—it's just that their epistemic value derives ultimately from the value of true belief. I will formulate the discussion of epistemic paternalism in what follows just in terms of interventions aimed at fostering true beliefs and avoiding false ones, keeping in mind that even on this monist picture, we can still count other things like understanding and intellectual virtues as derivatively valuable. Pluralists about epistemic value should not have any objection to the following discussion of epistemic paternalism; they'll just think that there is *more* to say as well.

Given the foregoing discussions of paternalism and epistemic value, I suggest that the following is a set of interesting sufficient conditions for epistemic paternalism:[8]

(1) A aims to bring it about that with respect to some state(s) of affairs, which concerns B's true-belief-involving epistemic good, B's choice or opportunity to choose is denied, diminished, or discouraged.
(2) A's belief that this behavior promotes B's good is a reason for A's behavior.
(3) A discounts either (i) B's actual refusal to authorize A's interference or (ii) the fact that B would not authorize the interference if B were to be relevantly informed of A's interference with her choices.

Condition (1) is (B1) with the addition that the good in question is a true-belief-involving epistemic good. Condition (2) is just (B2). Condition (3) is the modified (B3*). Together these conditions are sufficient for behavior to count as epistemically paternalist. I won't take a stand on whether the conditions are individually necessary.[9] All we need here is the claim that behavior which satisfies these conditions is epistemically paternalistic. With this set of sufficient conditions for epistemic paternalistic behavior in hand, we are now in position to address the *normative* question about the justification of epistemic paternalism. Is behavior that satisfies these conditions ever justified?

JUSTIFYING EPISTEMIC PATERNALISM INSTRUMENTALLY

Intrapersonal Epistemic Normativity

One way to approach the question of whether epistemic paternalism is ever justified is to begin with what explains the *intrapersonal* normative force of epistemic reasons. In other words: What makes it the case that you ought to hold beliefs that are supported by the epistemic reasons you possess? If the source of the intrapersonal normative force of epistemic reasons also explains why we can have normative reasons to promote epistemic goods in *other* people, then that will take us a long way toward an answer to the question of whether epistemic paternalist interventions are ever justified.

For simplicity, I assume here that epistemic reasons for belief are evidential reasons: they are reasons, which positively bear on the truth or falsity of propositions that we might believe.[10] The quality of the evidence on which beliefs are based is what makes beliefs *epistemically rational* or irrational, and so I assume that evidential reasons just are epistemic reasons. (The arguments about normative reasons discussed further below can still be made, albeit less straightforwardly, if we drop that assumption, and make only the more qualified and entirely uncontroversial assumption that evidence *very often*, or perhaps *typically*, provides epistemic reason for belief. Anyone who rejects a pure evidentialist view of epistemic reasons and rationality can read the arguments given below as only making claims about the kind of epistemic reasons that *are* evidential. We'll still get the result that some cases of epistemic paternalism are justified. To keep the discussion simple, I will proceed on the pure evidentialist assumption about epistemic reasons and rationality.) Epistemic reasons are not always *normative* reasons for holding beliefs. Sometimes the truth of a proposition is so uninteresting and unimportant to a person that it is not at all important for her to hold a belief in that proposition, even if she possesses excellent evidence indicating that the proposition is true. But normally, epistemic reasons are normative for us: it is usually at least a little bit interesting or important to us to get to the truth with respect to a proposition. And holding beliefs on the basis of the available evidence is the appropriate way for us to get true beliefs. Epistemic reasons, then, are at least very often *instrumentally* normative for us: they are normative for us because they represent the appropriate means to take for achieving important goals.

So the following is a plausible principle about the relation between having epistemic reason to believe that p and having a normative reason to believe that p:

> Necessarily, if A has a normative reason to get to the truth with respect to a proposition p, then if A has epistemic reason to believe that p, A has a normative reason to believe that p.[11]

Because epistemic reasons for believing p are evidential, they bear on the truth of p. So if A has a normative reason to get to the truth with respect to p, then A has a normative reason to take the appropriate means to get to the truth with respect to p—and that means forming a belief on the basis of the evidence A possesses regarding p.

Of course, even when epistemic reasons for believing p are normative for A, they can still be defeated by competing non-epistemic normative reasons for believing *not-p*. In general, normative reasons are *pro tanto*: they speak in favor of holding a belief or performing an action, but they can be overridden by contrary reasons for not holding the belief or performing the action. For example, suppose you accidentally make conflicting promises. Plausibly, each promise generates a normative reason to perform the promised action, but you cannot do both, so you ought to figure out which promise is more important, and let the other one go unfulfilled. (You might try to make up for it in other ways, but making up for the failure to fulfill a promise is not a way of fulfilling it.)

So there appear to be cases of conflicting normative reasons for action. And the same thing goes with normative reasons for holding beliefs. For example, we can imagine cases where holding the belief that p will be extremely psychologically damaging to A. In such a case, even if A possesses excellent evidence for p, and A cares about the truth of p (and A therefore has a normative reason to believe p), it might be that all things considered, A ought to withhold belief in p.

Note that the normative reason A has for getting to the truth with respect to p might be grounded simply in A's curiosity (e.g., A wonders: how many Jackson siblings were there?). But it's often grounded in much more than mere curiosity: our very survival and quality of life depends on our carefully cultivating a body of true beliefs in a variety of domains (e.g., what is the posted speed recommendation for this curve in the road near the cliff's edge?). Normative reasons grounded in mere curiosity might be easily defeated, while those that are grounded in survival and quality of life are much more difficult to defeat. But, in general, the importance of arriving at true beliefs, and avoiding false ones, makes our epistemic reasons normative—either because we are curious and just want to know the answer, or else for some other reason that has to do with our well-being, or perhaps to do with our practical and moral obligations.

So, on this picture, epistemic reasons are *instrumentally normative*: they are *good* reasons for belief when and because it is somehow important to achieve the goal of getting true beliefs and avoiding false ones on some topic. Believing what the available evidence supports is the appropriate means to take for the purpose of achieving that goal.

The importance of achieving true beliefs and avoiding false ones in a given case can also generate instrumental reasons to do other things, in addition to holding beliefs. In particular, it can generate a normative reason to conduct *further inquiry*, and acquire more evidence. If there is a good chance that we will be able to put ourselves into a better evidential situation with respect to a given proposition than we are in now, and if it is important to arrive at a true belief with respect to that proposition, then we have a good reason to go ahead and acquire that further evidence, if we can.

All of that is to say that the importance of arriving at a true belief with respect to a proposition can generate normative reasons for doing various things. And, as we will see in the next section, the ground of the instrumental normative reasons we can have for acquiring true beliefs and avoiding false ones in ourselves can also ground instrumental normative reasons for promoting true beliefs and preventing false ones in other people, too. Epistemic paternalist interventions can be justified by interpersonal instrumental normative reasons.

Justifying Epistemic Paternalism

If the aforementioned principle about intrapersonal epistemic normativity (i.e., about what gives us good reason to hold our beliefs on the basis of the evidence available to us) is correct, then it is plausible that there is also an analogous principle about the normative reasons we have for making interventions that will help other people to acquire true beliefs and avoid false ones. Here is one straightforward attempt at such a principle:

> Necessarily, if A has a normative reason to get B to have a true belief with respect to a proposition p, then if A has epistemic reason to believe that p, A has a normative reason to take appropriate steps to bring B to believe that p.

This principle mirrors the intrapersonal instrumental principle about epistemic normativity discussed earlier, and it is motivated by the same framework. This principle is fine as far as it goes, but it fails to accommodate some important cases of epistemic paternalism, and so it needs to be weakened to handle them.

In the intrapersonal case, when A possesses evidence that supports belief in p, and it is important that A get a true belief with respect to p, A has a normative reason to believe p. And some interpersonal cases will mirror that structure. Say, A possesses good evidence that indicates that p is true; A has good reason to get B to have a true belief with respect to p; and A has a good reason to try to get B specifically to believe that p. In this kind of case, the above principle entails that A has a normative reason to take appropriate steps to bring B to believe that p.

But other interpersonal cases are different. For example, A might not possess all of the relevant evidence. Or, A might occupy a social role that prevents A from directly trying to get other people to conclude that p. In such cases, although A would not have a good reason to try to get B to specifically believe that p, A might still have a good reason to promote B's acquisition of a true belief with respect to p, and to make paternalist interventions in B's deliberative processes, in the service of that goal. The case of the judge and jury discussed earlier exhibits this latter structure. The judge instructs that certain evidence be withheld from the jury in order to prevent their deliberations from becoming biased, so that they have the best chance of arriving at a correct judgment about the defendant's guilt or innocence. The judge does not aim to get the jury to arrive at a specific verdict, which he regards as true, or likely to be true; he only aims to do what he can to ensure that the evidence available to the jury is not misleading, so that they can avoid forming a false belief.

To account for cases like that, the principle should be weakened as follows:

> Necessarily, if A has a normative reason to get B to have a true belief with respect to a proposition p, then A has a normative reason to take the appropriate means to get B to have a true belief with respect to p.

This principle is plausible; it is really just a more determinate form of the general principle that when we have normative reason to achieve a goal, we have normative reason to take the appropriate means. But its apparent simplicity can be deceptive. For whether some means are appropriate to take for achieving a goal depends on a variety of factors, including at least the following: how important the goal is to achieve; how effective one can rationally expect those means to be; whether the means have any negative expected consequences or are pro tanto intrinsically wrong; and whether there are some other available means, which are more effective or have fewer negative expected consequences.

The conditions I've offered earlier as sufficient for epistemic paternalism follow Bullock's normatively neutral approach to general paternalism (2015), so behavior that falls under that category is not thereby shown to be intrinsically wrong. (Perhaps it is wrong, but that's a result that would need to be argued for; it doesn't follow immediately from the definition itself.) Note that the appropriate steps that A might take to promote B's formation of a true belief regarding p might take a variety of different forms, but they will in general be informed by an appropriate body of evidence. That body of evidence will sometimes be available to A; at other times, it will be available to B; and at still other times, the relevant body of evidence will be available to an appropriate third party. For an example of the latter kind of case, recall the legislator A, who corners another legislator B and confronts B with a summary of the IPCC's findings about global climate change, which B had wanted to avoid. In that case, the relevant evidence is possessed by the scientific community. A only knows about that evidence indirectly, and after their interaction, B now also knows about that evidence indirectly. But it is important that B come to have a true belief about the reality and the causes of climate change, because the consequences of ignorance are too severe for the future well-being of people on this planet.

This, I suggest, is a paradigm case of justified epistemic paternalism. It satisfies the sufficient conditions for epistemic paternalism provided earlier, so it counts as epistemic paternalism: (1) A is confronting B with evidence in such a way that B's opportunity to choose how to form beliefs about climate change is diminished (i.e., ignoring the IPCC's reports is no longer an option for B); (2) A believes that interfering in this way will help bring B to have more true beliefs about climate change; and (3) A discounts B's actual refusal to countenance A's interference (i.e., A discounts the fact that B would prefer to ignore this report, and that B does not want A to confront her in this way). And, because it is so important that legislators have true beliefs about the causes and the effects of global climate change, A has a strong normative reason to do what she can to bring B to have true beliefs on that subject—so her interference satisfies the condition for *justified* epistemic paternalism.[12]

Let's not forget that our reasons for making epistemic paternalist interventions can be overridden, when there is a more important reason to avoid interfering in other people's cognitive endeavors. Maybe the reasons for leaving people well enough alone, and letting people inquire and form beliefs as they will, *very often* override our reasons for intervening in order to promote people's acquisition of true beliefs. But there is no reason to think that our reasons for making epistemic paternalist interventions will *always* be overridden by contrary considerations. Sometimes, as in the case of the judge and jury, and the case of the two legislators, it is just too important that we do our best to ensure that other people arrive at true beliefs on a given question.

NOTES

1. I'm very grateful to Amiel Bernal, Guy Axtell, Benjamin Wald, and Jeremy Livingston for the very helpful comments and criticism they've provided on previous drafts of this chapter.

2. Note that the numbering, (D1) . . . employed here, and (B1) . . . employed next, are modified from the authors' own numbering.

3. Or, better: (ii) the *likelihood* that B would not authorize the interference if B were to be relevantly informed. For simplicity, I stick with Bullock's formulation, in terms of discounting the *fact* that B would not authorize the interference, in the main text. But strictly speaking one cannot discount future facts in one's deliberations; one can only discount one's *expectations* about what will become future facts, or one's *reasons for believing* that there will be some future facts.

4. Goldman (1991) contains a good discussion of withholding evidence from jurors for their own epistemic good.

5. For example, Goldman (1986; 1991; 1999) and Ahlstrom-Vij (2013b).

6. For example, Pritchard (2013) and Croce (2018).

7. Monists might say that *B1* and *B2* are equally epistemically valuable, though they needn't be committed to that. They might say that *B1* is more epistemically valuable, and the extra epistemic value derives from the fact that the beliefs in *B1* can be employed to acquire further true beliefs later.

8. By "interesting sufficient conditions," I mean a set of conditions which are clear, useful, and non-circular, and which suffice for an interesting class of cases. Note that these conditions are close to, but differ from, Ahlstrom-Vij's important recent analysis of epistemic paternalism. Unfortunately, there isn't space to discuss the differences here; I've proposed these conditions rather than Ahlstrom-Vij's in order to more closely parallel Bullock's (2015) plausible analysis of general paternalism.

9. Ryan (2016), for example, has argued that a condition like (2) is not necessary, because doxastic attitudes weaker than belief, such as merely suspecting or hoping that an intervention will promote B's well-being, can also make behavior paternalist. I am not convinced that attitudes weaker than belief really do make for paternalistic behavior; paternalism might very well require a "father knows best" type of attitude. That is, it might require that one really thinks that one has a grasp on what will be good for a person. But we can set that aside for now.

10. More precisely, it is A's evidence that bears on the truth of p, and A's higher-order evidence with respect to A's capacity to properly respond to the first-order evidence, which determines what attitude A ought to take. I ignore this wrinkle in what follows; it doesn't affect any of the points I want to make here.

11. Bondy (2018: 142). This is a modified version of a principle proposed by Steglich-Petersen (2011: 24). I have changed the lettering from "S" in the original to "A" here, to match the discussion in the previous sections.

12. Because I have appealed to the importance of promoting true beliefs as a means to achieving people's general well-being, in arguing in defense of epistemic paternalism, I have been articulating a version of "eudaimonistic epistemic paternalism." Bullock (2018) has argued that either eudaimonistic epistemic paternalism collapses into general paternalism, in which case there is nothing distinctively epistemic about it, or else it will conflict with general paternalism, and hence it will be unmotivated. There isn't space to fully address the objection here, but I think we should embrace the first horn of this dilemma: the kind of epistemic paternalism here does fall under general paternalism. Still, it is worthwhile to draw attention to it and to call it epistemic paternalism, because the direct goods being promoted here are epistemic goods (true beliefs, and the avoidance of false beliefs). One might naturally worry that there is something about epistemic goods that makes them off-limits for justified paternalist interventions, and it is important to see that that's not the case. (The objection might be: *sure*, paternalism in general is fine, but *epistemic* paternalism is a non-starter, because paternalism regarding epistemic goods is too close to thought-policing. The reply: no, epistemic paternalism is in some cases justified.)

BIBLIOGRAPHY

Ahlstrom-Vij, Kristoffer. *Epistemic Paternalism: A Defence*. Basingstoke: Palgrave Macmillan, 2013a.

———. "In Defense of Veritistic Value Monism." *Pacific Philosophical Quarterly*. 94 no. 1 (2013b): 19–40.

Bondy, Patrick. *Epistemic Rationality and Epistemic Normativity*. New York: Routledge, 2018.

Bullock, Emma. "A Normatively Neutral Definition of Paternalism." *The Philosophical Quarterly* 65, no. 258 (2015): 1–21.

Bullock, Emma. "Knowing and Not-Knowing for Your Own Good: The Limits of Epistemic Paternalism," *Journal of Applied Philosophy* 35, no. 2 (2018): 433–447.

Croce, Michel. "Epistemic Paternalism and the Service Conception of Epistemic Authority." *Metaphilosophy* 49, no. 3 (2018): 305–327.

Dworkin, Gerald. Paternalism. *The Stanford Encyclopedia of Philosophy* (Winter 2017 Edition), Edward N. Zalta (ed.), https://plato.stanford.edu/archives/win2017/entries/paternalism/

Goldman, Alvin I. *Epistemology and Cognition*. Cambridge, MA: Harvard University Press, 1986.

———. "Epistemic Paternalism: Communication Control in Law and Society." *The Journal of Philosophy* 88, no. 3 (1999): 113–131.

———. *Knowledge in a Social World*. Oxford: Clarendon Press, 1999.

Pritchard, Duncan. "Epistemic Paternalism and Epistemic Value." *Philosophical Inquiries* 1, no. 2 (2013): 9–37.

Ryan, Shane. "Paternalism: An Analysis." *Utilitas* 28, no. 2 (2016): 123–135.

Steglich-Petersen, A. "How to Be a Teleologist about Epistemic Reasons," in A. Reisner and A. Steglich-Petersen (eds.). *Reasons for Belief*, 13–33. Cambridge: Cambridge University Press, 2011.

Chapter 10

Epistemic Paternalism, Personal Sovereignty, and One's Own Good

Michel Croce

INTRODUCTION

In recent years, philosophical discussions about the nature and the legitimacy of paternalistic interferences have ventured into the epistemological domain, where questions have been raised in relation to a cognate practice, namely *epistemic paternalism*. Epistemic paternalism is the thesis according to which in some circumstances, we are epistemically justified in interfering with the inquiry of others for their own epistemic good without consulting them on the issue (Ahlstrom-Vij 2013: 4).

The bulk of the recent discussion on epistemic paternalism has concerned when and how interferences of this sort are legitimate or, to put it differently, when someone can be justified in undertaking them. Despite a widespread worry that epistemic paternalism is bound to be a practice that undermines our epistemic autonomy—if not our freedom, in general—several epistemologists have attempted to offer an account of legitimate or justified epistemic paternalism (Ahlstrom-Vij 2013; Bullock 2018; Goldman 1991; Pritchard 2013) or have inquired into who is rationally entitled to undertake epistemically paternalistic interferences, and in virtue of which features one inherits this entitlement (Croce 2018).

Somewhat less attention has been directed toward the issue of how to motivate epistemic paternalism, that is, of providing an explanation of *why* epistemically paternalistic interferences are justified. Addressing this question involves giving an account of the value of the epistemic improvements that these interventions are meant to bring about. In her "Knowing and Not-Knowing for Your Own Good: The Limits of Epistemic Paternalism," Emma Bullock raised a neat dilemma for epistemic paternalists, namely one that puts pressure on the very possibility of offering a motivation for paternalistic interferences in the domain of inquiry. In a nutshell, if epistemic paternalists contend that epistemic improvements contribute to one's well-being, then their view conflates with general paternalism. Instead, if they appeal to the notion of a distinctive epistemic value, their view is unjustified, in that concerns about epistemic value fail to outweigh concerns about personal sovereignty.

The goal of this chapter is to address Bullock's challenge in a way that safeguards the legitimacy of epistemic paternalism, albeit restricting its scope to a limited range of cognitive projects. After briefly recalling the definition of epistemic paternalism and reconstructing Bullock's dilemma in the following section, I shall attempt to fulfill the chapter's aim by way of two main moves. First, I shall take issue with the setup of Bullock's dilemma and, in particular, with how Bullock singles out cases to which the dilemma applies. Although I agree with her that the dilemma should not apply to standard educational settings involving young children—since in most cases of this sort, epistemic paternalism is justified—in section "Soft Epistemic Paternalism and the Case of Education" I shall point out that her proposed criterion for excluding these cases is highly problematic. Then, in section "Epistemic Paternalism Justified: On Personal Autonomy as Sovereignty" I shall offer a solution to the dilemma on behalf of those who find scope for justification of epistemic paternalism in the distinctive value of some interferences. Specifically, I shall argue that there is at least one reasonable way of interpreting the notion of "personal autonomy," which legitimates and justifies undertaking epistemically paternalistic interferences for one's epistemic good.

EPISTEMIC PATERNALISM DEFINED AND BULLOCK'S DILEMMA

According to Ahlsrom-Vij's (2013) recent definition, a paternalistic interferer (henceforth, PI) undertakes an epistemically paternalistic practice toward a subject interfered with (henceforth, S) by doing (or omitting to do) X if and only if the following conditions are met:

(i) Doing X interferes with the epistemic autonomy or freedom of S to conduct inquiry in whatever way S sees fit (*interference condition*);
(ii) PI does so without consulting S on whether S should be interfered with in the relevant manner (*non-consultation condition*);
(iii) PI does so for the purpose of making S epistemically better off (*improvement condition*).

Let us briefly comment on these requirements.[1] The interference condition individuates the nature of the phenomenon we are dealing with, that is, an intervention with the way in which someone else decides to manage her epistemic life. The non-consultation condition illustrates that for an interference to be epistemically paternalistic, PI does not ask S whether S welcomes PI's interference. Specifically, PI's interference is paternalistic irrespective of whether S would object to it, had S been consulted on the issue. The improvement condition sets the bar for the legitimacy of epistemic paternalism, as it specifies that the interference has to be aimed at bringing about an epistemic benefit for S—where this epistemic benefit can be cashed out along veritistic lines (Ahlstrom-Vij 2013; Goldman 1991) or along a broader perspective that encompasses S's growth in understanding or in intellectual virtues (Croce 2018; Pritchard 2013).

The main difficulty with any attempt to motivate epistemic paternalism concerns the general account of epistemic value from which paternalistic interferences inherit their justification and its relationship with the broader notion of one's own good or well-being. Bullock distinguishes two approaches to epistemic paternalism depending on how each determines what counts as a genuine benefit to the subject interfered with. *Eudaimonic* epistemic paternalism confers value to paternalistic interferences based on their contribution to S's *overall well-being*. *Strict* epistemic paternalism, in contrast, confers value to paternalistic interferences based on the *epistemic benefit* they generate for S. The two horns of Bullock's dilemma are basically arguments for why both views fail to provide a compelling motivation for undertaking paternalistic interferences in the epistemic domain.

Before introducing her arguments, it should be pointed out that Bullock's main targets are cases in which the individual interfered with is the one who benefits from the intervention—that is, cases of *direct* epistemic paternalism—and is mature enough to make decisions about their own inquiry—that is, cases of *hard* epistemic paternalism (2018: 434–435).[2]

Let us first consider Bullock's argument against eudaimonic epistemic paternalism. On this view, paternalistic interferences can generate epistemic improvements that are constitutive of well-being or merely instrumentally valuable to well-being if they simply increase the likelihood that S will be better off in terms of their well-being (437). Either way, Bullock argues, eudaimonic epistemic paternalists will have a hard time showing how their view distinguishes itself from general paternalism. For not only cases of general paternalism fulfill the interference condition and the non-consultation condition. If we read the improvement condition along the lines of eudaimonic epistemic paternalism, some general paternalistic interventions fulfill it too, insofar as generating epistemic improvements is just one of the ways in which an interference can improve S's well-being.

But why should epistemic paternalists worry about keeping a neat distinction between the eudaimonic account and general paternalism? As Bullock rightly notes, if epistemic paternalism collapses into general paternalism, it is no longer clear what role the improvement condition is supposed to play (438). For it may well be the case that some paternalistic interventions improve S's overall well-being at the cost of sacrificing S's epistemic welfare and that granting legitimacy to such interferences undermines the scope of epistemic paternalism.

To name just one of Bullock's examples, self-enhancement bias can contribute to one's well-being by favoring an overly positive conception of oneself and thereby diminishing the risks of depression (439). Eudaimonic epistemic paternalists seem committed to granting that there may be cases in which interferences that promote this cognitive bias are justified in virtue of their contribution to S's overall well-being, despite the fact that such bias reduces or obstructs S's self-knowledge.

Strict epistemic paternalism is well positioned to avoid this unwelcome consequence of the eudaimonic account, in that it assumes that epistemically paternalistic interferences fulfill the improvement condition to the extent that they bring about a genuine epistemic benefit for S. Thus, strict epistemic paternalists—at least, on the veritistic approach Bullock seems more concerned with—would not concede that promoting self-enhancement bias can constitute a legitimate paternalistic intervention in the epistemic domain. Nonetheless, strict epistemic paternalism has to face a challenge of its own, in that it has to explain whether and how epistemically paternalistic interferences can bring about epistemic benefits without damaging S's overall well-being. Bullock's contention is that strict epistemic paternalists fail to provide a compelling argument of this sort.

Available answers to the challenge for strict epistemic paternalism go in two different directions. One is offered by the *balancing goods condition*, according to which an epistemically paternalistic interference is justified insofar as PI has no good reason to suppose that their intervention will make S all-things-considered worse off. In other words, this condition requires that PI weighs the epistemic benefits of their intervention with its other possible non-epistemic effects and confers justification to it to the extent that the reasons for intervention outweigh the reasons against interfering.

This requirement provides two important advantages, in that it accommodates cases in which PI's interference aims at making S better off both epistemically and in some other relevant respect, and it avoids the risk that PI's interference be justified when it brings about an epistemic benefit for S at the cost of damaging other spheres of S's well-being.[3] However, as Ahlstrom-Vij points out, in several cases, weighing reasons might become an extremely difficult task because it might not be at all obvious how to put on the same scale different *quantities* of values that differ in *quality* too (2013: 116–117).

To avoid this problem, Ahlstrom-Vij suggests to replace the balancing goods condition with the *alignment condition*, according to which an epistemically paternalistic interference is justified only insofar as PI's epistemic reasons for the interference are aligned with PI's non-epistemic reasons for the interference, either by being additional reasons for intervening or by being neutral—that is, by not constituting reasons against intervening (117). Unlike the former condition, the alignment condition merely requires that PI only knows the valence of the reasons involved in the evaluation—namely, the direction for or against a given interference.

Yet, this condition is problematic too, as there might be cases in which a weak non-epistemic reason against intervening would commit us to deny that an interference in favor of which we have strong epistemic and non-epistemic reasons can be justified. For example, suppose the surgical procedure through which I can donate my bone marrow to a friend is potentially dangerous, given my actual medical conditions, and I tell the doctor I want to do it and do not want to be informed about any immediate or long-term side effect I could suffer from. The doctor initially consents to my request, but after acknowledging that the surgery went just fine and reflecting that my decision not to know will sit badly with my hypochondriac tendencies, she disregards my request and informs me about the positive results of the procedure.

In this case, the doctor has a weak non-epistemic reason against intervening, that is, my request not to be informed, and strong epistemic and non-epistemic reasons in favor of intervening, both having to do with the positive effects of knowing how the surgery went. It seems reasonable to suppose that the doctor's epistemically paternalistic interference is justified as the benefits of intervening override the harm of disregarding my request. If so, then the alignment condition fails to provide a necessary condition on justified epistemic paternalism. Ahlstrom-Vij is ready to concede that there might be a very minor range of situations to which the alignment condition does not apply. However, Bullock has shown that this weakness is more pervasive than Ahlstrom-Vij thinks. Basically, no paternalistic interference would be justified on this view because all interventions of this kind would have to outweigh one clear reason against interfering, namely the violation of S's personal sovereignty. For it should be clear that limiting or disrespecting one's personal sovereignty is a form of damaging one's well-being (Bullock 2018: 441–442).

According to Bullock, this problem undermines the alignment condition, for neither of the replies available to the strict epistemic paternalist meets the challenge. On the one hand, strict epistemic paternalists could deny that we have to respect personal sovereignty, but this is an extreme view that would need to be supported by a strong argument. On the other, they could contend that personal sovereignty is only pro tanto valuable but, in that case, only weighing reasons would allow us to determine whether in a given situation the concern with personal sovereignty is outweighed by other available reasons for interfering with one's inquiry.

Since the alignment condition cannot be rescued from its weaknesses, it looks as though strict epistemic paternalists will have to address the concern with personal sovereignty with the resources provided by the original balancing goods condition. In this scenario, Bullock argues that they could either take an *extreme* route and contend that bringing about an epistemic benefit for S is the only good that can outweigh personal sovereignty or opt for a *moderate* position. In particular, strict epistemic paternalists could argue that (a) the concern with personal sovereignty can be addressed by interventions that promote S's epistemic benefit *or* S's well-being, or (b) the concern with personal sovereignty can be addressed by interventions that promote *both* S's epistemic benefit *and* S's well-being (2018: 442).

All these views have their own problems. On the extreme position, it is far from clear why epistemic value should be the only kind of value that can outweigh personal sovereignty. Proponents of moderate option (a) shall show how the promotion of an epistemic benefit can trump personal sovereignty and the promotion of one's well-being when this contrasts with epistemic value. Finally, proponents of moderate option (b) shall show why it is necessary that an interference brings about both epistemic and non-epistemic value in order for epistemic paternalism to be justified.

The challenges for proponents of the moderate options, as Bullock admits, can in principle be met and therefore constitute the only available opportunity for epistemic paternalists—in fact, for strict epistemic paternalists—to solve the dilemma and justify epistemic paternalism as a legitimate practice (444). The remainder of this chapter will be devoted to outlining an argument in favor of this position.

SOFT EPISTEMIC PATERNALISM AND THE CASE OF EDUCATION

Before addressing the dilemma and outlining a potential way out for strict epistemic paternalists, I want to shed light on a general, yet related, issue that seems to be receiving less attention than it deserves in the current discussion on epistemic paternalism. As I pointed out in the last section, Bullock's dilemma takes stock of hard epistemic paternalism, that is, interventions aimed at bringing about some sort of epistemic benefit for a subject who is judged "to be worthy of having their decisions about their inquiry respected" (2018: 436). Bullock intentionally sets aside cases of soft epistemic paternalism, that is, circumstances involving individuals who lack the competence to make decisions about their own inquiry, and offers the case of a child's education as a paradigmatic example for this type of paternalistic interventions.

As I shall argue, in principle there is nothing wrong with this restriction in scope. For as we have already made clear, this phenomenon is in itself a violation of one's autonomy and therefore a prima facie problematic intervention. Thus, we should hope that the epistemically paternalistic interferences that take place in a given environment are meant to bring about an epistemic benefit only for individuals who lack the ability to make decisions about their own inquiry.

However, a closer look at the requirements of soft epistemic paternalism reveals that Bullock's criterion for distinguishing between hard and soft instances of epistemic paternalism looks more problematic than it initially appeared. The main problem with this criterion lies in the very notion of a competence to make decisions about one's own inquiry. Bullock takes education as a paradigmatic domain to clarify the distinction between the two kinds of epistemic paternalism, but education does not seem to fit the criterion. If it is clear that the child lacks the competence to make decisions about their own inquiry, it is not clear what it takes for a mature epistemic subject to have such competence.

Consider a case in which a parent moves a joke history book out of their child's reach to prevent them from acquiring inaccurate historical information (Pritchard 2013: 15), or a case in which a teacher refrains from providing a student with the answer to a geometry problem in order to let them work out a solution and develop analytical skills. It seems plausible to contend that both situations constitute cases of soft epistemic paternalism, in that the subjects interfered with lack of the competence to make decisions about their own inquiry and the educators' paternalistic interventions bring about an epistemic benefit for them.

Now consider another pair of cases involving mature epistemic subjects. In the first scenario, a brilliant math student based at MIT is approaching for the first time Hilbert's third problem—that is, the first of Hilbert's problems to be solved within a year of its formulation. The professor does not reveal to the student that this is one of Hilbert's solved problems, nor does she provide him with the solution because she judges that letting the student work on the problem on his own would allow him to develop a better understanding of the problem and improve their mathematical abilities. In the second scenario, two colleagues at a big company are in charge of recruiting 20 new employees and are evaluating a huge number of CVs to shortlist 40 applicants. Kate knows that Jerry has developed a bias against female applicants and therefore decides to provide him with blind CVs in order to prevent his bias from affecting his judgment. Should we consider these examples as cases of hard epistemic paternalism? That is: are the student and Jerry mature epistemic subjects who have the competence to make decisions about their own inquiry?

At first glance, it looks as though we should reply in the affirmative: the subjects interfered with are neither children nor individuals with limited awareness of their autonomy in both the practical and the intellectual sphere. However, their competence to make decisions in the respective domains is severely limited. Given the early stage of his career, presumably the math student does not know whether it would be epistemically better for him to get a straightforward solution to Hilbert's problem or to approach it as an extant problem in need of a solution. For he lacks the competence to evaluate what he could learn by dealing with the problem, what skills he would develop, and how this effort would reward him later in his career.

Similarly—in fact, even more dramatically—Jerry is completely blind to his cognitive bias. In this case, we should be wary of granting him the competence to decide about his own inquiry for two main reasons. First, because he lacks awareness of something relevant to possessing such competence. Second, because—as in the nature of biases in general—he would be reluctant to admit that he has developed one or is unable to change his epistemic conduct, were Kate to make him aware of his attitude toward female applicants.

Yet, if the characters of our toy examples lack the ability to choose what is epistemically better for them to do in the respective contexts, then it becomes at least dubious whether we should treat these cases differently than the ones involving children. As this argument illustrates, the boundaries between soft and hard epistemic paternalism become less and less neat. Hence, we are entitled to wonder what consequences this has on the kinds of epistemically paternalistic interferences that should be immune to Bullock's dilemma.

A tempting answer would be to extend the domain of soft epistemic paternalism so as to encompass many educational cases involving mature-yet-incompetent epistemic subjects. This move should not worry us too much, in that the overarching aim of education is no doubt epistemic and its main implications are typically confined to the intellectual domain.[4] The bad news for Bullock is that, as the cognitive bias example shows, the problem of separating soft and hard cases of epistemic paternalism can be pressing even outside education, where one's decisions may also affect the lives of others.

Thus, on the one hand, it seems as though there is scope for restricting the set of interferences that fall within soft epistemic paternalism as much as possible. On the other hand, Bullock's criterion for distinguishing between soft and hard cases of epistemic paternalism authorizes us to include a larger range of interferences in the set of soft cases, thereby exempting them from falling prey to Bullock's own dilemma. I must confess that I have no ready-made answer to this problem, which, to my knowledge, has been surprisingly overlooked to date. This problem, though, becomes somewhat relevant in relation to my proposed solution to Bullock's dilemma. So, I shall postpone any further comment on it until the concluding paragraphs of the next section and focus my attention on the discussion of Bullock's dilemma.

EPISTEMIC PATERNALISM JUSTIFIED: ON PERSONAL AUTONOMY AS SOVEREIGNTY

The solution I shall propose to escape the dilemma raised by Bullock constitutes an argument on behalf of strict epistemic paternalists embracing moderate option (a), as discussed in section "Epistemic Paternalism Defined and Bullock's Dilemma." More precisely, I will argue that in some cases, epistemic paternalism can be justified because the promotion of an epistemic benefit trumps the concern with personal sovereignty both when such epistemic benefit aligns with one's overall well-being and when it clashes with one's well-being.

Let me be clear from the start: I am not going to sell the balancing goods condition as an easy requirement to fulfill here, as I have already clarified that it is far from being so. My goal is rather to single out a set of cases of (hard) epistemic paternalism whose structure is such that they do not fall prey to Bullock's dilemma if one is willing to endorse a broader account of personal autonomy than mere personal sovereignty. This result might look modest to a demanding reader who seeks a wide spectrum treatment for the issue at stake. Yet, it will provide us with enough concrete instances of justified epistemic paternalism to manage and, as I argued in the previous section, we might well have good reasons to keep this list relatively short.

The *personal sovereignty model* of personal autonomy revolves around "the idea of having a domain or territory in which the self is sovereign" (Feinberg 1976: 52). The boundaries of this territory presumably include any self-regarding decision, that is, any decision that directly affects only the interest of the decision maker (56). Any violation of the boundaries by uninvited individuals is illegitimate. If we take this account by the book, the right of self-determination is as morally basic as the good of self-fulfillment. What is more, self-determination may lead one to harm oneself and yet nobody else has a right to interfere with one's decisions, in that "autonomy is even more important than personal wellbeing" (59).

Clearly, this model of personal autonomy allows no room for any sort of paternalistic interference, be it general or epistemic. It might well be the case that Jerry's epistemic agency, in our example, would benefit from having personal information about the applicants removed from their CVs, but his right of self-determination outweighs Kate's concerns with his epistemic welfare, despite the fact that it will lead him to provide a biased assessment of the CVs.[5] Thus, if this is how we conceive of personal autonomy, (epistemic) paternalism will never be justified.

However, other accounts of personal autonomy provide us with a different diagnosis of the relationship between self-determination and personal good, namely one in which personal sovereignty is only *pro tanto* valuable and, as a consequence, epistemically paternalistic interferences may be justified on specific grounds. Let us consider the *model of autonomy as a condition* outlined by Feinberg (1989), according to which autonomy is a *condition* that involves both the ability to make rational choices and de facto self-government, that is, the opportunity to exercise one's rights and capacities (31). According to this approach, autonomy requires several virtues: among them, Feinberg mentions moral authenticity, moral independence, integrity, self-discipline, self-reliance, but also those intellectual virtues that make one responsible for the self, namely intellectual courage, trustworthiness, reliability, and good judgment (44).

If we assess Jerry's example in light of this account, it is no longer clear that Jerry is such an autonomous individual. His overwhelming proneness to cognitive biases might undermine his ability to make rational choices and it certainly prevents him from displaying relevant virtues such as reliability, good judgment, and self-discipline—to the extent that being prone to his cognitive biases makes him "governed from the outside" (40).

However, if it is true that Kate's interference brings about an epistemic benefit for Jerry, our critic might still object that such benefit fails to counterbalance the violation of Jerry's right to self-determination (or personal sovereignty), which is necessary to provide strict epistemic paternalists with a way out of Bullock's dilemma. While this diagnosis does not suffice to settle the problem on its own, it points us in the right direction: as I shall argue in the remainder of this section, epistemic benefits trump concerns about personal sovereignty insofar as they contribute to one's overall personal autonomy, no matter whether on balance they also improve one's overall well-being.

Two brief remarks are in order here: first, following the model of autonomy as a condition, I assume that having autonomy is a matter of degree; second, I shall contend that becoming (more) autonomous may sometimes happen at the expense of one's well-being. Let me clarify these points while discussing another example involving a specific kind of social epistemic structure: *epistemic bubbles*.[6] Epistemic bubbles are structures of exclusion that prevent large groups of epistemic subjects from taking into due account some kinds of information. They impede distribution of a complete range of information by omitting relevant testimony from sources endorsing a rival perspective and therefore they distort the informational environment of their members. Bursting epistemic bubbles requires that some members are exposed to excluded information.

Epistemic bubbles are particularly interesting in the discussion of epistemic paternalism because they not only degrade the epistemic welfare of their members, but they are also likely to put members' personal autonomy at risk. Consider the following example:

THE CIA BUBBLE. Suppose Sarah has been raised in a small rural community that believes in all sorts of conspiracy theories regarding the corruption of the

US government and the involvement of the CIA in events such as 9/11, the Kennedy assassination, and Malala Yousafzai's attempted murder. Sarah has been convinced that these conspiracy theories are reliable by made-up data and evidence as well as by acknowledging that all members of her community endorse these theories. After living several years in a small village, Sarah moves to the city to work and befriends Mary, who does not seem to have a problem avoiding any conversation about the U.S. government and the CIA, as Sarah explicitly requests. One day, Mary overhears a phone call between Sarah and her family and figures out that Sarah belongs to a community with the aforementioned features. Mary decides to intervene by inviting Sarah for dinner and presenting her with pieces of counterevidence for her conspiracy theories as well as with journal articles detailing the mechanisms typical of epistemic bubbles and their likelihood to proliferate in communities with such and such features.

Sarah's community constitutes an example of an epistemic bubble, in that their members have not been exposed to any sort of counterevidence and foster their belief in these conspiracy theories by discussing these issues solely with insiders. Furthermore, no matter the outcome of Mary's interference, this story exemplifies a case of epistemic paternalism: Mary infringes Sarah's personal sovereignty and freedom to conduct her inquiries as she wishes to burst the bubble and improve her epistemic welfare. Is her interference justified?

On the personal sovereignty model of autonomy, Mary's intervention is clearly unjustified, as Sarah's right of self-determination is more valuable than her epistemic welfare and Mary's interference has infringed this inviolable right. Nonetheless, I believe that this diagnosis of the case is a complete loss. Intuitively, the epistemic gain of being freed from a deeply rooted detrimental condition—such as that of being trapped in an epistemic bubble—outweighs the harm of violating of one's right of self-determination. Moreover, Mary's intervention positively contributes to improving Sarah's personal autonomy, when conceived along the lines of the model of autonomy as a condition.

For it might well be the case that Sarah displays all the moral virtues that contribute to one's possession of autonomy, but she no doubt fails to display the required intellectual virtues. By omitting their members' exposure to all the available information and counterevidence, epistemic bubbles compromise the members' reliability and good judgment. By favoring interaction among like-minded individuals, epistemic bubbles bootstrap corroboration of the relevant theories or information, thereby deluding their members into believing that they are free to direct their own lives when, in fact, they are only exposed to a limited range of possibilities.

Thus, by bursting the epistemic bubble, Mary not only brings about an epistemic benefit for Sarah, but she also puts Sarah in a position to improve her personal autonomy. Sarah can now (i) acknowledge the functioning of epistemic bubbles and their detrimental effects on one's agency, (ii) inquire into the responsibility of those (if any) people who put her in the bubble and those who actively sustain this structure, and (iii) develop those virtues that are required to become an autonomous person. For these reasons, we can conclude that Mary's paternalistic interference is justified.[7]

Someone might rightly point out that, despite addressing the issue of whether epistemic value can trump one's personal sovereignty, my argument does not solve Bullock's dilemma, in that it remains silent about whether epistemic value can counterbalance considerations of well-being. As a matter of fact, nothing in THE CIA BUBBLE elicits the conclusion that this is a case in which Mary's epistemic reasons for intervening clash with the non-epistemic concern with Sarah's overall well-being.

As I anticipated early on in the section with the second remark, I concede that becoming more autonomous may negatively affect one's overall well-being. For example, it might be the case that, for an individual like Sarah, the non-epistemic value of becoming more autonomous fails to outweigh the psychological costs of getting out of such a longstanding bubble—for example, the affective costs of questioning the value of important personal relationships, combined with the distress and anxiety that this process generates. Sarah's life is just a mess now that she has realized that the community in which she has been raised was obstructing her access to knowledge and was instilling all this bullshit about the government's corruption and the CIA's bloody activities! No doubt she has grown in autonomy but, in the end, her discoveries did not change her life for the better, while the psychological effects of such discoveries changed her life for the worse.

This case exemplifies all the relevant features of Bullock's challenge for strict epistemic paternalists endorsing moderate option (a). For the epistemically paternalistic interference brings about an epistemic benefit and improves one's personal autonomy at the cost of violating one's personal sovereignty and conflicting with one's overall well-being. Would such interference be justified?

I would answer this question in the affirmative, for this reason: to the extent that an epistemically paternalistic interference contributes to fostering one's autonomy, it helps the subject interfered with to reach a position at which they can freely choose how to manage their own well-being. Thus, although the epistemic reasons in favor of interfering do not align with the non-epistemic considerations of one's well-being, they counterbalance this concern by freeing one from any external conditioning on how one should manage their own epistemic and non-epistemic life.

This way out of Bullock's dilemma has two important features: first, it allows strict epistemic paternalists to stick to the idea that epistemic value can trump the concern with one's personal sovereignty while taking into consideration the value of personal autonomy; second, it restricts the range of justified epistemically paternalistic interferences to those interventions that promote the autonomy of the subject interfered with. Thus, on this view, playing physics lectures to a sleeping individual to improve their epistemic welfare will not be justified because the interference, despite allegedly bringing about some epistemic benefit for S, does not contribute to S's overall personal autonomy (see Bullock 2018: 442–443).

As a conclusion to this contribution, I shall raise a final objection to the proposed solution to Bullock's dilemma. If PI's epistemic interference is justified insofar as it improves S's personal autonomy, so the objection goes, then it is not clear whether S had the competence to make decisions about S's own inquiry in the first place. But this undermines the argument I have proposed on behalf of strict epistemic paternalists because it means that the cases considered herein are instances of soft—rather than hard—epistemic paternalism.

We are finally back to the problem I raised in the previous section about the boundaries of the distinction between soft and hard cases of epistemic paternalism. There are two available conclusions to our journey. On one conclusion, I have offered an argument that grants justification to a restricted range of cases of hard epistemic paternalism, namely those that, besides improving one's epistemic welfare, foster one's personal autonomy. On the other, I have failed to do so because the cases of epistemic paternalism with which I was concerned are, by Bullock's own standards, cases of soft epistemic paternalism and therefore are already immune to Bullock's dilemma. Either way, the end of the story is a good one: for, besides standard cases in the educational domain, there is a relevant set of scenarios in which our due concerns with promoting one's epistemic welfare can justify our interventions despite the violation of one's personal sovereignty we inevitably incur.

NOTES

1. For a more detailed analysis of these conditions, see, for example, Bullock (2018: §1) and Croce (2018: §2).

2. Bullock contrasts these notions with those of *indirect* epistemic paternalism, that is, interferences with an individual that aim to benefit others, and *soft* epistemic paternalism, that is, interferences with an individual who lacks the competence to make decisions about their own inquiry.

3. Ahlstrom-Vij calls this form of interferences *mixed paternalism* (2013: 115). An example of mixed paternalism is a judge's decision not to reveal information about a defendant's past record of crimes both to prevent the jurors from developing a bias against the defendant (epistemic benefit) and to safeguard the welfare of the defendant themselves (non-epistemic benefit).

4. It remains a highly disputed question in the epistemology of education what constitutes the primary epistemic aim of education (e.g., see Baehr 2019; Kotzee, Carter, Siegel 2019; Siegel 2018). What matters for the purposes of this chapter is simply to note that, despite ongoing divergences, epistemologists of education agree that the primary or overarching aim of education is an epistemic one.

5. Notice, though, that Jerry's right of self-determination does not outweigh the candidates' right to receive a fair assessment of their suitability for the job. Thus, although it might not be legitimate for Kate to interfere with Jerry's agency for his own epistemic good, it might well be legitimate for her to intervene in order to protect the candidates' rights.

6. The following characterization of epistemic bubbles is taken from Nguyen (2018).

7. It is worth pointing out that a similar argument can be run for interferences with the agency of members of another detrimental epistemic structure, namely *echo chambers* (Nguyen 2018).

BIBLIOGRAPHY

Ahlstrom-Vij, Kristoffer. *Epistemic Paternalism: A Defence*. Basingstoke: Palgrave Macmillan (2013).

Baehr, Jason. "Intellectual Virtues, Critical Thinking, and the Aims of Education," in M. Fricker, P. Graham, D. Henderson, N. Pedersen, and J. Wyatt (eds.), *The Routledge Handbook of Social Epistemology*, 104–121. London: Routledge (2019).

Bullock, Emma. "Knowing and Not-Knowing for Your Own Good: The Limits of Epistemic Paternalism." *Journal of Applied Philosophy* 35, no. 2 (2018): 433–447.

Croce, Michel. "Epistemic Paternalism and the Service Conception of Epistemic Authority." *Metaphilosophy* 49, no. 3 (2018): 305–327.

Feinberg, Joel. *The Moral Limits of the Criminal Law Volume 3: Harm to Self*. Oxford: Oxford University Press (1989).

Goldman, Alvin. "Epistemic Paternalism: Communication Control in Law and Society." *The Journal of Philosophy* 88, no. 3 (1991): 113–131.

Kotzee, Ben, Adam Carter, and Harvey Siegel. "Educating for Intellectual Virtue: A Critique from Action Guidance." *Episteme* (2019). doi: 10.1017/epi.2019.10

Nguyen, Thy. "Echo Chambers and Epistemic Bubbles." *Episteme* (2018). doi: 10.1017/epi.2018.32

Pritchard, Duncan. "Epistemic Paternalism and Epistemic Value." *Philosophical Inquiries* 1, no. 2 (2013): 9–37.

Siegel, Harvey. *Education's Epistemology: Rationality, Diversity, and Critical Thinking*. New York: Oxford University Press (2018).

Chapter 11

Epistemic Care and Epistemic Paternalism

Fernando Broncano-Berrocal

Caring practices, such as those involved in parenting, health care or teaching, have epistemic dimensions. In raising our kids, we not only give them physical, emotional and social support, but also transmit them a lot of practical and propositional knowledge as well as other epistemic goods. In treating their patients, clinicians not only improve the well-being of their patients, but also inform them of their diseases, possible treatments, the risks they involve and alternative therapies. Finally, although not of all its aspects are epistemic, teaching is a paradigmatic form of *epistemic care*.

Such caring practices often involve *epistemically paternalistic acts*, that is, paternalistic acts aimed at making the subjects involved epistemically better off. Some examples of epistemically paternalistic acts include the following:

- Keeping a joke history book out of reach of your kids to prevent that they form false beliefs about history (Pritchard 2013: 27).
- Enrolling your son in college and paying for his tuition fees without letting him know to ensure that he keeps studying (Croce 2018: 305).
- Requiring the use of prediction models in clinical practice to make clinicians less susceptible to biases (Ahlstrom-Vij 2013: Ch. 6).
- Giving unwanted medical information to a patient (Bullock 2016: 3).
- Teaching false or incomplete theories to students in order to facilitate a better understanding of more complex theories (Bullock 2016: 2).

What is the relationship between epistemic care and epistemic paternalism? To what extent is epistemic care compatible with epistemic paternalism? Can some epistemically paternalistic acts be considered instances of epistemic care? To answer these questions, I will first give a brief characterization of the notions of epistemic care and epistemic paternalism. Then, after presenting some views in the literature about the justification of epistemically paternalistic acts, I will put forward my own positive proposal, which will show a relevant way in which epistemic care relates to epistemic paternalism: an epistemically paternalistic act is justified if it is an instance of proper epistemic care.

EPISTEMIC CARE

The phenomenon of care, in general, has been widely investigated in *care ethics*, a collection of approaches to ethics closely related to (if not overlapping with) feminist ethics that emphasize the moral and political significance of relationships, and especially of the attitudes and actions involved in personal relationships where a person fulfils the needs or interests of dependent or vulnerable persons she is responsible for, and toward whom she has duties of care.

In general, caring can be understood as a kind of practice whose range of application are relations of *dependence* (Collins 2015: Ch. 6). Accordingly, the following seems to hold true of care in general: (i) B, the care-receiver, has an unfilled need E; (ii) A, the care-giver, is in a better position *vis-à-vis* E than A; (iii) B depends on A to fulfil E.

As Berenice Fisher and Joan Tronto argue in their 1990 seminal paper, caring is a multifaceted phenomenon that involves several phases: *caring about others* (noticing their needs), *caring for them* (taking responsibility to ensure that these needs are met), *care-giving* (the actual care-giving work) and *care-receiving* (the response of the care-giver to the response of the care-receiver).[1] In this way, care, or at least proper care, not only involves the kind of *caring actions* that are relevant to giving and receiving care, but also certain *caring attitudes* on behalf of the care-giver (e.g., the attitude of caring about others). These actions and attitudes, if not necessary for care, are at least necessary for *proper* care.

Similarly, some authors (e.g., Engster 2005; Tronto 1993) think that care (or proper care for that matter) requires that care-givers manifest certain *virtues of caring* along the caring process. Tronto (1993), in particular, distinguishes four specific virtues corresponding to the caring-about, caring-for, care-giving and care-receiving phases. They are, in corresponding order: *attentiveness* (the disposition to proactively notice unmet caring needs and empathy for the care-receiver); *responsibility* (the willingness to take on the burden of meeting those needs); *competence* (skills and abilities needed to give successful care reliably); and *responsiveness* (the disposition to monitor the care-receiver's response after care is given and make adjustments if care is insufficient or improper).[2]

Epistemic care can be understood along the same lines, with the only main difference that the relevant needs are epistemic. In this way, the range of application of the practice of epistemic care are relations of *epistemic dependence*, such that (i) B, the epistemic care-receiver, has an unfilled epistemic need E; (ii) A, the epistemic care-giver, is in a better epistemic position *vis-à-vis* E than B; and (iii) B depends on A to fulfil E.[3] We should also expect (as we will see) that the same kind of actions, attitudes and virtues that are considered necessary for care, are also necessary for epistemic care—or at least for *proper* epistemic care.[4]

Notice that the fact that epistemic care can be distinguished as a phenomenon in itself, at least conceptually, does not mean that, in practice, it is found in isolation. On the contrary, epistemic care often occurs in the context of more general caring practices, that is, practices whose aims, and the needs they aim to meet, are not exclusively epistemic. To see this, let's consider some examples of epistemic care.

A person with a life-threatening infectious disease has the objective need to survive, but also the *epistemic need to know* what her condition and her life prospects are. In this way, a clinician may not only give health care to that person (e.g., by prescribing antibiotics), but also epistemic care by informing her patient about her condition and the effectiveness of the treatment. We also care for our kids, simpliciter, when we install socket covers at home, but also care for them *epistemically* when we let them *know* and make them *understand* why putting their fingers in an electrical socket is a dangerous activity. Teaching also involves a lot of care (e.g., ensuring that no one is left behind or that no injustices or abuses are committed among students) but also a great dose of epistemic care, which as any teacher or professor knows, not only consists in transferring knowledge or promoting understanding among one's students (e.g., by explaining to them what the main questions and answers in a certain field are), but also in facilitating that they develop a number of cognitive abilities and intellectual virtues such as curiosity, intellectual thoroughness or the skill of critical thinking, so they are able to ask the relevant questions and find the relevant answers for themselves.

In this way, the relevant *epistemic needs* of epistemic care include the *achievement of epistemic standings* (e.g., knowledge, understanding or justified belief) and the *development of cognitive abilities and intellectual virtues*. Epistemic care can be thus defined as a form of care that aims to meet these epistemic needs.

EPISTEMIC PATERNALISM

In his monograph on the topic, Kristoffer Ahlstrom-Vij (2013) offers the following definition of epistemic paternalism, which is itself inspired in Dworkin's general definition of paternalism (Dworkin 2010):[5]

A acts epistemically paternalistically toward B by doing (omitting) Φ if and only if:

(1) Φ interferes with B's freedom to conduct inquiry in whatever way she sees fit (*the interference condition*).
(2) A does (omits) Φ without consulting B on the issue of whether she should be interfered with in the relevant manner (*the non-consultation condition*).
(3) A does (omits) Φ for the purpose of making those interfered with epistemically better off (*the improvement condition*).

In some cases of epistemic paternalism, however, the non-consultation condition does not hold. This gives us reason to drop the non-consultation condition—or any condition that invokes lack of consent for that matter—from the definition of epistemic paternalism. As Shane Ryan (2016, 2018) argues more generally in the case of paternalism:

> [A Victorian] husband may put a stop to visits to his wife by a cousin who he regards as a bad influence on his wife. Even though he does this irrespective of the wishes of his wife, it may be the case that his wife also wishes that these visits end. That she also wishes this to happen doesn't undercut the intuition that the husband's action is paternalistic. (Ryan 2018: 64)

According to Ryan (2018), what makes the Victorian husband's action paternalistic is not that it involves lack of consent (or consultation), but its preemptory nature; the husband does not act conditional on or because of his wife's wishes, but irrespective of them. Another way to put it is this: the husband is *insensitive* to his wife's wishes in that, had they been different (e.g., if the wife had wished that her cousin did visit her), her husband would have acted in the same way.

The crux of the matter is that this kind of insensitivity that makes the husband's action paternalistic is both compatible with the wife actually consenting to the action and with being consulted upon it by him. After all, the husband would have acted in the same way regardless of whether or not his wife offered consent or whatever his wife's answer to his consultation was.

We can easily come up with analogous counterexamples involving epistemic paternalism. Just replace the cousin's visits in the previous example with a feminist book on the structural causes of women's oppression. The Victorian wife plausibly has the objective epistemic need to know about such causes (even if it might not be her wish).[6] Yet this is something that her husband prevents her from knowing when paternalistically getting rid of the book in the belief that what the book says is false and hence in the belief that it is on his wife's best epistemic interest not to read it. Such an action remains paternalistic even if the husband consults his wife about it, or even if she consents to it, so long as he would have acted in the same way had his wife's answer been different or had she refused to offer consent.

To avoid this kind of problem, Ryan (2016) offers a more comprehensive definition of paternalism which we can adapt for the more specific case of epistemic paternalism. Here is Ryan's definition of paternalism:

A acts paternalistically toward B by doing (omitting) Φ if and only if:

(1) A does so irrespective of what A believes the wishes of B may be.
(2) A does so just because A has a positive epistemic standing (e.g., a belief, a suspicion) that Φ may or will improve the welfare of B (where this includes preventing B's welfare from diminishing), or in some way promote the interests, values or good of B.

Notice that Ryan not only drops the non-consultation (or lack-of-consent) condition from his definition, but, unlike Dworkin's definition of paternalism (Dworkin 2010)—from which Ahlstrom-Vij's definition of epistemic paternalism derives—it no longer considers necessary that the freedom or autonomy of the agent is interfered with, because there are plausible cases of paternalistic acts where this does not happen.[7] Instead, he thinks that condition (2) already implies that there can be cases of paternalistic acts that threaten the freedom or autonomy of the interfered agent, while permitting cases of paternalism in which this is not the case. Ryan's more permissive definition of paternalism can be thus used to define epistemic paternalism as follows:

A acts epistemically paternalistically toward B by doing (omitting) Φ if and only if:

(1) A does so irrespective of what A believes the wishes of B may be concerning whether and how to conduct inquiry.
(2) A does so just because A has a positive epistemic standing (e.g., a belief, a suspicion) that Φ may or will make B epistemically better off (where this includes preventing B's epistemic position from diminishing), or in some way promote the epistemic goals of B.

The examples of epistemic paternalism detailed in the first section satisfy both conditions of the definition. In addition, they are also satisfied in the epistemic version of the Victorian wife case: (1) the husband gets rid of the book irrespective of what he believes his wife's wishes may be concerning whether and how to conduct inquiry on the structural causes of women's oppression; (2) the husband does so because he believes that getting rid of the book, whose contents he believes to be false, will prevent his wife's epistemic position from diminishing.

THE JUSTIFICATION OF EPISTEMIC PATERNALISM

A number of epistemologists uphold the view that, under certain conditions, it is justified to interfere with the inquiry of other agents for their own epistemic good regardless of what one believes their wishes may be concerning whether and how to conduct inquiry. Some of the conditions that have been defended or discussed in the literature include the following:

It is morally permissible that A acts epistemically paternalistically toward B by doing (omitting) Φ if:

- *Expert condition*: A is an expert on the relevant field of inquiry (Goldman 1991).
- *Virtue condition*: A is a virtuous paternalistic interferer for B, where this involves (among other things) displaying a wide range of novice-oriented abilities in judging how to intervene (Croce 2018).
- *Balancing-goods condition*: A is justified in believing that doing (omitting) Φ case is *not* or will *not* be all-things-considered worse off for B, compared to relevant alternatives to Φ (Ahlstrom-Vij 2013; Bullock 2016).
- *Alignment condition*: A's epistemic reasons for doing (omitting) Φ are aligned with her non-epistemic reasons in the sense that they are (a) both reasons for doing (omitting) Φ or, (b) if not-(a), they are silent on the issue by not constituting reasons for doing (omitting) Φ (Ahlstrom-Vij 2013: 117).
- *Burden-of-proof condition*: A is justified in believing that it is highly likely that doing (omitting) Φ makes or will make B epistemically better off, compared to relevant alternatives to Φ (Ahlstrom-Vij 2013: 122).

Here is not the place to adjudicate between these views.[8] Instead, in what follows, I will propose my own view, which shares some features with the views advanced by Ahlstrom-Vij (2013) and Croce (2018).[9]

MORALLY PERMISSIBLE EPISTEMIC PATERNALISM AS PROPER EPISTEMIC CARE

Consider some fairly clear examples of morally permissible paternalistic acts from Ryan (2016) along with corresponding cases in the epistemic domain. As I will suggest, the examples seem to share a common factor: they involve some form of (epistemic or non-epistemic) care. Accordingly, my proposal will be that what makes a case of (epistemic or non-epistemic) paternalism morally permissible is precisely that. This will show a relevant way in which epistemic care and epistemic paternalism are related.

Examples of paternalistic acts:[10]

(i) Not buying alcohol for someone who looks like they've already had too much to drink.
(ii) Not accepting an expensive gift from a friend who wants to give you that gift but who you know can ill-afford it.
(iii) Not sleeping with someone who wants to sleep with you because one suspects she could easily get hurt as a result of the action.
(iv) Reporting a person to the police in the belief that it will be better for that person if she is stopped now before she is caught doing something worse.
(v) Providing support for a friend who has asked not to be helped.
(vi) Prepaying for a doctor's appoint for one's elderly and ill parent because it seems the only way to get that parent to agree to see a doctor—she doesn't like the idea of money being wasted.

Corresponding examples of epistemically paternalistic acts:

(i) Not buying a creationist book for someone who is beginning to show creationist inclinations.
(ii) Not accepting your older brother's offer to help you prepare for your first-year final exams when you know he barely has time to prepare for his own last-year finals.
(iii) Not talking to someone who wants to talk with you about a complex topic you are not familiar with because you suspect that that person could easily get confused about it as a result of the interaction.
(iv) Reporting a classmate to a professor for having plagiarized a minor class assignment in the belief that she will be epistemically better off if she stops cheating at the beginning of the term than if she continues to do it for the whole course.
(v) Explaining the basics of logic to a friend who is struggling to pass a logic course but who has asked not to be helped (e.g., because he is too proud to admit that he needs your help).
(vi) Enrolling your son in college and paying for his tuition fees because it seems the only way to get him to agree to keep studying—he believes, falsely, that he is a bad student and doesn't like the idea of money being wasted.

Although some of the previous examples might need further details, it seems that all of them involve caring actions and attitudes. For instance, when explaining the basics of logic to your proud friend, you *care for*, among other things, your friend's epistemic position concerning logical matters. In addition, because you *care about* your son's education, you enrol him in college. In these kinds of cases, it seems morally permissible to take such epistemically paternalistic actions for the sake of ameliorating the impoverished epistemic positions of the people you care about. This helps motivate the following view:

> *Epistemic care condition*: It is morally permissible that A acts epistemically paternalistically toward B by doing (omitting) Φ if Φ is an instance of proper epistemic care on A's behalf.

What it takes for epistemic care to be proper? As we have seen, care, in general, and epistemic care, in particular, involve several phases: caring-about, caring-for, care-giving and care-receiving. We can think proper (epistemic) care as necessarily involving all of them. Accordingly, in a situation in which B (the epistemic care-receiver) has an unfilled epistemic need E, A (the epistemic care-giver) is in a better epistemic position *vis-à-vis* E than B, and B depends on A to fulfil E, A's action (or omission) Φ is an instance of proper epistemic care for B only if:

(1) A notices E (*caring about*)
(2) A takes responsibility to ensure that E is met (*caring for*).
(3) Φ significantly contributes to the fulfilment of E (*care-giving*).
(4) As a result of (1)–(3), E no longer represents an epistemic need for B (*care-receiving*).

However, while (1)–(4) seem necessary for proper epistemic care, they are not jointly sufficient. To start with, just as Ahlstrom-Vij (2013) argues in the case of epistemic paternalism, B's epistemic reasons for epistemically caring for A (helping A meet her epistemic needs) might not be aligned with her non-epistemic reasons, which could in fact be reasons for the opposite aim (i.e., not helping A fulfil her epistemic needs). Here is Ahlstrom-Vij's reasoning concerning epistemic paternalism:

> We can imagine a government with such complete control over government organs, news media outlets, educational institutions and so on that it is able to mandate the use of nothing but the most reliable scientific methods in virtually every domain of life, and remove from public consumption any misleading or biasing information. It might be that this would do epistemic wonders for the citizenry, and the government might to that extent be motivated to exercise the relevant form of control on epistemic grounds. But if so, what is it that stops the government, or any other sufficiently powerful body for that matter,

from going for anything short of an extremely strict epistemic regiment, forcing everyone to strive for epistemic perfection? ... [W]e might have non-epistemic reason against having a government exercise epistemic paternalism on such a great scale. (Ahlstrom-Vij 2013: 115)

A government constantly monitoring the epistemic needs of citizens and reliably meeting them at the cost of their welfare can be hardly described as caring about or as caring for its citizens, epistemically or not. This is because in forcing everyone to strive for epistemic perfection injustices (epistemic or non) are committed, and committing injustices is incompatible with caring. To amend this kind of problem, Ahlstrom-Vij puts forward the alignment condition for justified epistemic paternalism. It seems reasonable to understand proper epistemic care as requiring the same kind of condition. In this way, A's action (or omission) Φ is an instance of proper epistemic care for B only if:

(5) A's epistemic reasons for doing (omitting) Φ are aligned with her non-epistemic reasons in the sense that they are (a) both reasons for doing (omitting) Φ or, (b) if not-(a), they are silent on the issue by not constituting reasons for doing (omitting) Φ.[11]

However, conditions (1)–(5) are still not jointly sufficient for an action to represent an instance of proper epistemic care. The reason is that they might hold by luck. This especially applies to condition (3), that is, it can be the case that (1), (2), (4) and (5) hold, A does (or omits) Φ, Φ significantly contributes to the fulfilment of B's epistemic need E—so (3) holds too—and yet Φ cannot be considered an instance of proper epistemic care because E is met by luck. Consider the following case by Croce (2018):

A doctor breaks a patient's right not to know the result of a medical test, because she has a justified belief that the patient will benefit from knowing that he is in good health. Unbeknownst to her, someone replaced the result of the test with someone else's. As it turns out, the two tests had identical results. (Croce 2018: 320)

Let's assume that the patient has the objective epistemic need to form a justified true belief about the results of the test. The doctor's action significantly contributes to meet such a need: by reading the (coincidentally accurate) results of a test the doctor has very good reason to consider reliable, the patient forms a justified true belief as a result—condition (3) is thus satisfied. However, the doctor's epistemically paternalistic action can neither be considered a morally permissible action—after all, as Croce (2018) points out, the doctor's beliefs about the patient's health situation and the best way to intervene are true just because of luck—nor an instance of proper epistemic care—given the luck in play, too easily could the doctor have transmitted a false belief to the patient, thus diminishing her epistemic position.

Croce (2018) argues that cases of this sort motivate virtue-like conditions for justified epistemic paternalism (cf. his virtue condition in §4). Likewise, it seems reasonable to think proper epistemic care as requiring that epistemic care-givers manifest certain virtues of epistemic caring. As we have seen in §2, certain virtues of caring have been proposed in the care ethics literature: *attentiveness*, *responsibility*, *competence* and *responsiveness*. Epistemic virtues of caring are not different in kind, but only in the kind of goals they aim to promote.

In this way, to prevent lucky cases, we can include in our analysis of proper epistemic care a condition to the effect that the epistemic care-giver's action does not count as proper epistemic care unless its success in helping improve the epistemic position of the care-receiver (or in helping prevent it from diminishing) is due to or because of the exercise of her *epistemic care-giving competences* or *skills*. We can accordingly modify condition (3) as follows:

> (3)* Φ significantly contributes to the fulfilment of E because of the exercise of A's *epistemic care-giving skills* (i.e., A's reliable dispositions to give epistemic care).

What about condition (1)? What if the care-giver notices the care-receiver's epistemic needs by sheer luck? *At least for sustained practices of epistemic care*, we cannot talk of proper epistemic care unless the relevant epistemic needs are noticed virtuously, not by luck.[12] We can accordingly modify condition (1) as follows:

> (1)* A notices E because of the A's *attentiveness* (i.e., A's disposition to proactively notice unmet epistemic needs and empathy for B).

Similar considerations apply to condition (2). Here is the modified virtue-theoretic version:

> (2)* A takes responsibility to ensure that E is met because of A's being disposed and willing to take on such a burden.

Concerning the virtue of responsiveness (i.e., the disposition to monitor the care-receiver's response after care is given and make adjustments if care is insufficient or improper), we can plausibly modify condition (4) as follows:

> (4)* As a result of (1)*–(3)*, E no longer represents an epistemic need for B, and if E still represents (to some extent) an epistemic need for B, A manifests *responsiveness* by noticing it and making adjustments.

This completes our analysis of proper epistemic care. To summarize:

> In a situation in which B (the epistemic care-receiver) has an unfilled epistemic need E, A (the epistemic care-giver) is in a better epistemic position vis-à-vis E than B, and B depends on A to fulfil E, A's action (or omission) Φ is an instance of proper epistemic care for B if only if:
>
> (1)* A notices E because of the A's *attentiveness* (i.e., A's disposition to proactively notice unmet epistemic needs and empathy for B).
> (2)* A takes responsibility to ensure that E is met because of A's being disposed and willing to take on such a burden.
> (3)* Φ significantly contributes to the fulfilment of E because of the exercise of A's *epistemic care-giving skills* (i.e., A's reliable dispositions to give epistemic care).
> (4)* As a result of (1)*–(3)*, E no longer represents an epistemic need for B, and if E still represents (to some extent) an epistemic need for B, A manifests *responsiveness* by noticing it and making adjustments.
> (5) A's epistemic reasons for doing (omitting) Φ are aligned with her non-epistemic reasons in the sense that they are (a) both reasons for doing (omitting) Φ or, (b) if not-(a), they are silent on the issue by not constituting reasons for doing (omitting) Φ.

In light of this analysis, to know whether a given case is a case of proper epistemic care, we need to know details concerning the virtues of the epistemic care-giver and whether, if possessed, they are manifested in the relevant caring actions. In the epistemic version of the Victorian husband case, the morally impermissible epistemically paternalistic action of the husband does not obviously count as proper epistemic care mainly because the husband is not attentive (or sensitive) to his wife's epistemic needs: he would have acted in the same way irrespective of what those needs are. Other cases, such as the parents enrolling their son in university, also plausibly count as instances of proper epistemic care, as we may suppose that the parents are attentive, responsible, competent and responsive epistemic care-givers in so acting. In keeping with the epistemic care condition for justified epistemic paternalism, such an action counts as morally permissible. Similar considerations can be offered about the other epistemically paternalistic acts listed, which are plausibly cases of morally permissible epistemic paternalism too.

Obviously, proper epistemic care not only involves epistemically paternalistic acts. It often involves acts that are not paternalistic. But if the acts of caring are epistemically paternalistic, and they still count as proper epistemic care, they are morally permissible. In addition, there might be morally permissible epistemically paternalistic acts that are not cases of proper epistemic care—the view only states a sufficient condition for justified epistemic paternalism, not a necessary one. Be that as it may, epistemically paternalistic cases of proper epistemic care set the baseline for the moral permissibility of epistemic paternalism. Cases of epistemic paternalism that fall short in some respect of proper epistemic care may still be justified, but are less clearly justified than cases that don't. This, at any rate, is the view that I have put forward in this chapter.

NOTES

1. Tronto (2013) adds a posterior *caring-with-others* phase, which she defines as requiring "that caring needs and the ways in which they are met need to be consistent with democratic commitments to justice, equality, and freedom for all" (Tronto 2013: 23).

2. Engster (2005) adds *respect* to the list of virtues of caring, which he defines as the recognition that the care-receiver is worthy of attention and responsiveness.

3. For a taxonomy of types of epistemic dependence, see Broncano-Berrocal and Vega-Encabo (2019).

4. For instance, although the needs they aim to fulfil are different, the virtues needed to monitor an epistemic need (e.g., lack of knowledge) and the ones needed to monitor a non-epistemic need (e.g., lack of health) are of the same *kind*, that is, need-monitoring virtues.

5. For another seminal work on epistemic paternalism, see Goldman (1991).

6. We sometimes have objective epistemic needs that are opposite to our subjective preferences. For example, one has the objective epistemic need to know that if one continues drinking, one is going to die soon because of liver failure even though one is too afraid to acknowledge this and hence even though one explicitly refuses to know it.

7. See next for some examples; cf. also Shiffrin (2000: 213)

8. For criticism of the expert condition, see Croce (2018). For criticism of the balancing-goods condition, see Ahlstrom-Vij (2013) and Bullock (2016). For criticism of the alignment condition, see Bullock (2016).

9. For Ahlstrom-Vij (2013), the alignment condition *and* the burden-of-proof condition are jointly sufficient for an epistemically paternalistic act to count as morally permissible. Croce (2018) upholds the virtue condition and thinks that it entails the alignment and the burden-of-proof conditions, but also that it can account for some cases that Ahlstrom-Vij's view is unable to explain (see the case involving luck below).

10. Examples from Ryan (2016: 127–128). Ryan thinks that these are cases where the freedom or autonomy of the interfered agents is not violated, which explains why the intuition that they are justified is stronger than in other cases. Instead (albeit not unrelatedly), I think that what strengthens such an intuition is the fact that they involve care.

11. Bullock (2016) argues that a so formulated alignment condition might be too restrictive in the case of epistemic paternalism, as Ahlstrom-Vij (2013) acknowledges.

It might be overly restrictive in the case of epistemic care too. To fix this, (5) can be side-constrained with the following clause: (c) unless the epistemic and non-epistemic benefits of doing (omitting) Φ outweigh the non-epistemic harms. See Bullock (2016) for further discussion.

12. We can *perhaps* talk of proper care (epistemic or non) in cases in which a need is noticed fortuitously (not out of virtue) on a given occasion and competent and just care is given afterwards. However, if in giving sustained care the agent regularly fails to notice unmet needs, we can hardly talk of *proper* care. Thus, the existence of such one-time instances of proper care does not mean that proper care does not require virtuously noticing the relevant needs.

BIBLIOGRAPHY

Ahlström, Kristoffer. *Epistemic Paternalism: A Defence*. Basingstoke: Palgrave Macmillan, 2013.

Broncano-Berrocal, Fernando and Jesús Vega-Encabo. "A Taxonomy of Types of Epistemic Dependence: Introduction to the Synthese Special Issue on Epistemic Dependence." *Synthese*, September 2019. https://doi.org/10.1007/s11229-019-02233-6.

Bullock, Emma C. "Knowing and Not-Knowing for Your Own Good: The Limits of Epistemic Paternalism." *Journal of Applied Philosophy* 35, no. 2 (2016): 433–447.

Collins, Stephanie. *The Core of Care Ethics*. New York: Palgrave Macmillan, 2015.

Croce, Michel. "Epistemic Paternalism and the Service Conception of Epistemic Authority." *Metaphilosophy* 49, no. 3 (2018): 305–327.

Dworkin, Gerald. "Paternalism." *The Stanford Encyclopedia of Philosophy* (Fall 2019 Edition), Edward N. Zalta (ed.), https://plato.stanford.edu/archives/fall2019/entries/paternalism/

Engster, Daniel. "Rethinking Care Theory: The Practice of Caring and the Obligation to Care." *Hypatia* 20, no. 3 (2005): 50–74.

Fisher, Berenice and Joan C. Tronto. "Toward a Feminist Theory of Caring," in Abel, Emily K., and Margaret K. Nelson (eds.). *Circles of Care: Work and Identity in Women's Lives*. New York: State University Press, 1990.

Goldman, Alvin I. "Epistemic Paternalism: Communication Control in Law and Society." *The Journal of Philosophy* 88, no. 3 (1991): 113.

Pritchard, Duncan. "Epistemic Paternalism and Epistemic Value." *Philosophical Inquiries* 1, no 2 (2013): 9–37.

Ryan, Shane. "Libertarian Paternalism Is Hard Paternalism." *Analysis* 78, no. 1 (2017): 65–73.

Ryan, Shane. "Paternalism: An Analysis." *Utilitas* 28, no. 2 (2016): 123–135.

Shiffrin, Seana Valentine. "Paternalism, Unconscionability Doctrine, and Accommodation." *Philosophy and Public Affairs* 29, no. 3 (2000): 205–250.

Tronto, Joan C. *Caring Democracy: Markets, Equality, and Justice*. New York: New York University Press, 2013.

Chapter 12

Epistemic Autonomy, Epistemic Paternalism, and Blindspots of Reason

David Godden

ON THE PERMISSIBILITY OF EPISTEMIC PATERNALISM

Paternalistic interventions interfere with a person's choices for their own good; epistemically paternalistic interventions interfere with a person's epistemically oriented processes for their epistemic good.[1] Standard objections to paternalistic interventions claim they violate the autonomy of the interfered-with, and for this reason should be prohibited.

Yet, the merits of such objections depend on the nature of autonomy. And, autonomy may be understood in at least two ways: as autarkeia and as self-rule (May 1994). According to the former, autonomy is a kind of independence or self-reliance; according to the latter, it is the capacity to govern oneself according to a norm, by acting on the basis of a maxim, rule, or reason.

Some prevailing arguments about the permissibility of epistemic paternalism adopt a conception of epistemic autonomy as epistemic self-reliance. Kristoffer Ahlstrom-Vij (2013), for example, explains epistemic autonomy as "the freedom of inquirers to conduct inquiry in whatever way they see fit" (61). Similarly, Emma Bullock (2018) writes: "What I mean by 'epistemic autonomy' is sometimes referred to as 'epistemic self-sufficiency'" (447: note 58). So understood, external, non-consultative or non-consensual interferences with this "liberty of inquiry"—even those undertaken for the epistemic sake of the interfered-with—are prima facie violations of the inquirer's autonomy.

Following the lead of theorists like Robert Roberts and Jay Wood (2007: ch.10), Linda Zagzebski (2012, 2013), and Catherine Elgin (2013), this chapter argues that epistemic autonomy is better understood as epistemic self-governance rather than as self-reliance, and that, so understood, certain kinds of epistemically paternalistic interventions are permissible. Inquirers are engaged in the pursuit of knowledge, and are thus committed to the norm of belief (Adler 2002; Gibbons 2013). Their commitment to these norms can license paternalistic epistemic interventions, even in cases where the inquirer, in their present epistemic circumstances, would not consent to the interference—specifically, when their epistemic circumstance blinds them to the reasons licensing the intervention. This picture yields a new permissibility condition for paternalistic epistemic interventions.

PRELIMINARY CONSIDERATIONS

Alvin Goldman (1991) first characterized epistemic paternalism as occurring whenever, in an effort to improve another's epistemic well-being, an agent acts as an informational "gatekeeper," controlling the other's access to, or appraisal of, information by interposing their own judgment about the evidential value of that information, rather than allowing the other to exercise their own judgment (119).[2] Goldman focused on exercises of paternalistically motivated control that "weed out" information by preventing or limiting a cognitive agent's access to, or use of, it (120). Similarly, Ahlstrom-Vij (2013) construes epistemically paternalistic interventions as constraints on an inquirer's access to, or collection, use, or appraisal of the probative value of, information (cf. Bishop 2014). Yet, the control of information isn't limited to constraints like withholding or concealing (making information "available," though not readily discoverable or accessible by, for example, burying it in the fine print). Informational control can also include actively communicating information by calling another's attention to it, or presenting it in such a way as to help another make better sense of it (Grill and Hansson 2005). Rather than as acts of *censorship* or *constraint*, acts of epistemic paternalism are better conceived more broadly as efforts to *curate* another's informational environment (e.g., by selecting, ordering, and presenting information) for the end of their epistemic well-being.

The perspective offered by this broader conceptualization affords two important observations. First, our ordinary informational environments, including those that we might undertake to paternalistically curate, are, typically, already highly engineered, if not polluted. Regrettably, the regulatory systems for our informational economies often prioritize the interests of those making the intervention, rather than a concern for our well-being, epistemic or otherwise. While speedometers, like seatbelts, are there for the benefit of drivers (among others), roadside billboards distract drivers and seldom give information that is even remotely pertinent to their proximate epistemic concerns. Moreover, self-interested engineers of our informational environments have a motivation to—and will, if they're any good at what they do—exploit the very cognitive foibles in us that, according to Ahlstrom-Vij (2013), establish that we cannot rely on ourselves for our own epistemic improvement. Paternalistic interventions, then, do not merely protect us from ourselves. Rather, they additionally mitigate the interferences of non-paternalistically motivated actors.

As such, when considering the permissibility of epistemic paternalism, we should recognize that neither the context nor the default (resulting from non-action) of such decisions is neutral. Timid policies of paternalistic epistemic intervention that favor putatively "free," self-regulating, informational markets do not preserve the intellectual autonomy of inquirers in those informational environments. Instead, they allow non-paternalistically motivated interferences with the autonomy of inquirers, and relinquish control of the epistemic and social goods at stake to those actors already occupying positions of power in the informational economy. This observation yields an argument supporting Goldman's suggestion that "successful pursuit of epistemic ends depends not only on 'deregulation' at the highest levels, but on wise regulation at lower levels" (1991: 131).

Second, we should recognize that paternalistic epistemic interventions in our ordinary informational commerce (both interpersonal and institutional) are commonplace and often innocuous. We routinely "control" the flow of information to others in the course of our everyday interactions. Purposeful communication, including designing our acts of reasons-giving, is the curation of the presentation of information to another. And designing "choice architectures" in cognitively ergonomic ways, for example, with nudges, is to present reasons not to bypass reasoning (Levy 2019). Ordinarily, we do not resent such nudges or interruptions of our trains of thought and talk as infringements of our intellectual autonomy. Rather, they are just part of social life. Typically, it is only after such interventions that we judge them praiseworthy or condemnable, largely on the basis of whether their results were welcome.

Uncontroversially, some ordinary forms of epistemic paternalism, like "mansplaining," cause epistemic harms, and ought to be criticized on precisely these grounds (Rothman 2012; Solnit 2008). Indeed, if they undermine another's agency as a knower, acts of epistemic paternalism can cause, or consist in, epistemic injustices (Fricker 2007). Even when such acts are benevolently motivated, the beneficence of the act can be mitigated by other traits of the actor like intellectual hubris or reprehensible, pernicious ignorance. The very cognitive foibles motivating paternalistic interferences—our tendencies toward bias and overconfidence—can infect the intentions of the paternalistic interferer. Yet, granting all this, other ordinary forms of epistemic paternalism, from "whistle blowing" and warning labels to volunteering and demanding reasons, seems uncontroversially praiseworthy—exemplifying virtues like intellectual responsibility, courage, and open-mindedness, and enhancing the epistemic agency of others.

EPISTEMIC PATERNALISM

Michel Croce characterizes Goldman's conception of epistemic paternalism as having two fundamental features: protection and interposition (2018: 307). The paternalist interposes their judgment within another's process of inquiry for the sake of advancing the other's epistemic interests.[3] Ahlstrom-Vij (2013) similarly defines epistemic paternalism according to three individually necessary and jointly sufficient conditions (cf. Bullock 2018: 343). An epistemically paternalistic intervention

[1] interferes with the freedom of inquirers to conduct inquiry in whatever way they see fit (*the interference condition*)
[2] without consulting those interfered with on the issue of whether they should be interfered with in the relevant manner (*the non-consultation condition*), and . . .
[3] interferes—[whether] exclusively or not—for the purpose of making those interfered with epistemically better off (*the improvement condition*) (Ahlstrom-Vij 2013: 61).

Prima facie, and despite their beneficent motivations, such interferences seem to infringe on another's epistemic autonomy. And, as Gerald Dworkin writes about paternalism in practical affairs, "it is because of the violation of the autonomy of others that normative questions about the justification of paternalism arise" (1988: 123). Yet, in order to judge the permissibility of epistemically paternalistic interferences, we must consider the nature of intellectual autonomy.

INTELLECTUAL AUTONOMY

Rational autonomy, Immanuel Kant tells us, consists in our ability to make use of our understanding "without direction from another." According to R. S. Downie and Elizabeth Telfer (1971), "an autonomous agent, must be independent-minded . . . [and] not have to depend on others for being told what . . . to think or do" (301). Goldman (1991) characterizes rational autonomy as a kind of intellectual sovereignty, citing T. M. Scanlon's conception:

> To regard himself as autonomous . . . a person must see himself as sovereign in deciding what to believe and in weighing competing reasons for action. He must apply to these tasks his own canons of rationality, and must recognize the need to defend his beliefs and decisions in accordance with these canons. (Scanlon 1972: 215)

These descriptions sketch an ambiguous picture of autonomy, one aspect of which is autarkeia, the other self-rule (May 1994: 134).

Viewed as autarkeia, autonomy is a kind of independence or self-sufficiency whereby epistemic agency consists in not having to rely upon, confer with, or defer to others. Elizabeth Fricker describes the ideal of such an autonomous knower as someone who "takes no one else's word for anything, but accepts only what she has found out for herself, relying only on her own cognitive faculties and investigative and inferential powers" (2006: 225).[4] Understood as self-rule, autonomy is the capacity to govern oneself according to a norm, by acting on the basis of a maxim, rule, or reason, whereby epistemic agency consists in a kind of self-directed self-governance or self-regulation, according to norms that are not imposed upon one. On this ideal, Catherine Elgin describes: "Epistemic agents should think of themselves as, and act as, legislating members of a realm of epistemic ends: they make the rules, devise the methods, and set the standards that bind them" (2013: 135).

When constructing his argument for the permissibility of epistemic paternalism, Ahlstrom-Vij (2013) conspicuously takes the former conception of autonomy as independence as his primary target.[5] Perhaps his reason for doing so is that autonomy as independence makes the greatest claim to freedom from external interference. As May writes, while "autonomy as autarkeia views external factors as incompatible with autonomy . . . autonomy as self-rule allows external factors to influence the determination of action without eliminating the autonomy of the agent" (1994: 134). And, Ahlstrom-Vij concludes that even when understood as autarkeia, autonomy offers no conclusive grounds for objecting to paternalistic interferences.

In a certain sense, we are all epistemically self-reliant. "Self trust," as Zagzebski notes, "is a rational requirement" (2007: 58). Such epistemic self-reliance is part of what it is to have been conferred a berth on Neurath's ship. Yet, this is not to say that we are epistemically independent; quite the opposite (Hardwig 2005). Rather it is to say that we have to rely on our own competence in judging the limits of our own competence. Just as we must in judging when our belief-set stands in need of repair, we must rely on our own best rational lights when deciding whether, when, and whom to consult with and defer to (Zagzebski 2013). But this is to be epistemically self-guiding—not self-sufficient. May writes: "We, as the 'helmsmen' of our own lives, steer toward various forms of authority in certain facets of life, and away from authority in others. We are not self-sufficient, but this does not mean that we do not 'rule' our own lives" (1994: 135).

As J. Adam Carter (2017) argues, those who never allow their intellect to be guided by another disvalue epistemic dependence to their own detriment in ways that self-undermine their own intellectual agency: "virtuous intellectual autonomy simply cannot mean, as Roberts and Wood [2007: 259–260] put it, 'that one never relies on the intellectual labor of another.' " (2007: 259–260). Indeed, John Hardwig (2011) puts this point more strongly: "as long as epistemic autonomy brings with it epistemic variegation, it seems unlikely that *my* epistemic autonomy is a good thing for me. It would be epistemically better for me—assuming that I want true or justified beliefs—if I were a free rider on the autonomy of my predecessors and perhaps also that of my epistemic superiors."

Finally, as Zagzebski (2013) points out, a will can be heteronomous in at least two ways: "when it is controlled by a will *outside* of it," and "when it is determined by forces *within* the self *other than reason*—by *inclination* or *fancy*. . . . If we are not fully rational when our wills are pushed around, then we are not fully rational when our intellects are pushed around, whatever 'pushed around' amounts to" (247, 248, emphasis added). As such, we should be just as concerned about agent-internal causes of the loss, diminishment, and enhancement of our epistemic agency as we are about agent-external causes. That is, we should hold ourselves just as accountable for the care of our epistemic agency as we are inclined to do of those around us.

INTELLECTUAL AUTONOMY AND THE "FREEDOM" OF INQUIRY

As I read him, the picture of autonomy as autarkeia adopted by Ahlstrom-Vij (2013) seems closely tied to his interference condition for epistemic paternalism:

> Take the relevant kind of interference to be an interference with the extent to which an agent can *go about doing inquiry in whatever way she sees fit*. . . . Someone is interfering with the inquiry of another if the former is compromising the latter's *freedom to conduct inquiry in whatever way she happens to desire* and . . . someone is free to conduct inquiry thus if she is *free from constraints imposed by others on her ability to access, collect, and evaluate information in whatever way she happens to see fit*. (40–41, emphasis added)

So conceived, epistemic autonomy seems to consist in a "liberty of inquiry"— a freedom to conduct inquiry without external interference or encumbrance.[6] In this context, Ahlstrom-Vij (2013) summarizes his basic case for epistemic paternalism as follows: "our dual tendency for bias and overconfidence makes it unlikely that we can rely on ourselves for epistemic improvement, and that our best bet when it comes to promoting our epistemic good is to have external constraints imposed that restrict our freedom to conduct inquiry in whatever way we see fit" (177).

Yet, before asking whether any *external* constraints may restrict any freedom of inquiry, it is worth asking: What are the *internal* constraints? For example, are inquirers free to believe what they know to be, or what seems to them to be, false? May they believe on the basis of insufficient evidence? May inquirers ignore evidence? Are they free to believe by wishful thinking or form beliefs by inclination or fancy?

I answer: "No." "When engaging in inquiry," Ahlstrom-Vij (2013) claims, "we are engaging in a pursuit of epistemic goals . . . taking the formation of true belief and the avoidance of false belief to be the paradigm goals of epistemic practices" (40). The nature of belief prescribes its own norms (Adler 2002; Gibbons 2013). Belief aims at truth; and the truth-conditions for belief are transparent to, and grounded in, the truth-conditions of what is believed. So, to the extent that our propositional attitudes do not covary with what we apprehend as true, they cease to be beliefs. Relatedly, our epistemic justification is what we take to reveal, or make manifest, the truth of our beliefs. As such, to the extent that our credences are not proportioned to the strength of our justifications, they cease to be beliefs. And, in normal cases, to the extent that we cannot speak to our reasons for believing and hold ourselves answerable to our epistemic responsibilities, our beliefs cease to be rationally, or justifiably, held (Brandom 1998). As believers we are constitutively subject the norms of belief. Thus, epistemic autonomy properly consists in according one's believings to the norms of belief.

This, I contend, gets at a proper understanding of epistemic autonomy as epistemic self-governance.[7] The only beings capable of being *epistemically* interfered with, indeed the only beings capable of being *intellectually* autonomous, are *epistemic* agents: players in the knowledge game. As Wilfrid Sellars put it: "In characterizing an episode or a state as that of *knowing*, we are not giving an empirical description of that episode or state; we are placing it in the logical space of reasons, of justifying and being able to justify what one says" ([1956] 1997 §36). In virtue of our epistemic agency—by being believers, by engaging in inquiry, by making assertions and knowledge claims—we commit ourselves to the norm of belief. We may not simply "opt out" of the norms that constitute and govern the space of reasons without thereby relinquishing our very epistemic agency.

I take this to indicate an important disanalogy between epistemic autonomy and autonomy of the will, and thereby the resultant operation of paternalism in each domain. In practical affairs, paternalistic interferences can unjustifiably infringe on someone's autonomy simply because they don't want to improve their performance in the relevant (permissible but non-obligatory) activity or their realization of the relevant good. When you, having seen me play tennis badly, undertake to interfere with my liberty in order to make me a better tennis player (by, say, hiring a tennis coach for me), I may justifiably object: "I know I play tennis badly, but I don't want to play any better. I would rather pursue other, equally worthwhile, ends." There is no case to be made for your replying to my rebuff of your well-meant intervention by saying, "Well, you ought to want to be a better tennis player." By contrast, the same move is not available to me in the case of belief. I may not coherently, let alone justifiably, respond to your criticisms or resist your interventions for my *epistemic* improvement by claiming "I know I believe badly, but then I don't want to believe any better."[8] Such a response jeopardizes my standing as—if not renounces my claim to be—an inquirer and a believer. (Rather, any cause for my objection must instead be that your interventions won't make me a better believer.)

Any coherent understanding of the "liberty of inquiry" must preserve the nature of inquiry and the status of inquirers qua epistemic agents. Thus, countenancing disinclinations to epistemic improvement as reasons justifying refusals to consent to epistemically paternalistic interventions—whether under the guise of some putative "liberty of inquiry" or otherwise—risks the very epistemic agency and autonomy we are concerned to preserve in our worries about the permissibility of epistemically paternalistic interventions. Generally, believers and inquirers are not at liberty to withhold consent to paternalistic epistemic interventions. Rather, epistemic agents are constitutively and irrevocably committed to the norms, goods, and ends that generally motivate paternalistic epistemic interventions. This provides a presumptive (i.e., default but defeasible) reason for the general permissibility of paternalistic epistemic interventions and against their consisting in any objectionable infringement of the intellectual autonomy of inquirers.

PATERNALISTIC INTERFERENCES AND THE BLINDSPOTS OF REASON

As already noted, Ahlstrom-Vij's (2013) primary reason for the permissibility of epistemic paternalism is that our cognitive limitations and proclivities make it "unlikely that we can rely on ourselves for epistemic improvement" (177). One thing that makes us unable to rely on ourselves in certain epistemic situations is that each of us has epistemic blindspots—contingently true claims that are "idiosyncratically inaccessible" to us because of our constitution or situation (Sorensen 1988: 3).

The Permissibility of Epistemic Self-Censorship

An awareness of our epistemic blindspots can provide us with reason to consent to paternalistic epistemic interventions. To make this case, consider an example due to Roy Sorensen (2018), which gives an epistemic analog of Odysseus's prudential choice to have himself tied to the mast of his ship, voluntarily restricting his liberty in order to prevent his falling victim to the enchanting spell of the Sirens' call and thereby suffering a greater loss of his autonomy. Sorensen makes the case for the permissibility of acting against the principle of total evidence in cases where (i) we know that some specific evidence is misleading but (ii) we don't know how it is misleading, such that (iii) we are not in a position to correct for it. In such cases, he claims, we may engage in epistemic self-censorship, by ignoring relevant evidence.

In arguing for this claim, Sorensen considers the case of Miss Lead, a knowledge saboteur who is an occasional source of information that, if given, is unfailingly true, but is, undetectably to the recipient, misleading evidence to the matter under inquiry. Thus, Miss Lead is a source of apparently good, but undetectably bad, defeaters to one's knowledge claims and justifications. Miss Lead delivers her snippets of epistemic maleficence via sealed packets of (occasionally blank) documents, which we, knowing of Miss Lead's character and practices, must decide whether or not to open.

Consider now a situation where we correctly and justifiably take ourselves to be in a position to know that p, and, just as we are about to report what we know, we receive one of Miss Lead's infamous packets. Should we open it? Among the reasons against opening the packet are: First, "Keeping *yourself* ignorant of some facts can preserve knowledge of other facts," and, second, the following dominance argument:

> [Miss Lead's] packet either has no evidence or misleading evidence. If there is no evidence, you gain nothing. If there is misleading evidence, you lose the knowledge you have. So opening the packet leaves you either no better off or worse off. By not opening the packet you are guaranteed an outcome at least as good as offered by opening—and perhaps better. (Sorensen 2018)

The reasons in favor of opening the packet insist that even misleading evidence is evidence and thus, by the principle of total evidence, may not to be ignored. Moreover, individual pieces of misleading evidence can (sometimes) be combined (if properly arranged) so as to cancel out the misleading aspects of each, in order to point properly at the truth. So, by worsening our present epistemic position, we might be able to improve it in the future. Finally there's a dominance argument for opening the packet: Merely receiving the packet itself constitutes a defeater to our knowledge claim that p. Opening the packet might reveal a blank page, in which case our knowledge is restored. Thus, "those who refuse to open the packet lose their sole chance to really know. So you might as well open the packet and hope for the best!" (Sorensen 2018).

Importantly, Miss Lead exploits a permanent vulnerability of our (defeasibly justified) knowledge to misleading defeaters (Harman 1973). So long as there is a gap between justification and truth, Sorensen reminds us, "There will always be a truth whose discovery would undermine the knower's warrant." Richard Feldman (2003) elaborates on this point:

> If we can ordinarily know things, then there can be other truths such that if we learned them, we would undermine our justification for the thing we know. But some of these defeaters are misleading. That is, we actually know things, but we would not know them if we learned about these [misleading] defeaters. *We are lucky not to know about the defeaters.* (35–36, emphasis added)

Suppose we are faced with such an epistemic dilemma, what ought we do? How ought we to conduct our inquiry? While Sorensen advises us against opening Miss Lead's packet on the grounds that "your rationality is brought into question if you wittingly choose to enter a rationality trap," one would hope for a better option.

One such epistemically preferable option would be that, unbeknownst to us, A. "Lucky" Chance were to pass by and surreptitiously remove Miss Lead's packet before it came to our attention. (Ideally, Lucky would return with the packet once we were so positioned that we would not fall victim to the epistemic misfortunes that would befall us by presently discovering it.) Preferable even to Lucky's intervention would be that we should, having received Miss Lead's packet, promptly consult Count E.R. Rebuttal, who is on to Miss Lead's wily ways and can unfailingly provide us with a second packet containing a defeater for her misleading defeater. Should we know someone like the Count, we ought to consult them.

The morals of this story so far are these: First, according to Sorensen, it is sometimes rationally permissible to epistemically self-censor by ignoring relevant evidence so as to not risk losing knowledge due to misleading evidence. Second, this seems to be a case of rational, consensual epistemic self-paternalism. That is, it seems to provide us with reasons justifying our curation—indeed, censorship—of our epistemic surroundings for our own epistemic benefit. Third, there are recognizably better options to epistemic self-censorship, if only they were available to us.

FROM EPISTEMIC SELF-CENSORSHIP TO EPISTEMIC PATERNALISM

Despite its distinctive character as a "rationality trap," Sorensen's epistemic dilemma at least affords its victim the position to know that they are being misled, even though they are not in a position to do anything about it short of ignoring evidence. Here, we suffer from an epistemic blindspot, which, while recognizable to us, we cannot rely on ourselves to optimally correct for. Yet, knowing our epistemic circumstances, we are at least in a position to recognize that we ought to seek out epistemic guidance (or at least hope for some interference) as a way of improving our epistemic situation. That is, we are in a position to know that we ought to consent to certain kinds of epistemic interventions—specifically, ones that we judge will leave us epistemically better off.

A position worse than this is one where we are not even in a position to know that we are somehow being misled by the evidence. Now we have a blindspot we're not even aware of—a blindspot for our blindspot, if you will. Yet, importantly, other than that, our epistemic situation has not changed. In particular, the very same reasons that, when accessible to us, motivated and justified our seeking out the epistemic guidance of Count E. R. Rebuttal, remain—it's just that they're presently inaccessible to us. That is, while there *is* reason *for us* to consult or defer, the problem is that those reasons are not *apparent* to us.[9] Were we to *have* them (i.e., recognize them as reasons for us), they would motivate and justify our seeking external epistemic guidance. Moreover, something else that hasn't changed is *that* these reasons justify our seeking outside epistemic assistance. They are evidence of an epistemic problem that we cannot fix by ourselves. Yet, were those reasons accessible to an epistemic authority[10] who had our epistemic best-interests at heart—say, an epistemic paternalist—then *they* might be able to act on those reasons in our stead precisely because we cannot do so ourselves.

Suppose, for example, that Vic is the victim of a "blindspot blindspot." He's unaware of a blindspot of the sort we have been considering throughout the chapter (e.g., his inquiries are detrimentally affected in ways he cannot detect by internal biases, coercive agents, or a polluted informational environment that is also undetectable by him). Patty, the epistemic paternalist, is, and justifiably believes herself to be, an epistemic authority in a position to improve Vic's epistemic situation and reveal Vic's blindspots to him, yet only in ways that, in his present epistemic state, Vic would not consent to. To Vic, it seems that he has every reason to refuse Patty's intervention. May Patty intervene? From our point of view, the answer should be "Yes." Indeed she should. And Vic's commitment to the norm of belief, together with those reasons, inaccessible to him, for consenting to, indeed seeking out, external epistemic help, permits the intervention, even though he would not presently consent.

As I see it, this is the locus of the tension between epistemic autonomy and paternalistic epistemic intervention. While it seems to Vic as though he has no good reason to consent to Patty's intervention, in fact he does. According to the norm of belief, there is every reason for Vic to consent to Patty's epistemic intervention, even though he cannot access or recognize those reasons. Vic's problem is that he has (something like) the following additional epistemic blindspot: I believe that I have no good reason to consent to Patty's intervention, even though I do. Notice that, while true, Vic cannot coherently have this thought. Indeed, Vic's ignorance of this truth is explained by its idiosyncratic inaccessibility to him, given his present epistemic situation. Hence, *it* cannot constitute his reason for self-correction or seeking epistemic aid. Notice finally that Patty can coherently and justifiably have each of these thoughts, and that they supply her with good reasons to intervene in Vic's epistemic endeavors. Ironically, only Patty's intervention will allow Vic to recognize his blindspot(s), thereby making the reasons justifying the intervention accessible to him.

Consent After the Fact: *A Permissibility Condition for Paternalistic Epistemic Interferences*

According to Ahlstrom-Vij (2013), the epistemic paternalism is justified if it satisfies the *alignment* condition—that the epistemic reasons motivating the interference align with any non-epistemic reasons—and the *burden of proof condition*—that evidence indicates that the interference will leave those interfered with epistemically better off relative to other options (117, 122). Importantly, the burden of proof condition is stated in purely externalist terms. Neither the evidence indicating epistemic improvement nor the epistemic improvement itself need to be accessible to, let alone recognized by, the epistemically interfered-with. That is, we may, according to Ahlstrom-Vij, be paternalistically interfered with in ways that we never consent to even if the reasons behind both the intervention and its success or failure are perennially inaccessible to us. The condition of the interfered-with can be epistemically improved without their ever recognizing it.

Viewed in this way, perhaps we are right to worry about the permissibility of epistemic paternalism, since it really does seem to jeopardize our intellectual autonomy. While we might end up with an improved ratio of true beliefs to error and ignorance, we could hardly call those beliefs acquired via such interventions knowledge in anything but an externalist sense. Relatedly, our epistemic agency, understood as our capacity as a self-reliant, self-regulating knower, can hardly be said to have been enhanced. Rather, it seems to have been diminished.

The analysis offered herein suggests a new, higher standard for the permissibility of epistemic paternalism, which, I contend, better respects the epistemic agency of the paternalistically interfered-with. Such a standard incorporates some permissibility condition internally accessible from within the perspective of the interfered-with. Yet, given the nature of the epistemic blindspots addressed by paternalistic interventions, we cannot expect to satisfy this condition prior to the intervention itself. Instead, I suggest something along these lines: Paternalistic epistemic interventions are ideally permissible when, as a result of the intervention, the epistemic improvement afforded to the interfered-with provides them access to the reasons justifying the interference according to the norm of belief. Ideally, this will make visible to the interfered-with those blindspots that prevented them from being fully epistemically autonomous in this regard prior to the intervention. Also ideally, as a result of their recognizing these blindspots and coming to possess those reasons, the interfered-with will not only be in a position to—but indeed will come to—reflectively endorse the reasons for, and permissibility and benefits of, the paternalistic intervention (cf. Zagzebski 2013). But, they will come to grant this consent only after, indeed as a result of, the intervention itself.[11]

At the very least, raising the permissibility bar for paternalistic epistemic interventions hopes to impress upon epistemic paternalists that, rather than merely improving the epistemic *situation* of another agent, they ought to aim to enhance that agent's *agency*. One way that epistemic paternalists can do this is to hold themselves accountable to a standard of post-interference, reflective endorsement on the part of the interfered-with. Satisfying some condition of this sort is at least part of what I take to be involved in treating others as "legislating members of the realm of epistemic ends"—that is, as maximally autonomous epistemic agents, even in sub-optimal circumstances (Elgin 2013: 135).[12]

CONCLUSION

Paradoxically, acts of epistemic paternalism seem to interfere with another's intellectual autonomy, but for their epistemic sake. By interposing their judgment within another's process of inquiry, the epistemic paternalist aims to aid the interfered-with in acquiring some epistemic good, thereby improving their epistemic situation. So understood, both the possibility and the permissibility of epistemic paternalism depend, essentially, on our being epistemic agents and on the nature of epistemic autonomy. Epistemic autonomy, I have argued, is properly conceived of, not as epistemic self-sufficiency, but as self-governance according to the norm of belief—norms to which all epistemic agents are constitutively committed. This commitment supplies a presumptive reason permitting paternalistic epistemic interventions: Even without prior consultation or consent, inquirers cannot simply decline genuine efforts to improve their epistemic situation without thereby forsaking their epistemic agency. Yet, even successful paternalistic interferences can diminish another's epistemic autonomy should they go unrecognized. Thus, rather than merely improve another inquirer's epistemic situation, epistemic paternalists should also seek to enhance their epistemic agency. One measure for such agential enhancement is that as a result of the paternalistic interference, the interfered-with is in a position to reflectively endorse the reasons for, and the permissibility and benefits of, the paternalistic intervention.[13]

NOTES

1. In advocating for a *modest* epistemic paternalism, according to which "epistemic paternalism is not solely concerned with promoting a specifically epistemic kind of goodness," Duncan Pritchard (2013: 28f, 30) distinguishes several ways that epistemically paternalistic interventions might be motivated according to different ways that epistemic goods are valued. Against this, Emma Bullock (2018: 444) contends we lack good grounds for distinctively epistemically paternalistic interventions, writing "whilst the strict epistemic paternalist can avoid the collapse into general paternalism this comes at the cost of its plausibility."

2. Some theorists (e.g., Goldman 1991, Ahlstrom-Vij 2013, 2013a) offer an exclusively veritistic conception of our epistemic ends and interests. Goldman, for example, writes: "I have been equating epistemically valuable outcomes with true belief and error avoidance" (1991: 125). Others (e.g., Kvanvig 2003, 2005; Pritchard 2013; Bishop 2014; Carter 2017; Elgin 2017; Croce 2018) include goods like understanding and reasoning as having epistemic value. For example, Duncan Pritchard argues that "some epistemic standings [specifically understanding], over and above mere true belief, have a goodness which is good *simpliciter*" (20). In view of Jonathan Kvanvig's (2008) observations about "pointless truths" and Chase Wrenn's (2017) arguments on truth's intrinsic value, I am inclined to a conception of epistemic value that extends beyond mere true belief. Indeed, Michel Croce's case of Prof. Everyt Solved thoughtlessly providing her student the answer to an assigned problem he was still working out for himself provides a case of epistemic paternalism that satisfies the ends of inquiry, veritistically conceived, while not maximally improving the student's epistemic circumstance by allowing them discover for themselves, and thereby better understand the reasons for, the solution (2018: 312f). Plausibly, this does not maximally improve the student's epistemic well-being or enhance their epistemic agency. Relatedly, your feeding me a steady diet of *useful* truths which I thereby come to justifiably believe might nevertheless diminish my epistemic autonomy if, for example, my acquiring those true beliefs is not *creditable* to me. Despite my being better informed, my capacity as a knower, and thus my intellectual agency, is diminished (cf. Carter 2017; Pritchard 2010). While I am inclined to such broader conceptions of epistemic value, the case I make for the permissibility of epistemic paternalism seeks to succeed also under the narrower, exclusively veritistic conception.

3. Dworkin (1988) offers a similar pair of distinguishing characteristics, substitution and promotion, describing paternalistic acts as those which "attempt to substitute one person's judgement for another's, to promote the latter's benefit" (123).

4. Importantly, Fricker, together with virtually every author cited in this chapter who has written on the topic, ultimately rejects as untenable, if not incoherent, such a characterization of the ideal of epistemic autonomy as complete epistemic independence or self-reliance.

5. While Ahlstrom-Vij presents chapter 4 as an unsuccessful search for a conception of autonomy under which epistemic paternalism might be prohibited, each is characterized in terms of the independence of the epistemic agent.

6. "Freedom" of inquiry might be understood in a different sense. It might be said that there is a liberty to *undertake*, rather than *conduct*, inquiry freely—that is, to investigate whatever matters one deems worthy of inquiry to satisfy their intellectual curiosity or in pursuance of their practical ends. While some courses of inquiry might be criticized as frivolous, futile, inopportune, or immoral, there seems to be an important degree of liberty in selecting one's topics of inquiry. One might, for example, answer a criticism that one should rather inquire into this matter than that merely by saying, "But I'd rather investigate that than this; I find it more stimulating." Requiring or coercively incentivizing inquirers to direct their inquiries toward these permissible intellectual ends rather than those seems to infringe on an intellectual liberty.

7. I take this to be broadly consistent with Zagzeski's (2013) account of intellectual autonomy.

8. Cf. Wittgenstein's ([1929] 1956) distinction between judgments of absolute and relative value.

9. Cf. Robert Audi's (1986: 29) distinction between reasons to believe, reasons for S to believe, and reasons S has for believing.

10. By "epistemic authority" I have in mind the kind of epistemic superior—rather than expert—envisioned by Croce (2018). He defines an epistemic authority an epistemic agent who "has the capacity to help [another] achieve epistemic goals in [some, perhaps very local domain] that [the other] might not be able to achieve on [their] own" (315). Later, Croce elaborates: "On the broad conception of epistemic superiority endorsed here, one can be better epistemically positioned than another in a very local way—for example, by lacking a relevant bias or being able to spot it in other people in a given circumstance" (319).

11. Should this occur, they would have an additional reason not to object to the intervention as it occurs. Plausibly, among the principles we, believers, ought to subscribe to is one prescribing that we ought to defer our judgments to our epistemic superiors—those in a better position to know. And, should Patty intervene, Vic's future self would be in a better position to know whether her intervention would be epistemically justified and beneficial to him. Thus, Vic should defer his judgment to his future epistemic self.

12. Of course, even this permissibility condition is susceptible to pernicious, maleficent exploitation—gaslighting might be such an example.

13. Acknowledgments: For their generous and constructive comments that helped improve earlier versions of this chapter, I offer my thanks to Pat Bondy, John Grey, and the collection editors Amiel Bernal and Guy Axtell.

BIBLIOGRAPHY

Adler, Jonathan. 2002. *Belief's Own Ethics*. Cambridge, MA: MIT Press.
Ahlstrom-Vij, Kristoffer. 2013. *Epistemic Paternalism: A Defence*. New York: Palgrave Macmillan.
Ahlstrom-Vij, Kristoffer. 2013a. "In Defense of Veritistic Value Monism." *Pacific Philosophical Quarterly*, 94: 19–40.
Audi, Robert. 1986. "Reason, Belief, and Inference." *Philosophical Topics*, 14(1): 27–65.
Bishop, Michael. 2014. "Review of *Epistemic Paternalism: A Defence*." *Notre Dame Philosophical Reviews*, June 30, 2014.
Brandom, Robert. 1998. "Insights and Blindspots of Relaibilism." *The Monist*, *81*: 371–392.
Bullock, Emma. 2018. "Knowing and Not-Knowing for Your Own Good: The Limits of Epistemic Paternalism." *Journal of Applied Philosophy*, 35(2): 433–447.
Carter, J. Adam. 2017. "Intellectual Autonomy, Epistemic Dependence and Cognitive Enhancement." *Synthese*, doi: 10.1007/s11229-017-1549-y
Croce, Michel. 2018. "Epistemic Paternalism and the Service Conception of Epistemic Authority." *Metaphilosophy*, 49(3): 305–327.
Downie, R. S. and Elizabeth Telfer. 1971. "Autonomy." *Philosophy*, 46(178): 293–301.
Dworkin, Gerald. 1988. *The Theory and Practice of Autonomy*. Cambridge: Cambridge University Press.
Elgin, Catherine. 2013. "Epistemic Agency." *Theory and Research in Education*, 11(2): 135–152.
Elgin, Catherine. 2017. *True Enough*. Cambridge, MA: MIT Press.
Feldman, Richard. 2003. *Epistemology*. Upper Saddle River, NJ: Pearson.
Fricker, Elizabeth. 2006. "Testimony and Epistemic Autonomy," in Jennifer Lackey and Ernest Sosa (eds.). *The Epistemology of Testimony*, 225–250. Oxford: Oxford University Press.
Fricker, Miranda. 2007. *Epistemic Injustice: Power and the Ethics of Knowing*. Oxford: Oxford University Press.
Gibbons, John. 2013. *The Norm of Belief*. New York: Oxford University Press.
Goldman, Alvin. 1991. "Epistemic Paternalism: Communication Control in Law and Society." *The Journal of Philosophy*, 88(3): 113–131.
Grill, Kalle and Sven Ove Hansson. 2005. "Epistemic Paternalism in Public Health." *Journal of Medical Ethics*, 31(11): 648–653.
Hardwig, John. 1985. "Epistemic Dependence." *Journal of Philosophy*, 82: 335–349.
Hardwig, John. 2011. "Delight in Variegation: Individual Differences, Autonomy and the Pursuit of Knowledge." Unpublished manuscript presented at *Epistemic Autonomy* conference, August 8, 2011, Humboldt Universität, Berlin. Available via: http://web.utk.edu/~jhardwig/EpistAutonomy.pdf (accessed August 15, 2019).
Harman, Gilbert. 1973. *Thought*. Princeton: Princeton University Press.
Kvanvig, Jonathan. 2003. *The Value of Knowledge and the Pursuit of Understanding*. Cambridge: Cambridge University Press.

Kvanvig, Jonathan. 2005. "Truth Is Not the Primary Epistemic Goal," in *Ernest Sosa and Matthias Steup* (eds.), Contemporary Debates in Epistemology, 285–296, Oxford: Blackwell.

Kvanvig, John. 2008. "Pointless Truth." *Midwest Studies in Philosophy*, 32(1): 199–212.

Levy, Neil. 2019. "Nudge, Nudge, Wink, Wink: Nudging Is Giving Reasons." *Ergo*, 6(10): 281–302.

May, Thomas. 1994. "The Concept of Autonomy." *American Philosophical Quarterly*, 31(2): 133–144.

McMyler, B. 2011. "Doxastic Coercion." *Philosophical Quarterly*, 61: 537–557.

Pritchard, Duncan. 2010. "Cognitive Ability and the Extended Cognition Thesis." *Synthese*, 175(1): 133–151.

Pritchard, Duncan. 2013. "Epistemic Paternalism and Epistemic Value." *Philosophical Inquiries*, 1(2): 9–37.

Roberts, Robert and Jay Wood. 2007. *Intellectual Virtues: An Essay in Regulative Esdpistemology*. Oxford: Oxford University Press.

Rothman, Lily. 2012. "A Cultural History of Mansplaining." *The Atlantic*, November 1, 2012.

Scanlon, Thomas. 1972. "A Theory of Freedom of Expression." *Philosophy & Public Affairs*, 1(2): 204–226.

Sellars, Wilfrid. 1997 [1956]. *Empiricism and the Philosophy of Mind*. Cambridge, MA: Harvard University Press.

Solnit, Rebecca. 2008. "Men Explain Things to Me: Facts Didn't Get in Their Way." *TomDispatch*.com (The Nation Institute), April 13, 2008.

Sorensen, Roy. 1988. *Blindspots*. Oxford: Clarendon Press.

Sorensen, Roy. 2018. "Stealing Harman's *Thought*: Knowledge Saboteurs and Dogmatists." *Synthese*, doi: 10.1007/s11229-018-01945-5

Wittgenstein, Ludwig. ([1929] 1968). A Lecture on Ethics. *Philosophical Review*, 24: 3–12.

Wrenn, Chase. 2017. "Truth Is Not (Very) Intrinsically Valuable." *Pacific Philosophical Quarterly*, 98: 108–128.

Zagzebski, Linda. 2007. "Ethical and Epistemic Egoism and the Ideal of Autonomy." *Episteme*, 4(3): 252–263.

Zagzebski, Linda. 2012. *Epistemic Authority: A Theory of Trust, Authority, and Autonomy in Belief*. New York: Oxford University Press.

Zagzebski, Linda. 2013. "Intellectual Autonomy." *Philosophical Issues*, 23: 244–261.

Part IV

EPISTEMIC IN/JUSTICE, VICE, AND VIRTUE

Chapter 13

Epistemic Paternalism, Epistemic Permissivism, and Standpoint Epistemology

Liz Jackson

In most US states, it's illegal to drive without wearing one's seatbelt. Many recreational drugs are outlawed, even if used alone on one's own property. I enforce a strict no-technology policy for students in my classes. A public beach may disallow swimming without the presence of a lifeguard. These are all examples of paternalism, the practice of limiting the free choices of agents, without their consent, for the sake of promoting their best interests. Paternalism is frequently discussed in legal, ethical, and social contexts.[1]

A practice that has received less attention, however, is a strand of paternalism in the epistemic realm.[2] So-called epistemic paternalism is the practice of (i) interfering with someone's inquiry, (ii) without their consent, (iii) for their own epistemic good.[3] Conditions (i) and (iii) are unique to epistemic paternalism: you can engage in paternalism without interfering with someone's inquiry, and without having a distinctly epistemic motivation for doing so, as in many of the opening examples. Nonetheless, epistemic paternalism is a strand of general paternalism.

In this chapter, I concern myself with the question of whether epistemic paternalism is epistemically justified. First, I discuss the definition of epistemic paternalism is more detail and clarify this question about its justification. Then, I explore how two recent epistemological theses—epistemic permissivism and standpoint epistemology—answer this question. I argue they provide a sufficient condition for unjustified epistemic paternalism. Further, I note some remarkable parallels between epistemic permissivism and standpoint epistemology. I conclude that epistemic paternalism is unjustified in a certain class of cases, and, in general, we ought to exercise caution before engaging in epistemically paternalistic practices.

DEFINING EPISTEMIC PATERNALISM

Recall our definition:

Epistemic Paternalism: the practice of

(i) interfering with someone's inquiry,
(ii) without their consent, and
(iii) for their own epistemic good.

Let's consider each condition in more detail. Condition (i) refers to interfering with inquiry. I take inquiry to include both evidence-gathering and belief-forming practices. A common example of interference involves withholding evidence. For instance, juries aren't allowed to consider certain kinds of evidence because it is considered "inadmissible"— for example, evidence of a suspect's past crimes. If evidence is inadmissible or the jury is unlikely to weigh it properly, it is withheld, even though it is relevant—in the sense that, if properly weighed, it could make the jury's final verdict more accurate.[4] Another example of withholding evidence involves a professor who doesn't give her class an argument for moral relativism, knowing many of her students have relativist tendencies. Giving them this argument would likely reinforce those, and it might be epistemically better for them to instead see reasons why moral relativism is problematic.

One can also interfere with another's inquiry by manipulating the way they interpret or weigh their evidence. This enables one to influence another's beliefs without changing their evidence (or, without changing their evidence that bears on the target proposition). So, for example, if you are deciding which hypothesis best explains the evidence, I might make a particular hypothesis salient and not mention other possible explanations, to bias you toward my preferred explanation of the evidence. Or, when teaching, I might give the class a philosophical argument for p, but then strongly emphasize simplicity while purposefully leaving out discussion of the value of explanatory power. This could influence the students' conclusion about p without influencing their evidence that bears on p. Generally, then, one can engage in epistemic paternalism without attempting to change another's evidence.[5]

Condition (ii) is the non-consent condition, which is the same in both general and epistemic paternalism. This condition is relatively straightforward: one engages in the practice without consulting with the inquiring party. Alternatively, one might interfere explicitly against another's will.

Condition (iii) involves the motivation for epistemic paternalism—that is, for the inquirer's own epistemic good.[6] This raises the question: What is epistemically good? In the epistemic paternalism literature thus far, there has been a strong emphasis on true belief.[7] However, this emphasis strikes me as relatively narrow when considering the myriad of things epistemologists value (see DePaul 2001). For one, rational or justified beliefs, even if false, intuitively carry some epistemic value. In fact, Feldman (2000: 686) claims there is nothing epistemically valuable about true, unjustified beliefs. This is a strong claim. We can settle for a weaker one: epistemic justification confers epistemic value to beliefs, even to false beliefs (consider: a justified false belief seems epistemically better than an unjustified false belief). Thus, a potential motivation for epistemic paternalism involves increasing an inquirer's rational/justified beliefs.

JUSTIFYING EPISTEMIC PATERNALISM

Upon understanding the nature of epistemic paternalism, it is natural to turn next to normative questions. This chapter concerns the question that is the original focus of Goldman's (1991) paper: Is epistemic paternalism *epistemically* justified? Note that this question is about the epistemic justification of a particular practice, namely, interfering with inquiry. In this sense, "epistemic justification" (or "epistemically justified") is used in a somewhat non-standard way—it doesn't pick out the thing that turns true unGettiered belief into knowledge.[8] Here, "justification" indicates when a practice, on balance, promotes epistemic goods. This explains why most authors in the epistemic paternalism literature either implicitly or explicitly adopt a version of epistemic consequentialism.

Further, this question controversially assumes that epistemic norms can guide action.[9] However, it is reasonable to think some epistemic norms guide certain kinds of behaviors, such as how we get evidence (e.g., inquiry and evidence gathering) and what we do with our evidence (e.g., critical reasoning and reflection on our evidence).[10]

There are a variety of answers to the question of whether epistemic paternalism is epistemically justified. Consider the following options:

A1. Epistemic paternalism is always epistemically justified.
A2. Epistemic paternalism is never epistemically justified.
A3. Epistemic paternalism is always epistemically justified in ABC circumstances.
A4. Epistemic paternalism is never epistemically justified in XYZ circumstances.

A1 and A2 are hard to establish, especially against a backdrop of epistemic consequentialism. Given consequentialism, whether epistemic paternalism is justified depends on relevant outcomes. Nonetheless, this doesn't prevent us from giving an answer like A3 or A4—as others have already done. Ahlstrom-Vij (2013a), for instance, gives an answer in the form of A3; he provides two jointly sufficient conditions for justified epistemic paternalism.[11]

Here, I invoke a similar strategy, but unlike Ahlstrom-Vij, my answer is in the form of A4. I will argue that two recent theses in epistemology—epistemic permissivism and standpoint epistemology—provide us with a class of cases in which epistemic paternalism is unjustified. This doesn't amount to an answer as strong as A2, but it does give us reason to be cautious before engaging in an epistemically paternalistic practice and consider whether our situation might fall into that class of cases.

To sum up what we've covered so far, epistemic paternalism is the practice of interfering with someone's inquiry without their consent for their own epistemic good. I've focused on the question of whether epistemic paternalism is *epistemically* justified, and will argue that when a certain set of conditions are met, it is unjustified. With this background in place, I now turn to epistemic permissivism.

EPISTEMIC PERMISSIVISM

Epistemic permissivism is a thesis about epistemic rationality and evidence. Specifically, it is the view that there are evidential situations that rationally permit more than one attitude toward a proposition.[12] Here, *epistemic rationality* involves responding to one's epistemic situation appropriately, and it seems like certain evidential situations allow for multiple appropriate responses. For instance, paleontologists might share evidence but disagree about what killed the dinosaurs (Rosen 2001). Peter van Inwagen and David Lewis might share evidence but disagree about the nature of free will (van Inwagen 1996). Here, I will focus on a relatively weak version of permissivism called *interpersonal permissivism*: the view that there are evidential situations in which two (or more) agents can rationally adopt more than one doxastic attitude toward a proposition.

Interpersonal permissivism is commonly motivated by the idea that agents have differing epistemic standards (Schoenfield 2014). Epistemic standards are the means by which we evaluate, weigh, interpret, and process evidence. For instance, we might share evidence but rationally disagree about what hypothesis best explains the evidence. Or consider the two Jamesian epistemic goals: believe truth and avoid error. If I emphasize the value of believing truth, I may believe p with only a little evidence for p. If you emphasize the value of avoiding error, you might require significantly more evidence before you believe p. It doesn't seem like a particular weighing of these two goals is rationally required (Kelly 2013).[13]

What does any of this have to do with epistemic paternalism? Consider a natural reason one might engage in an epistemically paternalistic practice. I might think that my evidence E supports a particular proposition p.

However, I might suspect that another person, upon learning E, won't come to believe *p*—in fact, they might even come to believe not-p. On this basis, I withhold E from them. However, if interpersonal permissivism is true, then the fact that someone with my evidence would come to a different conclusion than me doesn't mean their belief is irrational or that they've misinterpreted the evidence. The possibility of permissive cases then undermines a reason that one might act paternalistically.

A specific example might make this point more concrete. A frequent case used in both the permissivism literature and the epistemic paternalism literature involves juries. Consider a judge who is deciding whether to act paternalistically by withholding some evidence from a jury. She is considering doing so because they would interpret evidence in a way that, to him or her, seems misguided. She suspects that, if she gave them the extra evidence, they would think it supports *p*, when she is convinced it supports not-p.[14] In a lot of these cases, what seems misguided to her might just be another epistemically legitimate way of interpreting the evidence. The jurors might invoke a different epistemic standard when weighing and interpreting the evidence—a standard that is epistemically acceptable, but results in a different conclusion about who is guilty (they may, for instance, conclude that another hypothesis best explains the evidence).

Of course, sometimes one might invoke an epistemic standard that is unlikely to produce rational beliefs. For instance, a jury might be disposed to make a basic math error or engage in a process of reasoning that is problematically biased. In these cases, the justification for epistemic paternalism is clear. However, these are also not cases of epistemic permissivism, as the jury is not invoking an epistemically legitimate standard, so the beliefs produced using that standard are not rational. The permissivist does not claim that any epistemic standard goes—merely that there are different but equally legitimate standards that can be applied to a body of evidence.

The possibility of interpersonal permissivism doesn't merely have implications for the practice of withholding evidence; it also speaks against interfering with the way another interprets or processes evidence. Consider again our judge who worries that some members of the jury would come to a different conclusion than she. Assuming they share evidence and are in an interpersonally permissive case, the fact that the jury would disagree with her does not give her grounds to interfere with the way they process the evidence.

Not only does interference in permissive cases fail to have epistemically good effects; it also can have epistemically bad effects. Interfering may stifle the jury's ability to think creatively and inquire freely. They might consider possible explanations of the evidence that had never occurred to the judge; for example, the judge might be convinced that Smith did it, but the jury might employ another standard that makes salient the possibility that Jones, Smith's butler did it (Douven 2009). Both beliefs are rational, given the evidence, but if the judge had paternalistically imposed her epistemic standard on the jurors, the latter explanation may never have been considered. Co-existing epistemic standards lead to epistemic diversity that improves our collective epistemic position in the long run. For this reason, in permissive cases, not only is there no clear justification for paternalism, but there is positive reason not to engage in a paternalistic practice. Interfering with another's epistemic standard will often have long-term negative epistemic effects, and, in permissive cases, is epistemically unjustified.

It is worth noting that certain defenders of epistemic paternalism may agree with this conclusion. For example, Ahlstrom-Vij argues that for paternalism to be justified, the one interfering needs to have good reason to believe that their interference is epistemically *pareto efficient*: it will make no one epistemically worse off and at least one person epistemically better off.[15] Given that Ahlstrom-Vij and I are both merely arguing for sufficient conditions for justified and unjustified epistemic paternalism, respectively, it isn't surprising that our arguments aren't strictly inconsistent. My argument, however, provides reason to think that certain interferences that *seem* epistemically pareto efficient may not be—interpreting the evidence well and concluding p doesn't provide ground to interfere with another because they conclude not-p. Thus, even if Ahlstrom-Vij's conditional claim is correct, my argument narrows the range of cases in which it applies—the pareto condition isn't met in permissive cases.

I have been arguing that in permissive cases, epistemic paternalism is not epistemically permitted. One might worry that epistemic permissivism concerns epistemic *rationality*—but rationality doesn't guarantee truth. Permissivism wouldn't speak to epistemic paternalism concerned with promoting true beliefs, rather than rational ones. I could be in a permissive case and acknowledge that another's beliefs are perfectly rational, but act paternalistically for the sake of promoting true beliefs.

In response, the problem here is that from the perspective of the agents in a permissive case, the evidence does not make the truth obvious. Some have likened permissive cases to cases of underdetermination in science (Jackson & Turnbull forthcoming)—in these cases, the evidence underdetermines what one ought to conclude. When I find myself in a permissive case, I'm not in a position to know whether my paternalistic action would be alethically valuable for another. Thus, permissivism also undermines the alethic justification for epistemic paternalism.

In this, my claims about the permissibility of permissivism take the agent's perspective seriously. This raises the question: Does one have to *know* they are in a permissive case? but one has no idea; is paternalism unjustified for that person?[16] In response, while the simplest case in one in which agents know or justifiedly believe their case is permissive, the applicability of my argument goes beyond these straightforward cases. If the probability that the case is permissive is high enough, then the expected epistemic utility of the interference often won't be justified on balance (depending on the expected gains and losses of the interference).

Generally, many disagreements are pervasive, and open-mindedness is difficult to cultivate. It is hard to see when someone who disagrees with you is employing another, equally legitimate epistemic standard, as this often requires epistemic empathy that involves "taking on" their perspective. Because this can be so challenging, I worry that there are cases where one might think one is engaging in legitimate epistemic paternalism—helping out another epistemically. However, one is instead ruling out another adequate way of interpreting the evidence. And this could have long-term bad effects—for example, stifling new ideas and free inquiry. Thus, we have reason to exercise caution and consider whether we might be in an epistemically permissive case before engaging in epistemic paternalism.

Of course, some deny that permissive cases ever occur.[17] While I've motivated interpersonal permissivism with epistemic standards, the permissivism debate is complex and has a growing literature, and I cannot fully settle it here. If one were convinced permissive cases are impossible, then this argument won't have purchase for them (although they need a response to the argument for permissivism from epistemic standards).

Also note that there is a distinction between moderate and extreme permissivism. Extreme permissivists maintain that there are evidential situations in which all doxastic attitudes toward a proposition are permitted (e.g., belief, withholding, and disbelief; all credences between [0,1]). Moderate permissivists maintain merely that there are evidential situations in which a subset of those doxastic attitudes is permitted (e.g., only belief and withholding; only credences between [0.9, 0.7]).[18] In moderately permissive cases, it may be justified to engage in paternalism to move others away from the impermissible attitudes. For example, if you and I are in an evidential situation that permits belief in p and withholding on p, but not disbelief, I may be justified in paternalistically nudging you away from disbelief.[19] Nonetheless, paternalism is unjustified when it draws others away from the permitted attitudes.

My main claim is as follows:

Strong claim: If, given their evidence and a proposition p, agents are in an epistemically permissive case with respect to attitudes A1-An in p, it is *always* epistemically wrong for any of them to paternalistically interfere to change the other's attitude A1-An in p.

I've provided several reasons to think this claim is true. However, the assumption of epistemic consequentialism makes it challenging to establish in a short chapter. It requires that, in the permissive cases described, there is no epistemic good (even in the long run) that outweighs the losses associated with interfering with another's inquiry. I've tried to explain earlier why I think there are serious losses associated with this kind of interference, and also why other possible epistemic goods (e.g., true beliefs) won't outweigh these losses in permissive cases. I realize, though, that all might not be convinced. In this case, there are two weaker claims to fall back on:

Weak claim 1: If, given their evidence and a proposition p, agents are in an epistemically permissive case with respect to attitudes A1-An in p, then a potential justification they might have for interfering with each other's inquiry is undermined.

Weak claim 2: If, given their evidence and a proposition p, agents are in an epistemically permissive case with respect to attitudes A1-An in p, it is *often* epistemically wrong for any of them to paternalistically interfere to change the other's attitude A1-An in p.

Note that the first weak claim asserts that permissivism simply undermines a potential positive justification for paternalism but doesn't necessarily claim we have positive reason not to do it. The difference between the second weak claim and the strong claim is the scope of the cases involved. I hope I've at least convinced the reader of these claims.

Generally, then, the possibility of permissive cases undermines a justification for epistemic paternalism, and renders epistemic paternalism unjustified, at least in most permissive cases. Now, I turn to another epistemological thesis that also speaks against a class of paternalistic interferences—standpoint epistemology.

STANDPOINT EPISTEMOLOGY

Standpoint epistemology comes in many forms.[20] Here, I focus on a general version that states that one's social position affects the epistemic goods that one can access. More precisely, standpoint epistemology is the view that one's social situation gives one unique access to epistemic goods (such as information/evidence, concepts, ways of interpreting or weighing evidence, etc.) that people in other social situations cannot access.[21] In other words, two different people can come to very different conclusions about the same matter, either because they end up having different evidence, or because they end up interpreting or weighing evidence quite differently. Standpoint epistemologists argue that one's social situation affects both what one in fact knows (or rationally believes), but also what is knowable (or rationally believable) for them. There are two versions of this thesis:

Global standpoint epistemology: one's social situation affects *all* of their (epistemically) rational beliefs/knowledge.
Local standpoint epistemology: one's social situation affects *some* of their (epistemically) rational beliefs/knowledge.

I sense that most standpoint epistemologists endorse the local thesis, rather than the global one.[22] For example, one's gender might not affect their beliefs about the weather tomorrow, but it may affect their views on divorce, abortion, or labor economics. The local thesis also helps with the worry that standpoint epistemology leads to a problematic global subjectivism, an objection that has been discussed extensively, especially in terms of implications for scientific objectivity and progress.[23] Thus, I will focus on the local thesis.

Standpoint epistemology has been linked to various other epistemological theses; for instance, Toole (2019) likens it to pragmatic or moral encroachment, as she focuses on how non-epistemic social facts can affect knowledge. At the same time, it appears to have quite a bit in common with epistemic permissivism, especially the interpersonal strand of permissivism discussed earlier.[24] One's social situation can affect, shape, and potentially even partially constitute one's epistemic standard, and thus the way one weighs and processes evidence. In fact, standpoints and epistemic standards might be two ways of describing the same phenomenon. Two people may share evidence, but due to their distinct social situations, process that evidence very differently and come to incompatible conclusions. In the same way, there isn't always a unique most-rational standpoint, there isn't a unique most-rational standard. Thus, it seems natural for advocates of standpoint epistemology to adopt a permissivist epistemology; similarly, advocates of intrapersonal permissivism might find themselves sympathetic to standpoint epistemology.

Given that standpoint epistemology and interpersonal permissivism have some notable similarities, it makes sense that standpoint epistemology would also render epistemic paternalism unjustified, at least on the matters affected by the standpoint. The basic idea is this: A might consider acting paternalistically (e.g., withholding evidence from B or interfering with the way B processes evidence) because B would come to a completely different conclusion if B had that evidence or processed that evidence according to B's standpoint. However, if both standpoints are epistemically legitimate ways of interpreting evidence, then A can't justify paternalism because B would have more rational beliefs if A interfered. Further, because in most of these cases, A also won't have access to the truth of the matter, the interference can't be veritistically justified either. And again, the interference will often lead to epistemically bad results—stifling distinct perspectives and the values associated with epistemic diversity. So, there are epistemic negatives associated with interfering, and epistemic positives associated with not-interfering. Thus, standpoint epistemology also renders epistemic paternalism unjustified.

Here is a way to see my overall argument in this section. Standpoint epistemology is closely related to interpersonal permissivism. We've already seen that epistemic paternalism is unjustified in permissive cases. Thus, the same considerations apply to situations where one's standpoint affects one's epistemic attitudes.

One might object that it is possible to endorse standpoint epistemology but deny permissivism. Maybe a standpoint has a single purpose, that is, changing what evidence one has, and two people with different standpoints will always have different evidence. My response is twofold. First, on this view, one's standpoint has a relatively limited function; all it does is affect what evidence one has. There is a reason to think that this is not the only function of the standpoint. A natural alternative picture is a permissivist standpoint epistemology, on which the standpoint also affects the way one weighs or processes evidence—especially given the apparent similarities between standpoints and epistemic standards.

A second reply is that standpoint epistemology might, on its own, render epistemic paternalism unjustified, whether or not permissivism is true. For example, there might be something epistemically valuable about the fact that different standpoints provide different bodies of evidence. Consider the literature on the cognitive division of labor, which supports the idea that researchers pursing a large variety of different projects is long-term epistemically best. This diversity is valuable even if, from our current perspective, some of those projects have a low probability of success (or the hypotheses they are testing have a low prior probability; see Kitcher 1990, 1993). The epistemic value of diverse perspectives is emphasized in this literature. Muldoon (2013: 123–124) summarizes, "In several of the models of the division of cognitive labor . . . diversity plays an important and positive role . . . it encourages differences in agents, and as more diversity is generated, we can make a finer-grained division of labor." Epistemic diversity—including the diversity of various standpoints—leads to breakthroughs in the context of collective inquiry, and paternalistically interfering with others to promote a monistic way of thinking stifles this. This speaks against interfering with the inquiry of people with other standpoints, whether or not permissivism is true.

Second, one might object that standpoint epistemology is disanalogous to permissivism because standpoint epistemology privileges certain standpoints. For instance, many standpoint epistemologists would claim that the female standpoint should be *privileged* over, not merely considered alongside of, the male standpoint when it comes to questions like abortion.[25] In response, this is analogous to the way permissivists view epistemic standards, since permissivists don't maintain that any epistemic standard produces rational beliefs. Their view is not that that any standard goes. At the same time, both permissivists and standpoint theorists posit that there are multiple, equally epistemically good standpoints; even if the female standpoint should sometimes be privileged over the male standpoint, we also shouldn't assume all women have the same standpoint—not all women agree on whether and when abortion is morally permitted, for instance. As Bowell (2019: sec. 7a) says, "Feminist standpoint theories can also be misunderstood as proposing a single, monolithic feminist standpoint . . . [but they] are clearly not committed to the project of formulating a homogenous women's or feminist standpoint." Thus, on both views, certain viewpoints are privileged, but multiple equally good viewpoints sometimes arrive at competing verdicts.

CONCLUSION

On many epistemic theories, such as permissivism and standpoint theory, there isn't one privileged way of interpreting a body of evidence. I've pointed out that this shared commitment highlights a noteworthy connection between standpoint epistemology and epistemic permissivism, and suggested that prominent versions of standpoint epistemology have much in common with interpersonal permissivism.

I've also argued that this points us to a class of cases in which epistemic paternalism is epistemically unjustified. We might be quite confident that we are doing someone an epistemic favor, when in reality, we are imposing our own standards on them. In these cases, epistemic paternalism can have bad long-term consequences: squelching valuable perspectives and promoting a monistic way of thinking. Thus, we ought to exercise caution before engaging in epistemically paternalistic practices, and consider whether we might be in a permissive case or imposing our standpoint on another.[26]

NOTES

1. For philosophical discussions of paternalism, see Mill (1869), Dworkin (2010), Grill and Hanna (2018).

2. Discussions of epistemic paternalism include Goldman (1991), Ahlstrom-Vij (2013a, 2013b), Pritchard (2013), Ridder (2013), Bullock (2018), and Croce (2018).

3. This definition is found in Ahlstrom-Vij (2013a: 51) and Bullock (2018: 434).

4. This example features prominently in Goldman (1991). However, it is unclear that withholding information from a jury counts as epistemic paternalism in many real-life cases, since, upon agreeing to be on a jury, one should realize that evidence might be withheld from them, due to the relevant laws about inadmissible evidence in courtrooms. Thus, it is plausible that, upon agreeing to be a juror, one is consenting to have evidence withheld from them. Thanks to Kirk Lougheed.

5. See Jackson (forthcoming-a) and Jackson and Turnbull (forthcoming) for further discussion of the ways that one's broader epistemic situation can affect one's beliefs without affecting one's evidence.

6. This raises the question: Does an action count as epistemic paternalism if it is done partially for one's epistemic good and partially for their moral and/or practical good? This question deserves more attention but goes beyond the scope of this chapter; see Bullock (2018: 443) and Jackson (forthcoming-b) for discussion. Thanks to Seth Lazar.

7. See, for example, Goldman (1991) and Ahlstrom-Vij (2013a). Pritchard (2013) discusses ways that epistemic paternalism might promote both true beliefs and understanding.

8. Thanks to Pamela Robinson.

9. Feldman (2000) Kelly (2002: fn. 30), and Berker (2018) argue that there aren't epistemic reasons for action.

10. See Tidman (1996), Hookway (1999), Friedman (2019), and Jackson (forthcoming-b).

11. See Ahlstrom-Vij (2013a: 134). For a criticism of his account, see Bullock (2018: 440–442).

12. Defenses of epistemic permissivism include Kelly (2013), Meacham (2014), Meacham (2019), Schoenfield (2014), Schoenfield (2019), and Jackson (forthcoming-a).

13. For further examples of ways epistemic standards might differ, see Nolan (2014) and Meacham (2014).

14. There is a question of how often judges employ this sort of reasoning to justify paternalism in real life. In the United States, for instance, the withholding of information is often formal and procedural; for example, juries cannot see a defendant's criminal record. I don't want to rule out the possibility, however, that judges also withhold information for non-procedural reasons, for example, because from their point of view, it will mislead the jury. Further, my points can be applied to many cases that don't involve courtrooms; the courtroom case is merely to illustrate a more general point. Thanks to Guy Axtell. (See also note 4).

15. See Ahlstrom-Vij (2013a: 134). Thanks to Amiel Bernal.

16. Thanks to Justin D'Ambrosio.

17. White (2005), Matheson (2011), White (2013), Greco (2016), Horowitz (2019), and Stapleford (2019).

18. This distinction is found in White (2005). For a defense of moderate permissivism, see Roeber (forthcoming); for an argument against moderate permissivism, see Horowitz (2014).

19. Thanks to Klaas Kray.

20. Standpoint epistemology was developed from Marxist epistemology by Smith (1974), Hartsock (1983), Rose (1983), and Harding (1986). For recent discussions, see Wylie (2003), Kukla (2006), Solomon (2009), and Toole (2019). See also the 2009 (vol. 24, no. 4) symposium on standpoint theory in *Hypatia*, introduced and summarized by Crasnow (2009).

21. Many standpoint epistemologists affirm several additional claims, for example, (a) that these epistemic goods are not merely passively received, but are often actively sought after and constitute an achievement, (b) that there is unique epistemic advantage associated with powerlessness, and, a normative claim, (c) that we ought to embrace the valuable contributions to knowledge that differing standpoints provide.

22. Solomon (2009) and Toole (2019).

23. See especially Crasnow (2013) but also Harding (1986), Harding (1993), and Kourany (2009).

24. Thanks to Janine Jones. An interesting area for further research is whether standpoint epistemology could also be linked with diachronic *intrapersonal* permissivism, if one's standpoint/epistemic standard changed over time.

25. Thanks to Justin D'Ambrosio.

26. Acknowledgments: Thanks to Amiel Bernal, Guy Axtell, Seth Lazar, Justin D'Ambrosio, Nic Southwood, Matthew Kopec, Kirk Lougheed, Klaas Kray, Chris Dragos, and audiences at the 2019 Canadian Philosophical Association, Australian National University, and Michigan State University. Research on this chapter was supported by Australian Research Council Grant D170101394.

BIBLIOGRAPHY

Ahlstrom-Vij, K. *Epistemic Paternalism: A Defence*. London: Palgrave Macmillan, 2013a.

Ahlstrom-Vij, K. "Why We Cannot Rely on Ourselves for Epistemic Improvement." *Philosophical Issues* 23 (2013b) 276–296.

Berker, S. "A Combinatorial Argument Against Practical Reasons for Belief." *Analytic Philosophy* 59(4) (2018): 427–470.

Bullock, E. C. "Mandatory Disclosure and Medical Paternalism." *Ethical Theory and Moral Practice* 19(2) (2016): 409–424.

Bullock, E. C. "Knowing and Not-Knowing for Your Own Good: The Limits of Epistemic Paternalism." *Journal of Applied Philosophy* 35(2) 2018: 433–447.

Bowell, T. "Feminist Standpoint Theory." *Internet Encyclopedia of Philosophy*, 2019.

Crasnow, S. "Is Standpoint Theory a Resource for Feminist Epistemology? An Introduction." *Hypatia* 24(4) (2009): 189–194.

Crasnow, S. "Feminist Philosophy of Science: Values and Objectivity." *Philosophy Compass* 8(4) (2013): 413–423.

Croce, M. "Epistemic Paternalism and the Service Conception of Epistemic Authority." *Metaphilosophy* 49(3) (2018): 305–327.

DePaul, Michael. "Value Monism in Epistemology," in Matthias Steup (ed.) *Knowledge, Truth, and Duty: Essays on Epistemic Justification, Responsibility, and Virtue*, 170–183. Oxford: Oxford University Press, 2001.

Douven, I. "Uniqueness Revisited." *American Philosophical Quarterly* 46 (2009): 347–361.
Dworkin, G. "Paternalism," in E. Zalta (ed.), *The Stanford Encyclopaedia of Philosophy*, 2010.
Feldman, R. "The Ethics of Belief." *Philosophy and Phenomenological Research* 60(3) (2000): 667–695.
Friedman, J. "Inquiry and Belief." *Noûs*, 53(2) (2019): 296–315.
Goldman, A. I. "Epistemic Paternalism: Communication Control in Law and Society." *The Journal of Philosophy* 88(3) (1991): 113–131.
Greco, D. H., Brian. "Uniqueness and Metaepistemology." *The Journal of Philosophy* 113(8) (2016): 362–395.
Grill, K., & Hanna, J. *The Routledge Handbook of the Philosophy of Paternalism*. New York: Routledge, 2018.
Harding, S. *The Science Question in Feminism*. Ithaca, NY: Cornell University Press, 1986.
Harding, S. "Rethinking Standpoint Epistemology: What Is 'Strong Objectivity'?" in L. Alcoff and E. Potter (eds.), *Feminist Epistemologies*. New York: Routledge, 1993.
Hartsock, N. "The Feminist Standpoint: Developing the Ground for a Specifically Feminist Historical Materialism," in M. B. Hintikka and S. Harding (eds.), *Discovering Reality: Feminist Perspectives on Epistemology, Metaphysics, Methodology, and Philosophy of Science* (Vol. 161). Dordrecht: Springer, 1983.
Hookway, C. "Epistemic Norms and Theoretical Deliberation." *Ratio* 12(4) (1999): 380–397.
Horowitz, S. "Immoderately Rational." *Philosophical Studies* 167(1) (2014): 41–56.
Horowitz, S. "The Truth Problem for Permissivism." *The Journal of Philosophy* 116(5) (2019): 237–262.
Jackson, E. "A Defense of Intrapersonal Belief Permissivism." *Episteme*, forthcoming-a. https://www.cambridge.org/core/journals/episteme/article/defense-of-intrapersonal-belief-permissivism/7B561E7581C9813C5984918BB10EF709
Jackson, E. "What's Epistemic about Epistemic Paternalism?" in K. Lougheed and J. Matheson (eds.), *Essays in Epistemic Autonomy*. New York: Routledge, forthcoming-b. https://philarchive.org/archive/JACWEA
Jackson, E., & Turnbull, M. G. "Permissivism, Underdetermination, and Evidence," in C. Littlejohn and M. Lasonen-Aarnio (eds.), *The Routledge Handbook of the Philosophy of Evidence*. New York: Routledge, forthcoming.
Kelly, T. "The Rationality of Belief and Some Other Propositional Attitudes." *Philosophical Studies* 110(2) (2002): 163–196.
Kelly, T. "Evidence Can Be Permissive," in M. Steup, J. Turri, & E. Sosa (eds.), *Contemporary Debates in Epistemology*, 298–311. Oxford: Wiley-Blackwell, 2013.
Kourany, J. "The Place of Standpoint Theory in Feminist Science Studies." *Hypatia* 24(4) (2009): 209–218.
Kukla, R. "Objectivity and Perspective in Empirical Knowledge." *Episteme* 3(1) (2006): 80–95.

Matheson, J. "The Case for Rational Uniqueness." *Logos & Episteme* 2(3) (2011): 359–373.
Meacham, C. J. "Impermissive Bayesianism." *Erkenntnis* 79(6) (2014): 1185–1217.
Meacham, C. J. "Deference and Uniqueness." *Philosophical Studies* 176(3) (2019): 709–732.
Mill, J. S. *On Liberty*. London: Longman, Roberts & Green, 1869.
Nolan, D. "The Dangers of Pragmatic Virtue." *Inquiry,* 57(5–6) (2014): 623–644.
Pritchard, D. "Epistemic Paternalism and Epistemic Value." *Philosophical Inquiries* 1(2) (2013): 9–37.
Ridder, J. D. "Is There Epistemic Justification for Secrecy in Science?" *Episteme* 10(2) (2013): 101–116.
Roeber, B. "Permissive Situations and Direct Doxastic Control." *Philosophy and Phenomenological Research*, forthcoming. 10.1111/phpr.12594.
Rose, H. "Hand, Brain, and Heart: A Feminist Epistemology for the Natural Sciences." *Signs* 9(1) (1983): 73–90.
Rosen, G. "Nominalism, Naturalism, Epistemic Relativism." *Philosophical Perspectives* 15 (2001): 69–91.
Schoenfield, M. "Permissivism and the Value of Rationality: A Challenge to the Uniqueness Thesis." *Philosophy and Phenomenological Research* 99(2) (2019): 286–297.
Schoenfield, M. "Permissivism and the Value of Rationality: A Challenge to the Uniqueness Thesis." *Philosophy and Phenomenological Research*, forthcoming. https://doi.org/10.1111/phpr.12490
Smith, D. "Women's Perspective as a Radical Critique of Sociology." *Sociological Inquiry* 44 (1974): 1–13.
Solomon, M. "Standpoint and Creativity." *Hypatia* 24(4) (2009): 226–237.
Stapleford, S. "Intraspecies Impermissivism." *Episteme* 16(3) (2019): 340–356.
Tidman, P. "Critical Reflection: An Alleged Epistemic Duty." *Analysis* 56(4) (1996): 268–276.
Toole, B. "From Standpoint Epistemology to Epistemic Oppression." *Hypatia* 34(4) (2019): 598–618.
van Inwagen, P. "It Is Wrong, Everywhere, Always, and for Anyone, to Believe Anything upon Insufficient Evidence," in J. Jordan and D. Howard-Snyder (eds.), *Faith, Freedom, and Rationality*, 137–154. Lanham, MD: Rowman & Littlefield, 1996.
White, R. "Epistemic Permissiveness." *Philosophical Perspectives* 19(1) (2005): 445–459.
White, R. "Evidence Cannot Be Permissive," in M. Steup, J. Turri, and E. Sosa (eds.), *Contemporary Debates in Epistemology*, 312–323. Oxford: Wiley-Blackwell, 2013.
Wylie, A. "Why Standpoint Matters," in R. Figueroa and S. G. Harding (eds.), *Science and Other Cultures: Diversity in the Philosophy of Science and Technology*. New York: Routledge, 2003.

Chapter 14

Silencing, Epistemic Injustice, and Epistemic Paternalism

Valerie Joly Chock and Jonathan Matheson

Members of oppressed groups are often silenced. One form of silencing is what Kristie Dotson calls "testimonial smothering." Testimonial smothering occurs when a speaker limits her testimony in virtue of the reasonable risk of it being misunderstood or misapplied by the audience. Testimonial smothering is thus a form of epistemic paternalism since the speaker is interfering with the audience's inquiry for their benefit without first consulting them. In this chapter, we build on Dotson's account of testimonial smothering by exploring the connections between epistemic injustice and epistemic paternalism through the phenomenon of silencing. We argue that when you silence your testimony as a result of epistemic injustice, it is a form of epistemic paternalism and that it is epistemically permissible. The chapter will explain epistemic paternalism and the criteria for permissible paternalism, explain the phenomenon of epistemic injustice and testimonial smothering, and proceed to demonstrate how silence due to testimonial smothering is a permissible form of epistemic paternalism. In fact, examples of such silencing provide clear cases of permissible epistemic paternalism. In doing so, we bring together work in two emerging literatures, the literature on epistemic paternalism and the literature on epistemic injustice in a way that is fruitful for debates in each area.[1]

EPISTEMIC PATERNALISM

Our epistemological endeavors are inherently social. We rely on the inquiry and testimony of others for a great deal of what we believe. The beliefs of others place checks and balances on our own beliefs.[2] Alvin Goldman, a leading figure in social epistemology, maintains that these social features of our epistemological projects make epistemic paternalism necessary, and at least sometimes desirable (1991: 127). While broader paternalistic practices have been scrutinized for some time, it is only fairly recently that *epistemic* paternalism has been analyzed. Goldman coined "epistemic paternalism" to capture the phenomenon that occurs whenever a communication controller interposes their own judgment (in place of the audience's) in order to improve the epistemic states of the audience (119). Kristoffer Ahlstrom-Vij (2013) further develops epistemic paternalism and advances three necessary and jointly sufficient conditions for a practice to be epistemically paternalistic: (i) the interference condition, (ii) the non-consultation condition, and (iii) the improvement condition. According to these criteria, S acts in an epistemically paternalistic way toward H just in case:

(i) *The interference condition*: S affects H's inquiry regarding some matter,
(ii) *The non-consultation condition*: S interferes with H's inquiry without consulting H on the matter or receiving H's consent, and
(iii) *The improvement condition*: S interferes, at least in part, so as to make H epistemically better off (39).[5]

The interference condition can be satisfied in a number of distinct ways. First, information can be paternalistically *given* to someone. An example of such interference in inquiry is some health education measures. In such cases, the subject is given a great deal of information, where perhaps there was no interest on the subject's part to receive that information.[3] Second, information can also be paternalistically *withheld* from a subject. Common examples here are when evidence is withheld from jurors during a trial, or certain information (like young earth creationism) is left out of a school's curriculum.[4] In both cases, the relevant subject's inquiry has been affected, with the likely result of the subject having different beliefs than they otherwise would have—having new beliefs they otherwise would not have had, or failing to have beliefs they otherwise would have had.[5]

The non-consultation condition is familiar enough. Paternalistic practices, epistemic or otherwise, do not involve getting prior consent from the subject. Paternalistic practices remove the subject's own agency from the picture in that they do not first consult the subject for their prior approval regarding the intervention. For instance, in the school curriculum example mentioned earlier, the students were not first consulted regarding what should be in the curriculum, nor was their prior approval sought. The decisions to interfere in their inquiry were made by independent parties—the communication controllers.

Finally, the improvement condition requires that the epistemically paternalistic act be aimed at the epistemic improvement of the subject. Paternalistic practices must aim to make the affected parties better off, and *epistemically* paternalistic practices concern *epistemic* improvements, even if the subject may be affected in other ways as well. What makes a subject epistemically better off will depend upon one's account of epistemic value. In the literature on epistemic paternalism, epistemic improvements have typically been cashed out in a veritistic way. On the veritistic picture, a subject is made epistemically better off by acquiring true beliefs or avoiding false beliefs. For the veritist, all other epistemic goods are merely instrumentally valuable—valuable only in their propensity to bring about true beliefs or avoid false beliefs. However, epistemic paternalism can also accommodate broader accounts of epistemic value.[6] It is necessary that an epistemically paternalistic act aims to make the subject better off epistemically, but epistemic paternalism itself is silent as to what counts as an epistemic good.[7]

Examples of epistemic paternalism can make the satisfaction of these conditions clear. Goldman's core example of epistemic paternalism comes from the Federal Rules of Evidence—a set of rules set to provide fair, speedy, and just trials, where the truth is ascertained. According to Goldman,

> It is apparent that the framers of the rules, and judges themselves, often wish to protect jurors in their search for truth. If, in the framers' opinion, jurors are likely to be misled by a certain category of evidence, they are sometimes prepared to require or allow such evidence to be kept from the jurors. This is an example of what I shall call epistemic paternalism. The general idea is that the indicated rules of evidence are designed to protect jurors from their own "folly," just as parents might keep dangerous toys or other articles away from children, or might not expose them to certain facts. (Goldman 1991: 118)

So, the Federal Rules of Evidence provide an *epistemic* rationale for excluding various pieces of evidence from doxastic decision makers, in this case, the jurors (116). Since jurors are likely to misevaluate the evidential import of certain pieces of evidence (e.g., the past criminal record of the defendant, a withdrawn guilty plea, and testimonial hearsay), such evidence is allowed to be withheld from the jury, and it is often *required* to be withheld. Rules to this effect, thus, *protect* jurors in their role as inquirers; these rules are in place for the *epistemic* benefit (protection) of the jurors.[8]

It is also worth noting that in this example, *truths* are being withheld from the jurors. The Rules of Evidence differ from other epistemically paternalistic legislation like laws against false advertising. Legislation prohibiting false advertising is in place to prevent *falsehoods* from negatively affecting the audience's beliefs. It is easy enough to see how preventing the spread of falsehoods can have positive epistemic effects. However, in the Federal Rules of Evidence, certain *truths* are withheld from the jurors. Truths about a defendant's criminal past, and truths regarding a withdrawn guilty plea can all be withheld from the jury for their own epistemic benefit. In these cases, it is these further truths that can reasonably be thought to epistemically harm the subjects (the jurors), by making certain epistemic errors on their part more likely.

Is epistemic paternalism *epistemically* justified? Ahlstrom-Vij gives two jointly sufficient conditions for an epistemically paternalistic act to be justified:[9]

i) *The alignment condition*: The epistemic and non-epistemic reasons S has for so acting are not in conflict (117).
ii) *The burden-of-proof condition*: The evidence S has indicates that it is highly likely that the paternalistic act will epistemically benefit all the affected parties (122).

The alignment condition ensures that the epistemic rationale for an epistemically paternalistic practice is not trumping other non-epistemic normative considerations (moral, prudential, etc.) that push in another direction. Two reasons are aligned when they either point to the same end, or one points to an end that the other is silent about (117). The alignment condition thus avoids any worries about how to weigh reasons of different kinds against one another. When there are no non-epistemic reasons in conflict with the epistemic reasons, the alignment condition is met. So, while there may be justified acts of epistemic paternalism where one does have non-epistemic reasons that are in conflict (though outweighed by the epistemic reasons), the alignment condition would not be met in those cases. Recall that the alignment condition is simply one of two jointly sufficient conditions for an epistemically paternalistic act being justified. Meeting the alignment condition is not necessary for an epistemically paternalistic act to be epistemically permissible.

The burden-of-proof condition requires that the communication controller be reasonable in believing that the improvement condition is met for all affected parties. Rationality is fallible, so a justified act of epistemic paternalism needn't be successful. However, the burden-of-proof condition requires that from the intervening subject's perspective, the intervention is highly likely to succeed in bringing about its intended epistemic improvements. Here too, it may be that other epistemically paternalistic acts are justified since they overwhelmingly benefit the affected parties though it is clear that some will not be benefited. The burden-of-proof condition too is not a necessary condition for a justified act of epistemic paternalism, but simply one of two jointly sufficient conditions.

Applied to the case of the Federal Rules of Evidence, it looks like both jointly sufficient conditions for the permissibility of an epistemically paternalistic act are met. First, withholding certain pieces of evidence is not in conflict with the non-epistemic reasons present. In fact, the epistemic reasons here align with the moral reasons we have to arrange for a fair trial and to have the jury arrive at the correct verdict. Second, it is reasonable to believe that the restrictions placed on jurors will have their intended epistemic benefits. Given what we know about the common cognitive errors that we make, a misevaluation of the excluded evidence is sufficiently likely.[10]

EPISTEMIC INJUSTICE AND SILENCING

Philosophers have become more and more concerned with how one's social position can affect one's epistemic position.[11] One issue here is how one's social position has epistemic effects in testimonial exchanges. The term "epistemic injustice" was introduced by Miranda Fricker to refer to "a kind of injustice in which someone is wronged specifically in her capacity as a knower" (2009: 20).[12] At the core of this idea is the thought that power structures create or preserve a given social order, which impedes a speaker's capacity as an epistemic agent by restricting her access to epistemic exchanges. Fricker argues that the epistemic injustice that results from such a social order is originated and sustained by identity prejudices held by the audience. The kind of identity prejudices that are important for epistemic injustice are "tracker prejudices" about the social group to which the speaker belongs. These prejudices are systematic in that they "track" a speaker of a particular social group across various contexts of social activity (e.g., economic, professional, political, and religious) (27). When tracker prejudices lead to epistemic injustice, the injustice is *systematic* because it is systematically connected to other types of injustice experienced by people of a given identity group.

Fricker distinguishes two kinds of injustice: *testimonial injustice* and *hermeneutical injustice*. Testimonial injustice occurs when a speaker is given an unjustified, unfair credibility assessment—for Fricker, that is a prejudicial *credibility deficit*.[13] That is, when the speaker is given less credibility than she deserves. Fricker claims, "The speaker sustains a testimonial injustice if and only if she receives a credibility deficit owing to identity prejudice in the hearer" (28). An example discussed by Fricker is Harper Lee's *To Kill a Mockingbird*, where an all-white jury fails to believe the black defendant's testimony because of the racial prejudices they hold. Hermeneutical injustice occurs when there are conceptual lacunae in which members of a social group lack the conceptual resources to understand and describe particular social experiences. An example of this kind of injustice is the one suffered by victims of sexual harassment before the 1970s who had trouble-making sense of and expressing the behavior they were subject to given that the term "sexual harassment" had not yet been coined.

Kristie Dotson (2011) expands on Fricker's account of testimonial injustice, distinguishing two ways in which members of oppressed groups are silenced with respect to giving testimony: *testimonial quieting* and *testimonial smothering*. Testimonial quieting occurs when the audience fails to recognize the speaker as a knower, thus failing to fairly assess the speaker's credibility. Testimonial smothering occurs when a speaker recognizes her audience as unwilling or unable to appropriately interpret her testimony, and in response, limits her testimony in virtue of the reasonable risk of it being misunderstood or misapplied by the audience. While Dotson argues that both of these silencing practices are forms of epistemic violence[14] with comparable epistemic effects, given the purpose of this chapter, we focus here on the latter species of silencing—testimonial smothering.

Dotson defines epistemic violence in testimony as a "refusal, intentional or unintentional, of a hearer to communicatively reciprocate a linguistic exchange owing to pernicious ignorance" (238). According to Dotson, *reciprocity* is a necessary condition for a successful linguistic exchange. She takes this from Jennifer Hornsby's (1995) model, in which reciprocity "requires that an audience understand a speaker's words and understand what the speaker is doing with the words" (237). Thus, epistemic violence in testimony takes place in failed linguistic exchanges. That is, when the audience fails to understand the speaker's claims due to pernicious ignorance, which refers to "any reliable ignorance that, in a given context, harms another person (or set of persons)" (238).[15]

Dotson describes testimonial smothering as a coerced self-silencing that amounts to the "truncating of one's own testimony in order to ensure that the testimony contains only content for which one's audience demonstrates testimonial competence" (244). According to Dotson, there are three conditions for a case of testimonial smothering:

(1) the content of the testimony must be unsafe and risky,
(2) the hearer must demonstrate testimonial incompetence with respect to the content of the testimony to the speaker, and
(3) testimonial incompetence must follow from, or appear to follow from, pernicious ignorance (244).

In cases of testimonial smothering, a speaker "smothers" her own testimony due to these factors being met. Regarding the first condition, Dotson defines unsafe and risky testimony as one that "an audience can easily fail to find fully intelligible," running the risk of "leading to the formation of false beliefs that can cause social, political, and/or material harm" (244). Thus, in cases of testimonial smothering, the omitted testimony is unsafe and risks causing negative effects in virtue of being unsafe. Dotson gives the example of women of color's silence around occurrences of domestic violence.[16] There is often a possibility for women of color's testimony about domestic violence to be understood as corroborating the stereotype of the "'violent' black male" (245). The distorted public perception brought about by this stereotype in turn brings about harm to the African American community as a whole. It is because of this harm that testimony about domestic violence by women of color is often unsafe and risky. Further, it is because this testimony is often unsafe and risky that the pressure to remain silent about domestic violence exists for women of color.

To explain the second condition of testimonial smothering, Dotson introduces two terms: "accurate intelligibility" and "testimonial competence." "Accurate intelligibility" refers to the audience's ability to understand the content of a speaker's testimony, as well as their own ability to detect a failure to understand. Thus, a testimony that is accurately intelligible is one that is comprehensible and defeasibly intelligible to the audience. "Testimonial competence" refers to the speaker's positive assessment of an audience's ability to find potential testimony accurately intelligible. Thus, the audience demonstrates testimonial *incompetence* with respect to the content of the speaker's testimony (condition (2)) when they fail to demonstrate accurate intelligibility.[17] To make this condition clear, Dotson uses one of the stories from Cassandra Byers Harvin's article "Conversations I Can't Have."[18] Here Harvin describes an encounter with a white woman who demonstrated a racial microaggression by asking her how raising black sons is any different from raising white sons. The tone in which the woman asked the question indicated that she believed Harvin was "making something out of nothing,"[19] which, in turn, demonstrates that the woman is not equipped to have such conversation. Further, Harvin's encounter also meets condition (3) because the woman's testimonial incompetence seems to follow from pernicious ignorance on her part. The woman is ignorant with respect to racially different experiences of child-rearing in the United States. According to Dotson, the woman's ignorance is pernicious because her differing social situation (e.g., economic, educational, political, and cultural) is what have led her to have a different understanding of the world as one in which the difference at question is nonexistent. Important to Dotson's argument is that if the testimonial exchange were to happen, it would be worse than merely unfruitful due to the audience's ignorance—it would also be harmful.

In summary, Dotson argues that testimonial smothering takes place when there is a failed linguistic exchange in which the content of the potential testimony is unsafe and risky, and the audience demonstrates testimonial incompetence to the speaker grounded in their own pernicious ignorance. With this understanding of testimonial smothering in hand, we turn to examining how such instances of self-silencing are instances of epistemic paternalism, and why they also meet Ahlstrom-Vij's criteria for instances of permissible epistemic paternalism.

SILENCING AS PATERNALISM

When someone self-silences as a result of testimonial smothering, they act in an epistemically paternalistic way toward their audience. Cases of withheld testimony due to testimonial smothering meet all of Ahlstrom-Vij's three conditions for epistemic paternalism. *The interference condition* is met because the speaker affects the audience's inquiry regarding some matter. As outlined earlier, the interference condition can be met by giving or *withholding* information, as is the case when certain types of evidence are withheld from jurors in a trial. In cases of testimonial smothering, the speaker limits her testimony and thus withholds information from the audience, interfering in their inquiry. Since the withheld testimony affects which beliefs the audience would have, the speaker has affected the audience's inquiry.

Plausibly, not every instance of not testifying meets the interference condition.[20] For one's testimony to be *withheld*, there plausibly must be some expectation to receive it or some plan to give it. So, cases where an individual simply doesn't feel like talking might not be cases of epistemic paternalism, but they also are not cases of self-silencing. To be a case of self-silencing, the speaker refrains from saying *what they otherwise would have said*. So, self-silencing is an importantly distinct type of not testifying. Not all cases of evidence *not being given* are cases of evidence being *withheld*. The Federal Rules of Evidence prevent evidence that *otherwise would have been presented* from being heard by the jurors, and cases of self-silencing prevent evidence that *otherwise would have been spoken* from being heard. In each case, the interference condition is met since evidence is withheld—evidence that *would otherwise have been given* is not given.

The non-consultation condition is met since the speaker withholds their testimony without first consulting and receiving the consent of the audience. In cases of testimonial smothering, the speaker makes an evaluation of the audience's conversational fitness and makes this assessment on their own. While this assessment of conversational fitness is informed by how the audience has conducted themselves in conversation, the audience is not also consulted as to whether they could correctly handle the potential testimony. Finally, cases of withholding testimony due to testimonial smothering also meet *the improvement condition*. This condition is met when the speaker withholds their testimony, at least in part, to make the audience epistemically better off. In cases of testimonial smothering, testimony is withheld because it is likely to lead to a false and harmful belief. Recall that for Dotson, testimony is withheld in such cases due to the risk of it "leading to the formation of false beliefs that can cause social, political, and/or material harm" (244).

Recall Dotson's domestic violence example. Dotson claims that self-silencing like this often occurs because of the possibility for it to be understood as corroborating the harmful stereotype of the "violent black male." This makes the aim of the silence primarily about protecting the image of black men rather than about making the audience epistemically better off. Nonetheless, the audience ends up being epistemically better off because the silencing protects them from having, or reinforcing, a false belief. Further, there is a necessary connection to making the audience epistemically better off since that is the avenue by which the image of black men (in this case) is protected. As with the jurors who are likely to misevaluate the evidential import of certain pieces of evidence, the audience in this case is likely to misevaluate the testimony coming from women of color regarding instances of domestic violence. While the epistemic betterment of the audience is not the *primary* goal in such self-silencing, it does still occur, and it is the means by which the primary goal is achieved. So long as the epistemic betterment of the audience is *at least in part* the reason why the speaker withholds her testimony, the third condition of epistemic paternalism is also satisfied.[21]

In addition, when someone self-silences as a result of testimonial smothering, their paternalistic withholding of information is a particularly clear case of permissible epistemic paternalism. Such withholding of testimony meets Ahlstrom-Vij's proposed set of sufficient conditions for an epistemically paternalistic act to be epistemically permissible. Recall, Ahlstrom-Vij claimed that acts of epistemic paternalism are epistemically justified whenever they meet both the alignment condition and the burden-of-proof condition. *The alignment condition* is met in these cases, since in being silent, the speaker's reasons for withholding their testimony do not conflict. In cases of testimonial smothering, the speaker has both epistemic and moral reasons to withhold their testimony. They have epistemic reasons to withhold their testimony because their testimony would bring about a false belief in the audience or raise their confidence in a false proposition. These are epistemically bad outcomes that are being avoided. The speaker also has moral reasons to withhold their testimony. Since the audience's testimonial incompetence is due to pernicious ignorance on their part, the speaker's testimony comes with moral consequences as well. Recall that for Dotson, in cases of testimonial smothering there is a reasonable risk that one's testimony would have led to beliefs that "cause social, political, and/or material harm" (244). So, the harms that are avoided by self-silencing are not merely epistemic harms, there are also possible moral, social, political and material harms to be avoided. In cases of testimonial smothering, these reasons to remain silent all align. There is no need to weigh the epistemic reasons against the moral reasons since all the relevant reasons point in the same direction—to restrict one's testimony.

In cases of testimonial smothering, *the burden-of-proof condition* is also met. In such cases, the speaker is reasonable in believing that the audience would misinterpret or misapply their testimony. According to Dotson's second condition, for an instance of testimonial smothering, the audience must have demonstrated their testimonial incompetence to the speaker with regard to the content of the potential testimony. If the audience has demonstrated such an incompetence, then it will be reasonable for the speaker to believe that the improvement condition is met. Since the audience has demonstrated their incompetence, it is reasonable for the speaker to believe that further testimony would only lead to bad outcomes—that self-silencing would lead to better outcomes (epistemic and moral). These reasons do not *guarantee* that the audience would have misinterpreted or misapplied the testimony, but they do suffice for making the intervention epistemically permissible.

Dotson's domestic violence example is again helpful in making this clear. First, in many cases, the women's non-epistemic reasons to withhold their testimony are not in conflict with their epistemic reasons. Their epistemic reasons to remain silent are to prevent their audience from acquiring or reinforcing a false belief about black males. Women of color often self-silence to prevent the audience from believing the "violent black male" stereotype, or from reinforcing this false belief of theirs. Their non-epistemic reasons to be silent are to avoid further unnecessary harm to their community: harm that would result from reinforcing the black male stereotype. Thus, their epistemic and non-epistemic reasons are not in conflict because they both point toward self-silencing. Second, in many cases, it is reasonable for the women of color to believe that their silencing about occurrences of domestic violence will have the intended epistemic benefits. Given what they know about how people misevaluate the relevant testimonies, it is often reasonable for women of color to believe that their silencing will prevent false beliefs, and thus prevent the reinforcement of the "violent black male" stereotype. This is particularly true when the audience has demonstrated their unfitness for such a conversation. Since such a demonstration is a necessary condition for a case of testimonial smothering, the burden-of-proof condition will be met whenever one self-silences due to testimonial smothering.

CONCLUSION

Recent epistemology has seen a greater attention paid to issues concerning epistemic paternalism and issues concerning epistemic injustice. However, these developing literatures have not yet been brought together. In this chapter, we have shown how a kind of epistemic injustice, self-silencing due to testimonial smothering, offers a vivid case of permissible epistemic paternalism. Such self-silencing clearly meets the criteria for an epistemically paternalistic act, as well as Ahlsrom-Vij's set of sufficient conditions for the permissibility of an epistemically paternalistic act. Further, the epistemic permissibility of such self-silencing is independently plausible. When someone is the victim of epistemic injustice, it is clearly permissible for them to withhold further testimony to those who have demonstrated testimonial incompetence regarding the subject due to their pernicious ignorance. To think otherwise would be to think that individuals are required to provide testimony that will contribute to even more epistemic injustice (as well as non-epistemic injustice) when they are in the midst of experiencing epistemic injustice themselves. Such a requirement is simply not plausible. So, cases of self-silencing due to testimonial smothering help us see the permissibility of some acts of epistemic paternalism.

NOTES

1. Riley (2017) brings insights from the literature on epistemic injustice to debates about paternalism more broadly (and nudging in particular), but insights from epistemic injustice have not yet been brought to bear on debates about epistemic paternalism. However, things are changing. See Green (2020) in this volume and Smith (manuscript).

2. The epistemology of disagreement is relevant here. See Matheson (2015).

3. See Bullock (2016a and 2016b).

4. See Bullock (2016a), Goldman (1991), and Ahlstrom-Vij (2013).

5. So, the interference condition is quite weak and easy to meet. We will return to this issue later.

6. Additional epistemic improvements may come from the subject becoming more reliable (see Ahlstrom-Vij 2013) or developing in epistemic virtue/understanding (see Pritchard 2013).

7. See Pritchard (2013) for more on the connection between epistemic paternalism and epistemic value.

8. See Goldman (1991), 118. As Goldman notes, in the legal case, the defendant is the primary object of protection, but the defendant's protection comes by way of protecting the jurors from their own biases and errors in judgment.

9. In claiming that these conditions are jointly sufficient, Ahlstrom-Vij claims that any time both conditions are met, the act of epistemic paternalism will be permissible, while leaving open that there are other instances of permissible paternalism.

10. For Goldman, the permissibility of an act of epistemic paternalism is a matter of the veritistic outcomes. Goldman lists the following factors as relevant to the epistemic outcomes of a case of epistemic paternalism: "A number of variables are relevant, especially: (1) the characteristics of the controller (or 'gatekeeper'), (2) the characteristics of the speakers who wish to send messages via the communication

channel, (3) the controller's criterion of selection among speakers or messages, (4) the characteristics of the audience, and (5) the availability of alternate channels that address the same topic" (124).

11. See Collins (2008), Fricker (2007), Medina (2012), Mills (1997), Pohlhaus Jr. (2012), Toole (2019), and Wylie (2003) for some examples.

12. More recently, Gerken (2019) persuasively argues that epistemic injustice is better captured by a broader account. According to Gerken, epistemic injustice occurs when someone is harmed as an epistemic subject. Since there are ways to be harmed as an epistemic subject that do not involve knowledge, Gerken's account is more inclusive and does better at capturing the intended phenomenon.

13. Medina (2011) and Lackey (2018) forcefully argue that credibility excesses also lead to epistemic injustice.

14. Dotson uses the term "epistemic violence" instead of "epistemic injustice." However, the way in which she defines and uses the concept bear similarities to Fricker's broad account of epistemic injustice.

15. *Reliable ignorance* here refers to ignorance that is consistent or follows from a predictable epistemic gap in cognitive resources. This kind of ignorance need not be harmful. Reliable ignorance may be benign in one epistemic agent while being pernicious in another. Dotson argues that whether the ignorance is pernicious depends on the context, where the social location and power level of the agents is relevant. She argues that pernicious ignorance should be determined according to the ways that the ignorance causes or contributes to harmful practices of silencing such as testimonial smothering.

16. Dotson takes this example from Kimberlé Crenshaw (1991).

17. Note here that the speaker's assessment of her audience's testimonial competence is not contingent upon the audience's *actual* ability to find the speaker's testimony accurately intelligible. It depends only on whether the audience gives the appearance of being able to find the testimony accurately intelligible (whether this is the case or not).

18. See Harvin (1996).

19. Harvin (1996), 16.

20. Thanks to Amiel Bernal for raising this point.

21. This point is also made by Ahlstrom-Vij (2018: 264).

BIBLIOGRAPHY

Ahlstrom-Vij, Kristoffer. *Epistemic Paternalism: A Defence*. Basingstoke: Palgrave Macmillan, 2013.

Ahlstrom-Vij, Kristoffer. "Epistemic Paternalism," in K. Grill and J. Hanna (eds.) *The Routledge Handbook of the Philosophy of Paternalism*, 261–274. New York: Routledge, 2018.

Bullock, Emma. "Knowing and Not Knowing for Your Own Good: The Limits of Epistemic Paternalism." *Journal of Applied Philosophy* 35(2) (2016a): 433–447.

Bullock, Emma. "Mandatory Disclosure and Medical Paternalism." *Ethical Theory and Moral Practice* 19(2) (2016b): 409–424. DOI 10.1007/s10677-015-9632-2

Collins, Patricia Hill. *Black Feminist Thought: Knowledge, Consciousness, and the Politics of Empowerment*. New York: Routledge, 2008.
Crenshaw, Kimberlé. "Mapping the Margins: Intersectionality, Identity Politics, and Violence against Women of Color." *Stanford Law Review* 43 (1991): 1241–1299.
Dotson, Kristie. "Tracking Epistemic Violence, Tracking Practices of Silencing." *Hypatia* 26(2) (2011): 236–257.
Dotson, Kristie. "Conceptualizing Epistemic Oppression." *Social Epistemology* 28(2) (2014): 115–138.
Fricker, Miranda. *Epistemic Injustice: Power and the Ethics of Knowing*. Oxford: Oxford University Press, 2007.
Gerken, Mikkel. "Pragmatic Encroachment and the Challenge from Epistemic Injustice." *Philosopher's Imprint*, 19(15) (2019): 1–19.
Goldman, Alvin. "Epistemic Paternalism: Communication Control in Law and Society." *Journal of Philosophy* 88(3) (1991): 113–131.
Green, Adam. "Paternalism and Epistemic (Non-)Violence," in A. Bernal and G. Axtell (eds.) *Epistemic Paternalism Reconsidered: Conceptions, Justifications and Implications*. Lanham, MD: Rowman & Littlefield, 2020.
Harvin, Cassandra Byers. "Conversations I Can't Have." *On the Issues: The Progressive Woman's Quarterly* 5(2) (1996): 15–16.
Hornsby, Jennifer. "Disempowered Speech." *Philosophical Topics* 23(2) (1995): 127–147.
Lackey, Jennifer. "Credibility and the Distribution of Epistemic Goods," in K. McCain (ed.) *Believing in Accordance with the Evidence*, 145–168. New York: Springer, 2018.
Matheson, Jonathan. *The Epistemic Significance of Disagreement*. London: Palgrave, 2015.
Medina, José. "The Relevance of Credibility Excess in a Proportional View of Epistemic Injustice: Differential Epistemic Authority and the Social Imaginary." *Social Epistemology* 25 (2011): 15–35.
Medina, José. "Hermeneutical Injustice: Social Silences and Shared Hermeneutical Responsibilities." *Social Epistemology* 26(2) (2012): 201–220.
Mills, Charles. *The Racial Contract*. Ithaca, NY: Cornell University Press, 1997.
Pohlhaus Jr., Gaile. Relational Knowing and Epistemic Injustice: Toward a Theory of Willful Hermeneutical Ignorance." *Hypatia* 27(4) (2012): 715–735.
Pritchard, Duncan. "Epistemic Paternalism and Epistemic Value." *Philosophical Inquiries* 1(2) (2013): 9–37.
Riley, Evan. "The Beneficent Nudge Program and Epistemic Injustice." *Ethical Theory and Moral Practice* 20 (2017): 597–616.
Smith, Leoni. "Epistemic Nudging and Paternalism: the Permissibility of Epistemic Interventions in Preventing Epistemic Injustice," manuscript.
Toole, Briana. "From Standpoint Epistemology to Epistemic Oppression." *Hypatia: A Journal of Feminist Philosophy*, 34(4) (2019): 598–619.
Wylie, Alison. "Why Standpoint Matters," in Robert Figueroa and Sandra G. Harding (eds.) *Science and Other Cultures: Diversity in the Philosophy of Science and Technology*. New York: Routledge, 2003.

Chapter 15

Epistemic Paternalism as Epistemic Justice

Amiel Bernal

The central wrong of epistemic injustice is epistemic objectification. Epistemic objectification arises when people are disrespected or treated unfairly as knowers, due to stereotyping or structural gaps in collective understanding, respectively (Fricker 2007). Interference in another's inquiry suggests a failure of respect for that individual's intellectual faculties or decision-procedure. As such, there is a prima facie tension between epistemic paternalism and achieving epistemic justice. If epistemic justice requires appropriate respect for individuals as knowers, or fair conditions of inquiry, interfering with an agent's inquiry may be a form of epistemic injustice. To date, the literature connecting epistemic paternalism to epistemic justice is couched in terms of the *distribution* of epistemic goods, such as knowledge (Coady 2010; Medvecky 2018). In keeping with Miranda Fricker's (2007, 2013) conceptualization of epistemic injustice, this chapter returns the analysis of epistemic injustice to considerations of respect for epistemic agents, rather than the distribution of epistemic goods.[1] To resolve the apparent tension between epistemic paternalism and epistemic justice, I argue that epistemic paternalism can be a form of epistemic justice insofar as applications of epistemic paternalism respect persons as actual knowers, facilitate their epistemic capacities, and ameliorate epistemic injustice. By interfering in the conditions of inquiry, agents can benefit from moral and epistemic improvements, thereby supporting the foundations of our normative significance.

This chapter will proceed as follows. First, epistemic paternalism is defined, and its justificatory conditions are presented. To avoid redundancy, this section will be brief. Second, exegesis of Fricker's work shows that harm is only a secondary consideration; disrespect and unfair conditions are the primary wrongs of epistemic injustice. Recognizing this motivates the tension between epistemic paternalism and epistemic justice, developed in the third section. I argue that epistemic paternalism is compatible with epistemic justice. I show this by invoking the distinction between ideal and non-ideal theory. While Fricker's deontological commitments suggest ideal theory, the nature of social epistemology and the possibility of epistemic injustice presuppose non-ideal theory. As such, the questions of epistemic paternalism and epistemic in/justice must be assessed in accord with non-ideal theory. The ostensive tension between epistemic paternalism and epistemic justice dissolves once we recognize this distinction. With this distinction in place, the penultimate section develops two examples of epistemic paternalism as epistemic justice. Indeed, in some special cases, epistemic paternalism amounts to a form of restorative epistemic justice.

EPISTEMIC PATERNALISM, CONDITIONS, AND JUSTIFICATIONS

Epistemic paternalism is characterized by three jointly sufficient conditions: (1) interference in the inquiry of another (2) without their consultation or consent (3) with the intended purpose of epistemically improving the subject of interference (Ahlstrom-Vij 2013).

Interference can follow active or passive strategies. Active interference changes content, or who is presenting that information. Passive strategies include withholding pertinent information and changing background conditions to motivate "nudges." To constitute withholding of evidence in keeping with interference, the information must be *pertinent*. It would be absurd to imply that any withholding of information is interference. Determining pertinence is a contextual matter, but there are a number of features characteristic of pertinent information. Information is clearly pertinent if it would play a decisive role in the inquiry. Weaker still, it may merely prove relevant to the inquiry to count as pertinent.

Second, it is necessary that the subject is not consulted about the interference or does not consent to interference in their inquiry. This condition may arise by not informing someone of an intended application of interference strategies. It may also occur if the other party asks for non-interference, but you do so anyway. It is not paternalistic to withhold information from a person if they asked for that information to be withheld. Likewise, it is not interference if you are asked to passively interfere.

Third, epistemic improvement of the agent must be an objective of the interferer's epistemic intervention. The interferer intends to realize some greater epistemic values in the interfered upon. Successful improvement need not occur. A bumbling parent is still paternalistic even if they fail to improve their child as they intended. Likewise, a teacher can be epistemically paternalistic by framing content to improve student understanding (without consultation), irrespective of whether the student benefits epistemically.

The two prevailing standards of improvement are consequentialist or virtue theoretic. The veritistic view is a quintessential form of epistemic consequentialism. Veritism holds that, all things being equal, an increase in true beliefs is good (Goldman 1999). As such, "epistemic improvement" directly correlates with an increase in the number of true beliefs held by either an individual or population. Alternatively, a virtue-theoretic reliabilist identifies epistemic improvement with an agent's propensity to draw justified true inferences, or otherwise hone their intellectual abilities. Improvements regard the agent's epistemic reliability (Greco 1999). On a reliabilist view, one can enjoy epistemic improvements without increasing the quantity of true beliefs they possess. If their inference procedure improves, for example, epistemic improvement occurs. Identifying a characteristic form of error (e.g., prejudicial bias) constitutes epistemic improvement insofar as the person is thereafter less prone to commit the same mistake. Being a less prejudiced recipient of testimony constitutes improvement of an intellectual character trait, even if no new true beliefs result from this change. Of course, this improvement will tend to make the recipient more reliable in their assessment of testimony and thereby more likely to hold true beliefs.

I will opt for the reliability standard here. This is a higher standard. It is more valuable to become the sort of person who reliably makes sound inferences than it is to gain another true belief. It is also the case that the reliable epistemic agent is more likely to hold and promote justified true belief. Further, this standard more fundamentally regards the cognitive/epistemic features of agents, rather than what they believe at a given time. As will be shown, this focus better corresponds to the relevant concerns of Fricker, regarding conditions of respect and fairness for epistemic agents.

To review, if the *interference, non-consultation*, and *improvement* conditions are met, then epistemic paternalism occurs. Justifying institutional or personal engagement in epistemic paternalism is a separate matter.

Ahlstrom-Vij stipulates two normative conditions for justified applications of epistemic paternalism. First, the *alignment condition* stipulates that the epistemic values realized by engaging in epistemic paternalism align with non-epistemic considerations. As such, epistemic improvement cannot justifiably come at the expense of moral or prudential values. My interference in another's inquiry is unjustified if I make them or the world worse-off. Epistemic paternalism is unjustified if it comes at the price of morality. This resolves normative tensions between epistemic and moral considerations in favor of moral considerations. Moral considerations are *defeater*s, overriding epistemic improvement. This motivates the second justificatory condition.

Second, justification of a paternalistic intervention requires that the burden-of-proof condition is met. Ahlstrom-Vij states that the burden-of-proof condition is met when "our evidence suggests that it is highly likely that the relevant proportion benefits" (2013: 120). Here "proportion" refers to the ratio of a population which is epistemically improved. It must be the case that most people interfered with are highly likely to epistemically benefit. This burden-of-proof requires would-be paternalists to know relevant empirical literature on effective interventions to assess the likelihood of improvement. Rather than relying on subjective appraisals, Ahlstrom-Vij opts for "statistical probabilities of the kind typically provided by way of scientific studies about human behavior from the fields of social and cognitive psychology" (2013: 121). So, the burden-of-proof condition requires that a would-be paternalist has good reason to believe that the person(s) in question will benefit from interference. Therefore, there is a responsibility to know relevant social psychology and effective pedagogy. We ought to know, in scientific terms, what sort of interventions work on our respective target individual or population in order to be justified in engaging in epistemic paternalism. By setting the standards of justified epistemic paternalism in this way, Ahlstrom-Vij avoids two standard objections.

First, there is a generic concern that interference will be *counterproductive*. Interference will do more harm than good. The alignment-condition and burden-of-proof condition jointly avoid this problem. The alignment-condition establishes that epistemic paternalism is unjustified if the interfered upon is worse off. Ahlstrom-Vij opts for an epistemic Pareto-improvement standard demanding "an improvement along one epistemic dimension (such as reliability) that does not entail a deterioration with respect to any other epistemic dimension (for example, question-answering power)" (53). Epistemic paternalism cannot come at the expense of greater goods or other people's epistemic faculties, as per the alignment condition.

Why should we believe that stipulation of the alignment condition protects against excessive interference? To assert the problem: an analytic definition does not entail successful application of paternalistic intervention. This leads to a second problem. Namely, that people will believe that they have met the two justificatory conditions due to cultural or cognitive bias. J. S. Mill worried that the standard of assessment for paternalistic interference would be public opinion resulting from power dynamics. Anticipating Marx, Mill states, "In any country that has a dominant class, a large portion of the morality of *the country* emanates from *that class*" (4). People are prone to impose their own cultural and personal biases when interfering. Generally speaking, imposing personal or cultural norms has a weak coincidence with epistemic improvement. In our case, the concern is that people's conception of achieving the alignment-condition is acculturated, rather than based on epistemically robust factors. These genealogical considerations regarding the origin of people's beliefs regarding the two justificatory conditions provide reasons to doubt that paternalists can reliably achieve the alignment and burden-of-proof conditions. The origins of their "common" beliefs reflect dominant views, not the most justified views.

But, the burden-proof condition requires the interferer to understand relevant empirical content to ensure effective interventions. It is not enough to know what most people believe, and that one person disagrees. One must also have good reason to expect their interference to be efficacious for that person, and that their methods (or beliefs) are well justified, without coming at any comparable cost. The would-be paternalist does not meet the burden-of-proof condition if they invoke only dominant opinion. Of course, people may still err in their judgments, but these conditions forestall the theoretical objections to epistemic paternalism. One could offer a slippery-slope argument, maintaining that the justifying paternalistic interference lowers the standards of future interference, such that unjustified interventions become socially permissible.

Two related points undermine this concern. First, this slippery-slope worry applies to any inter-personal or social interference. So, a detractor of paternalistic interference must motivate why epistemic paternalism is uniquely worrisome. Teachers, among many others, are frequently epistemically paternalistic without serious moral hazard. Any applied ethicist could be criticized on these grounds. There is no *special* problem with epistemic paternalism, so far as I can tell. Second, the anti-paternalist must show why, despite meeting all of the descriptive and normative conditions mentioned earlier, we would have good reason to expect epistemic paternalists to devolve to unjustified interference despite ostensibly meeting the two normative conditions. Justificatory conditions provide some extra assurances against abuses of epistemic paternalists. While rank abuse of epistemic paternalism is still possible, the special concern directed toward it seems unwarranted. I briefly review these concerns, and explain why they are being considered at all, before considering objections to epistemic paternalism motivated by deontological considerations of respect for people as knowers.

Note that both of these objections are consequentialist. The worries are either that people will be harmed by interference (due to ignorance, bias or acculturation), or that justifying paternalistic interventions in some circumstances will lead to further unjustified interventions. I hope to have shown that neither problem is compelling. Ultimately, there is empirical uncertainty. Whether these objections obtain depends on specific choices and reactions. Nonetheless, erring in the implementation of justice (or epistemic paternalism) does not show that attempts to implement justice are inherently problematic, or that the concept of justice is itself problematic. The next objection

I motivate is not contingent in this way. Rather, the deontic focus of Fricker motivates a concern that, irrespective of the harms or distribution of epistemic goods, epistemic paternalism is objectifying. So, even if agents are more reliable after interference, there may be an intractable element of unfairness or disrespect in any instantiation of epistemic paternalism. Rebutting these consequentialist objections thereby directs us to another problem that cannot be resolved to likely outcomes. Ultimately, this worry will be resolved by recognizing a difference in theoretical frameworks; the standards of fairness and respect found in ideal theory are inappropriate for the purposes of social epistemology and considerations of epistemic in/justice.

A brief exegesis of Miranda Fricker's work on epistemic injustice will develop the case for a non-consequentialist reading of epistemic in/justice, which focuses on proper respect, and fair conditions for persons as epistemic agents. This reading, in turn, motivates the tension between epistemic justice and epistemic paternalism. The ostensive tension will be resolved in the final section.

EPISTEMIC INJUSTICE: FROM OBJECTIFICATION TO DISRESPECT AND UNFAIRNESS

The conclusion of this section is that the bad-making features of Fricker's two types of epistemic injustice are the disrespect and unfairness entailed in testimonial injustice, and hermeneutical injustice, respectively. While Fricker's (2007) work has a large secondary literature, few of these developments emphasize the non-consequentialist bent of her thesis. To develop this case, I present each type of epistemic injustice, then analyze their distinctive bad-making features. The theoretical and methodological advantages of moving from "objectification" to unfairness and disrespect are developed afterward.

Testimonial injustices are prejudicial credibility deficits. They occur when a speaker is granted less intellectual authority than they deserve due to the listener's prejudicial stereotyping. As a result, the speaker is wrongfully under-credited as an epistemic authority, in a communicative exchange. For example, if a man disregards the testimony of a woman, just because she is "an emotional woman," this is a testimonial injustice. Most characteristically, the social salience of these prejudicial stereotypes results in the persistence of testimonial injustice across contexts. These sorts of stereotyping are more harmful because of their prevalence and recurrence. Nonetheless, these harms are not the primary wrong of epistemic injustice.

Fricker maintains that testimonial injustices are epistemic injustices just because they disparage a central feature of our status as people; that is, our capacity as knowers. As Fricker laments, "To be wronged as a knower is to be wronged in one's capacity essential to human value" (44). It is for this reason that Fricker differentiates between primary and secondary harms. To be disrespected as a knower is to be degraded as a person, irrespective of tangible costs or benefits. Fricker denotes the primary harm of testimonial injustice of "epistemic objectification." Invoking Kantian language, she writes, "It wrongfully deprives the subject of a certain fundamental sort of respect . . . this deprivation [is] also a form of *objectification*" (132).[2] The primary wrong is not a matter of consequentialist considerations. Instead, it follows a deontic reasoning. One errs to testimonial justice if they assess others as mere bodies whose gender, for example, dictates their epistemic abilities.

Secondary harms are the practical and epistemic effects of an epistemic injustice. So, in the above case of testimonial injustice, the primary wrong is objectification of the speaker as person qua epistemic agent. The secondary harms the adverse personal effects, including the epistemic harms. For example, the speaker may become more reticent to share her testimony after being flatly and repeatedly rejected. This harms her capacity as a sharer of information. This is just one dimension of her epistemic agency. Without the venues or practice to communicate one's experience, gaps in collective understanding may arise.[3] This leads to Fricker's second form of epistemic injustice.

Hermeneutical injustices occur when collective gaps in understanding and a lack of communicative resources inhibit one's understanding of their experience, or their ability to convey their experience to others intelligibly.[4] These conditions place the marginalized knower in an undeserved disadvantaged position. They lack useful interpretative resources, or the ability to influence which terms are collectively understood, or the conditions necessary to be understood. As Fricker (2016) states, "Hermeneutical marginalization will manifest itself in the unfair deficit of intelligibility that constitutes a hermeneutical injustice" (164). These hermeneutical lacunas are due to socio-epistemic processes involving the sharing and uptake of concepts. Asymmetries in power and privilege dictate which conceptual resources are circulated and collectively adopted.[5] For example, someone afflicted by combat-induced post-traumatic stress disorder (PTSD) may have difficulty negotiating these experiences without the appropriate vocabulary and understanding. The competing conceptions of a shellshock, battle fatigue, cowardice, and PTSD lead to different self-understandings and qualitative outcomes. The low-ranking enlisted soldier is in no position to influence military or medical doctrine on this subject, and so they are relatively powerless to inform collective understanding regarding combat trauma. This deficit in available hermeneutic resources undermines the soldiers' ability to understand their experience. This may lead them to interpret their ongoing trauma as cowardice, rather than a treatable medical condition. So, the hermeneutical injustice arises when "the subject is rendered unable to make communicatively intelligible something which it is particularly in his or her interests to be able to render intelligible" (2007: 162). The unintelligibility may be a matter of self-understanding, or others not understanding one's claims due to their unfamiliarity with the concepts invoked. Hermeneutical injustice is the situated unfair asymmetry in resources needed to understand oneself or needed for others to understand the person's experience.

The distinctly epistemic dimension of an epistemic injustice regards our capacities as epistemic agents, and the conditions pertaining to the development of that central capacity. The conditions that are pertinent to testimonial injustices are the credibility assessments of others, and prevailing stereotypes. In the case of hermeneutical injustice, it is socio-epistemic conditions that dictate whether one's testimony or experiences will be intelligible.[6] It is not merely a loss of net true beliefs circulated but "exclusion from the pooling of knowledge" (162). We are less able to exercise our capacities as epistemic agents and be recognized as such. Structural unfairness produces hermeneutical injustice, and a type of interpersonal disrespect constitutes testimonial injustice.

While disrespect implies intentionality, unfairness does not. Structural conditions can unfairly limit one's ability to understand or explain their experiences without any individual being disrespectful. Yet, both unfairness and disrespect are agent-centered considerations. They regard individual worth and desert, rather than an assessment of abstracted quantities of goods, epistemic or moral. This point will be central to recognizing the tension between epistemic justice and epistemic paternalism.

Before turning to this tension, I offer further methodological reasons for interpreting "objectification" as disrespect and unfairness. First, objectification is a "relatively loose cluster-term" (Nussbaum 1994: 258). Some forms of objectification lack a negative moral valence. As Nussbaum distinguishes, instrumentalization of another person may be permissible, if their subjectivity and autonomy are respected. As Nussbaum reminds us, "[objectification] could be a wonderful part of sexual life" (274). Unfairness and disrespect have negative denotation capturing what is problematic about objectification. They explain its bad-making features in basic terms. Second, using conceptions of respect and fairness allows the useful comparison between and moral/political philosophy and normative social epistemology, which will be our focus in the final sections of the chapter. This comparison demonstrates relevant differences between the two aforementioned types of theory, ideal and non-ideal.

THE APPARENT TENSION BETWEEN EPISTEMIC JUSTICE AND EPISTEMIC PATERNALISM

Engaging in epistemic paternalism suggests epistemic superiority. Someone engages in paternalism because they believe they know better, or they believe they know the conditions, which are in the epistemic interests of the inquirer. The burden-of-proof condition implies epistemic superiority, both regarding the relevant truth-claims and appropriate means of interference. Choosing to forgo consultation indicates that the matter is too important for the inquirer to determine for themselves or that their current faculties will not lead them rightly. This superiority is characteristic of *disrespect,* consistent with Fricker's conception of testimonial injustice. If epistemic paternalism is disrespectful or unfair to persons as knowers, it is epistemically unjust. The primary wrong of epistemic injustice seems to arise in cases of epistemic paternalism, as the interfered-upon is "objectified." Their agency seems to be disrespected, even if the intervention does not come at any greater costs and is likely to be successful. To put the point differently, this line of deontic reasoning holds that epistemic paternalism precludes the possibility of satisfying the alignment condition just because non-consultation is inherently disrespectful. Instead, the paternalist determines what ends are most appropriate, and that move subordinates the other party's epistemic faculties to match what the paternalist expects. This "derivatizes" the uninformed party, as they become a means in the ends of the epistemic paternalist (Pohlhaus 2014: 105). Even when they interfered-upon benefits, their faculties are used for the paternalist's goals. The paternalist does not respect the other party's current actual autonomy or epistemic abilities. Next, I show how epistemic paternalism might be considered *unfair* for the same reasons hermeneutical injustice is unfair.

Manipulating conditions without the inquirer's consent risks interpersonal unfairness. A person is in a position of relative epistemic powerlessness if another person is interfering in their inquiry without consent. The inquirer is placed in modified conditions of inquiry without having any means to assess whether the conditions are in their interest. Much like hermeneutical injustice, they are deprived of influence over their own understanding when subjected to epistemic paternalism. Notice that all epistemic paternalism inherently precludes this possibility of symmetrical influence, as a necessary condition of epistemic paternalism is that the relevant party is not consulted or consenting. As such, these agents or inhibited from using their intellectual abilities to determine what constitutes their epistemic interests.

Contrast this with Rawls's (1999) conception of pure procedural justice, in the case of dividing a pie (75). The division of pie is fair just if one person cuts the pie once and the other can choose either piece. Both parties understand this procedure in advance. Either party can cut the pie, and both know that the other party gets priority picking if they cut the pie. Because each party knows the initial procedure and has symmetrical (if not the same) influence over outcomes, it is fair, for Rawls.

One might object that Rawls's pure procedural justice regards the *distribution* of goods, and this chapter focuses on non-distributive objections to epistemic paternalism. Yet, this procedure underpins a "respect for persons" as evidenced by their equal bargaining power, knowledge and influence (Rawls 455). The basis for determining a "fair" distribution is the presumed moral equality of agents. (I will return to this point later to show a relevant difference between moral philosophy and normative social epistemology.)

To extend the pie-cutting analogy to paternalism, a procedure employed by a pie-paternalist would involve cutting the pie without consulting the other party and giving them the piece deemed best for them. This asymmetry in influence and knowledge of the procedure seems unfair, following Rawls's reasoning, irrespective of the actual quantity of pie received by either party. This is for purely structural, procedural reasons. I will not belabor applying this to epistemic paternalism explicitly, as this is an objection to the practice *in principle*, rather than outcome-oriented objection. Apart from the empirical results of any given intervention, there is a prima facie case that epistemic paternalism is *unfair* and *disrespectful* to persons as knowers. This is the essence of epistemic injustice.

RESOLVING THE TENSION: IDEAL THEORY AND NON-IDEAL THEORY

Successfully resolving the tension between epistemic paternalism and epistemic justice requires showing why the basis of appraisal used in moral theory and political philosophy is inappropriate for normative social epistemology. The distinction between ideal and non-ideal theory is instrumental to this end. Rawls's work will be taken as one illustrative example of ideal theory, though the key assumption of *moral equality* is common to nearly all moral philosophy after Plato. The standards of fairness and respect in contexts of epistemic in/justice must be based on relevant information about the parties involved, unlike in Rawls's Original Position.

To distinguish ideal from non-ideal theory, I will use Valentini's (2012) differentiation of (i) full compliance vs. partial compliance theory; (ii) utopian vs. realistic theory; and (iii) end-state vs. transitional theory. The former of each pair is characteristic of ideal theory. For Rawls, people's conduct and attitudes conform to the principles of justice, and the basic institutions of society are just. As such, it is a full compliance and end-state theory.[7] There is little need for amelioration of injustice, merely the perpetuation of justice.[8] Agents recognize the contingencies inherent in the birth-lottery, and so endorse a procedure, which deprives them of knowledge about their actual social situation when deciding how to distribute the benefits and burdens of society. This is the veil of ignorance. Rawlsian agents are fair-minded. Symmetrical influence in bargaining during the original position follows from the moral equality of persons. This is fair because asymmetrical influence in our actual world is overwhelmingly due to morally irrelevant factors, such as the wealth of one's parents, and other forms of natural fortune.

The principles of justice generated in this initial idealized situation serve the role of regulative ideals by which current conditions are assessed. Rawls writes, "Existing institutions are to be judged in the light of this conception and held to be unjust to the extent that they depart from it without sufficient reason" (246). Idealized agents generate an ideal of justice and use it to assess actual institutions. It is a top-down approach.[9]

By contrast, non-ideal theory accounts for partial compliance to agreed-upon norms (e.g., the principles of justice), and when social institutions are unjust. Non-ideal theory is transitional as it serves to redress these problems. *In the context of social epistemology, non-ideal theory is much more apt*. This claim follows from three considerations. These are: (1) the nature of social epistemology; (2) considerations about the types of injustice addressed within normative social epistemology; (3) the epistemic characteristics of our current basic institutions. Each will be considered in order of mention.

Broadly, "social epistemology" regards the study of how knowledge is collectively generated and justified. From this perspective, we must recognize that actual people do not reliably conform to the ideals of justified inference and testimonial assessment. People inherit beliefs from their parents and culture. People are not fully compliant with norms of justified inference, from the perspective of ideal epistemology of either the empiricist or rationalist traditions. For example, provision of counterevidence to one's beliefs often reinforces that belief in a process called "cognitive immunization" (Kube et al. 2019). In general, there are vast literatures on human irrationality (e.g., Ariely 2008; and Sunstein and Thaler 2008). Indeed, much of this volume is motivated by such considerations. So, social epistemology studies *partial compliance*. Within this context, people sometimes culpably err. Epistemic injustices are predictable forms of error.

Testimonial injustice presupposes non-ideal theory, insofar as agents err in their inferences due to unwarranted credibility attributions. They do not apportion their belief to available evidence. Instead, they rely on heuristics of prejudice and convenience. Notice that possibility of testimonial injustice presupposes epistemic non-ideal theory. The person committing testimonial injustice is engaging in an *epistemic* and *moral* mistake. They are partially compliant with norms of inference and of respectful treatment of others. Likewise, hermeneutical injustice entails conditions, which favor the understandings of others, merely due to power asymmetries. In an idealized (e.g., Cartesian) epistemology, such factors are to be disregarded or controlled-out entirely. Yet, any ameliorative strategy for epistemic justice must address these actual conditions.

Finally, current social institutions are not epistemically directed. Misinformation is a common strategy of persuasion and manipulation among corporate and governmental institutions. Profit-motives have led major distributors of information, such as Facebook and Google, to prioritize advertisement income over epistemic considerations. For citizens of the twenty-first century, this point is too obvious to belabor.

So, the question of epistemic paternalism only applies to our actual world as part of a non-ideal social epistemic theory. The assumption of equality is an axiomatic commitment of moral and political philosophy that is ill-suited for social-epistemic interactions. While social location, natural intellect, and educational opportunity are morally irrelevant, *they are obviously epistemically relevant*. One's epistemic agency is contingent on facts about the relevant parties. Epistemic agency is not fully and spontaneously exhibited by persons. Rather, it is developed and cultivated socially. These considerations put pressure on the assumption that fairness and respect entail an equality of treatment and influence. In this world, the normative assumption of epistemic equality and the normative expectation of symmetrical influence are unwarranted. Realizing epistemic justice, as a form of normative social epistemology, requires a bottom-up approach. Ensconced in a world full of actual people and institutions requires this. To demonstrate this point, I offer two cases of epistemic paternalism that are epistemically just insofar as they serve to prevent further epistemic injustice, and as they share a proper respect and fair treatment for the interfered-upon.

Cases of Epistemic Paternalism as Epistemic Justice in Non-Ideal Theory

First, consider a case of two friends. Alex recognizes that her friend Steve engages in a pattern of testimonial injustice. Steve is prone to dismiss the testimony of women and minorities in STEM fields. Steve was raised in a prejudicial household in which "Affirmative Action" was used as a rationale for the success of any minority. Alex, recognizing this unfortunate circumstance, makes a point of exposing Steve to evidence, which will help redress his prejudice. Alex watches videos of leading scientists of color when she is around Steve. By not foisting these videos on Steve, Alex hopes to draw

Steve's interest. Alex does not consult Steve, manipulates conditions of inquiry, and is motivated by the justified belief that Steve will become less prejudiced with increased exposure to different peoples who exemplify their expertise and epistemic merit in the sciences.

Insofar as this remediation eliminates a Steve's testimonial injustice, it constitutes a case of epistemic paternalism as epistemic justice. Steve is not coerced, or otherwise disrespected. He is not put in unfairly disadvantaged epistemic context. Yet, there is something manipulative about Alex's strategy. She is tactically using her knowledge about Steve's background and natural curiosity to make him epistemically better off. Steve is now less likely to commit testimonial injustice.

Second, consider the case of a veteran Marine who served multiple tours during the occupation of Afghanistan by the United States. Ensconced in masculinist warrior-culture, symptoms of combat induced post-traumatic stress are dismissed as "just part of the job." Worse yet, military institutions discourage seeking the help of a clinical psychologist as doing so risks future promotion and medical discharge from enlistment. Mental healthcare is merely evidence of mental infirmity, as "some people can't hack it." This scenario is characteristic of hermeneutical injustice, as discussed earlier. The Marine is placed in a position of relative powerlessness regarding how to interpret their experience in a way that is likely detrimental to them. They are epistemically marginalized. In this context, a friend discreetly places a pamphlet for veteran-group therapy in the Marine's line of sight, at home. Or, they may share posts with the Marine on social media, to encourage them to interpret their post-combat symptoms as a treatable and common result of war. Again, this is characteristic of epistemic paternalism. The friend is intervening to fill a gap in interpretive resources, so that the Marine may better understand their experience, and better realize their agency (epistemically and in general). The Marine is not consulted, as he would almost certainly dismiss such efforts as emasculating. Yet this passive epistemic paternalism is empowers the Marine to better cope, and to better understand their own experience (e.g., that they are not blame-worthy for their PTSD).

These cases do not smack of unfairness or disrespect. They are remediations of conditions that were unfair or disrespectful to people as knowers. In the first case, Alex redresses Steve's childhood exposure to white-supremacist ideology before they are able to critically think for themselves. In the second case, toxic echo chamber of the American military culture regarding mental healthcare is countered to enable the Marine to better flourish, epistemically and otherwise. These interventions are poised to positively contribute to epistemic agency of persons. Steve will be able to assess testimony more reliably, while the Marine will have the additional conceptual resources instrumental in their readjustment to civilian life.

A FINAL ANALYSIS

The upshots of this account are numerous. Considerations of epistemic paternalism account for the frailty and contingency of our epistemic faculties, placing the practice of epistemic paternalism within the framework of non-ideal theory. From this theoretical perspective, we can recognize the asymmetries and knowledge and influence, which undermine persons' capacities as epistemic agents and try to remediate problematic conditions. Yet, this account does not give a categorical answer to the question of whether epistemic paternalism is justified. It depends. This requires a contextualist view; we are not working with axiomatic assumptions about individuals' faculties, adherence to norms of inference, or rationality. We cannot presuppose that some set doctrine is adequate. Finally, this account shows that epistemic paternalism might serve to remediate the most widely recognized and characteristic forms of epistemic injustice. So, Fricker's deontic commitments must be attenuated to the foibles of actual agents. There is no inherent tension between epistemic justice and epistemic paternalism. Our duties to actual people are clearly different than our duties to idealized agents.

NOTES

1. A limitation of this approach is that mentions of "epistemic paternalism" will almost exclusively consider interpersonal cases, rather than institutional or structural varieties of epistemic paternalism.

2. Pohlhaus (2014) persuasively maintains that this process is better understood as "derivative subjectification." The epistemic injustice which occurs is not merely one in which a person is being read like an object, such as a thermometer. Instead, the person who engages in testimonial injustice expects her interlocutors to adhere to their preexisting (racialized, sexist, classist, etc.) worldview. The person committing testimonial injustice recognizes the other as an epistemic agent, but she expects that other to present views which correspond to her expectations. In either case, the problem is one of respect for others as epistemic agents, and thus their personhood. I will use "objectification" for simplicity, despite the more apt "derivative subjectification." For our purposes, this semantic difference is inconsequential, as *disrespect* is the central concern.

3. Fricker (2007) illustrates this with the case of "sexual harassment" as a term that lacked social salience and circulation due to women's recurring experience of testimonial injustice regarded unwanted workplace advances (149–151).

4. This raises a question of hermeneutical desert, implying that people *deserve* to be able to understand and be understood. This point has not been addressed in the literature.

5. Dotson (2011) and Medina (2012) note that there are numerous epistemic communities such that a hermeneutical resources may be full hermeneutical resources may be fully intelligible in one social context, while remaining unintelligible in general, or in dominant public narratives.

6. Of course, there are many culpable forms of interpersonal injustice which produce the structural hermeneutical disadvantages characteristic of hermeneutical injustice. For two examples, see Dotson's (2012) contributory injustice and Pohlhaus's (2012) willful hermeneutical ignorance.

7. Of course, the Original Position is an initial procedure and not an end-state. Yet after development of the initial procedure, Rawls engages in end-state theorizing as institutions and peoples are basically just.

8. See Sandel's (1982) critique of Rawls's for being problematically utopian.

9. Rawls recognizes that actual agents may not be so rational and well informed. He asserts that "principles of paternalism are those that the parties would acknowledge in the original position to protect themselves against the weakness and infirmities of their reason and will in society" (219). Idealized agents in the Original Position recognize that actual agents sometimes need paternalistic redirection, for their own good.

BIBLIOGRAPHY

Ahlstrom-Vij, Kristoffer. *Epistemic Paternalism: A Defence*. Basingstoke: Palgrave-Macmillan (2013): 207.
Ariely, D. *Predictably Irrational: The Hidden Forces That Shape Our Decisions*. New York: HarperCollins (2008): 269.
Coady, D. "Two Concepts of Epistemic Injustice." *Episteme*, 7(2) (2012): 101–113.
Dotson, K. "Tracking Epistemic Violence, Tracking Practices of Silencing." *Hypatia*, 26(2) (2014): 236– 257. https://doi.org/10.1111/j.1527-2001.2011.01177.
Dotson, K. "A Cautionary Tale: On Limiting Epistemic Oppression." *Frontiers: A Journal of Women Studies*, 33(1) (2012): 24–47. https://doi.org/10.1353/fro.2012.0008
———. "Conceptualizing Epistemic Oppression." *Social Epistemology*, 28(2), (2014): 115–138. https://doi.org/10.1080/02691728.2013.782585
Fricker, M. *Epistemic Injustice: The Power and Ethics of Knowing*. Oxford: Oxford University Press (2007): 188.
Fricker, M. "Replies to Alcoff, Goldberg, and Hookway on Epistemic Injustice" (January, 2012): 164–178. https://doi.org/10.3366/E1742360010000894
Fricker, M. "Epistemic Justice as a Condition of Political Freedom?" *Synthese*, 190(7) (May 2013): 1317–1332. http://www.jstor.org/stable/41931810
Fricker, M. "Epistemic Injustice and the Preservation of Ignorance," in R. Peels & Blaauw Martijn (eds.), *The Epistemic Dimensions of Ignorance*. Cambridge: Cambridge University Press (2016): 160–178.
Greco, J. "Agent Reliabilism," in J. Tomberlin (ed.), *Philosophical Perspectives* (Volume 13: Epistemology). Atascadero, CA: Ridgeview Press (1999): 273–296.

Goldman, A. I. *Knowledge in a Social World*. Oxford: Clarendon Press (1999): 424.

Kube T., Rief W., Gollwitzer, M., Gartner T. "Why dysfunctional expectations in depression persist—Results from two experimental studies investigating cognitive immunization." *Psychological Medicine*, 49:9, July (2019), 1532–1544.

Medvecky, F. "Fairness in Knowing: Science Communication and Epistemic Justice." *Science and Engineering Ethics* 25 (5) (2018): 1393–1408. doi:10.1007/s11948-017-9977-0

Mill, J.S., *On Liberty*. London: Longman, Roberts & Green, 1869; Bartleby.com, 1999. www.bartleby.com/130/.

Pohlhaus, G. "Relational Knowing and Epistemic Injustice: Toward a Theory of Willful Hermeneutical Ignorance." *Hypatia*, 27(4) (2012): 715–735. https://doi.org/10.1111/j.1527- 2001.2011.01222

Pohlhaus, G. "Discerning the Primary Epistemic Harm in Cases of Testimonial Injustice." *Social Epistemology*, 28(2) (2014): 99–114. https://doi.org/10.1080/02691728.2013.782581

Rawls, J. *A Theory of Justice: Revised Edition*. Cambridge, MA: Harvard University Press. (1999): 538.

Sandel, M. *Liberalism and the Limits of Justice*. Cambridge: Cambridge University Press. (1982): 231.

Sunstein C., & Thaler, R. *Nudge: Improving Decisions about Health, Wealth and Happiness*. New York: Penguin Books. (2008): 309.

Valentini, L. "Ideal vs. Non-Ideal Theory: A Conceptual Map." *Philosophy Compass*, 7 (9) (2012): 654–664.

Chapter 16

Epistemic Vices and Epistemic Nudging: A Solution?

Daniella Meehan

"Bad" epistemic behavior is unfortunately commonplace. Take, for example, those who believe in conspiracy theories, trust untrustworthy news sites or refuse to take seriously the opinion of their epistemic peers. Sometimes this kind of behavior is sporadic or "out of character"; however, more concerning are those cases that display deeply embedded character traits, attitudes, and thinking styles (Cassam 2016). When this is the case, these character traits, attitudes, and thinking styles are identified by vice epistemologists as epistemic or *intellectual* vices. Considering that these vices often block or subvert the acquisition of epistemic goods such as knowledge or truth, it is important for epistemologists to understand how these kinds of traits can be most effectively mitigated. One currently unexplored way in which we might go about doing so is by employing *epistemically paternalistic* strategies, particularly the strategy of "epistemic nudging" (here on EN)—the practice of altering an agent's decision-making capacities toward a desired outcome (Thaler and Sunstein 2009).

By bringing together two underexplored areas of epistemology yet to be discussed in connection to one another, this chapter will examine whether epistemic nudging can be employed as a successful practice to combat our epistemic vices. Despite prima facie appeal, I will argue that epistemic nudging at the very best amounts to a superficial and short-lived way of addressing epistemic vices. Additionally, I argue that the practice of EN can often lead to the creation of further vices, specifically the vice of epistemic laziness, as identified by Ian Kidd (2017).

This debate has important ramifications for the literature on both vice epistemology and epistemic paternalism. If EN can assist in the mitigation of epistemic vices, this is a great advantage in terms of advancing the debate for EN and for vice epistemology with regard to providing a solution to the problem of epistemic vices. However, if my argument is correct and EN not only is unsuccessful at mitigating epistemic vices but more worryingly leads to the creation of more epistemic vices, then arguably this is a problematic objection to the field of EN.

EPISTEMIC NUDGING INTRODUCED

Epistemic paternalism is the thesis that in some circumstances we may intervene with the inquiry of another for their own epistemic good, without consulting them on the issue (Ahlstrom-Vij 2013). One way in which someone may interfere with another's ability to conduct inquiry is through the practice known as "epistemic nudging." The standard and most prominent account of EN is offered by Thaler and Sunstein. By their definition, an epistemic nudge "alters people's behavior in a predictable way without forbidding any options or significantly changing their economic incentives" (Thaler and Sunstein 2008: 6). Thaler and Sunstein's definition of a nudge implicates some need to change people's behavior into making better choices. This follows the ideology that assumes that human behavior is not always rational and can therefore profit from a paternalistic point of view (Kahneman and Tversky 1972). With this in mind, epistemic nudging allows institutions to attempt to influence an agent's behavior and to steer their choices in directions, which will improve their welfare.

EN is further defined by Thaler and Sunstein as a form of "liberal paternalism." It is libertarian insofar as the interventions and strategies of EN are employed to guide people's decision without taking away their freedom of choice and the nudges can be easily resisted. EN is "paternalist" in the sense that it steers people toward one choice as opposed to another, where the individual's choices are interfered with for the individual's own epistemic good. Examples of epistemic nudging can be found in architecture, educational programs, bureaucracies, propaganda and so forth. Common types of epistemic nudging can include disclosing particular information, using social norms, reminders, warnings and informing people of the nature and consequences of past choices (Sunstein 2014). One example of epistemic nudging may be the use of the educational tool of "lying-to-children" which is viewed as an interference to schoolchildren's inquiry. This educational tool, according to Stewart and Cohen (1997) involves teaching false or incomplete theories to students in order to facilitate a better understanding of the more complex theories. For example, a student might first be taught that Newtonian mechanics provides a complete account of the laws of motion, in order to make it easier for them to learn quantum mechanics.[1]

EPISTEMIC VICES INTRODUCED

The next section of this chapter will discuss the nature of epistemic vices and lay groundwork for the exploration of the relationship between EN and epistemic vices.

A flourishing but relatively new field of social epistemology is vice epistemology. Modeled off the recent trend in virtue epistemology, vice epistemologists have turned their attention to epistemic.[2] Epistemic vices are the systematic study of character traits, attitudes or ways of thinking that obstruct the acquisition of knowledge (Cassam 2016). One of the central aims of vice epistemology is to guide human inquiry. This aim is often referred to as "regulative epistemology," which has the overall aim of improving our epistemic conduct. As Alvin Goldman notes, "If we wish to raise our intellectual performance, it behooves us to identify those traits which are most in need of improvement" (Goldman 1978: 511). The traits that need improvement are those which are of interest to vice epistemologists, and it is in this sense that the study of these character traits attitudes and thinking styles are imperative to the study of human inquiry, and by extension, to epistemology.

While there has yet to be any literature exploring the connection between epistemic vices and epistemic paternalism or nudging, the shared concern for making humans better off epistemically by overcoming certain kinds of characteristic weaknesses in thinking, provides a clear starter for how the two domains overlap. In particular, it seems plausible that if EN is considered a successful strategy at making positive shifts to our epistemic behavior, then EN could be an extremely useful tool with regard to the mitigation of certain epistemic vices.

Of course, if EN proves to be successful at mitigating our epistemic vices, this would be a huge benefit both to the field of EN and vice epistemology. The advantage of being able to combat epistemic vices, as already defined by vice epistemologists as serious threats to human inquiry, adds strength to the practice of EN and the plausibility of it as an epistemic tool. Additionally, vice epistemologists will have a solution for the mitigation of epistemic vices, which would be of great benefit to epistemic communities. However, if we find that EN is unsuccessful in combating epistemic vices, and more concerningly, can *cause* the existence of vices, then this will be a great concern for the practice of EN as a useful and acceptable epistemic tool.

With this in mind, the remainder of this chapter will explore the connection between EN and epistemic vice, focusing on the potential role that EN can play with regard to the combating of epistemic vices.

EPISTEMIC NUDGING AS SUCCESSFUL VICE COMBAT

As EN is employed in response to flaws in the human decision-making process, and as epistemic vices are perceived as flaws we possess in our capacity as inquirers, it is clear to see how prima facie EN can successfully combat and mitigate the effects of some of our epistemic vices.[3] We can also discuss the following examples that demonstrate how EN can combat certain vices:

Harry, your flatmate, frequently forms false beliefs based on unreliable and untrustworthy news sources from right-wing newspapers and websites. He never reads any other news sources and is unwilling to do so. Harry's behavior fits the definition of the epistemic vice of closemindedness, in the sense that it is a character trait that obstructs him from gaining knowledge about the true events occurring in the world (Cassam 2019).[4] In response to Harry's vice of closemindedness, over the course of a month, you decide to nudge him away from forming any more irresponsible beliefs from untrustworthy news sources. Some of the measures you take include offering him a discount for the subscription service for a well-trusted newspaper, warning him about the reliability and trustworthiness of the sources he reads his news from, and leaving neutral, unbiased news programs on the TV.[5]

This example satisfies Thaler and Sunstein's definition of EN. While we are aiming to incline the target toward a subsequent action or outcome, we still leave the nudgee's previously salient options on the table (Harry is still able to access whatever news sources he may choose to) and Harry is able to resist our efforts to change his vice if he chooses to do so. It is also important to note here that as epistemic vices are *systematic*—one-off cases of closemindedness or merely defective instances of epistemic behavior do not count as epistemic vices—for EN to successfully combat epistemic vice they must be able to affect one's epistemic character traits.[6] It appears that by using EN, we are ridding Harry's character trait (not just a singular case of closemindedness), in the sense that we are employing multiple nudges over a series of time.

Another example that seemingly demonstrates how EN can combat displays of epistemic vice concerns a well-debated example of EP, which involves responses to the anti-vaccination movement. Vaccine denialists manifest the epistemic vice of dogmatism (when a subject claims to hold a belief or knowledge, which is not based on evidence or supporting reasons) when they seek to avoid engaging in the giving and taking of reasons about vaccines with their pediatricians. For example, vaccine denialists often go to great lengths to find healthcare providers who will not challenge their beliefs. They replace their children's pediatricians with naturopaths, homeopaths, and chiropractors whose training in alternative therapies often makes them predisposed to reject evidence-based forms of medicine, and less willing to challenge parents' preconceptions.[7]

In response to this vice of dogmatism, some states in the United States have employed EN to put in places strategies in order to minimize the risks anti-vaccinators pose and to attempt to change their mind about the risk of vaccinations. The Michigan model, referred to as the *Inconvenience Model*, aims to increase the burden of those who chose to exempt children from vaccinations, by ensuring that anyone who applies for it must attend education sessions about vaccines at the local public health department. In comparison to 2014 reports, this measure had successfully lowered exemption rates by 39% statewide and 60% in the Detroit area (Higgins 2016). By employing a default system but allowing the vaccine denialists the option to opt-out if they attend education classes, options are still left open to the vaccine denialists, meaning this program successfully counts as a case of EN, which successfully overcame the vice of dogmatism.

From these two examples, it seems plausible that EN can be employed to mitigate our epistemic vices and interventions such as the Michigan model have already successfully assisted in doing so.

EPISTEMIC NUDGING AS INSUFFICIENT FOR THE MITIGATION OF VICE

Despite the perceived success of EN with regard to aforementioned examples of vice mitigation, I argue that at best EN amounts to a superficial and temporary elimination of epistemic vice. More concerningly, I also argue that EN can make us worse off epistemically by leading to the *creation*, not mitigation of epistemic vices. The remainder of this chapter will explore these two claims, drawing from literature in vice epistemology concerning the vice of epistemic laziness (Kidd 2017) and "deep" epistemic vices (Cassam 2019; Kidd 2019).

A "DEEP" UNDERSTANDING OF EPISTEMIC VICE

I argue that upon closer examination, EN fails to address the root of epistemic vices and only succeeds in masking them. This is based on the argument that EN fails to acknowledge the depth of epistemic vices, which often consist of deep psychological dispositions and heavily embedded social structures (Cassam 2019; Kidd 2019).

In his recent publication, *Vices of the Mind* (2019), Cassam discusses the explanatory depth of vice explanations. I will draw upon this literature here to demonstrate how EN fails to acknowledge the depth of our epistemic vices. Cassam contrasts explaining people's actions through vice with explanations that appeal to "structural influences" (Tilly 2002). For example, by explaining gender inequality with regard to pay, we can appeal to the economic structure, which disadvantages women relative to men with regard to childcare and part-time work (Haslanger 2015). No appeal to character traits or thus epistemic vices is needed to explain this behavior. Similarly, structural explanations may explain how some people are close-minded, considered the structural influence of education for example. Again, we do not need to appeal to character vices to explain how people exhibit their close-mindedness, meaning that vice explanations could be replaced with structural explanations. The objection toward vice explanations then is that they underestimate the importance of structural factors whilst exaggerating the importance of character traits. Vice explanations seem superficial attempts at explaining one's behavior, which ignores the deeper, structural influences that truly shape our epistemic acts.

However, one response to this threat that Cassam puts forth is that structural influences need not be considered as a threat to vice explanations as often the two explanations are intertwined, meaning the same phenomenon can be explained with reference to epistemic vice and structural factors. This claim is also supported by Tanesini, who argues that vice and structural explanations are complementary as opposed to competitors, in the sense that sometimes actions can be explained by appealing to both explanations (Tanesini 2019).

Putting the debate between structural and vice explanations aside, what this discussion highlights is the complicated and deep structure of epistemic vices. Often our vices stem from due to unfortunate and epistemically depriving economic and educational structures, for example, which play an important role in shaping the nature of the vice and our understanding of how to "treat" them.

Additionally, Kidd's recent work *A Deep Conception of Epistemic Vice* (2019) makes similar claims to the complicated nature of epistemic vices. Kidd argues for a "deep" reading of epistemic vices, which he defines as follows:

Deep Epistemic Vices (DEV): "a deep conception of epistemic vice is one whose identity and intelligibility is determined by the set of practices, projects, or contexts within which it is embedded" (Kidd 2019: 15).

When studying the nature of epistemic vices we need to appeal to their "deeper features" to fully understand their nature. "Shallow" explanations of vices will only identify the status of a vice by locating it within the practices in which it is typically manifested or the projects of inquiry it obstructs. Alternatively, a "deep" explanation of a vice is one in which the identity and form of a vice can only be understood in relation to a deeper, underlying conception of human nature, or by appealing to a "worldview" of the vice.

By discussing both Cassam's and Kidd's work on the nature of epistemic vice, it becomes clear that the identity of epistemic vices should be understood as consisting of deep psychological dispositions, which are heavily influenced by various societal structures, as well as being embedded in various contexts, which pertain to wider conceptions of human understanding. This is important for our discussion on the mitigation of vice, in the sense that any attempt to combat our vices must take this reading into account. However, I argue that cases where EN may seem to vitiate our vices (as discussed above) are based on a shallow reading of epistemic vices, which results in epistemic vices only being masked, not mitigated as we may have initially believed.

We can explain how EN fails to successfully combat epistemic vice by drawing from the literature on dispositions (Johnston 1992). Take the following example. A vase, which has the disposition of fragility is wrapped in bubble wrap to present it from shattering. By protecting the vase with bubble-wrap, we haven't vitiated its fragility, but just masked it in the sense that while it is packaged in bubble-wrap, it is not fragile. We haven't done anything to remove the disposition itself, the vase is still made from glass and prone to shattering if damaged and if the bubble-wrap were removed then the disposition would still be present.

I believe this type of "masking" of dispositions can successfully explain why EN fails to suffice as a successful practice of ridding of epistemic vice. When EN claims to have successfully mitigated a vice, like the examples presented earlier, what has really happened is that EN has merely *masked* the epistemic vice at hand. EN can only mask epistemic vices as the deep nature of vices remains present. EN does not change the vice in any way, just like the bubble wrap did not change the fragility of the vase, but only masks it, and when EN practices are not employed the vice is still present, just like how the fragility of the vase still remains when the bubble-wrap is removed.

Let us apply this objection to the previously discussed example of Harry, our close-minded flatmate. It initially appeared that through employing various forms of epistemic nudging, we could combat his epistemic vice. However, when we are not epistemically nudging Harry, his vice is still present and will continue to manifest itself. This is because EN does nothing to change the vice itself, but only masks it for the duration that various EN techniques are employed. The deepness of the vice of close-mindedness, its real identity, is still present and cannot be mitigated through EN.

EPISTEMIC LAZINESS

Kidd, in his paper "Capital Epistemic Vices," introduced the vice of epistemic laziness. He defines these vices as "as a culpable failure to acquire or exercise the epistemic capacities required for enquiry" (Kidd 2017: 16). Furthermore, Kidd states: "Such laziness lies at the root of a whole range of vices characterized by failures to do epistemic work—think of vices like inaccuracy or rigidity, both of which are, ultimately, failures to do the work needed to ensure accuracy or revision of one's beliefs" (Kidd 2017: 16).

One example of how epistemic laziness manifests itself, as outlined by Kidd, is when someone may not care enough about the status of their beliefs in order to put in the epistemic work—they become epistemically lazy. I want to further suggest that the vice of epistemic laziness can manifest itself as a result of epistemic nudging. I argue that epistemic nudging can hinder one's epistemic capacities when agents either become too dependent on EN, or EN is employed in too many situations.

One way to demonstrate how EN can lead to the vice of epistemic laziness is to turn to the material on EN and epistemic injustice. Take Evan Riley's paper "The Beneficial Nudge Program and Epistemic Injustice" (2017), who argues against the concept of EN on the basis that it contributes to *reflective incapacitational injustice*. Riley introduces the notion of reflective incapacitational injustice by referring to our epistemic capacity to reason critically. Our epistemic capacities are ones which are properly exercised in cases of knowledge, such as reasoning soundly or trusting a genuinely reliable peer. Riley claims that having the fully developed capacities associated with reasoning critically and energetically is necessary for being a robustly and epistemically developed person. Accordingly, denying or neglecting to provide people with the support, opportunities, or means necessary to develop those capacities, or making it relatively more difficult to develop and exercise those capacities, is unjust. In addition, the character of this general kind of wrong cannot be made fully explicit without reference to the epistemic nature of the victim. When our capacity to think critically and reasonably is therefore denied, according to Riley we have a clear case of an epistemic injustice—a reflective incapacitational injustice.

According to Riley, one practice in which our capacities to reason and think critically is hindered and thus gives way to reflective incapacitational injustice is EN. The main reasoning for this claim is that EN does not merely accidentally fail to engage the critical deliberative faculties of their targets, but purposefully seeks to bypass reflective deliberation entirely. Take the educational tool example outlined earlier, where teachers nudged students toward effective inquiry by teaching incomplete theories to facilitate a better understanding of their complexities. As Riley would note, this form of EN seeks to bypass a genuine open reflective deliberation, meaning for one to nudge successfully in this case (and many others)[8] one must at the time of the nudge, not invite, seek or start any critical reflection or deliberation. As epistemic justice demands that we treat people as the reasoning beings we properly are and our communities, states, and social institutions should be actively fostering the capacities for reasoning well, it is clear how epistemic nudging ordinarily fail to pay due respect for this. Therefore, Riley concludes that typical nudging is structurally prone to violations of epistemic justice when it refuses to allow agents to engage in critical deliberation and reflection.

Riley's material on EN and epistemic injustice clearly highlights how EN can deny agents critical and reasoning capacities. In light of this, Riley argues that her objection demonstrates how EN in its current state is morally impermissible and must be radically revised. Similar concerns have been discussed with regard to the effect that EN on our overall autonomy which, in turn, can affect our epistemic capacities (Ahlstrom-Vij 2013; Enoch 2016). I wish to take these objections to EN one step further, and argue that by hindering our epistemic capacities, EN can *create* epistemic character vices, specifically the vice of epistemic laziness. Arguably, this vice is created even in cases where EN does not just prevent agents from creating certain epistemic capacities as Riley argues, but also in cases where agents already possess those capacities but fail to exercise them as a result of EN.

EN can give way to the vices of epistemic laziness when epistemic capacities fail to be exercised, or are nulled. As we have seen through the definition of epistemic laziness presented by Kidd, epistemic laziness occurs when we fail to exercise our epistemic capacities; so any tool that blocks or hinders us from doing so, such as EN, can lead to the creation of such vices. Arguably, the key contention here between EN and EV are the constraints that EN puts on our epistemic capacities and freedom to exercise them when we choose to do so, and this hinders our ability to exercise autonomy over our epistemic capacities. The concern, therefore, is arguably with the "libertarian" aspect of EN, as defined by Thaler and Sunstein. We should therefore assess whether EN truly does restrict our freedom to exercise our epistemic capacities, and if so, what this means for the claim that EN can assist in combatting our epistemic vices.

It could be argued that EN can allow for people to exercise their epistemic capacities in a non-restricted sense. This, in turn, would make the problem I raise that EN leads to the creation of epistemic laziness, redundant. However, this does not seem a plausible possibility.

As we have already seen, Riley argues that it is within the very definition of EN that it halts our epistemic capacities to reason and think critically, in the sense that EN requires at the time of the nudge that no critical reflection or deliberation is employed. In response to objections over the agency of EN, Sunstein argues "when nudges are in place, human agency is retained (because freedom of choice is not compromised)" (Sunstein 2015: 513). However, as Riley rightly argues, this response is unconvincing to the extent that we take autonomous human agency to involve considerably more than just liberty of choice.

In addition to Riley's objections to EN, further literature can be found, which criticizes EP and EN on the basis that it is not as autonomous as it implies. Take Hausman and Welch's criticisms found in their paper *To Nudge or Not to Nudge* (2010) who argue that Thaler and Sunstein wrongly define EN as autonomous and respecting of the nudgee's liberty. The reality, Hausman and Welch argue, is that in most cases of EN listed by Thaler and Sunstein autonomy is diminished, stating that "The paternalistic policies . . . are prima facie as threatening to liberty, broadly understood, as is overt coercion" (Thaler and Sunstein 2010: 130). They also claim that when cases of nudging concern an agent's rationality (arguably many cases of EN), autonomy is rarely respected; when speaking of the character and significance of our deliberative capacities, Hausman and Welch warn "one should be concerned about the risk that exploiting decision-making foibles will ultimately diminish people's autonomous decision-making capacities (the government) . . . should take care not to undermine its capacity to persuade people rationally" (Hausman and Welch 2010: 135).

The argument between EN and autonomy is extensive and cannot be covered in this chapter alone. However, it is worth noting that one response to the objection is to argue that in cases where autonomy is violated, often it is for a greater good, which gives cases of EN permissibility. For example, the "Toxic Release Inventories" case presented by Thaler and Sunstein, required firms to publish their toxic release inventories. This allowed the media and environmental groups to produce an "environmental blacklist." While firms only had to disclose what hazardous chemicals they are storing or releasing into the environment, the requirement makes possible heavy social sanctions for polluting. This nudge was effective precisely because it significantly increased the costs of polluting, a positive outcome, which arguably outweighed the seemingly lack of autonomy over the information that the firms possessed.

While this position may be defended by some, I argue that it cannot be employed in cases of EN and epistemic vice combat, precisely because the consequences of autonomy violations will result in the vices of epistemic laziness. If decisions are made for us or we are pushed to make certain decisions, despite being for the best (e.g., being less dogmatism), the violation of autonomy gives way to new vices, as argued, specifically the vices of epistemic laziness. Therefore, despite the possibility of epistemically beneficial consequences, as far as EN is employed for the mitigation of our vices, it fails, for as we have noted, the lack of autonomy generally results in the vice of epistemic laziness. It is also worth noting that even if we grant that EN respects the autonomy of an agent, the vice of epistemic laziness can still be formed. This is because laziness, like most character traits, is gradient. Making one depend on certain nudges over time will lead certain epistemic capacities to atrophy thus resulting in the vice of laziness. Like how muscles are lost overti me if they are not exercised, epistemic capacities that are not exercised due to the practice of EN will also be lost, leading to the creation of epistemic laziness.

CONCLUDING REMARKS

To conclude, this chapter has discussed both epistemic nudging and epistemic vices and the potential role that EN may have with the mitigation of epistemic vices. Despite initial signs of plausibility with reference to the role that EN may have with shaping our epistemic character, I objected to this possibility. I argued that EN could only mitigate a shallow interpretation of epistemic vices at best and not the accurate understanding of epistemic vices as deep psychological dispositions, influenced by various societal structures and embedded in various contexts, which pertain to wider conceptions of human understanding. This shallow reading of epistemic vice meant that EN only masked, not mitigated, the existence of epistemic vices. Furthermore, and more concerningly, I demonstrated how EN can result in the creation of the vices of epistemic laziness. I appealed to literature on EN and epistemic injustice to highlight how EN restricts our autonomy as epistemic agents, which, in turn, results in the vices of epistemic laziness, which arises when agents fail to exercise the capacities to do epistemic work. I also argued that the response to this objection—that the benefits achieving epistemic goods outweighs restricting one's autonomy—does not apply if such a restriction results in the creation of more epistemic vices. Finally, I stated that objections to EN and autonomy aside, EN still leads to the creation of epistemic laziness. This is because epistemic laziness prevents our epistemic capacities from being exercised and thus becoming atrophied. While it appears that EN may not be successful in combating our epistemic vices, we can arguably be generally optimistic in other practices that hint toward this possibility, such as the various methods employed via critical education, which aims to cultivate and promote certain epistemic virtues.[9]

ACKNOWLEDGMENTS

I would like to thank the volume editors of this chapter for their constructive comments on a previous version of this chapter.

NOTES

1. This example is borrowed from Emma Bullock's paper "Knowing and Not-Knowing for Your Own Good: The Limits of Epistemic Paternalism" (2016).
2. See Zagzebski 1996, Sosa 2009, and Greco 1993.
3. I will not discuss arguments as to whether EN is a successful practice or not—the purpose of my chapter is to discuss, *if* EN is successful, can it be used to combat our epistemic vices?
4. I am aware that the nature of close-mindedness as an epistemic vice is contested (Battaly 2018).
5. This example displays the three EN techniques of default rules, warning, and increasing ease and convenience (Sunstein 2014).
6. For a discussion on how EN may affect our epistemic character, see Alfano, Cheong and Carter "Technological Seduction and Self Radicalization" (2018) and Alfano "Character as Moral Fiction" (2013). However, literature on this topic is scarce and predominately concerns the relationship between EN and epistemic virtue as opposed to vice.
7. Edzard Ernst, "Rise in Popularity of Complementary and Alternative Medicine: Reasons and Consequences for Vaccination," Vaccine 20 (2001): S90–S93.
8. See Sunstein's (2014) cases of "Flies," "Less Drinking," and "Save More," which all merit the same criticism.
9. See Jason Baehr "Intellectual Virtues and Education" (2016).

BIBLIOGRAPHY

Ahlstrom-Vij, Kristoffer. *Epistemic Paternalism: A Defence*. Basingstoke: Palgrave Macmillan. 2013.
Alfano, Mark, J. Adam Carter, and Marc Cheong. "Technological Seduction and Self-Radicalisation." *Journal of the American Philosophical Association*, 4 (3): (2018): 298–322.
Alfano, Mark. *Character as Moral Fiction*. Cambridge: Cambridge University Press. 2013.
Baehr, J. *Intellectual Virtues and Education: Essays in Applied Virtue Epistemology*. London: Routledge. 2016.
Battaly, Heather. "Can Closed-Mindedness Be an Intellectual Virtue?" *Royal Institute of Philosophy Supplement*, 84: (2018): 23–45.
Bullock, E. C. "Knowing and Not-Knowing for Your Own Good: The Limits of Epistemic Paternalism." *Journal of Applied Philosophy*, 35(2): (2016): 433–447.
Cassam, Quassim. "Vice Epistemology." *The Monist*, 99 (2): (2016): 159–180.
Cassam, Quassim. *Vices of the Mind*. Oxford: Oxford University Press. 2019.
Enoch, David. "II—What's Wrong with Paternalism: Autonomy, Belief, and Action." *Proceedings of the Aristotelian Society*, 116 (1): (2016): 21–48.
Ernst, Edzard. "Rise in Popularity of Complementary and Alternative Medicine: Reasons and Consequences for Vaccination." *Vaccine*, 20 (1): (2001): S90–S93.

Goldman, Alvin I. "Epistemics: The Regulative Theory of Cognition." *The Journal of Philosophy*, 75 (10): (1978): 509–523.
Greco, John. "Virtues and Vices of Virtue Epistemology." *Canadian Journal of Philosophy*, 23(3): (1993): 413–432.
Haslanger, Sally. "Social Structure, Narrative and Explanation." *Canadian Journal of Philosophy*, 45: (2015): 1–15.
Hausman, Daniel M. and Brynn Welch. "Debate: To Nudge or Not to Nudge." *The Journal of Political Philosophy*, 18 (1): (2010): 123–136.
Higgins, Lori. "More Michigan Parents Willing to Vaccinate Kids." Detroit Free Press. (2016). Accessed June 16th 2019. https://eu.freep.com/story/news/education/2016/01/28/immunization-waivers-plummet-40-michigan/79427752/
Johnston, Mark. "How to Speak of the Colors." *Philosophical Studies*, 68: (1992): 221–263.
Kahneman, Daniel and Amos Tversky. "Subjective Probability: A Judgment of Representativeness." *Cognitive Psychology*, 3 (3): (1972): 430–454.
Kidd, Ian James. "Capital Epistemic Vices." *Social Epistemology Review and Reply Collective*, 6 (8): (2017): 11–16.
Kidd, Ian James. "Deep Epistemic Vices." *Journal of Philosophical Research*, 43: (2018): 43–67.
Riley, Evan. "The Beneficent Nudge Program and Epistemic Injustice." *Ethical Theory and Moral Practice*, 20 (3): (2017): 597–616.
Sosa, Ernest. "A Virtue Epistemology: Apt Belief and Reflective Knowledge, Volume I." *Analysis*, 69 (2): (2009): 382–385.
Stewart, I. and J. Cohen. *Figments of Reality: The Evolution of the Curious Mind.* Cambridge: Cambridge University Press. 1997.
Sunstein, Cass R. "Nudges Do Not Undermine Human Agency: A Note." *Journal of Consumer Policy*, 38 (3): (2015): 207–210.
Sunstein, Cass R. "Nudging: A Very Short Guide." *Journal of Consumer Policy*, 37 (4): (2014): 583–588.
Tanesini, Alessandra. "'Vices of the Mind' by Quassim Cassam. Oxford: Oxford University Press (2019): xiv + 202." Review of *Vices of the Mind*, by Quassim Cassam.
Thaler, Richard H. and Cass R. Sunstein. *Nudge: Improving Decisions about Health, Wealth and Happiness.* London: Penguin. 2009.
Thaler, Richard H. and Cass R. Sunstein. *Nudge: Improving Decisions about Health, Wealth, and Happiness.* New Haven, CT: Yale University Press. 2008.
Tilly, Charles. *Stories, Identities, and Political Change.* Lanham, MD: Rowman & Littlefield. 2002.
Zagzebski, Linda Trinkaus. *Virtues of the Mind: An Inquiry into the Nature of Virtue and the Ethical Foundations of Knowledge.* Cambridge: Cambridge University Press. 1996.

Chapter 17

Paternalism and Epistemic (Non-)Violence

Adam Green

There are a variety of ways one might motivate epistemic paternalism. I will be concerned with only one here. Epistemic injustice arises from epistemic violence, and epistemic violence causes harm. One of the traditional justifications for paternalistic interventions is harm.[1] Thus, one might well wonder whether there is a route from our being harmed as knowers by epistemic injustice to paternalistic interventions of an epistemic sort. It is one thing to ask whether we must put up with the stupidity of our neighbor. It is quite another when the stupidity of one's neighbor manifests itself in wrongs committed against us.

In this chapter, I will not be arguing that epistemic paternalism is impermissible. What I will try to highlight, however, is that paternalistic interventions in the context of epistemic injustice are at significant risk of committing wrongs of the sort they seek to redress. Epistemic injustice is rooted in epistemic violence, but paternalism can take the form of violence. By contrast, I will be arguing that non-violent resistance offers us a novel model for thinking about how one could oppose a putative epistemic injustice without putting oneself at risk for committing one.

In the first section, we will look more closely at the route to justifying epistemic paternalism from epistemic injustice. In the second, we will turn our attention to the trade-offs in moral risk that attend different approaches to paternalistic intervention, drawing out where the temptation to epistemic violence arises from. In the third and final section, I will present a non-violent alternative as well as two different kinds of non-violent intervention that can be implemented to resist epistemic injustice.

THE ROUTE OF EPISTEMIC INJUSTICE

It is hard to oppose paternalistic interventions across the board. Rules that keep us from harming ourselves and others shape the world we live in. When it comes to harms that others inflict on us either intentionally or in virtue of their poor life choices, we may even feel that paternalistic intervention is not simply permissible or advisable but that it is demanded by justice. Since feminist epistemology has drawn our attention to the fact that there are injustices that are uniquely epistemic, this should cause us to ask whether epistemic injustice too can justify paternalistic interventions of an epistemic nature.

Miranda Fricker brought the term "epistemic injustice" to prominence in her 2007 book by that title. For Fricker, an epistemic injustice covers a range of harms that one suffers qua knower. Epistemic injustices subdivide into harms that one encounters in coming to know things and harms that concern what one can do with the knowledge one has. Fricker's book focuses on one specific variant of each type of injustice: hermeneutical injustice and testimonial injustice respectively.

Testimonial injustice involves not having one's credibility as a knower acknowledged through a proper receptivity to one's testimony due to prejudice. The wrong may have implications for what the sufferer of injustice can come to know, but what it directly concerns is what one can do with the knowledge one has. Hermeneutical injustice is Fricker's example of an epistemic injustice pertaining to the gaining of knowledge.[2] The person who suffers a hermeneutical injustice is blocked from understanding her experience due to prejudice. The specific way in which one is blocked is due to the impoverishment of the conceptual resources available for making sense of that experience.[3] One of Fricker's main examples of the phenomenon is experiencing sexual harassment before that concept had made its way into the social imagination. Being able to conceptualize an experience as not simply unwanted flirtation or rudeness but as a species of harassment helps one capture the legitimacy and moral seriousness of one's desire not to be so treated.

A limitation in Fricker's framework that Kristie Dotson in particular has highlighted is that it is not true that society shares some single social imagination. Rather, there are social imaginations. Different groups work with different conceptual repertoires, and marginalized groups are perfectly capable of having their own. Women certainly didn't need the permission of the wider culture to begin describing their experiences in terms of sexual harassment.

In light of this important modification, Dotson introduces the idea of "contributory injustice." A contributory injustice is one in which an agent fails willfully "to recognize or acquire requisite alternative hermeneutical resources" (Dotson 2012: 32). The resources that we bring to bear on our experience to make sense of it are not simply a given, conditioning experiences downstream of their existence. How one uses one's agency influences what categories will be available. The person who does not expose herself to differing viewpoints may not commit testimonial injustice very often because she does not often encounter out-group testimony on matters of dispute.[4] Likewise, she may not experience hermeneutical injustice or at least not experience it as an injustice if she lives more or less at peace within the cognitive framework of her group. By way of contrast, it will be nearly impossible for the cognitive xenophobe to avoid being complicit in contributory injustice. For instance, the xenophobe will not seek out other perspectives responsibly, will be disposed to reject them without understanding them or for bad reasons, and will fail to share or to flag resources that put others in touch with alternative perspectives.[5]

Failing to listen when one ought to is one way of silencing others, and Dotson thinks of silencing as a kind of violence. According to Dotson

> Epistemic violence is a failure of an audience to communicatively reciprocate, either intentionally or unintentionally, in linguistic exchanges owing to pernicious ignorance. Pernicious ignorance is a reliable ignorance or a counterfactual incompetence that, in a given context, is harmful. (Dotson 2011: 242)

For Dotson, epistemic violence is intimately related to the silencing of individuals. The aim of Dotson's account of epistemic violence is to provide "a mechanism for identifying on-the-ground practices of silencing" (237). Dotson builds on work by Jennifer Hornsby focusing on a lesson we can learn from pornography. The violence depicted in pornography silences women (237; cf. Hornsby 1994). According to Hornsby, pornography encourages men not to hear a "no" from a woman as a real no. There is a refusal of uptake on the part of the hearer, which can have the effect of silencing a woman. It violates the bounds of a woman's appropriate agency for her word not to be received appropriately and in that sense is a kind of violence committed against women generally. Dotson, then, seeks to expand on that idea.

Dotson's characterization is geared toward the context of testimony specifically, but one might broaden it still further in this way.

> (E-Violence) = Epistemic violence is perpetrated by x anytime x undermines the uptake of y's perspective in a way directed toward the silencing of y and/or undermines the development of an independent perspective by y that could be a candidate for uptake in the first place.

In the most straightforward case, x and y would be individuals, but x could be a group, an institution, a policy, or even an ideology. For the purposes of this chapter, I will not take any stance on whether all the acceptable values of x can be reduced to individuals and individual agency. Likewise, y need not stand for a particular individual.

Many actions might indirectly silence another person. The pulling of a fire alarm can have the effect of silencing conversations that one doesn't know about. When a publisher passes on a manuscript for legitimate reasons, it contributes to the silencing of the author but not necessarily in order to silence her. Just as it is useful when discussing physical violence to focus not simply on bodily contact that causes harm but on intentional behavior whose aim is to harm, so too our concern here is the committing of epistemic violence understood as intentional activity directed toward the silencing of others.

One can see how epistemic violence shows up in each of the three forms of injustice discussed. In testimonial injustice, there is a refusal of uptake for a testifier's credentials. This does violence to their status in the epistemic community and expresses disrespect for them as a knower. It is directed toward the silencing of the testifier by refusing her the credentials necessary to command dialogical engagement if not belief. Likewise, the difference between a hermeneutical injustice and a mere gap in our knowledge is that the gap in our hermeneutical resources is not simply due to bad luck or human finitude. Rather, agency has been expressed in a society over time in such a way that a category that should exist or be more widely appreciated is not. Finally, contributory injustice, the failure to seek out and engage with a reasonably diverse set of perspectives, silences others by proceeding as if they were not there to begin with.

In sum, epistemic violence harms people. If harm in general can be used to justify paternalistic intervention (e.g., mandating safety procedures that preclude harm; shaming people who cause harm; abrogating the rights or privileges of those that threaten harm), then it would seem that the epistemic violence committed in acts of epistemic injustice should license paternalistic intervention. Thus, one might think that epistemic injustice and the epistemic violence which underlies it provide good reason to endorse a range of paternalistic interventions to guide our epistemic lives, that is, to endorse epistemic paternalism. It ends up, however, that there are a number of relevantly different ways of thinking about epistemic paternalism.

KINDS OF PATERNALISM

Paternalism can take different forms, and epistemic paternalism is no exception.[6] Even if we grant that all epistemic paternalisms will follow the contours of a particular account like that of Ahlstrom-Vij (2013), there is ample room for variety. Ahlstrom-Vij's account consists of three components (61). A practice is epistemically paternalistic for him if and only if it interferes with someone's freedom of inquiry, does so without consulting them, but aims to make the person interfered with better off epistemically. Interfering in someone's freedom of inquiry, however, can take different forms that each admit of more and less extreme forms. One can interfere prior to, during, or after an enquiry, for instance. Epistemic improvement can target different kinds of epistemic goods, and as Ahlstrom-Vij himself is sensitive to, there are a variety of ways to relate to someone else's interests, which could be described as having non-consultation in common.

One should not assume that kinds of paternalism are all alike in moral cost. After all, when a judge suppresses misleading evidence in a courtroom in accordance with the official duties and prerogatives of her office, this counts as paternalism. Ideologically motivated indoctrination also counts.[7] Intervening in the cognitive life of another without their consent, albeit for what one takes to be their benefit, covers a multitude of potential sins. And in fact, Ahlstrom-Vij's defense of epistemic paternalism only claims that "we are sometimes justified in interfering with the inquiry of another without her consent but for her own epistemic good" and specifies that this epistemic improvement must be "aligned" with relevant non-epistemic values as well (Ahlstrom-Vij 2013: 114, 134–135).

As non-epistemic forms of paternalism readily illustrate, even an intervention aimed at redressing or preventing a clear and egregious harm can come with a moral cost that is too high a price to pay, and indeed, a paternalistic intervention can cause more harm than the harm it seeks to address. Parents have a duty to intervene in the life of their children for their own good. Yet, the way some parents punish their children is abusive, and indeed, it may be abusive even if the child's behavior is, in fact, egregious and even if the parents really think that what they are doing is for the child's own sake.

The moral cost of intervention is especially important in cases of paternalistic intervention wherein the values being promoted by the intervention or their interpretation are not shared by the target of the intervention.[8] This is a distinct issue from that of consent. If one's partner admits to being an alcoholic and has a higher order desire to quit, then pouring a discovered bottle of brandy down the sink may be a defensible intervention. If, on the other hand, one is a teetotaler who simply wishes that no one would drink alcohol and one's partner is neither an alcoholic nor a teetotaler, the same intervention looks much less defensible.

To the extent that an intervention requires a more drastic violation of the autonomy of the other person, intervening despite a dispute over the moral, if not the material, facts of the case is more costly and less defensible. For instance, if the teetotaler simply refused to pick up alcohol when he's doing the grocery shopping, that may be irritating to the partner that enjoys a drink on occasion, but arguably there's nothing wrong with that. If the teetotaler threatens bodily harm to the partner should the devil's drink cross their threshold again, that's something else. The paternalistic intervener has gone from themselves being someone to put up with to someone committing wrongs that need to be redressed.

Paternalisms can vary in their ends and in their means, and both matter to discerning moral cost and likely effectiveness.[9] Epistemic paternalism might take as its object a change in belief (or desire), in belief-forming process, or in the social expression of one's epistemic agency. Trying to get the target to use a good belief-forming process is not as inherently problematic as trying to get them to hold a given belief by some means or another. The reason for this is the same as the reason that epistemologists prize goods beyond mere true belief. Etiology matters. Likewise, many epistemologists value the etiology of a belief reflecting virtuous or reasonable or properly functioning agential processes.

Once we factor in the fallibility of the intervener, the gap between aiming to induce good process and just aiming to provoke a true belief or an appropriate behavior widens. If an intervener with a false belief provokes critical reflection in the target, the intervener has still brought an epistemic good into the world. If the intervener, by contrast, uses an epistemically illicit process to bring about a belief in the target that corresponds to that of the intervener, then the epistemic value of the intervention for the believer is capped at the value of mere true belief. Moreover, if the intervener is wrong, there is no epistemic consolation prize such as rationality or justifiedness left for the target. They just have a bad belief arrived at badly. Thus, though it is possible to run aground in the paternalistic support of good process, one should expect that paternalism runs more moral and epistemic risks to the extent that the object of paternalistic intervention is merely true belief. Holding a true belief is an agentially thin state rather than something thick enough to imply some form of agential excellence.

In the case of an epistemic intervention into just the social expression of someone's epistemic agency, by contrast, it's hard to see how such an intervention counts as *epistemically* good for the target at all. If the intervener takes the target to have a bad belief and the intervention is aimed not at changing that belief or inspiring better cognition but just in restricting its dissemination, then at best, the target would benefit by being guilty of causing less harm, though it's not clear that there is such a thing as purely epistemic, as opposed to moral, guilt. More plausibly, an intervention just at the level of social expression is an intervention on behalf of a collective, not the individual subjected to the intervention. This would be akin to locking up an incorrigibly violent individual whose quality of life is thereby diminished by being imprisoned. When an intervention is undertaken that doesn't benefit the individual whose autonomy is compromised, the moral cost is higher, and one should at best be reticent to engage in substantive interventions of this type without some very strong counter-vailing reason (e.g., that the incorrigibly violent person would maim people if allowed to roam free).

The means used to affect a paternalistic intervention can vary in type as well. Some methods are more epistemically, physically, or emotionally violent than others. One could publicize the rational grounds that recommend the belief one wants to instill in the target. This need not count as being violent in any way. It is notable that appealing to the reason of those we disagree with is not usually thought of as paternalistic even when proffering said reasons is done as an unasked for intervention with the intent of changing someone's mind.[10] This, in effect, is a way of targeting a belief change but in a way that implies good process. One might alternatively seek to enhance the psychological salience of epistemically relevant considerations already available to the target with the aim of making someone more likely to reason or intuit their way to the correct belief. One might harness prudential reason apart from pure epistemic rationality by, for instance, creating contexts in which having the wrong belief costs more and having the right belief is rewarded. One could engineer contexts that temporarily mask the expression of someone's prior belief through framing effects or local social pressure so as to create a window friendly for belief reconsideration if not revision.[11] Likewise, even if one were to give up on the project of changing the mind of the target, one could, once again, seek to neutralize their effects on others.

If one were only concerned with making a psychological impact, one should combine techniques. One should seek to make sure that the intervention's targets heard the correct belief early. One should supply the target with hard evidence and psychologically moving experiences that supported belief. Contrary perspectives should either not be encountered or encountered in a way that foregrounded why they are bad. The social consequences of not adopting the right belief and acting on it in canonical ways should be clearly communicated and so on. If effectiveness is what we're after, one should manage every aspect of whether and how someone ecounters the perspective that the intervener opposes. In short, a paternalism guided only by the end of affecting the desired epistemic change would easily become epistemically violent.

Even when not combined, the farther we get from the attempt to promote good process in the target, the more paternalistic methods are likely to resemble or be identical with exactly the sort of behaviors highlighted when describing the wrongs of epistemic injustice. For instance, suppose that one was placed behind the proverbial veil of ignorance. Suppose, that is, that one did not already know which side of a cultural conflict one was rooting for or to which moral tribe one had fealty. All one is told is that one group is manipulating incentives to exclude and quarantine the perspective of another group and that they are doing so because they considered the other group an epistemically if not morally malignant influence. I do not want to claim that one could not possibly learn anything of relevance to our moral and epistemic evaluation by pulling back the veil. Yet, it seems quite clear that the scenario as described from behind the veil would apply to cases that we recognize as being epistemically unjust and that it captures essential aspects of these situations that make them unjust. The fact that the attempted silencing is done as a paternalistic intervention should go no distance toward reassuring the person behind the veil that what we have is not a case of epistemic injustice. Rather, there should be a strong presumption from behind the veil of ignorance that the intervention is epistemically unjust, and the intervener would bear the burden of proof to show this was not so.

Being willing to commit epistemic violence that one would clearly think of as epistemically unjust if perpetuated by the other puts a lot of pressure on (a) the intervener's claim to represent the correct belief, the correct values, and the correct interpretation of the situation and (b) the idea that we can contain the use of epistemic violence in this situation in a way that can be differentiated in a principled manner from the kind of epistemic violence being redressed. I will not take a stance here on whether one might overcome (a) and (b) in particular cases. As a generalizable practice, however, it seems clear that (a) and (b) are a significant obstacle to a generalizable practice of paternalistic intervention.

As regards (a) consider, for instance, the way in which our fallibility can be accentuated by ideologically laden group disagreements. We are prone to motivated reasoning and confirmation bias on our own. If how we think about an issue is framed by our group, our group makes group-reinforcing resources easy to access and digest, and the rewards of group membership as well as the costs of being at variance with one's group provide a set of (dis)incentives that overlay one's decisions about how to conduct one's inquiry, one should, indeed, expect our cognitive limitations to be heightened.

As regards (b), the veil of ignorance argument already provides us with reason to worry. The trade-off between the effectiveness of a violent intervention and the degree of violence it involves is another reason to worry. The more violent an intervention, the harder it will be to differentiate it from the bad violence being redressed in a justified manner. Yet, one could be forgiven for thinking that the interventions that cost the least are least likely to be effective, especially if the harms that we are trying to root out are deeply engrained in the character or view of the world of the other. Epistemic injustices often are grounded in their perpetrators sense of identity, their view of the world, and their habitual coping strategies. The kinds of epistemic injustice that Fricker and those after her have been concerned with influence what one takes to be evidence and how one interprets evidence. Moreover, they are usually thought to be resistant to counterevidence as a defining feature. For instance, in her definition of prejudice, she says that they "display some (typically, epistemically culpable) resistance to counter-evidence owing to some affective investment" and then, as regards identity-prejudicial stereotypes in particular that they display "resistance to counter-evidence owing to an ethically bad affective investment" (35). Thus, they should be hard to control without serious measures being taken and thus without non-trivial degrees of epistemic violence.

In conclusion, paternalism is always at risk of actively suppressing the production and expression of deviant perspectives, that is, of engaging in silencing. The motive for being violent may be that the paternalist thinks it is what is in the best interest of either the individual targets or society generally, but it would still be violence. On any reasonable view, not all violence is justified, even when the cause is just. Thus, it is very important to either find a robust check on paternalistic violence or an alternative to it. Thus, one should worry that effective paternalism will frequently run high moral costs. That worry is exacerbated only when the target of paternalism is epistemic injustice.

NON-VIOLENT PATERNALISM?

Something we learn from the previous section is that, all other things being equal, the moral and epistemic cost of a paternalistic intervention goes up the greater the violation of autonomy required,[12] the smaller the good brought about, the more that the values animating the intervention deviate from those of the target of the intervention, and the less directly the subject of the intervention is benefited. Moreover, there is reason to believe that for an epistemic paternalism that employs violence, considerations of effectiveness will push interventions in the direction of high moral and epistemic costs. But must epistemic paternalism be violent?

The history of non-violent resistance in the twentieth century suggests another path forward. Although often cited as the bloodiest century in human history, the twentieth century was also witness to a remarkable number of significant social changes and the de-escalation of long-running conflicts through organized non-violence.[13] Non-violent resistance has been successful in so many situations and so many types of situation that many with no intrinsic tie to non-violent methods use the method simply because of its effectiveness, though it seems fair to say that most serious practitioners associate it with intrinsic values such as the dignity or equality of persons (cf. May 2015). Physical non-violence does not, of course, entail epistemic non-violence, but it provides an alternative model for intervention.

Non-violent resistance of the traditional sort has, of course, used a wide array of techniques, but one might boil them down into two categories. The first is the denial of material support. This family of tactics identifies the ways in which one participates in systems that are then used to perpetuate injustice. The non-violent party then strategically refrains from doing so. It is premised on the idea that the oppressor cannot rule the oppressed without the large-scale acquiescence of the latter. In Gandhi's time, for instance, there were a lot more Indians than British soldiers occupying India. If enough Indians did not cooperate, Gandhi knew that British rule would become infeasible.

As applied to epistemic injustice, one could, of course, seek to deny the other material support so as to silence them, but one could also do so for the sake of not participating in the silencing behavior of the bad actor. Doing so is consistent with participating in alternative practices or institutions that do allow the bad actor or better representatives of his perspective a fair chance to be heard. One could, of course, not participate in a practice for the sake of not being complicit in an injustice. That, by itself, would not qualify as a form of epistemic paternalism. If one's denial of material support is directed toward making someone's silencing behavior infeasible or ineffective, then we have a kind of epistemic paternalism. The difference between a violent and a non-violent form of denying material support is that the action is not directed toward the silencing of the unjust person so much as to negating the impact of their silencing behavior. In practice, it will sometimes be hard to separate the two but only sometimes. The non-violent actor will react differently to de-escalation on the part of the violent opponent, for instance, by making room for their participation in civil dialogue so long as it is non-violent.

The second family of tactics common among non-violent campaigns is undertaking strategically symbolic actions that present the opponent with a choice either to make the violence of their position more public and more stark, or else to engage with the non-violent party in a way that formally respects the dignity of the non-violent party. The engagement may come in the form of demanding concessions, but it can also come by way of an invitation to dialogue, debate, or negotiate.[14]

The symbolic action has a function beyond simply obstructing the projects of the opponent. The action should embody a message. The symbolic meaning helps unify the non-violent actors and informs message discipline in a way that something perceived as a mere tactic could not do. A skillfully crafted symbolic action has more potential to garner the attention and sympathy of third-party observers, packaging the values of the non-violent party in a palpable way framed in contrast to the violence of the other side. Finally, the message of the symbolic action paired with a willingness to suffer violence has power to communicate one's moral seriousness and sincerity to the violent party, providing them an opportunity to reassess how they think about the nature of the conflict and the moral status of their allegiances. In fact, there is reason to think that the key factor in whether a non-violent resistance movement will be successful is whether one is able to sap the will of the ground-level enforcers of violence to engage in violence before the discipline of the resistance to engage in organized non-violence breaks.[15]

As applied to the epistemic realm, non-violent, symbolic resistance amounts to putting the other in a position where they must choose between engaging in conspicuous silencing or else make cultural space for fair engagement with or the independent existence of the other.[16] To pluck an example from the history of non-violence with a significant epistemic dimension, consider the "Asociación Madres de Plaza de Mayo" women who gathered in front of the presidential residence in Argentina in the 1970s and 1980s to protest the abduction and disappearance of their loved ones (cf. Guzman Bouvard 2002). Although the protest was also directed at what the military regime was presumed to have done to their loved ones, it was focused on an epistemic injustice, an unjust gap in the public's knowledge. These mothers were demanding to know what had happened to their loved ones and have it publicly acknowledged. If the regime was going to make opponents of the regime disappear, they were invited to extend their silencing to these maternal figures who were publicly shaming the regime, and, of course, several of the mothers were abducted and murdered. The regime's manifesting its violent silencing of opposition in this way, however, only helped to bring the regime down in the end. Indeed, it is hard to imagine that there was a violent alternative open to this group of women that would have been as effective as their non-violent protest in not only bringing down the regime but in remedying the specifically epistemic injustice of not knowing what happened to their loved ones.

The problem with just offering evidence and arguments in the face of epistemic injustice is that epistemic injustice comes with a biased means of identifying and processing evidence, and it's hard to break through. This leads to a temptation to meet violence with violence. Yet, the cost of an epistemic intervention goes up the more violence the intervention involves. The thickness of the agential good potentially brought about goes down the greater the scope of the violent intervention. Non-violent action holds out promise as a way of avoiding this tension between ineffective and violent intervention.

The target of a well-executed non-violent intervention has to choose between more deeply listening to the perspective of the other person or else more starkly experiencing one's impulses to silence others. Either can be a powerful tool for provoking at least a fresh look at one's position and one's biases. Yet, non-violent symbolic engagement is not epistemically violent. It shouldn't require silencing and indeed, it could act as a foundation for a reciprocal engagement where both parties come to understand the other better. Non-violent symbolic engagement aims at thick agential goods without violence but, when done well, captures some of the psychological salience that makes for a good "nudge." Indeed, to borrow the language of nudging, a non-violent intervention presents the target with an epistemic "choice architecture" where one must choose between conspicuous silencing and an openness to the perspective and co-existence of the other party.[17]

Let us, then, set the account of epistemic violence side by side with the non-violent strategies of epistemic paternalism that I have advocated for in this chapter.

> (E-Violence) = Epistemic violence is perpetrated by x anytime x undermines the uptake of y's perspective in a way directed toward the silencing of y and/or undermines the development of an independent perspective by y that could be a candidate for uptake in the first place.
>
> (Non-Violent Material Support) = A putative epistemic injustice by x is responded to by y through y's withholding material support that enables x to commit the epistemic violence at the root of x's injustice and does so in a way that makes reasonable accommodation for x to advocate for the uptake of x's perspective fairly.
>
> (Non-Violent Symbolic Nudging) = A putative epistemic injustice by x is responded to by y through a course of action that puts x in a position where x must choose either to relate to y in a way that makes reasonable accommodation for y to advocate for the uptake of y's perspective or else engage in silencing behaviors whose egregiousness is more conspicuous to x or other observers.

As with the initial introduction of epistemic violence, x and y can be individuals, but they could stand in for groups as well.

CONCLUSION

On a final note, even in the best case scenario, one might think that the moral cost of violence, physical and epistemic, varies quite a bit depending on whether one is in fact in the right. Even if one is allowed to shoot a burglar breaking into one's home, the moral cost of being wrong about whether the person in question is a burglar is heartrendingly high. Yet, we are often in the wrong, even when we think we are on the side of justice. Violent reprisals walk that very fine line between permissibility and grievous error. By way of contrast, there is reason to hope that mistaken non-violent resistance can actually bring more good into the world. If you make yourself vulnerable by repressing the impulse to silence those you think will silence you and instead make yourself visible with your concerns and protests, if you do that before the demonized other and find yourself engaged with honestly and fairly, then it will be easier to realize that you have been in the wrong and to update accordingly. There are potential costs, of course. The withdrawal of material support can cause indirect harm, for instance. The most likely result of a mistaken non-violent intervention is shame and embarrassment. The most likely result of a mistaken violent intervention, however, is more harm being added to the world, potentially of just the sort that inspired the intervention.

NOTES

1. Famously, John Stuart Mills states, "The only purpose for which power can be rightfully exercised over any member of a civilized community, against his will, is to prevent harm to others" (9).

2. For simplicity, the discussion will be conducted in terms of knowledge, but here as elsewhere the discussion would apply to other epistemic goods such as understanding as well.

3. Fricker seems to associate hermeneutical injustices with absences of concepts that should be there. That is certainly an important form that hermeneutical injustice can take, but it is too narrow as a characterization of the general phenomena. If, for example, one is provided with a tainted stereotype for making sense of one's experience or the necessary concept exists but there are social mechanisms in place that prevent or punish one for using it, then I think it is still apt to describe what is going on in terms of hermeneutical injustice.

4. Contributory injustice should probably also be extended to belief-forming practices. As Lorraine Code noted long ago, we are "conservers and modifiers of practices." They are "neither self-generating nor self-sustaining" (1987, 193), and thus we may participate in injustices in the belief-forming practices we lend our agency to as well.

5. Jose Medina's discussion of "meta-insensitivity" and the need for "virtuous interpretive responsiveness" that meets the demands of "polyphonic" contexts involves a similar critique and evolution of Fricker's framework (cf. Medina 2013, 90ff).

6. The most common distinction in paternalisms is between soft and hard paternalism (cf. Feinberg 1986, 12), where, roughly, hard paternalism seeks to prevent voluntary self-harmful behavior and soft paternalism opposes only non-voluntary self-harm. Even examining this distinction closely leads to a proliferation of possible approaches, however, as the nature and relevance of voluntariness and self-harm is complicated (cf. Hanna 2018a).

7. Indeed, the court case example occupies the first 10 pages of Goldman 1991's introduction of the topic. (It is also the guiding example of Ahlstrom-Vij's 2018 handbook article on the subject.) Interestingly, though Goldman then turns to the case of creationism in public schools to illustrate paternalistic exclusion of ideology, the possibility that an ideologue could seize the mantle of epistemic paternalism does not show up. The closest that Goldman gets is a very short paragraph stating that one should be concerned about epistemic paternalism exercised by the state "for historical reasons" (127).

8. Jason Hanna, a defender of "pro-paternalism," calls this "the objection from value imposition" (cf. Hanna 2018b, 87ff).

9. For example, both Conly (2013, 102–112) and Sunstein (2014, 63–71) draw attention to paternalism that focuses on the means taken in the pursuit of one's own ends and contrast that with a paternalism that picks ends for one.

10. For instance, consider this clause from Seana Shiffrin's well-regarded account of what paternalism is. According to Shiffrin, a paternalistic act "involves the substitution of X's judgment or agency for Y's" (2000, 218). The intuition here is that the defining feature of paternalism might be that it takes away an agent's opportunity to engage in good agential processes, substituting the agency of the intervener instead.

11. Of course, the nature of one's method might itself be disputable. For example, the pro-life proponents of a policymaking pregnant women have to witness an ultrasound before having an abortion is probably thought by those pro-lifers to be a paternalistic intervention that makes the woman attend to relevant and psychologically powerful evidence. That is not, of course, what most pro-choice persons would think of that intervention.

12. What the exact nature of autonomy is, how it relates to moral value, and how one ought to think through the relationship between autonomy and paternalism generally are all, of course, deep philosophical questions that take us beyond what can be addressed here. For instance, autonomy plays an important role in every essay in Coons and Weber's 2013 collection on paternalism. I limit my claim here to the claim that the moral cost of an intervention goes up the more it violates someone's autonomy. I do not think that claim should be too controversial. Even Sarah Conly's provocatively titled *Against Autonomy* only goes so far as arguing that the value of autonomy is not "inviolable."

13. For popular but well-researched surveys, cf. Ackerman and Duvall 2000; Kurlansky 2006.

14. To borrow a description of Jurgen Habermas's position from Alfred Moore, "The 'orientation toward agreement' was not about achieving the outcome of consensus, but about the means by which communicative influence was exercised, namely, without using coercion and manipulation in the pursuit of one's goals" (2017, 11). So too here, I am not claiming that a non-violent approach avoids conflict but rather that it eschews many of the natural expressions of conflict to which we are attracted.

15. This is the conclusion of Sharon Nepstad's 2011 comparative analysis of non-violent revolutions that succeed and that fail controlling for the kind of government being opposed.

16. Consider in this connection Sally Haslanger's recommendations (2008, 219) for promoting work by women and minorities in philosophy. I take it that it is three-pronged—soliciting information regarding what dynamics within philosophy are problematic, providing material support for places with supportive dynamics, and encouraging high-profile academics to submit work identifying itself as being from the margins to high profile journals which challenges the mainstream to either make room or engage in conspicuous silencing.

17. I do not claim that such non-violent interventions always qualify as nudges in exactly the Thaler-Sunstein sense. They usually are not "easy and cheap to avoid" for example (Thaler and Sunstein 2008, 6).

BIBLIOGRAPHY

Ahlstrom-Vij, Kristoffer. *Epistemic Paternalism*. London: Palgrave Macmillan, 2013.
Ahlstrom-Vij, Kristoffer. "Epistemic Paternalism," In *The Routledge Handbook of the Philosophy of Paternalism*, edited by Kalle Grille and Jason Hanna, 261–273. New York: Routledge, 2018.
Ackerman, Peter and Jack Duvall. *A Force More Powerful*. New York: St Martin's, 2000.
Code, Lorraine. *Epistemic Responsibility*. London: University of New England, 1987.
Conly, Sarah. *Against Autonomy*. New York: Cambridge University Press, 2013.
Coons, Christian and Michael Weber. *Paternalism: Theory and Practice*. New York: Cambridge University Press, 2013.
Dotson, Kristie. "Tracking Epistemic Violence, Tracking Practices of Silencing." *Hypatia* 26, no. 2 (2011): 236–257.
Dotson, Kristie. "A Cautionary Tale: On Limiting Epistemic Oppression." *Frontiers* 33, no. 1 (2012): 24–47.
Fricker, Miranda. *Epistemic Injustice*. New York: Oxford University Press, 2007.
Goldman, Alvin. "Epistemic Paternalism: Communication Control in Law and Society." *The Journal of Philosophy* 88, no. 3 (1991): 113–131.
Guzman Bouvard, Marguerite. *Revolutionizing Motherhood: The Mothers of the Plaza de Mayo*. New York: Rowman & Littlefield, 2002.
Hanna, Jason. "Hard and Soft Paternalism," In *The Routledge Handbook of the Philosophy of Paternalism*, edited by Kalle Grille and Jason Hanna, 24–34. New York: Routledge, 2018a.
Hanna, Jason. *In Our Best Interest*. New York: Oxford University Press, 2018b.
Haslanger, Sally. "Changing the Ideology and Culture of Philosophy: Not by Reason (Alone)." *Hypatia* 23, no. 2 (2008): 210–223.
Hornsby, Jennifer. "Illocution and Its Significance," In *Foundations of Speech Act Theory*, edited by Savas Tsohatzidis, 187–207. New York: Routledge, 1994.
Kurlansky, Mark. *Nonviolence: The History of a Dangerous Idea*. New York: Random House, 2006.
May, Todd. *Nonviolent Resistance*. New York: Wiley, 2015.
Medina, Jose. *The Epistemology of Resistance*. New York: Oxford University Press, 2013.
Mill, John Stuart. *On Liberty*. Indianapolis, IN: Hackett, 1978.
Moore, Alfred. *Critical Elitism*. New York: Cambridge University Press, 2017.
Nepstad, Sharon. *Nonviolent Revolutions*. New York: Oxford University Press, 2011.
Shiffrin, Seana. "Paternalism, Unconscionability Doctrine, and Accommodation." *Philosophy & Public Affairs* 29, no. 3 (2000): 205–250.
Sunstein, Cass. *Why Nudge?* New Haven, CT: Yale University Press, 2014.
Thaler, Richard and Cass Sunstein. *Nudge*. New Haven, CT: Yale University Press, 2008.

Chapter 18

Paternalistic Knowers and Erroneous Belief

Shaun O'Dwyer

Recent studies such as Miranda Fricker's book *Epistemic Injustice* have promoted greater understanding of the varieties of injustice which infringe on disadvantaged people's ability to know, and which prevent them from being taken seriously as knowers, in efforts to make sense of and overcome the class, gender and racial discrimination generating their disadvantage.[1] These *epistemic* injustices, far from being peripheral to the deprived material circumstances of those discriminated against, rather function systematically to prevent their disadvantages and discriminations from being recognized and remedied. The people subjected to these disadvantaged conditions suffer two epistemic rights deprivations. They are deprived of their *rights to know* accurately and truly the causal factors generating their conditions of deprivation and discrimination, and of their *rights to be taken seriously* as knowers concerned with truthful, accurate assessment of those conditions and with their amelioration. The aim of this chapter is to highlight and suggest remedies to conflicts which arise when an epistemic paternalism aiming to redress deprivations of the right to know impacts unjustly upon the right to be taken seriously.

Consider first the epistemic injustice associated with deprivation of "the right to know." This occurs through *distributive epistemic injustice*, an injustice in the distribution of "epistemic goods," such as true information and knowledge.[2] Instances of such injustice arise wherever poverty, class, sexual and racial discrimination close off from someone the opportunities to acquire further education. She is then deprived of access to high-quality information and inquiry methods for developing reliable, truthful insight into her disadvantaged situation, and for avoiding erroneous beliefs about that situation. As a result of such deprivations, she will lack the conceptual resources for accurately comprehending her situation.

Hermeneutical injustice can then occur in situations where, by reason of a lack of status and authority, a discriminated against person is denied access to and indeed is unable to influence the ways in which extant hermeneutical resources are used to conceptualize her experience.[3] She is thus unable to influence or change dominant understandings, which fail to conceptualize adequately her experiences of, say, gendered and racial abuse, and which also obstruct her from conceptualizing those experiences to herself as discrimination and making them intelligible to others.

In these circumstances, such a person is also likely to be deprived of her right to be taken seriously. One expression of this deprivation is *testimonial injustice*. Suppose that a testifier is Black, female, and lacks university education credentials, professional employment and class-based status. In interactions with authority-holding individuals and institutions, she may be vulnerable to an a priori prejudice, which stigmatizes her epistemic competence in virtue of attributed properties of low intelligence and poor education. Authority-holding figures in her life may also silence her by denying her any epistemic credibility and trustworthiness. She will thus be excluded from the knowledge community deliberating over her circumstances.[4] Such silencing can alternatively occur through objectification based on her attributed status, as at best a passive, uncomprehending witness and information source rather than equal participant in inquiry.[5]

Finally, this testifier will suffer what Kristie Dotson calls *contributory injustice*. Suppose she possesses hermeneutical resources through which she *does already* make sense of her life conditions, which are distinct from "structurally prejudiced hermeneutical resources" reflecting institutionally dominant ways of knowing. Injustice arises when, for instance, institutional authorities refuse out of "situated ignorance" to acknowledge the epistemic value of these distinctive hermeneutical resources she possesses and her articulation of her experience through them.[6]

One problem with the apparently integrated account of epistemic injustices outlined earlier is that its four different perspectives are in tension with each other. David Coady has pointed out one such tension. Suppose that distributive epistemic injustice impinges upon someone's right to know better about her world in two senses. First, she is placed, or left in a situation where she is wrong about something she is entitled to be right about; she is unable to evade a false belief that she has a right to evade. Or she is placed or left in a situation where she is ignorant of something that she "has a right to know"; she is unable to know what she is entitled to know.[7] Fricker's account of epistemic injustice focuses on unjust devaluation of the knowledge and expertise of testifiers, and of unjust distributions in hermeneutical resources that prevent marginalized groups from making their disadvantaged situation intelligible.

Yet suppose as a matter of distributive epistemic injustice a member of the oppressed group happens to be wrong in her assessment of her situation, or is unable to render the injustice in her experience intelligible to others or to herself as a result of hermeneutical injustice. In this case, the distinctive claims of testimonial, hermeneutical and contributory injustice lose persuasive force. It would be right not to give credibility to this member's beliefs that are false or arise out of ignorance, though this situation is a result of injustice. It would also be of no concern that she cannot (yet) make intelligible claims about her situation, since she is less likely to be able to express true statements about it anyway. Moreover, the "alternative epistemologies and countermythologies" that a particular community uses to make sense of its experience may not be vital hermeneutical resources for them to articulate their distinctive sense of belonging and their oppression as *knowledge*. They may rather be instances of erroneous, adaptive preferences as Amartya Sen defines them: "adaptation[s] of desires and preferences to existing inequalities viewed in terms of perceived legitimacy."[8] Intervention by nongovernmental organizations (for instance) is required both to inform oppressed individuals of the truth, and to educate them in the skills they need for fulfilling, on their own, their "right to know."

However, such interventions could exacerbate rather than alleviate the tensions between the two types of epistemic injustice, by giving rise to what I term *judgmental epistemic paternalism*, derived from Jonathon Quong's definition of judgmental paternalism. In judgmental paternalism, an agent is motivated to try and improve the "welfare, good, happiness, needs, interests or values" of another agent. Yet the agent does so on the basis of a "negative judgment" about the latter's ability to decide competently on those matters in a deliberative problem she faces. When such paternalism is directed toward a mentally competent adult, Quong holds that it is "presumptively wrong." It diminishes her dignity and equal standing as a citizen by treating her like a child, incapable of formulating, pursuing and revising her own good for herself.[9] The profound tension the epistemic variety of this paternalism gives rise to is that similarly motivated efforts to ameliorate the structural, discriminatory conditions that violate an agent's right to know x can also impinge on her right to be taken seriously. On the basis of negative ascriptions about her current cognitive skill level grounded in judgments about her educationally deprived, discriminated against status, paternalistic agents presume that she is not *yet* competent to know x. She is therefore not in a position to deliberate over her good regarding x, and is not even aware of the present cognitive and informational deprivation that prevents her from knowing x. She is then potentially vulnerable to testimonial, hermeneutical and contributive injustice. This is because her epistemic credibility is devalued, and her right to participate on equal terms in any community of knowers considering her plight denied, until such time as she is educated sufficiently to exercise her own "right to know."

A brief semi-autobiographical sketch by African-American writer Richard Wright crystalizes these concerns. He relates a horrifying incident from his childhood in early twentieth-century Jim Crow Mississippi, in which his mother, an impoverished domestic worker, beat him until he "had a fever of one hundred and two" after he was injured in an unequal fight with white boys whose parents she worked for. He described her as belting into him "gems of Jim Crow wisdom," including that he was not to fight with, act up against, or disrespect white folks, on whom they depended for their livelihood.[10]

These beliefs of Wright's mother, conditioned by her oppressive life conditions, could be, from the point of view of contributory injustice analysis, an "alternative epistemology." It is a folk knowledge, which is a hermeneutical resource conducive to survival in desperately oppressive circumstances. Yet its value in such circumstances is distorted by the use liberal humanitarian or socialist observers make of "structurally prejudiced hermeneutical resources" to peremptorily dismiss Wright's mother's understanding as false consciousness. Imagine middle-class socialist outsiders telling her that her situation deprives her of true understanding of her and her son's oppression and that she should acquire such understanding under their tutelage. Surely the anguished retort would have been "What do you know? I just want my boy to stay alive!"

I will argue here that this tension may be overcome, and that judgmental epistemic paternalism is avoidable. I will explain further how an ethically motivated doxastic regard for the instrumental value of beliefs in sustaining individual self-worth or the social cohesion and survival of oppressed minorities can be distinguished from epistemic regard for beliefs that are evidentially justified and true. Incorporated into that epistemic regard is an ideal standard of epistemically respectful rebuttal of erroneous beliefs. This standard acknowledges the cognitive capabilities of those subjected to such rebuttal—acknowledgement that is due to them as mentally competent adults, irrespective of race, class or gender.

TWO IDEAL DOXASTIC DOMAINS

Let us first consider two ideal doxastic domains for belief fixation, maintenance and transmission informed by "different, incompatible sets of hermeneutical resources."

In doxastic domain "A," there is a set of beliefs about what is and isn't so in the world, how things, events and their relations in it are classified and ordered, and how they were so classified and ordered with reference to specifiable things, events and things in the past, the present and the future. These beliefs are fixed by largely unreflective individual inclination or collectively observed custom, and in the latter case, adherence to them is enforced by collective shaming and punishment of unorthodox belief holders or dissenters. There is also a set of values guiding and constraining actions toward these beliefs, regarding which beliefs should be regarded as sacrosanct or sacrilegious. These values, which I will call *thumetic* values (after the Greek *thumos*, "feeling," "spirit," or "passion"), include piety, faith, reverence and loyalty. In this domain, belief change does occur, but such change is for the most part gradual and unreflective, with a largely unconscious alteration of belief in the course of intergenerational transmission.

In domain "B," there is also a set of beliefs about what things, events and relations justifiably are and aren't known to be so in the world and how they are ordered and classified, with reference to specifiable events and things in the present, the past and the future. In this domain, beliefs are not fixed by inclination, custom or by the fiat of authority. They are fixed through methods of inquiry guided by the conviction that—as Charles Peirce once put it—"there are Real things, whose characters are entirely different from our individual opinions about them (that) affect our senses according to regular laws" and that through careful, disciplined observation of those laws we can discern "how things really and truly are."[11] In this domain, there are values that guide processes of elaborating and choosing hypotheses for how those events and things stand in their properties and relations, for assembling and assessing evidence or proofs to test them and for forming beliefs that are conducive to truth or informed opinion. These values are *epistemic* in character. They include values instantiated in practices of inquiry, such as verifiability, credibility, logical coherence and facticity, justification, informed opinion, warranted assertability and truth. They also include "thick," specifically agent-relative values, or, as some would say, epistemic virtues of intellectual curiosity, open-mindedness, truthfulness, honesty, objectivity and impartiality. Belief change in this domain can be both reflexive and rapid, as beliefs once held to be true, or offered up as candidates for truthfulness, are examined and found in light of evidence to be incredible, unverifiable and untrue.

In formulating these model doxastic domains, I take a leaf out of Charles S. Peirce's book that there are a plurality of means for fixing belief about how things and events are in the world. These means can be guided by epistemic as well as non-epistemic values with thumetic values constituting a subset of the latter. On this view, epistemic and thumetic values are, however, commensurable; they can be compared and ranked against each other, and the priority of epistemic values asserted in matters of knowing.

However, no one can live and thrive in a world where beliefs are wholly governed by domain A or domain B. A scientific community may hold certain beliefs—what Wittgenstein called "hinge propositions" including Charles Peirce's conviction in "real things"—which have high heuristic value in their discipline. These propositions delimit the boundaries of acceptable hypothesis and theory elaboration in the context of discovery, and delimit the scope of admissible evidence for verification in the context of justification. Sociologists of science and feminist critics may reveal the degree to which thumetic values of faith in those propositions, in-groupist loyalties to fellow (mostly male) adherents who share that faith and reverence by junior scholars for seniors who exemplify such faith enforce the boundaries of belonging in actual communities of knowers.[12] These values elevate the acceptable bar for, and impose potential disciplinary costs upon, pursuit of inquiry to question those beliefs, and delimit the scope of what is at any time "acceptable" theory.[13]

The distinguishing feature of values from Domain B is that they guide cognitive processes that are conducive to truth as the over-arching epistemic value or to approximations to it such as informed belief. They also have built-in reflexivity about their own capacity (or incapacity) to guide those processes. In scientific controversy, non-epistemic thumetic values serving the in-group biases and affiliations of knowledge communities will come under scrutiny once it is realized that they obstruct inquiry.[14]

AN IDEAL SCHEMA FOR THE REBUTTAL OF ERRONEOUS BELIEF

Now I want to consider two hypothetical scenarios where beliefs potentially consistent with values in domain A and B are disputed and rebutted. The distinguishing feature of these scenarios is a clear refusal to accord *epistemic* recognition to "alternative hermeneutical resources" associated with domain A values. This is because, from the point of those rebutting them, *those resources are considered as non-epistemic in character and therefore irrelevant to epistemic justification.* Such scenarios *could* provide instances of what may be taken to be the contributory injustice described by Kristie Dotson and of the testimonial injustice described by both Miranda Fricker and Dotson. For in such instances, the beliefs subject to rebuttal are held by members of discriminated against communities and minorities. My aim in presenting these scenarios is to show that epistemic and ethical injustices can both arise in such efforts at rebuttal, but they need to be carefully delineated and kept conceptually distinct from each other. The hypothetical scenarios are as follows.

1. A close friend diagnosed with stage 4 pancreatic cancer has rejected conventional medical treatment for an alternative health remedy, which

prescribes vitamin pill dosages as a cancer cure. I (a man) present her with multiple research findings demonstrating that such vitamin cures for cancer have been scientifically discredited, and will make no difference to the course of the illness.
2. Members of a marginalized and impoverished indigenous group hold a local mountain to be sacred, and blame a recent, disastrous earthquake on a failure to adequately propitiate the mountain's spirit. A seismologist representing government emergency services rebuts their belief, informing them of the results of regional seismological studies that provide the sole, credible explanation for the occurrence of the earthquake. The seismologist urges them to accept state assistance in adopting earthquake mitigation, safety and evacuation measures consistent with that explanation.

The ideal schema R for such rebuttals would be as follows:

1. Speaker S states to Listener L the proposition P, knowing that L does not believe P is true.
2. S states E1 and E2 as evidence in support of P.
3. S appeals to epistemic values V1 and V2 as action-guiding in the demonstration that E1 and E2 are credible, verified and stand in a relation of evidential justification to P.
4. S proceeds with steps 1–3 on the belief that (A) L is capable of accepting V1 and V2 as action-guiding; and that therefore (B) L is capable of accepting E1 and E2 as credible and verified; so that (C) L is also capable of accepting that E1 and E2 thereby stand in a relation of evidential justification for P; and finally that (D) L is capable of offering counter-arguments in support of an alternative proposition not-P, potentially justified by counterevidence appealing to V1 and V2.

Note that for reasons of brevity, I have not included L's counter-arguments against P or justifications for a rival proposition like not-P. Implicit in (4) is S's acknowledgement of L's capability (and implicitly, right) to assert such counter-arguments or justifications. In scenarios 1–2, I argue that injustices can arise, but care must be taken to distinguish epistemic from ethical injustice; and to show that epistemic injustice and the unwarranted epistemic paternalism that is its expression alone arises from infelicities, or failures, arising in the four-step schema discussed above, which I will discuss next.

Where is such epistemic failure or infelicity likely to occur in the four steps outlined earlier? I would argue that possibility for such failure arises in S's attitude to what I will term the *sincerity* conditions stated in step 4 of schema R. These conditions state assumptions through which S sincerely attributes epistemic capabilities to L, recognizing in her what is her due as an epistemic agent and partner in inquiry, rather than subjecting her to the epistemic objectification characteristic of testimonial injustice. They also recognize her ability to hold certain epistemic values as "shared hermeneutical resources" for inquiry. S acknowledges that L therefore understands how these are action-guiding in the selection and confirmation of information which can then be potentially recognized as evidence justifying P—that L disagrees with—and that L in turn is in principle capable of justifying a counter-rebuttal of P and of providing evidential support for a rival proposition not-P.

Rebuttal of L's belief may therefore fall short of success at any of the following steps. L may accept being guided by epistemic values V1 and V2 or be persuaded to accept them, but refuse to admit their application as action-guiding with respect to one or more items of evidence E1 and E2. Or she may argue that E1 or E2 do not stand in a sufficiently justificationary relation to P, compared to the items of evidence, which she believes—supposedly under guidance from V1 and V2—stand in a more robust justificationary relationship with the alternative proposition, not-P. In all these cases, rebuttal will not result in L accepting the truth of P, but it may result in a still desirable epistemic state from S's point of view. That is, L may be persuaded to (1) at least open her mind to the possibility that P is true; or (2) accept the possibility that E1 or E2 are *potentially* factual, credible, and verified even if singly or collectively they fall short of L's own justificationary threshold with respect to P; or (3) at least accept the possibility that V1 and V2 are potentially action-guiding and applicable in a domain of belief where L had previously excluded them. Alternatively, there is a prospect that S will open his own mind to the possibility that P is false, following from L's response to his attempted rebuttal.

Yet in accordance with a judgmental epistemic paternalist stance, S may alternatively proceed with steps 1–3 in a truncated form, reducing or completely omitting the argumentative and justificatory moves in 2–3 and cutting off L from issuing counter-arguments. S will do this because he is not committed to the sincerity conditions stated in (4), presuming L to be epistemically deficient. This negative judgment on L's epistemic capacities may arise from S's conviction that L has succumbed to dogmatism in her refusal either to accept P or even to open her mind to the possibility of P. For S, this dogmatism conceivably arises out of (1) L's *epistemic inconsistency*. That is, L understands V1 and V2 and is committed to their application in other belief domains, but is unwilling to apply them consistently to the particular domain of belief where P is in question. L will be unwilling to accept E1 or E2 under guidance from V1 and V2, and may supply counterevidence for her own belief that is inconsistent with her professed commitment to V1 and V2. Therefore, she will be unwilling in conditions of argumentation to submit to refutation and accept P as justified, or to at least open her mind to the possibility that P is justified. Or S may proceed from the conviction that L has succumbed to (2) *epistemic nullity*, that L is either unwilling or incapable of entertaining any recognizable epistemic criteria for why she should or should not hold her beliefs. She is unwilling or incapable of comprehending V1 and V2 in any domain of belief, and does not grasp or is unable to grasp the evidential standing of E1 or E2 in light of V1 and V2 in relation to P. She just has a tenacious "faith" that they are true.

Either way, S will proceed to use the epistemic resources available not with the intention of persuading L with an argument based on evidence to accept P, or to at least open her mind to its possible truth, but with different, or interrelated, intentions to dismiss, silence, ridicule, shame or denounce L's beliefs and assert P over the top of them. S does one or all of these things based on the negative judgment that L is not a competent knower, at least in the domain of belief at hand. There may be ameliorative intent in such actions. S may intend to shame L into a more epistemically responsible attitude toward P, or at least toward a more consistent and informed attitude to epistemic values (facticity, veracity, truth, etc.) that would be consistent with open-mindedness toward P. On the face of it, such conduct does not by itself provide sound reasons for thinking that S is committing testimonial injustice against L. There are some beliefs so wrong and also so pernicious in their effects—beliefs about racial supremacy, for instance—that polemical ridicule, dismissal, and denunciation are the most epistemically just responses to them.

However, considered in light of the discussion of Schema R, there are two potential reasons for epistemic injustice occurring when the sincerity conditions specified in (4) are not met. Firstly, S may hold a priori what Fricker calls a "negative identity-prejudicial stereotype": a common "disparaging association" between a social group and attributes, which presume the inherent (but possibly reformable) epistemic inconsistency, nullity or lack of epistemic credibility in members of that group.[15] We can argue that this prejudicial stereotype is an epistemically blameworthy attribute, because it is a stable disposition arising out of defects in psychology and epistemic character for which the agent can reasonably be held responsible for.[16] S should "know better" than to hold such prejudices, but is resistant to counterevidence because of a prior "affective investment" in the belief that any individual member of that group will lack competence and credibility as a knower.

This is one source of epistemic injustice against a knower, but it ties it to that knower's membership in a systematically discriminated against group. I want to add that there is also a less systematic interpersonal epistemic injustice, also arising from a blameworthy epistemic deficiency. It is an injustice in which S, without prior confirmation or inquiry, presumes in advance the inconsistency or nullity in L's belief on grounds *unrelated to L's membership in any discriminated against group*, and proceeds to rebuttal without commitment to the sincerity criterion outlined in step 4 in Schema R. These grounds will relate to particular, unreasonable assessments of L's epistemic competence in general or with respect to the particular domain of belief in question. For instance, S disparages L's competence because L is not an elite university graduate—independently of whether or not L belongs to a group that is also the subject of prejudice concerning the epistemic capabilities of its members.

In respect of Schema R earlier, epistemic injustice will occur once S devotes epistemic resources to rebut L's belief if (and only if)

A) out of "negative identity-prejudicial stereotype" or more particularized, culpable misrecognition of L's epistemic competence, S does not commit himself to the sincerity conditions stated in step 4 of schema R; and
B) thereby asserts P while unreasonably truncating or omitting altogether argumentative and justificationary moves outlined in steps 1- 3 of schema R.

These instances of epistemic injustice find expression as judgmental epistemic paternalism insofar as S, out of an unwarranted, a priori negative judgment refuses to recognize in L the cognitive capacities that is due to her as a mentally competent adult. S not only truncates or omits steps 1–3 of schema R as a means for inducing belief change in L, but also asserting his own superior cognitive ability, his "say so" that he knows better than L as the sole reason for why L should accept P as true. In doing so, he silences and epistemically objectifies L, attempting to disqualify her from being an equal participant in and contributor to inquiry, or to a knowledge community that—for instance—is deliberating over her own good.

EPISTEMIC AND ETHICAL INJUSTICE IN REBUTTALS OF ERRONEOUS BELIEF

This leaves the criteria for distinguishing *ethical* from *epistemic* injustice. I will briefly consider hypothetical scenarios 1–2 stated earlier in light of the criteria for epistemic injustice, and suggest ways in which they can be distinguished from ethical injustice.

In scenario 1, epistemic injustice occurs if I unreasonably presume in advance, on the basis of gender-based prejudice or more individualized personality judgment, my friend's rejection or inconsistent uptake of epistemic values in considering information that might disconfirm her faith in a vitamin cure. Rather than outlining in good faith the case against her current belief by presenting her with evidence that disproves it and explaining its credibility and veracity, I make perfunctory reference to such evidence.

Alternatively, I proceed directly to dismiss her belief as quackery, and ignore her counter-arguments. This is an instance of epistemic injustice since I owe it to my friend to presume her competence as an epistemic agent, and not to paternalistically assert my own belief in conventional medical approaches and demand her acceptance of them, while brusquely dismissing her beliefs.

Suppose I do proceed scrupulously with a commitment to the "sincerity" criteria in schema R in rebutting my friend's belief and hearing out her response, thereby fulfilling my duty to attribute to her the epistemic competence that is her due as an adult. Something may still be "off" or even cruel in this course of action. Imagine I find her still tenacious in clinging to her beliefs, and now also deeply distressed. My rebuttal may have proceeded from ignorance of, or an unwillingness to consider, the distress it may cause to someone terrified at the prospect of her impending death and clinging to any hope of a "miracle" cure. I have forgotten that I owe to her, as *my friend*, a certain forbearance regarding her belief, particularly if her preferred "cure" involves no likelihood of physical harm and incurs no great financial expense.

There may, in other words, be good reasons for respecting other people's faith in beliefs that we know to be erroneous—and thus to forbear from trying to refute them—but these are non-epistemically motivated reasons. We may feel bound by relational ties of love, loyalty and friendship to see such forbearance as something that is due to someone as a family member or friend. A case *could* thus be made that there is, in some cases, ethical injustice in even scrupulous, epistemically just rebuttal of beliefs that are central to the friend's or loved one's psychological well-being in a time of personal crisis. These are beliefs guided by thumetic values of faith or piety.

In scenario 2, similar considerations apply, though an attitude of forbearing silence will not be desirable when information vital to a community's welfare needs to be communicated. The seismologist owes it to the indigenous community's members the presumption that they are epistemically competent agents. So she should present her data and the values guiding it on the assumption that they do share sufficient of her hermeneutical resources to be at least open minded to her explanation for the occurrence of the earthquake. She would then also be bound to hear out their counter-arguments and accept them as equal participants in an inquiry in which they can also open her mind to new information. Epistemic injustice occurs when, out of "negative identity-prejudicial stereotype," the seismologist does not commit to the sincerity condition in schema R, if she makes no sincere effort to outline evidence in favor of a scientific explanation for the earthquake, and for the epistemic values informing it. This injustice finds expression in a judgmental epistemic paternalism asserting the superiority of this explanation and of scientific knowledge, dismissing and ridiculing their beliefs and their responses to her as childish "superstition" that must be immediately dismissed for the sake of their own good.

Yet a scrupulous, sincerely conducted rebuttal may also be "off" in this case. The seismologist's rebuttal could still be conducted in ignorance or, or out of unwillingness to consider that the indigenous group's animist belief in the mountain's spirits are vital for the group's social cohesion and self-respect. Thumetic values of faith, piety and reverence are in this case critical for sustaining beliefs central to a minority's communal belonging, in the face of a wider society that is indifferent to or contemptuous of their way of life.

Such a rebuttal will therefore come off as insensitive and disrespectful to those thumetic values and to the beliefs that they guide. It will likely be seen by members of the indigenous group as the latest round in a series of disrespectful actions aimed by "expert" members of the dominant society against them, and as another iteration of a colonial power extinguishing their culture. This, I would argue, amounts to a type of ethical rather than epistemic injustice. To avoid it, the seismologist's efforts at persuasion must engage the community's members in an inquiry over how to accommodate an attitude of cultural and tradition respect with absorption of the scientific viewpoint she urges. Such efforts would have to proceed from an understanding of the instrumental importance of traditional beliefs for the indigenous community's social cohesion and self-respect. The better alternative would be for scientifically educated members of that indigenous community who also remain conversant with its traditions to take on this persuasive role instead of her.

CONCLUSION

The conclusion to be drawn from the arguments above is as follows. Practices for fixing belief guided by thumetic values and practices for fixing belief guided by epistemic values are commensurable. They and their guiding values can be ranked against each other, and in matters of deciding truth those guided by epistemic values will be ranked higher because they are the most reliable means for arriving at truth. I have sought to provide an ideal schema for evaluating efforts at persuading members of disadvantaged groups to inquire into, modify, or abandon demonstrably erroneous beliefs, to confirm whether such efforts are themselves epistemically unjust, because proceeding from and shaped by epistemically paternalist motivations. I have tried to do so while confronting the contentious issue of how such beliefs, often central to the social cohesion, self-respect, and even sense of survival of marginalized, discriminated groups can still be accorded doxastic, if not epistemic respect.

NOTES

1. Miranda Fricker. *Epistemic Injustice: Power and the Ethics of Knowing* (Oxford: Clarendon Press, 2007).
2. David Coady. "Two Concepts of Epistemic Injustice." *Episteme* 7, no. 2 (2010), pp. 101–113.
3. Fricker, *Epistemic Injustice*, 147–176.
4. Ibid., 41–60.
5. Ibid., 132–133.
6. Kristie Dotson. "A Cautionary Tale. On Limiting Epistemic Oppression." *Frontiers* 33, no. 1 (2012): 31–33.
7. Coady, "Two Concepts," 109–111.
8. Amartya Sen. "Gender Inequality and Theories of Justice," in *Women, Culture and Development: A Study of Human Capabilities*, edited by M. Nussbaum and J. Glover (Oxford: Oxford University Press, 1995), pp. 262–263.
9. Jonathon Quong, *Liberalism without Perfection* (Oxford: Oxford University Press, 2012), pp. 100–101.
10. Richard Wright. *Uncle Tom's Children* (New York: HarperCollins, 1938), pp. 2–3.
11. Charles Peirce. "The Fixation of Belief," in *Philosophical Writings of Peirce*. Edited by J. Buchler (New York: Dover), p. 18.
12. For an overview of this debate, see Anthony Brueckner, "Hinge Propositions and Epistemic Justification," *Pacific Philosophical Quarterly* 88, no. 3 (2007): 285–287.
13. For discussion of different approaches to the status of epistemic and non-epistemic values in epistemology and philosophy of science, see Heather Douglas "Values in Science" in *The Oxford Handbook of Philosophy of Science*, edited by P. Humphries (Oxford: Oxford University Press), pp. 610–633.
14. See, for example, Keith Ashman, "Measuring the Bubble Constant" in *After the Science Wars* edited by K. Ashman and P. Barringer (London: Routledge, 2001), pp. 97–117.
15. Fricker, *Epistemic Injustice*, 35.
16. On such a responsibilist account of attributing "epistemic vice," see Ian Kidd, "Charging Others with Epistemic Vice," *The Monist* 87 (2016): 181–197.

BIBLIOGRAPHY

Ashman, Keith. "Measuring the Bubble Constant," in *After the Science Wars*, edited by K. Ashman and P. Barringer 97–117. London: Routledge, 2001.

Brueckner, Anthony. "Hinge Propositions and Epistemic Justification," *Pacific Philosophical Quarterly* 88, no. 3 (2007): 285–287.

Coady, David. "Two Concepts of Epistemic Injustice." *Episteme* 7, no. 2 (2010): 101–113.

Dotson, Kristie. "A Cautionary Tale. On Limiting Epistemic Oppression." *Frontiers* 33, no. 1 (2012): 31–33.

Douglas, Heather. "Values in Science," in *The Oxford Handbook of Philosophy of Science*, edited by P. Humphries 610–633. Oxford: Oxford University Press, 2014.

Fricker, Miranda. *Epistemic Injustice: Power and the Ethics of Knowing*. Oxford: Clarendon Press, 2007.

Kidd, Ian. "Charging Others with Epistemic Vice," *The Monist* 87 (2016): 181–197.

Peirce, Charles. "The Fixation of Belief," in *Philosophical Writings of Peirce*, edited by J. Buchler, 5–23. New York: Dover, 1955.

Quong, Jonathon. *Liberalism without Perfection*. Oxford: Oxford University Press, 2012.

Sen, Amartya. "Gender Inequality and Theories of Justice," in *Women, Culture and Development: A Study of Human Capabilities*, edited by M. Nussbaum and J. Glover 259–274. Oxford: Oxford University Press, 1995.

Wright, Richard. *Uncle Tom's Children*. New York: HarperCollins, 1938.

Chapter 19

Paternalism and Intellectual Charity

Charlie Crerar

THE PUZZLE OF CHARITY

"Be charitable." This is a familiar refrain among philosophers. It is the exhortation that we make to students as they encounter the work of easily caricatured historical figures. It is the advice that we offer to the teaching assistant who is struggling to engage with their seminar group. It is the plea that we make to colleagues as we present a new paper for the first time.

Intellectual charity, these interactions suggest, is a good thing. More specifically, it is an *epistemically* good thing. When we expound the value of intellectual charity, we are not (merely) encouraging people to be nice to each other. Rather, we are presenting intellectual charity as part of good, responsible epistemic practice. Part of what it is to be a good philosopher—a good reader of philosophy, a good teacher of philosophy, a good interlocutor about philosophical issues—is the ability and willingness to be charitable with the views of those with whom we disagree. Indeed, while my focus here will primarily be charity within academic settings, its importance extends far beyond these. Entrenched polarization and partisanship, "take-down" and "pile-on" culture on social media, breakdowns in inter-cultural dialogue: we are all familiar with the problems afflicting public discourse in societies across the world. A greater willingness to be charitable across viewpoints would be no panacea for these problems, but it might help.[1]

In this chapter, I treat charity as a putative intellectual virtue. I employ a virtue epistemological framework because it naturally lends itself to an exploration of charity's positive epistemic status, and to distinguish the charitable dispositions I am interested in from charity as an interlinguistic principle or interpretative tool.[2] Nothing crucial hangs on this designation of charity as a distinct intellectual virtue, though. At the very least, it seems uncontroversial that charitable is something the intellectually virtuous agent should be, at least on occasion.

This claim about the epistemic value of charity may be uncontroversial, but it is also somewhat puzzling. After all, when we stop and think about what being charitable actually involves, there is something prima facie suspect about it. Consider some paradigmatic manifestations of intellectual charity: the student who resists the temptation to dismiss Kant on the basis of her peers' concerns about axe-murderers, instead stopping to consider whether anything can be said in his defense; the colleague who, determined to be helpful with their feedback, tries to read an incoherent-seeming paper again with fresh eyes; the tourist who suspends judgment on an apparently nonsensical cultural practice on the assumption that "there must be some justification for it, even if I cannot see what it is." In each case, an agent is assessing the epistemic merits of some view or position. They judge that, on the basis of the evidence available to them, this view or position ought to be dismissed. Charitably, however, they display a willingness to look beyond this evidence, to try and find a way of viewing this position in a more favorable light.

This willingness of the charitable agent, to lend credence or other cognitive resources in disproportion to their evidence, clashes with some basic epistemic precepts. Take the following principle, as formulated by Alvin Goldman:

Requirement of Total Evidence (RTE): A cognitive agent X should always fix [their] beliefs or subjective probabilities in accordance with the total evidence in [their] possession at the time.[3]

RTE is a principle concerning the fixation of belief, but structurally similar principles concerning the distribution of other cognitive resources—how we should apportion credence, say, or where we should assign time and effort in epistemic practice—are equally plausible. The general idea invoked here is that, in our epistemic activities, we should be sensitive to, guided by, and accommodating of the evidence available to us. To be clear, I do not intend to explicitly commit myself to this evidential ideal. Rather, I think it represents a reasonable default standard, a plausible apportioning of the burden of proof. If we find ourselves espousing the value of an epistemic practice that requires, as in paradigmatic manifestations of intellectual charity, that one purposefully disregards their assessment of the available evidence, then we better have some story to tell about what makes doing so epistemically worthwhile.

The aim of this chapter is to undertake this vindicatory task as it applies to intellectual charity. That is, my aim is to explain why it is a good thing to be charitable, even if it sometimes requires that one disregards their assessment of the available evidence. One initially attractive way of doing so, I will note, is by way of an appeal to the other-regarding benefits of charitable interactions. This defense interprets intellectual charity as a form of epistemic paternalism, and looks to justify charity in the same way that paternalistic interventions are justified. I offer two objections to this solution, before presenting my own account of charity as a corrective virtue. I conclude by comparing these two accounts, and offering some final thoughts on the connections between epistemic paternalism and intellectual charity.

CHARITY AS PATERNALISM

Goldman's discussion of RTE offers a potentially helpful starting point for our discussion. His main concern is with a related principle, one that can be reached by an apparently straightforward extension of the logic underpinning RTE. What RTE implies is that beliefs fixed in accordance with all of the available evidence are epistemically better than beliefs fixed in accordance with only part of the available evidence. If we grant this, then it seems a small step to the claim that it is also better to have more evidence available than less. And, if *that* is granted, then it is presumably also best if those who control one's access to evidence make as much evidence available as possible. This reasoning leads Goldman to the "control" version of RTE:

Control RTE (C-RTE): If agent X is going to make a doxastic decision concerning question Q, and agent Y has control over the evidence that is provided to X, then, from a purely epistemic point of view, Y should make available to X all of the evidence relevant to Q which is (at negligible cost) within Y's control.[4]

Goldman's thesis is that, despite the initially plausible nature of the reasoning underpinning C-RTE, as a principle it is sometimes—perhaps often—false. One of his central examples concerns the admissibility of evidence in criminal trials. Assume that the central task of a jury is to reach a correct determination of a defendant's guilt. If C-RTE is right, then the best way of facilitating this would be to provide jurors with as much evidence relevant to this question as possible. In practice, however, this is not always what happens. Instead, judges in many jurisdictions can exclude evidence from proceedings if they believe that hearing that evidence might mislead the jury. For example, a judge might rule that the court cannot hear evidence about the defendant's prior involvement in similar crimes. This evidence is surely relevant to the jurors' task, since an ideally rational agent who heard this evidence would assign a higher subjective probability to the defendant's guilt. Nonetheless, a judge may decide that hearing this evidence would have *too much* of an impact on the jurors' deliberations—this evidence is relevant, but not so relevant as the jurors would likely think it—and opt to exclude it on this basis. Contrary to C-RTE, in other words, the judge might determine that the jurors are better placed to carry out the epistemic function assigned to them if they have access to only part of the available evidence.

The judge's actions in cases like these constitute a now classic example of epistemic paternalism. By restricting the pool of evidence to which the jurors have access, the judge is interfering with their ability to conduct inquiry in ways that the jurors see fit. Her actions thus satisfy the *interference condition*, one of the three definitional conditions that Kristoffer Ahlstrom-Vij has identified for acts of epistemic paternalism.[5] Ahlstrom-Vij's other two conditions specify when such an interference counts as epistemically paternalistic.

First, a paternalistic interference will meet the *non-consultation condition*. A paternalistic interference is one carried out without consulting or seeking permission from the target of the intervention. The judge, in Goldman's case, imposes this restriction on the jurors. Had she done so at their request or following consultation, these restrictions would not count as paternalistic.

Second, a paternalistic interference will meet the *improvement condition*. Such an interference will be undertaken with the intent of making the targeted agent(s) epistemically better off. For Ahlstrom-Vij this means improving access to true beliefs, though we can also identify other forms of epistemic improvement; Michel Croce, for example, focuses on improvements in a subject's understanding of some topic or in their level of epistemic virtue.[6] Whatever the nature of the improvements anticipated, it is these that serve to justify the paternalistic act. The judge is only warranted in restricting the pool of information available to the jurors insofar as she justifiably believes that doing so will facilitate their making a correct judgment about the defendant's guilt. If she had nefarious ulterior motives or if her belief in the epistemic benefits of these restrictions was unjustified then her paternalistic intervention would lack justification on epistemic grounds.

The broadly consequentialist defenses of epistemic paternalism by Goldman and Ahlstrom-Vij show how there can sometimes be an epistemic justification for violating intuitive principles about the acquisition and use of evidence. Perhaps we can say something similar about the prima facie questionable evidential practices involved in intellectual charity. Perhaps, in other words, the reason we value a charitable disposition is because, like epistemic paternalism, it brings about epistemic benefits for others.

This explanation seems promising in cases like the following. A student in an undergraduate ethics class attempts a criticism of Kantian deontology. Their objection is a tired one, which has been covered in class *ad nauseum* and for which there are a number of available responses. Rather than treat the question dismissively, however, the instructor charitably picks up on a more fruitful interpretation of what the student meant, albeit one that is at most tangentially related to the student's clear intent in asking the question. What justifies her in purposefully misinterpreting the student in this way, presumably, is just the thought that doing so would be pedagogically useful; that, rather than bluntly clearing up a simple misunderstanding, taking the question off on a tangent would help the class as a whole come to a greater appreciation of the nuances of the topic at hand, while also preserving the intellectual confidence of the questioner. In other words, just as in cases of epistemic paternalism, the instructor is motivated by the epistemic improvements on offer, both for the questioner and for the class in general.

In fact, a stronger claim about the connection between intellectual charity and epistemic paternalism is open to us here. Note that, in the case just provided, the two other conditions on epistemic paternalism are *also* met. The student wished to inquire about a particular aspect of Kant's view, but the intervention of the instructor meant that they ended up discussing something quite different. The instructor has thus interfered with the student's freedom to conduct inquiry as they see fit, satisfying the interference condition. Her doing so also satisfies the non-consultation condition, since she acts without consulting the student first.[7] In short, it is not just that the instructor's interference is justified in the same *way* as epistemic paternalism; rather, her interference just *is* a form of epistemic paternalism.

A similar analysis can be deployed to vindicate the value afforded to a charitable disposition in other contexts. Think about practices of charity in peer feedback, for example, or even in historical interpretation: in each instance, the charitable agent takes pro-active steps to shift their focus from what they take to be the most *likely* or obvious interpretation of a position, and attempts to engage with what, in their eyes, represents the *best* interpretation of that position. From the perspective of the charitable agent, viewed as someone whose main interest is in building an accurate understanding of their interlocutor's view, this is an odd thing to do. Maybe, though, this is not the perspective we should be viewing the charitable interaction from; or, if it is, we shouldn't be understanding their motives in this way. Like other forms of epistemic paternalism, perhaps the value of being charitable derives not from any good effects that it brings about for the charitable agent but from the benefits it confers upon its recipients.

THE PATERNALISTIC ACCOUNT: PROBLEMS

My evidence for this is largely anecdotal, but I suspect that an appeal to other-regarding benefits underpins the value that many philosophers attribute to charity in pedagogy, peer feedback, and historical interpretation.[8] What's more, this account does seem to have a fair amount going for it. It tells a clear vindicatory story about intellectual charity, one that can make sense of many of its paradigmatic manifestations. By drawing the connection with epistemic paternalism, it can make use of an established theoretical framework. And, perhaps most interestingly, it can explain the connection between intellectual charity and other forms of charity. A charitable donation, roughly, is a donation that goes beyond what is strictly owed by the donor to the recipient, and that is made ostensibly in an effort to benefit the recipient. *Intellectual* charity, on the paternalistic account, similarly involves bestowing upon someone (or something) more of some good than the charitable agent thinks is strictly due. What makes this form of charity intellectual is simply that the goods in question—credence, credibility, other cognitive resources—are all broadly intellectual.

Nonetheless, there are also some significant problems with this account. First, recall the improvement condition on epistemic paternalism. For Ahlstrom-Vij, this is a condition about the motives of the interfering agent: a paternalistic act must be undertaken with the intent of eliciting epistemic improvements in the target of the intervention.[9] As we have seen, the paternalistic account of intellectual charity derives much of its initial plausibility from the observation that this motive is present in many charitable interactions. However, it is not present in all. When we encourage our students to be charitable when thinking about classic texts in the history of philosophy, for example, the suggestion isn't that they should go out of their way to *improve* these views. Rather, often we are encouraging charity as a way of arriving at a better *understanding* of the text in question, by moving past tempting misreadings or hasty dismissals. Similarly, calls for people to be more charitable on social media or when discussing controversial topics "across the aisle" are surely motivated by more than just the thought that, if one does so, one can improve the views of one's interlocutor. There is something arrogant or duplicitous about the person who resolves to be charitable with their political opponents only because they believe that, by doing so, they can help them to "improve" their views.

The whiff of arrogance that pervades this case leads us to a second, closely related objection to the idea of intellectual charity as a form of epistemic paternalism. Recall the observation that this account situates intellectual charity on a continuum with other forms of charity. In non-epistemic contexts, there is something implicitly hierarchical about charitable giving. To put this point crudely, typical instances of charitable donation take place between the "haves" and the "have-nots": those with a surplus of some resource go beyond what is required of them in sharing that resource with those in need of it. It thus makes sense that an account of intellectual charity understood, similarly, as a form of charitable giving works best in contexts where there is some clear *intellectual* hierarchy that situates the charitable agent above their beneficiary; most straightforwardly in teacher–student relationships, but also in practices of peer feedback where there may be disparities in specific skills or knowledge bases. Difficulties arise when we turn our attention to relationships of supposed peerhood (public discourse among citizens of a democracy, for example), or where the established intellectual hierarchy places charitable agent in a position of relative inferiority (say, an undergraduate in a history of philosophy class). Interpreting charity as a form of paternalism in these cases generates an air of arrogance because doing so is to impute an unwarranted presumption of intellectual superiority on behalf of the charitable agent.

The arrogance of assuming a position of intellectual superiority when you lack one is only part of the worry here. The deeper point is that, unless the charitable agent does occupy some relevant position of superiority, the paternalistic defense of charity cannot perform the task for which it was called upon: namely, to vindicate the epistemic value that we afford to a charitable disposition. For a paternalistic interference to be justified, the paternalistic agent must be in a position to know what's epistemically best for those with whom they are interfering. This requirement is quite explicit in Croce's claim that the paternalistic interferer must be "better epistemically positioned" than the target of their interference,[10] and is at least implicit in Goldman's identification of epistemic paternalism as the preserve of experts[11] and Ahlstrom-Vij's stipulation that the paternalistic agent must have a justified belief in the efficacy of their intervention.[12] In the kinds of cases presently under discussion, where the charitable agent can make no justifiable claim to being epistemically better-placed than the target of their charity, this condition is unlikely to be met. As such, even if the charitable agent is paternalistically motivated, their paternalism will not be justified. This provides scant vindication for the value of intellectual charity.

CHARITY AS CORRECTIVE

At the beginning of the previous section, I suggested that it was an attraction of the paternalistic defense of intellectual charity that it establishes a structural symmetry between this and other forms of charity. At this point, we might question whether establishing this asymmetry is really so attractive. After all, note that both of the difficulties just identified arise from aspects of charitable giving that are central to other forms of charity: namely, the requirement of an other-regarding motive, and the position of superiority presumed by the charitable agent.[13] Perhaps, then, the key to a more compelling vindication of intellectual charity will be to identify an appropriate *asymmetry* with other forms of charity. In this section, I will sketch an account that builds upon this line of thought.

The asymmetry in question concerns whether charity operates as a *self-* or *other-regarding* virtue. The distinction between these two types of virtue is well-established within virtue theory.[14] Traditionally, it is taken to pick out a distinction between the prime beneficiaries of a particular virtue, with self-regarding virtues primarily benefiting the virtuous agent themselves and other-regarding virtues primarily benefiting other people. Alternatively, it can be interpreted as marking a distinction in the object of one's virtuous thoughts, feelings, and actions: whether virtue is directed at the virtuous agent or at others.[15] On either interpretation, the moral virtue of charity falls out as a clear example of an other-regarding virtue: to be morally charitable is to be concerned with and to take steps to promote the well-being of others, and it is those others who typically benefit. So too does the intellectual virtue of charity, understood as a form of epistemic paternalism: the charitable agent is concerned with improving some other agent's epistemic situation, and it is this other agent who benefits if their intervention is successful.

It is this identification of intellectual charity as an other-regarding virtue, of course, that ultimately led to difficulties for the paternalistic account. My suggestion, then, is that we reconceive intellectual charity as a self-regarding virtue, at least on the second way of interpreting this distinction (that is, as a virtue directed toward the self), and possibly also on the first (a virtue that primarily benefits the self). Specifically, my suggestion is that we understand intellectual charity as a *corrective* virtue. Corrective virtues help us to correct for certain natural or typical human shortcomings. Philippa Foot famously suggested that all virtues take this form, of "[standing] at a point where there is some temptation to be resisted or deficiency of motivation to be made good."[16] The suggestion that all virtues can be analyzed in this way—that courage and temperance, for example, only count as virtues because human nature is such as to be easily distracted by fear or the desire for pleasure—is controversial, though this need not concern us here. Even if we do not accept this strong claim, the idea that certain traits might derive their virtuous status from their role in the making good of deficiencies is a helpful one.

If charity is a corrective virtue, what is it correcting *for*? The most straightforward answer, one might think, is that intellectual charity corrects for the tendency to be *un*charitable, but this answer really only takes us so far. The dispositionally charitable person might be said to have the virtue of charity, but the dispositionally uncharitable surely doesn't have a vice of "uncharity." Aside from the clumsiness of the term, the important point here is that being uncharitable does not provide us with a characterological explanation of someone's behavior. Rather, someone's tendency to be uncharitable can—perhaps must—be explained by appeal to any of a whole host of further vices. If someone habitually offers uncharitable interpretations, it might be because they are intellectually lazy or cowardly, because they are arrogant or closed-minded, because they are cynical or impatient. The virtue of intellectual charity, conversely, might provide a corrective to any of these failings.

We can build upon this insight to offer the following vindication of a charitable disposition. Like all corrective virtues, intellectual charity derives its status as a virtue from the role it plays in correcting for a natural or typical human shortcoming. What is distinctive about intellectual charity is that, rather than providing a bulwark against a specific motivational deficiency or harmful passion, it is concerned with shortcomings *elsewhere in one's intellectual character*. Intellectual charity is a kind of corrective intellectual meta-virtue. Being charitable helps to correct for (or, at least, mitigate) a tendency to be too dismissive in one's intellectual assessments and evaluations, where this tendency is itself borne of some shortcoming in virtue. A willingness to afford a view or interlocutor more credence than you think it actually deserves makes epistemic sense if you have reason to think that your initial judgments are generally too dismissive of views or interlocutors of this type.

CHARITY AND PATERNALISM: FINAL THOUGHTS

How does the corrective account of charity fare, as compared to the paternalistic account? The most notable advantage is that it provides plausible verdicts on the kinds of cases that troubled the paternalistic defense. Take the student in the history of philosophy class, who is inclined to be dismissive toward Kant (who else?) on the basis that his ethics is implausibly rigid and moralistic. *Should* this student try to be more charitable? This depends. Suppose that this student is maximally virtuous: she has been patient and thorough in her reading, open-minded in her reflection, autonomous and fair in her critique, and so on. If so, then I think the encouragement to be more charitable would, in fact, be puzzling. If she has reached her judgment in a fashion that is entirely epistemically responsible, why should she then make a special effort to change that judgment? That being said, virtue of this degree is exceedingly rare. I suspect that part of the reason why instructors call for charity when teaching easily caricatured figures is the suspicion that students are often too quick in their dismissals or rejections. A greater degree of patience, open-mindedness, and autonomy needn't necessarily make you more sympathetic to Kant, but it would at least mean that one's dismissal is adequately grounded. Where these virtues are in shortfall, charity is a helpful workaround.

Trickier for this account, perhaps, are the other kinds of cases we looked at, those that seemed to fit quite readily with the paternalistic defense. Indeed, while I noted the limited scope of this defense, I never sought to directly undermine the explanation it gives of those cases that inspire it, such as a teacher being charitable with their students or a colleague providing charitable feedback. The suspicion at this point might be that there are two quite different contexts in which charity has a role to play: other-regarding contexts, where the charitable agent is aiming to epistemically benefit the recipient; and self-regarding contexts, where the charitable agent is aiming to improve their own epistemic situation. If the paternalistic defense only works in the first context and the corrective defense only in the second then maybe what I've really established is that there are *two* virtues of intellectual charity: one an other-regarding virtue, the other a self-regarding virtue. Both virtues might manifest themselves in similar ways, but their epistemic utility is vindicated on the basis of quite different considerations.

A twin-track account of intellectual charity is one option. However, we can also aspire to a greater degree of theoretical unity via my corrective defense. Recall the two explications I presented of the other- and self-regarding distinction, as a distinction in the prime *beneficiaries* of a virtue and as a distinction in the agent at which the virtue is *directed*. The corrective account conceives of charity as an attitude to one's own characterological shortcomings, and as such is straightforwardly self-regarding in the latter sense. It is less clear whether it even *can* be classed as self-regarding or other-regarding on the first explication. As a corrective meta-virtue, intellectual charity can correct both for deficiencies in those virtues that primarily benefit the self (as we have seen), and for deficiencies in those virtues that primarily benefit others.

To see how this works, let's return one last time to our charitable instructor. Their goal in teaching Kant, we can start by noting, is different from the goal of the undergraduate studying Kant. Whereas the main target for the latter is to acquire epistemic goods in the form of a greater understanding of Kant's work, the instructor is not aiming to understand Kant, or the student, or to acquire any epistemic good for herself. Rather, her goal is other-regarding: to try and bring about epistemic improvements in her student. Achieving this goal will involve undertaking acts of epistemic paternalism, and performing these activities successfully will require an array of different virtues, ranging from intellectual generosity and care to patience, impartiality, and attentiveness. The ideal instructor, cognizant of her other-regarding goals and possessing each of these virtues to a maximal degree, wouldn't be appraising a student's contribution in terms of its bare philosophical robustness in the first place, and thus wouldn't be tempted by a quick dismissal or blunt response. Rather, they would be instinctively attuned to the pedagogical opportunities generated by a student's interjection and the productive ways in which it could be used. Like the maximally virtuous student, then, the maximally virtuous instructor shouldn't need to be charitable in order to facilitate their (in this case, other-regarding) goals. The maximally virtuous instructor, however, is probably just as rare as the maximally virtuous student. Given that this is the case, charity can help pick up some of the slack.

This, then, hints at a different connection between intellectual charity and epistemic paternalism, albeit a less ambitious one than we started with. It may not be right to say that being charitable just is a form of epistemic paternalism; certainly, I have argued that we don't *need* to describe it as such, even in other-regarding contexts. However, on the basis of what I have just argued, it does seem that intellectual charity will be a valuable virtue to cultivate for those with paternalistic ends, or who are looking to engage in paternalistic practice.[17] Perhaps the best-case scenario would be if all such people—judges, teachers, policy makers, and the like—were maximally patient, impartial, epistemically generous, and so on. Failing that, they could do worse than be charitable.[18]

NOTES

1. This point is not uncontroversial; Lorna Finlayson, for example, has argued that demands for charity in political discourse serves to obscure deep disagreement and prejudice discussion in favor of the liberal status quo. See her *The Political Is Political: Conformity and the Illusion of Dissent in Contemporary Political Philosophy* (2015).

2. On charity as an interlinguistic principle, see, for example, Donald Davidson (1973). On charity as a principle of historical interpretation, see, for example, Tom Stern (2016).

3. Alvin Goldman "Epistemic Paternalism" 1991, 113.

4. Goldman, "Epistemic Paternalism," 114.

5. Kristoffer Ahlstrom-Vij, 2013.

6. Michel Croce, 2018.

7. That the student might *welcome* this interference is not relevant. All that matters for an interference to be paternalistic is that it is instigated without the prior approval of the target. See Ahlstrom-Vij, *Epistemic Paternalism*, 44–45.

8. Stern, for example, suggests that the desire to ensure that there is "better philosophy around" is one of the main drivers of the principle of charity in the history of philosophy. See Stern, "Some Third Thing," 297.

9. Ahlstrom-Vij, *Epistemic Paternalism*, 49, 63.

10. Croce, "Epistemic Paternalism," 320.

11. Goldman, "Epistemic Paternalism," 128.

12. Ahlstrom-Vij, *Epistemic Paternalism*, 113–114.

13. The superiority invoked here is typically superiority in a very localized, non-moral sense. The idea is just that it makes no sense to make a charitable donation of some good if you think that the recipient of that donation has more of that good than you do.

14. Mill carves up the moral virtues along these lines in *On Liberty*; as, more recently, do two seminal texts in contemporary virtue ethics: Philippa Foot, 2002; and Michael Slote, 1992. Jason Kawall (2004) discusses this distinction from a virtue epistemological perspective.

15. The significance of these different interpretations comes to the fore with epistemic virtues. Open-mindedness, for example, might be self-regarding in the sense that it primarily confers benefits on the open-minded agent, but other-regarding in the sense that it concerns how they interact with others.

16. Foot, *Virtues and Vices*, 8. From a virtue epistemological perspective, this idea is also suggested in Roberts and Wood, *Intellectual Virtues: An Essay in Regulative Epistemology* (2007). Miranda Fricker presents some of the virtues of epistemic justice as corrective of the vices of epistemic injustice in her *Epistemic Injustice: Power and the Ethics of Knowing* (2007).

17. Croce, "Epistemic Paternalism," argues that for epistemic paternalism to be justified, the paternalistic interferer *must* possess and exercise certain relevant virtues. This condition is too strong, since it makes the justification for specific acts of paternalism dependent on quite general facts about one's character. In other words, it precludes non-virtuous people from ever conducting justified acts of epistemic paternalism, even if acting "out of character."

18. Acknowledgments. This chapter was inspired by a round-table discussion at an intellectual humility workshop at the University of Connecticut, and in particular by some suggestive comments from Jason Baehr. My thanks to Jason for discussion then and subsequently, and to the other participants in this roundtable. Thanks also to Maxime Lepoutre, Jessica Tizzard, Lani Watson, audiences at the University of Roehampton and the *Rhode Island Philosophical Society*, and the editors of this collection.

BIBLIOGRAPHY

Ahlstrom-Vij, Kristoffer. *Epistemic Paternalism: A Defence*. New York: Palgrave Macmillan, 2013.

Croce, Michel. 2018. "Epistemic Paternalism and the Service Conception of Epistemic Authority." *Metaphilosophy* 49 no. 3 (2018): 305–327.

Davidson, Donald. "Radical Interpretation." *Dialectica* 27, no. 3–4 (1973): 314–328.

Finlayson, Lorna. *The Political Is Political: Conformity and the Illusion of Dissent in Contemporary Political Philosophy*. Lanham, MD: Rowman & Littlefield, 2015.

Foot, Phillipa. *Virtues and Vices: And Other Essays in Moral Philosophy*. Oxford: Oxford University Press, 2002.

Fricker, Miranda. *Epistemic Injustice: Power and the Ethics of Knowing*. Oxford: Oxford University Press, 2007.

Goldman, Alvin. "Epistemic Paternalism: Communication Control in Law and Society." *The Journal of Philosophy* 88 no. 3 (1991): 113–131.

Kawall, Jason. "Other-Regarding Epistemic Virtues." *Ratio (new series)* XV, no. 3 (2004): 257–275.

Roberts, Robert C. and W. Jay Wood. *Intellectual Virtues: An Essay in Regulative Epistemology*. Oxford: Oxford University Press, 2007.
Slote, Michael. *From Morality to Virtue*. Oxford: Oxford University Press, 1992.
Stern, Tom. "'Some Third Thing': Nietzsche's Words and the Principle of Charity." *The Journal of Nietzsche Studies* 47 no. 2 (2016): 287–302.

Notes on Contributors

Aude Bandini is assistant professor in philosophy at Université de Montréal, and president of the Canadian Society for Epistemology. Besides her interests in epistemology at large, her current work focuses on the issue of conflicting expertise in clinical practice, and the dispute over legitimate epistemic authority in the relationships between healthcare professionals and patients living with a chronic illness.

Lee Basham has authored numerous articles on academic, media and political responses to allegations of conspiratorial political manipulation. Basham is among the first philosophers offering a broad defense of the epistemic and democratic legitimacy in Western-style societies of public suspicions of extensive and routine hierarchical deception. Basham is professor of philosophy at South Texas College and the University of Texas.

Patrick Bondy is assistant professor in the Department of Philosophy at Wichita State University. He works mainly in epistemology. He is the author of *Epistemic Rationality and Epistemic Normativity* (2018, Routledge) and co-editor of *Well-Founded Belief: New Essays on the Epistemic Basing Relation* (2020, Routledge).

Fernando Broncano-Berrocal is a talent attraction fellow at the Autonomous University of Madrid, Spain. He works mainly in epistemology, with an emphasis on virtue epistemology, philosophy of luck, social epistemology, and collective epistemology. His work has appeared in such places as *Philosophical Studies, Analysis, Synthese,* and *Erkenntnis.*

Clinton Castro is assistant professor in the philosophy department at Florida International University in Miami, Florida. His primary areas of study are epistemology and information ethics.

Valerie Joly Chock graduated from the University of North Florida with a BA in philosophy and a BFA in graphic design & digital media.

Charlie Crerar is assistant research professor at the University of Connecticut. He works primarily on issues in virtue and social epistemology. Recent publications include a collection on *Harms and Wrongs in Epistemic Practice* (co-edited with Simon Barker and Trystan Goetze), and papers on epistemic injustice, snobbery, and intellectual vice.

Michel Croce (Ph.D.) is a FCT junior researcher at the University of Lisbon and has previously held an Early Stage Marie Curie Fellowship at the University of Edinburgh. His main research interests include epistemology, moral philosophy, and the philosophy of education.

David Godden (Ph.D. McMaster University, 2004) is associate professor of philosophy at Michigan State University. His research program, located at the intersection of logic, epistemology, and normative theories of reasoning and argument, integrates work in social epistemology and applied logic with argumentation-theoretic considerations. He has published widely on topics including: deep disagreement, corroborative evidence, argumentation and extended cognition, virtue argumentation, presumption, and common knowledge.

Adam Green is associate professor of philosophy at Azusa Pacific University. He works at the intersection of social and virtue epistemology as well as in the philosophy of religion and the philosophy of the human sciences. His work in epistemology focuses on the epistemic impact of pro-social traits and the social aspects of epistemic ones.

Liz Jackson is a research fellow at Australian National University and assistant professor at Ryerson University. Her research focuses on issues at the intersection of formal and traditional epistemology. She has recently published work on the belief-credence connection, epistemic permissivism, and pragmatic and moral encroachment. Her research interests also include social epistemology, decision theory, and philosophy of religion. She completed her PhD in philosophy at the University of Notre Dame.

Stephen John is Hatton Trust Senior Lecturer in the Philosophy of Public Health, Department of History and Philosophy of Science, University of

Cambridge. He mainly works on topics at the intersection of philosophy of science, political philosophy and public health policy, with a particular interest in issues around scientific communication and expertise.

Jonathan Matheson is associate professor of philosophy at the University of North Florida. He works mainly in epistemology with a focus in the epistemology of disagreement.

Robin McKenna is a lecturer in philosophy at the University of Liverpool. Most of his work is in epistemology, but he is also interested in philosophy of language, philosophy of science and ethics. Current topics of interest include ideal and non-ideal theory in epistemology, the epistemology of climate change denial (and of "dysfunctional epistemologies" more broadly), epistemic injustice and social constructivism.

Fabien Medvecky is a senior lecturer in science communication at the University of Otago. His work sits at the interaction between values, science and knowledge. He is especially interested in ethical and justice issues around knowledge (who gets to know what and who should get to know what, etc.) and the roles of values in decision making around contentious or controversial issues in science and technologies (gene tech, alternative medicine, etc.).

Daniella Meehan is a Ph.D. student and member of the epistemology research centre, COGITO, at the University of Glasgow. Her thesis focuses on vice epistemology and epistemic responsibility, examining what it takes for epistemic vices to be deemed blameworthy. Other areas of research are also concerned with the "non-ideal" in epistemology, including epistemic injustice, epistemic rights and distrust.

Shaun O'Dwyer is associate professor in the Faculty of Languages and Cultures at Kyushu University. He has published widely on political and moral philosophy, philosophy of education and feminist philosophy. His book *Confucianism's Prospects* was published in 2019 by State University of New York Press.

Adam Pham is a Ph.D. candidate in the Department of Philosophy at the University of Wisconsin–Madison, where he teaches philosophy, legal studies, and communication classes. His research interests are focused on topics at the intersection of value theory and social science.

Shaun Respess is a Ph.D. candidate in the Alliance for Social, Political, Ethical, and Cultural Thought Program at Virginia Tech. He also teaches for the

Department of Philosophy. His work implements moral philosophy to reveal and critically respond to social unrest. Current research projects specialize in blending care ethics with mental health care reform.

Alan Rubel is associate professor in the Information School and director of the Center for Law, Society & Justice at the University of Wisconsin–Madison. He works on moral and legal issues related to information and data, including on privacy and surveillance, transparency, and algorithmic decision systems.

Marion Vorms is Marie Curie Research Fellow, and senior lecturer in philosophy at Pantheon-Sorbonne University in Paris. Her research, including a present project to study the notion of "reasonable doubt," lies at the crossroads of the philosophy of science, epistemology, and the psychology of reasoning.

About the Editors

Guy Axtell is professor of philosophy at Radford University and works primarily in social epistemology, and philosophy of the sciences. His *Knowledge, Belief, and Character* (Rowman & Littlefield, 2000) was the first edited collection in the area of virtue/vice epistemology; he has since published two monographs: *Objectivity* (Polity, 2015) and *Problems of Religious Luck: Assessing the Limits of Reasonable Religious Disagreement* (Lexington Books, 2019).

Amiel Bernal received his PhD from Virginia Tech's ASPECT Program (The Alliance for Social, Political, and Economic Thought) in 2018. Currently, he teaches at Colorado State University and Arapahoe Community College. His research focus is on social epistemology, epistemic injustice, and ethics.

Index

A/B testing, 33
accurate intelligibility, 225
Against Autonomy (Conly), 267n12
Ahlstrom-Vij, K., 6, 8, 9, 36, 62, 67, 73n3, 80, 81, 86–87, 88, 98, 102n7, 108, 109, 145, 152n8, 158–59, 167n3, 171, 173, 174, 176–77, 180n9, 180n11, 183, 184, 185, 186, 187, 188–89, 190, 194, 197n5, 205–6, 208, 220, 226, 227, 235–36, 266–67, 296, 299
akathisia, 110
alignment condition, 8, 109, 111, 158–60, 174, 177, 180n9, 180n11, 194, 222, 227, 235, 236, 241
anti-psychotic medications, 114
antipsychotics, 117
attention scarcity, 87
attentiveness, as caring virtue, 170, 178, 179
attitudes, 34–35, 249, 251; caring, 170, 171; charity as, 302; doxastic, 34, 35, 36, 37, 152n9, 206, 209; forbearing silence, 289; inauthentic, 35, 37–38; paternalistic, 123, 126, 152n9
autonomy: assumption, 81; as autarkeia, 183, 187; conception, 186–87; Demoting Fake News and, 37, 38; freedom of inquiry, 188–90;

paternalistic interferences, 188–90; personal, 8, 163–67; as self-reliance, 183, 187; as self-rule/self-governance, 183, 187, 189

balancing-goods condition, 8, 119, 160, 163, 174, 180n8
Bandini, Aude, 7
Basham, Lee, 5
Bayesian inference, 54
Bayesian theories, 49
BBC, 82, 83
Beeby, Laura, 119n10
beliefs, 189; doxastic domains, 282–84; erroneous, 284–90; truth-conditions for, 189; values, 283–84
"The Beneficial Nudge Program and Epistemic Injustice" (Riley), 256
Bernal, Amiel, 10
biosociality, 114
black hole, 82–83
blinding, 2
blindspots of reason, 190–92
Bowell, T., 213
British rule and Indians, 272
Broncano-Berrocal, Fernando, 8, 119n9

Bullock, Emma, 8, 20–21, 24, 109, 118n1, 141, 142, 143, 144, 151, 153n12, 155–62, 166–67, 167n2, 180–81n11, 183, 196n1
burden-of-proof condition, 8, 109, 111, 174, 180n9, 222, 227, 228, 236, 237, 241

"Capital Epistemic Vices," 255–56
carbon emissions, 95
care/caring, 168–80; attentiveness, 170, 178, 179; competence, 170, 178; concept, 170–71; condition, 8, 176, 179; dependence, 171; ethics, 8, 115–16; knowing/knowledge and, 116–18; model of justice, 117; morally permissible paternalistic acts, 174–80; needs, 171; obligations of, 115; overview, 169–70; paternalistic acts, 169, 171–73; phases, 170; proper, 170, 174–80, 181n12; responsiveness, 170, 178, 179; schema, 116; theories, 115; virtues of, 170, 178–79
care-giving, 170
Carel, Havi, 128, 130
caring about others, 170
caring actions, 170
caring attitudes, 170
caring for them, 170
Carter, J. Adam, 188
cascaded inference, in complex evidential reasoning, 49–51
Case Assessment and Interpretation (CAI), 54–56
Castro, Clinton, 5
Catholic Index, 71
charity as intellectual virtue. *See* intellectual charity
child abuse, 70
Chock, Valerie Joly, 9
Christman, John, 34
chronic diseases, 130
Click-Gap, 34
Coady, David, 280
Code, Lorraine, 113, 275n4

cognitive bias, 158, 164
cognitive division of labor, 212
Cohen, J., 250
common knowledge, 45, 50, 56
communication: controllers, 79; science, 80, 82–84
communities, 112
Conly, Sarah, 276n12
consent, 2, 9, 21, 193–94, 226; informed, 18–19, 124; inquiry of another, 190, 234, 241, 267; interfering with someone's choices/actions, 96–97, 142–44, 172–73; interpersonal unfairness, 241; of users on Facebook, 32–33, 37
consequential false belief, 91–102; climate change, 93–96; combatting problem of, 96–102; de-idealized social epistemology, 6, 91, 92–93; overview, 91–92; rational persuasion to solve problem of, 98–102
contractual interference, 87–88
contributory injustice, 264–65, 266, 275n4, 280, 281, 282, 284
Control-RTE (C-RTE), 294–96
"Conversations I Can't Have" (Harvin), 225
Cook, John, 93
Cook, Robert, 54, 55
corrective virtue, 11
courtroom, expert advice in. *See* criminal trials, experts in
credibility and relevance: expert witnesses, 48–51; medical relationships, 112–13; scientific reports, 52–54; testimonial evidence, 51–52
credibility deficit, 223
Crerar, Charlie, 8, 11
criminal trials, experts in, 5, 48–51; CAI model, 54–56; credibility and relevance, 48–54; scientific reports, 52–54; testimonial evidence, 51–52
Croce, Michael, 6, 8, 109, 113, 116, 177–78, 180, 186, 196, 197n10, 296, 299, 304n17
curation of information, 4–5, 21

The Daily Me, 29
Dalmiya, Vrinda, 117
decision-making, expert advice in, 45–57; CAI model and, 54–56; complex evidential reasoning, 49–51; credibility and relevance, 48–54; inductive risk, 46–47; informing *vs.* prescribing, 46; moral paternalism, 47–48; overview, 44; pragmatic issues, 51–52; scientific reports, 52–54; testimonial reports, 51–52
de-idealized social epistemologist, 6, 91, 92–93
democracy, 61–71; deception by commission *vs.* omission, 63–64; epistemic elites/elitism, 64–66; epistemic paternalist, 62–63; fundamental feature and motive, 63; overview, 61–62; pathologizing project, 63–66, 69–81; toxic truths and rule by crisis, 66–69
Demoting Fake News, 34–39; harm reduction, 38; as policy, 38–39; purveyors, 37–38; user autonomy, 38
descriptive reading, 6
Dewey, John, 12n3
Diagnostic and Statistical Manual of Mental Disorders (DSM-5), 112
digital technology, 5
Dilling, Lisa, 93, 96
distributive epistemic injustice, 279, 281
diversity, 212
doctor–patient relationships, 7, 123–35; in chronic illness context, 131–32; epistemic justice in, 135; experiential knowledge, 132, 133–34; expert/partner patients, 133–35; as object of scientific scrutiny, 134
domestic violence, 9, 225
Dotson, Kristie, 9, 219, 224–28, 230nn14–16, 247n5, 264–65, 280, 284

Douglas, Heather E., 47
Downie, R. S., 186
doxastic attitudes, 34, 35, 36, 37, 152n9, 206, 209
doxastic disconnection, 119n11
doxastic domains for beliefs, 282–84
Dworkin, Gerald, 34, 142, 171, 173, 186, 197n3

Elgin, Catherine, 183
elitism, 65
epistemic bubble, 5, 30, 39, 39n1, 164–66
epistemic capacities, 256
epistemic care. *See* care/caring
epistemic costs to knowing, 82
epistemic environment, 96
epistemic goods, 144–47
epistemic injustice, 9–10, 263, 279; contributory injustice, 264–65, 266, 275n4, 280, 281, 282, 284; disrespect and unfairness, 236–38; distributive epistemic injustice, 279, 280, 281; medical paternalism, 128–30; route, 264–66; silencing, 223–26; as tracker prejudices, 223. *See also* hermeneutical injustice; testimonial injustice
Epistemic Injustice (Fricker), 279
epistemic justice, 3, 9, 10, 102n7, 304n16; distribution of epistemic goods, 233; epistemic paternalism as, 233–46; ideal *vs.* non-ideal theory, 242–45; literature on, 4; nudging and, 256–57; patient-doctor relationships, 135; restorative, 234; science communication and, 80
epistemic nudging (EN), 10, 249–59; autonomy and, 258; concept, 250; as liberal paternalism, 250; Riley's objections to, 256–58; types of, 250
epistemic objectification, 113
epistemic obligations. *See* obligations
epistemic paternalism, 1–4; conditions, 80, 108–9, 146–47, 186; defense of, 2, 4, 88, 127–28, 153n12,

267; defined, 79–80, 107, 204–5; emotional aspects of, 70; epistemic goods, 144–47; hard, 157, 160, 161, 162, 163, 167; indirect, 167n2; justifying, 98–102, 204–6; literature, 61; as a normative thesis, 1–2; ordinary forms, 185–86; permissibility, 183–95; as a practice, 2; proponents and critics, 107; social uncertainties, 109; soft, 160, 161, 162, 167; as a two-step dance, 79; viewed as suspicion, 79, 80–81

Epistemic Paternalism, a Defence (Ahlstrom-Vij), 62. *See also* alignment condition; balancing-goods condition; burden-of-proof condition

epistemic scarcity, 82, 83, 87

epistemic solidarity, 22–25

epistemic value, 57n3, 81, 145–46, 156, 157, 160, 166–67, 196n2, 205, 212, 221, 229n7; value of the epistemic compared with, 4

epistemic vices: combating/mitigating, 252–59; concept, 251; defined, 251; laziness, 255–59; overview, 249–50

epistemic violence, 10, 230n14; silencing as, 265–66; in testimony, 224

Epistemocracy, 64

epistocracy, 64–65; epistocrats, 65; individual liberty and, 12; vertical conversation eliminators, 72; vertical *vs.* horizontal communication, 72. *See also* skepticism (distrust) about expertise

epistemological individualism, 112

epistemologists, 92

"Epistemology Naturalized" (Quine), 92

epistocrats, 65

equal risk assumption, 23

erroneous belief, rebuttals of, 284–90; epistemic and ethical injustice in, 288–90; ideal schema for, 284–88

Estlund, David, 64–65

eudaimonistic epistemic paternalism, 153n12

eudaimonistic view, 24

evidence-based approach, 6

evidential reasoning, 45

experiential knowledge, 132, 133–34

expert advice in decision-making, 45–57; CAI model and, 54–56; complex evidential reasoning, 49–51; credibility and relevance, 48–54; inductive risk, 46–47; informing *vs.* prescribing, 46; moral paternalism, 47–48; overview, 45; pragmatic issues, 51–52; scientific reports, 52–54; testimonial reports, 51–52

expert condition, 8, 174, 180n8

Facebook, 4, 5; Audience Network policy, 38; Click-Gap, 34; fighting misinformation, 36–37; psychological experiment, 31–32

fake news, 33–39; Facebook Audience Network policy, 38; harmful movements, 38; purveyors of, 37–38

false beliefs, 268; avoidance of, 145, 150, 153; consequential, 91–102; epistemic value to, 205; public policy and, 6; self-silencing and, 227, 228; unsafe and risky testimony, 224–25, 227

Federal Rules of Evidence, 221–23, 226

Feinberg, Joel, 164

Feldman, Richard, 192

fingerprints, 52–53

Fisher, Berenice, 170

floating standards conception, 47

fluid expertise, 120n15

Fogle, Jenna, 110

Forensic Science Service in England and Wales, 54

freedom of inquiry: limits on, 20–21; right to, 21

Fricker, Elizabeth, 187, 197n4

Fricker, Miranda, 102, 112–13, 128, 223–24, 233–34, 235, 238–39, 241, 246, 264, 270, 275n3, 279, 279, 284, 287

Gandhi, M. K., 272
Gelfert, Axel, 82
global warming, 92, 93–96; framing, 95; misinformation, 94–95; mitigation policies, 95; political ideology, 94
Godden, David, 8–9
Goldman, Alvin, 2, 6, 79–81, 85, 86–87, 108, 109, 112, 113, 118, 119n4, 145, 184, 185, 186, 205, 214n4, 218–20, 221, 229n8, 229n10, 251, 275n7, 294, 295. *See also* expert condition
Goodin, Robert E., 119n13
Google, 4
Gosselin, Abigail, 113, 114, 117
Green, Adam, 10
Grill, Kalle, 86–87
Gulf of Tonkin, 66, 68, 72
Gupta, Kristina, 114

Habermas, Jurgen, 276n14
Hanna, Jason, 275n8
Hansson, Sven Ove, 86–87
hard epistemic paternalism, 157, 160, 161, 162, 163, 167
Hardwig, John, 188
Harvin, Cassandra Byers, 225
Haslanger, Sally, 276n16
Hausman, Daniel M., 258
health care, 109
Hempel, Carl G., 46
hermeneutical injustice, 112, 117, 223, 238, 239–40, 241, 244, 245, 264, 275n3, 280, 281
hermeneutical marginalization, 119n10, 239
hermeneutical resources, 117, 247n5, 264–65, 280–82, 284, 286
hinge propositions, 284
Hornsby, Jennifer, 224, 265
Husting, Ginna, 70–71

improvement condition, 80, 84, 108, 156, 157–58, 172, 186, 220–21, 226–27, 228, 235, 241, 296, 297
inauthentic attitudes, 35, 37–38

Indians, 270; and British rule, 272
indirect epistemic paternalism, 167n2
inductive risk, 4, 45, 49, 50, 52–53, 56, 57n2; as a challenge to expert advice neutrality, 46–47; values, 46–47
inequality, 113
infectious diseases, 130
inference networks, in complex evidential reasoning, 5, 45, 49–51
informational environments, 184–85
information control, 184; obligation-first approach to, 18–20
information technologies, 133–34
informing *vs.* prescribing, 46
inoculation theory, 95
instrumentally normative reasons, 148, 149
intellectual charity, 11, 293–303; as corrective virtue, 299–301, 302; and epistemic justice, 304n16; as other-regarding virtue, 300; overview, 293–95; paradigmatic manifestations, 294; as paternalism, 295–97; as self-regarding virtue, 300
intellectual virtue of sensitivity, 116
intention/intentionality to interferences, 84–86
inter-cultural dialogue, 11
interference condition, 62, 79, 80, 108, 156, 157, 172, 186, 188, 220, 226, 296, 297
interferences, 82–84; contractual, 87–88; intention/intentionality, 80–86; language of, 6; negative, 3; non-consultative, 83–84; positive, 3; testimony and, 82; trivial, 82
Intergovernmental Panel on Climate Change (IPCC), 145
interpersonal permissivism, 206; standpoint epistemology and, 211–13. *See also* permissivism
intrapersonal normativity, 147–49; justifying epistemic paternalism, 149–52

Jackson, Liz, 9
Japanese attack on Pearl Harbor, 66–68

Jim Crow, 282
John, Stephen, 4–5, 47, 57n2, 57n4, 58n8, 58n13
judgmental paternalism, 11, 281–82; Quong's definition, 281

Kahan, Dan, 101
Kant, Immanuel, 186
Kidd, Ian, 128, 130, 249, 254–56, 257
To Kill a Mockingbird (Lee), 223
Kimmel, Husband E., 67
Kittay, Eva Feder, 115
"Knowing and Not Knowing for Your Own Good: The Limits of Epistemic Paternalism" (Bullock), 155–56
knowing/knowledge: caring and, 117–18; common, 45, 50, 56; demand for, 82, 83; ecosystem, 107–8, 112; epistemic costs to, 82; epistemic scarcity, 82, 83, 87; experiential, 132, 133–34; material costs to, 82

labor, cognitive division of, 212
Lackey, Jennifer, 80, 230n13
laziness, vices of, 255–59; epistemic nudging (EN) and, 256–59; manifestation, 256
leadership in Western-style democracies, 68–69
Lee, Harper, 223
Lewy, Guenter, 68
Lippert-Rasmussen, Kasper, 65

machine learning algorithm, 30
Mad in America, 110
Manson, Neil, 18
marketing methods, 6
Mary, Rachel, 61
material costs to knowing, 82
Matheson, Jonathan, 9
May, Thomas, 187–88, 189
McCollum, Arthur, 66–67
McKenna, Robin, 6, 8

medical paternalism, 4, 6–7, 123–35; chronic disease management, 131–32; epidemiologic transition, 130–31; epistemic injustices, 128–30
medical model of psychiatry, 113
Medina, Jose, 275n5
Medvecky, Fabien, 6
Meehan, Daniella, 10
mental health care, 6–7, 107–18; credibility, 112–13; discrimination and inequality, 114; epistemic paternalism, 107–9; ethical obligations, 115–16; Gosselin's approach to, 117; knowing/ knowledge, 117–18; knowing patient, 111–15; medical model, 113; model of justice, 117; overview, 107–8; pharmacotherapy, 110–11; professionals and practitioners, 107; psychotic disorder, 110
Mill, John Stuart, 1, 236, 275n1
mixed paternalism, 142, 144, 167n3
Mol, Annemarie, 119n14
Moore, Alfred, 276n14
moral equality, 242, 243
morally permissible paternalistic acts, 174–80
Moser, Susanne C., 93, 96
Mosseri, Adam, 36
Mueller Report, 29
Muldoon, R., 212

Nazi Germany, 66
negative interferences, 3
Negroponte, Nicholas, 29
Nelson, Lynn Hankinson, 112
Nepstad, Sharon, 276n15
New Evidence Scholarship, 49
News Feed, 36
non-compliant patients, 7, 114, 125

non-consultation condition, 80, 82, 84, 108, 156–57, 172, 173, 186, 220, 226, 235, 241, 267, 296, 297
non-violent paternalism/resistance, 271–74
normative reading, 6
normative reasons, 141–42; instrumentally, 148, 149; intrapersonal, 147–52; non-epistemic, 148; principle, 148–50; *pro tanto*, 148
normative thesis, 1–2
nudge/nudging, 97–98, 111, 119n7, 185, 234. *See also* epistemic nudging (EN)
To Nudge or Not to Nudge (Hausman and Welch), 258

Obama, Barack, 30
objectification: epistemic, 113; patients, 114
obligations, 17–25; care/caring, 115; ignorance, 25; other-directed, 18, 20; self-directed, 18; solidarity, 22–25
O'Dwyer, Shaun, 11
offence-level propositions, 55
O'Neill, Onora, 18
other-directed obligations, 18, 20

Pariser, Eli, 30
paternalism: characterization in general, 142–44; descriptive profile, 2, 12n2, 22, 237; kinds of, 266–71; non-epistemic forms, 267; non-violent, 271–74; normative/prescriptive stance, 1–2, 4, 6–10, 12n3, 65, 91, 118, 141–42, 143, 147–51, 186, 205, 222, 233, 235, 237, 240, 242, 243, 244. *See also* epistemic paternalism
paternalistic attitudes, 123, 126, 152n9
paternalistic interference. *See* interferences
pathologizing project, 63–66, 69

patients: with chronic diseases, 131–32; cognitive abilities, 131; epistemic capacities, 131; experiential knowledge, 132, 133–34; expert/partner, 133–35; information technologies and, 133–34; knowing, 111–15; non-compliant, 7, 114, 125; objectification, 114; self-disciplining, 114. *See also* care/caring; mental health care
Pearl Harbor, Japanese attack on, 66–68
Peirce, Charles S., 283, 284
permissibility of epistemic paternalism, 183–95; blindspots of reason, 190–92; conditions, 194–95; intellectual autonomy, 186–90; overview, 183–85; paternalistic intervention, 186, 192–94; preliminary considerations, 184–86; self-censorship, 191–92. *See also* alignment condition; balancing-goods condition; burden-of-proof condition; expert condition
permissivism, 8–9, 203, 206–10; interpersonal, 206; permissibility, 208–9; rationality, 206, 208; standpoint epistemology and, 211–13
personal autonomy, 163–67; as a condition, 163–64; epistemic bubbles, 164–66; personal sovereignty model, 163; virtues, 164
personalized medical information, 23
personalized predictions, 23
personalized medicine (PM), 17–25; duties of ignorance, 25; epistemic obligations, 18–20; epistemic paternalism, 20–22; epistemic solidarity, 22–25; overview, 17–18
personal sovereignty, 159–60, 163–67. *See also* personal autonomy
persuasion, 91; rational, 6, 98–102
Pham, Adam, 5
pharmacotherapy, 110–11
physical non-violence, 271
Plato, 1

political epistemic paternalism, 5,
   61–71; commission *vs.* omission,
   63–64; emotional mechanisms,
   70–72; Estlund on, 64–65; Lippert-
   Rasmussen on, 65; as nation-centric,
   68; overview, 61–62; pathologizing
   project, 69–71; public trust and toxic
   truths, 66–68; *realpolitik*, 61; rule by
   crisis, 68–69; terror management, 71
political piety, 71
pornography, 265
Portes, Louis, 128
positive interferences, 3
Post, Robert, 110
post-traumatic stress disorder (PTSD), 239
prediction techniques, 23
prescribing *vs.* informing, 46
Pritchard, Duncan, 4, 119n1, 152n6,
   155, 157, 161, 169, 196n1–2, 214n7,
   229n7
proper care, 170, 181n12
psychiatric interventions/treatment. *See*
   mental health care
psychosis, 117
psychotic disorder, 110. *See also* mental
   health care
public trust, 68
Puig de la Bellacasa, María, 115

Quine, W. V. O., 92
Quong, Jonathon, 11

racial prejudices, 223
Radnitzky, Gerard, 82
rational fear, 71
rational persuasion, 6, 98–102
Rawls, J., 241–43, 247n9
reading: descriptive, 6; normative, 6
rebuttals of erroneous belief, 284–90;
   epistemic and ethical injustice in,
   288–90; ideal schema for, 284–88
reciprocity, 224
reflective incapacitational injustice,
   10, 256
regulative epistemology, 251. *See also*
   epistemic vices

reliable ignorance, 230n15
Requirement of Total Evidence (RTE),
   81, 294; Control-RTE (C-RTE),
   295–96
Respess, Shaun, 6–7
responsiveness, as caring virtue, 170,
   178, 179
rights to be taken seriously as knowers, 279
rights to know, 279
Riley, Evan, 229n1, 256–58
Roberts, Robert, 183, 188
Rochefort, Joseph, 67
Rubel, Alan, 5
Rudner, Richard, 46
Ryan, Shane, 35, 36, 152n9, 172, 173,
   174, 180n10

Sanders, Bernie, 30
Scanlon, T. M., 2, 186–87
Schroepfer, Mike, 33
Schum, David, 49, 50, 51
science: black hole, 82–84;
   communication, 80, 82–84; value-
   free ideal of, 47
scientific reports, 52–54
self-censorship, 191–92
self-directed obligations, 18
self-disciplining, 114
self-enhancement bias, 158
self-harmful behavior, 275n6
self-silencing, 224–28. *See also*
   testimonial smothering
self trust, 187
Sellars, Wilfrid, 189
Shiffrin, Seana Valentine, 276n10
silencing: epistemic injustice, 223–25;
   self-silencing, 224–28. *See also*
   testimonial smothering
situationist psychology, 4. *See also* vice
   epistemology
skepticism (distrust) about expertise, 111
social epistemology, 10, 109
soft epistemic paternalism, 160, 161,
   162, 167
Sorensen, Roy, 191–92
source-level propositions, 54

Index

sovereignty. *See* personal sovereignty
standpoint epistemology: concept, 210–11; permissivism and, 210–12; versions, 210
Stewart, I., 250
Sunstein, Cass R., 10, 29, 97, 250, 252, 258
survival strategy, 114

Tan, Sor Hoon, 12n3
tardive dyskinesia, 110
Telfer, Elizabeth, 186
terror management, 71
testimonial competence, 225
testimonial evidence, 51–52
testimonial incompetence, 225, 228
testimonial injustice, 112, 117, 223, 224, 280, 281; concept, 238–39; as prejudicial credibility deficits, 238; primary harms, 239; secondary harms, 239. *See also* epistemic injustice
testimonial practice, 79, 80–82, 86, 88
testimonial quieting, 224
testimonial smothering, 9, 219; conditions, 224–28; withholding information, 226–28
testimony: defined, 80; interference and, 82; silencing, 9; unsafe and risky, 224–25; violence, 224
Thaler, Richard H., 97, 250, 252, 258
thumetic values, 11, 283–84, 289, 290
Toole, Briana, 211
tracker prejudices, 223
Tronto, Joan C., 116, 170, 180n1
truth-conditions for beliefs, 189
Tsai, George, 98–102

United States (US): Japanese attack on Pearl Harbor, 66–68; mental disorders, 110, 113; Vietnam war, 68

value-free ideal of science, 47
value judgments, 45, 47, 48, 56
van der Linden, Sander, 94
vice epistemology, 4, 10, 12, 249–50, 251–59
Vietnam, 68
violence. *See* epistemic violence
virtual communities of patients, 133–34
virtue epistemology, 12, 178, 251, 280, 283
virtues: caring, 170, 178–79; as condition, 8, 174, 180n9; intellectual charity as, 299–301, 302. *See also* epistemic justice
virtuous interferer, 109
Vorms, Marion, 5

Warren, Elizabeth, 30
Welch, Brynn, 258
well-being, 24
Western-style democracies, leadership in, 68–69
Whitaker, Robert, 110, 119n8
Wood, Jay, 183, 188
World Health Organization (WHO), 110
World War II, 66–68
Wright, Richard, 282

YouTube, 30

Zagzebski, Linda, 183, 187, 188

www.ingramcontent.com/pod-product-compliance
Lightning Source LLC
Chambersburg PA
CBHW031544300426
44111CB00006BA/174